São Paulo

Time Out Guides Ltd
Universal House
251 Tottenham Court Road
London W1T 7AB
United Kingdom
Tel: +44 (0)20 7813 3000
Fax: +44 (0)20 7813 6001
Email: guides@timeout.com
www.timeout.com

Published by Time Out Guides Ltd, a wholly owned subsidiary of Time Out Group Ltd.
Time Out and the Time Out logo are trademarks of Time Out Group Ltd.

© Time Out Group Ltd 2009

10 9 8 7 6 5 4 3 2 1

This edition first published in Great Britain in 2009 by Ebury Publishing.
A Random House Group Company
20 Vauxhall Bridge Road, London SW1V 2SA

Random House Australia Pty Ltd 20 Alfred Street, Milsons Point, Sydney, New South Wales 2061, Australia

Random House New Zealand Ltd 18 Poland Road, Glenfield, Auckland 10, New Zealand

Random House South Africa (Pty) Ltd Isle of Houghton, Corner Boundary Road & Carse O'Gowrie, Houghton 2198, South Africa

Random House UK Limited Reg. No. 954009

For further distribution details, see www.timeout.com.

ISBN: 978-1-84670-126-9

A CIP catalogue record for this book is available from the British Library.

Printed and bound by Firmengruppe APPL, aprinta druck, Wemding, Germany.

The Random House Group Limited supports The Forest Stewardship Council (FSC), the leading international forest certification organisation. All our titles that are printed on Greenpeace approved FSC certified paper carry the FSC logo. Our paper procurement policy can be found at http://www.rbooks.co.uk/environment.

Time Out carbon-offsets its flights with Trees for Cities (www.treesforcities.org).

Contents

Introduction

Poet Mário de Andrade called São Paulo 'the hallucinated city', and his words are a fitting description of this enormous metropolis. The city is 455 years old, but its soul remains still young and restless. Shaking off 300-plus years of sloth-like growth, it careered through the 20th century at breakneck speed, and continues to grow. So it's not surprising, perhaps, that a huge number of expats are now calling the city home, and are bristling if anyone thinks they're hallucinating. São Paulo is a giant that slumbers no more.

Sampa, as locals call the city, is the only Brazilian city that can truly call itself cosmopolitan, due to a history of immigration on the same scale as New York. First came the Portuguese colonisers, the Spaniards and the African slaves, then the Italians, Japanese, Germans, European Jews, Lebanese and Syrians. The most recent influxes have been Bolivians and Koreans, adding to the 11 million people already here.

The city is amazingly diverse in its environment and architecture. There are remnants of a rainforest, the Mata Atlântica, as well as Gothic churches, Brutalist buildings and futuristic parks. Step on to Avenida Paulista, the city's most celebrated thoroughfare, and you may think you're in Manhattan, while the hilly, well-heeled streets of Jardim Paulista will erase any preconceptions you may have about dirt and congestion south of the equator.

São Paulo's population exploded in the late 19th century when it became an industrial powerhouse. It's the working class that deserves the laurels for the city's present-day stature, although the poor still struggle to avoid the *cortiços* (tenements) and *favelas* that push against the city's perimeter, while middle-class Paulistanos have settled in green, leafy neighbourhoods. It's a tropicopolis that is at once gritty and flashy – you'll see amazing feats of graffiti alongside multi-million-*real* high-rises, and you'll find working-class *lanchonete* snack bars serving juice and pastries along with some of Latin America's finest restaurants.

Paulistanos revel in their city's uniqueness as a non-homogenised, party-mad colossus, and the town certainly leaves other Brazilian cities in the dust when it comes to cultural life, with cutting-edge theatres, bars and frenzied clubs and a staggering art scene just for starters. It's also a sunrise-to-sunrise city: if you really want to experience São Paulo, you'll be out all day and up all night. *Anna Katsnelson, Editor*

São Paulo in Brief

IN CONTEXT

Founding Jesuits, migrants and immigrants, anarchists, Communists and military dictators are just some of the pivotal players in São Paulo's history. Starting with the city's roots, while also casting an eye on the architectural and economic blueprints of the 20th century, this opening series of essays examines a city high on ambition and riddled with contradictions.

▶ *For more, see pp14-44.*

SIGHTS

In a city as large as this one, the sights are varied and spread out. Here you'll find neighbourhood highlights, stand-out museums, Baroque churches, modern cultural institutions and monuments that give São Paulo its feel. Chapters are dedicated to São Paulo's major areas, and are filled with independent venue reviews written by *Time Out*'s local writers.

▶ *For more, see pp45-91.*

CONSUME

From *açaí* stands and snack counters to exclusive restaurants and Amazonian retreats hidden in the urban jungle: the city has an amazing variety of tastes. We help you search out the best of Paulistano hotels, shops, restaurants and – of course – cafés and bars, where *cachaça*, *caipirinha* and *cerveja* are the three magic words.

▶ *For more, see pp92-158.*

ARTS & ENTERTAINMENT

Rio's partying gets all the press, but *Carnaval* aside, even Cariocas will admit São Paulo has the nightlife edge. You'll find a sophisticated music scene: jazz, rock, electronica and samba. Add to that one of the most ardent football followings in the world and the country's most important arts centre, and this city promises to hold your interest like no other in the southern hemisphere.

▶ *For more, see pp159-214.*

ESCAPES & EXCURSIONS

When and if the metropolis makes you long for the Brazil of your dreams – lovely beaches, sun-kissed skin and swaying palm trees – you need only remember that São Paulo is just an hour away from some of the most gorgeous stretches of the Atlantic coastline. Whether you're looking to sip *caipirinhas* or walk along cobblestoned streets, there's plenty here to entice.

▶ *For more, see pp215-230.*

São Paulo in 48 Hrs

Day 1 Jungle Trekking

10AM Begin your São Paulo exploration in **Jardim Paulista** on **Rua Oscar Freire** (*see p70*). Brazil's most glamorous street makes for a pleasant first impression of the city. Order an espresso at one of the tables outside **Santo Grão** café (Rua Oscar Freire 413, www.santograo.com.br); from there, watch upwardly mobile locals chat on their Blackberries and navigate their bulletproof SUVs.

11AM Window-shop on Alameda Lorena before walking up the seven steep blocks to **Avenida Paulista** (*see p67*), the most iconic of the city's streets. Stop at the **Livraria Cultura** (*see p148*), the largest bookstore in São Paulo, for a brief browse.

11.30AM Wander into the **Parque Siqueira Campos/Trianon** (*see p69*), a remnant of the rainforest native to this part of Brazil. The Mata Atlântica is alive and well in this luscious hideaway; you may even forget that you're in South America's largest city.

NOON Across the street from the park is the **Museu de Arte de São Paulo** (*see p70*). The most impressive museum in the city is filled with fantastic art. Take a half-hour to eat a colourful and affordable buffet lunch at the restaurant on the lower level.

3PM Take a walk on Avenida Paulista, towards Brigadeiro metrô station and catch one of a number of buses to **Parque do Ibirapuera** (*see pp73-75*). Ramble along the park's paths and drop in at a number of its cultural institutions, such as the historically influenced **Museu Afro Brasil** (*see p74*) or the **Museu de Arte Moderna** (*see p75*).

6PM From Ibirapuera, walk over to the **Unique Hotel** (*see p99*), when you can admire the daring designs of Ruy Ohtake. Enjoy a drink at the equally striking bar inside the building, which resembles a vast slice of watermelon.

8PM Head back to Jardim Paulista; dining at the delicious Bahian-flavoured **Capim Santo** (*see p120*) is the way to begin your evening. From there, grab a cab to the neighbourhood of Pinheiros for a samba-filled night at **Ó do Borogodó** (*see p194*).

NAVIGATING THE CITY

São Paulo was built sporadically, and the various growth spurts have contributed to a city with many parallel and diagonal streets. Ask for directions if you're lost or confused; people may not speak English, but they will usually try their best with non-verbal signals.

For a city of this size, the public transport is not particularly user-friendly. Bus maps are only available online, and the metrô does not cover every area. Still, if you follow the street maps in this guide (*see pp239-52*), take the metrô and use the buses that we suggest, the city is quite navigable. São Paulo's metrô, the largest in the country, is modern, clean, quick and safe. For more information on public transport, *see pp224-25*.

Day 2 Destination Centre

10AM If you won't have a chance to explore Brazil's UNESCO-protected colonial towns, begin your day inside the **Museu de Arte Sacra** (*see p56*). This museum, inside an 18th-century monastery, is a great example of colonial architecture.

11AM Outside the museum, turn left for the **Parque da Luz** (*see p55*), a gem of a sculpture garden. The park is also home to the **Pinacoteca do Estado** (*see p56*), a renovated turn-of-the-century museum with the second-best collection of art in the city, housed in an impressive space.

1PM Across the street is **Estação da Luz** (*see p55*), São Paulo's English-built train station.

2PM Hungry yet? If so, walk south-east to the **Mercado Municipal** (*see p156*), the city's giant, restored old market. Try the mortadella sandwiches, *pasteis* with cheese or Middle Eastern kibbeh, followed by rainbow-coloured Amazonian fruit from the many stalls.

4PM Spend the afternoon wandering around the old colonial centre-turned-financial stronghold. Don't miss the two iconic churches and surrounding *praças*, **Mosteiro de São Bento** (*see p49*) and **Catedral Metropolitana** (*see p49*). Relax at the **Parque Anhangabaú**, the city's most European-looking plaza, with a gorgeous fountain and views of the **Teatro Municipal**, São Paulo's striking opera house (*see p204*).

6PM From here you can walk down to the Japanese neighbourhood of **Liberdade** (*see p60*) and either grab some sushi or tempura, or just take in the atmosphere of the area, home to the largest Japanese community outside Japan.

8PM You can now decide between dinner or music. If you want food, take the metrô back to Jardim Paulista and try **Brasil a Gosto** (*see p119*). If you're ready for music with appetisers, stay in the Centro. **Bar Brahma** (*see p192*) has some of the best traditional tunes in town; between bossa nova, jazz, samba and *pagode*, you're bound to find something you= like inside its inviting maze of music rooms.

SEEING THE SIGHTS
Most of São Paulo's important sites are in close proximity to each other and the metrô. For sights that are further out, consult the municipal bus website, www.sptrans.com.br, or take a taxi. Most cultural centres and museums are free or charge low admission prices, and even the MASP can be visited one day a week free of charge.

GUIDED TOURS
A number of guided tours are available through agencies around town. Try Matueté (3071 4515, www.matuete.com) for customised tours around the city, and Easygoing Brazil for half or whole day tours around the major sights (3801 9540, www.easygoing.com.br). For trips to the immigrant areas, try Number One Tours (3081 4004, www.numberonetours.com).

GUANABARA
RECOMMENDS

HOT
SPOTS SÃO
IN PAULO

BAR BRAHMA
www.barbrahmasp.com

ORIGINAL
www.baroriginal.com.br

PIRAJÁ
www.piraja.com.br

BAR DO JUAREZ
www.bardojuarez.com.br

The soul of Brazil in
the heart of London

GUANABARA ◉
BRAZILIAN MUSIC DRINK FOOD CULTURE
WWW.GUANABARA.CO.UK

São Paulo in Profile

CENTRO

The most historic part of São Paulo is also the city's business nucleus. The colonial centre has been transformed into a financial powerhouse, and its abundant, leafy *praças* are crowded with business people during the working day. Splendid skyscraper views of the city can also be found here, from either the Edificio Itália or the Banespa buildings.

▶ For more, see pp44-53.

LUZ & OTHER DISTRICTS

The *bairros* of **Brás** and **Mooca** were labour centres during the industrial revolution in São Paulo. The neighbourhood of **Luz** is home to the spectacular Pinacoteca do Estado, a wonderful museum filled with a fabulous array of Brazilian landscape painting and portraiture. **Bom Retiro** was the centre of the garment industry; once a Jewish neighbourhood, it's now home to a large number of Korean immigrants.

▶ For more, see pp54-58.

BELA VISTA & LIBERDADE

Directly south of Centro lies the Japanese neighbourhood of **Liberdade**; come here for great sushi and curious novelty items. Southwest of Liberdade, **Bela Vista** was once home to the Italian community; remnants of the cuisine and culture can still be found in São Paulo's Little Italy.

▶ For more, see pp59-62.

CONSOLAÇAO & HIGIENOPOLIS

Encircling the western edge of the Centro district is the newly hip and attractive neighbourhood of **Consolação**. It's fast becoming a buzzy restaurant and bar area, frequented by media types. Neighbouring **Higienópolis** is a green, garden-like urban retreat for the city's wealthier residents.

▶ For more, see pp63-65.

AVENIDA PAULISTA & JARDINS

The snazzy neighbourhood of **Jardim Paulista** is a high-class, leafy sanctuary. Rua Oscar Freire is the Melrose Place and Madison Avenue of São Paulo. The adjacent, skyscraper-lined **Avenida Paulista** is an urban jungle, of concrete and greenery, and has a first-rate art attraction in the Museu de Arte de São Paulo, more commonly known as the MASP.

▶ For more, see pp66-72.

Offset your
flight with
Trees for Cities
and make your
trip mean
something for
years to come

www.treesforcities.org/offset

Trees for Cities
Charity registration number 1032154

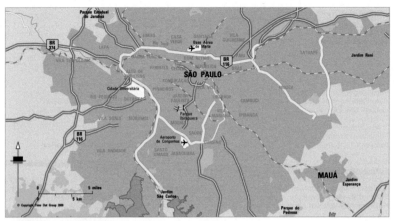

PARQUE IBIRAPUERA

São Paulo's most famous park is home to the largest number of attractions per square mile anywhere in the city. You can use the park for sports or for panoramic vistas of the city, but most visitors explore it for its museums and the festivals it hosts throughout the year.

▶ For more, see pp73-75.

PINHEIROS & VILA MADALENA

Head to **Pinheiros** and **Vila Madalena** for a taste of bohemian São Paulo, a pair of easygoing neighbourhoods that are full of great music venues. The city's crowded bar central is to be found at the crossing of Rua Aspicuelta and Rua Mourato Coelho.

▶ For more, see pp76-78.

ITAIM BIBI & VILA OLIMPIA

South of **Pinheiros** and west of **Jardins**, these neighbourhoods are filled with condominiums and high-class malls for the rich. Nevertheless, with cash comes (some) culture, and there's no shortage of museums and restaurants to explore as well.

▶ For more, see pp79-81.

BROOKLIN, BUTANTA & MORUMBI

The metropolitan area of the city's outer edges on either side of the Pinheiros river has supplanted favelas, and is dotted with glass-walled skyscrapers and financial centres, shopping malls and luxury hotels.

▶ For more, see pp82-84.

SOUTH OF CENTRO

The city's massive sprawl extends to the point where parks and palaces are incorporated by the growing city. In Vila Mariana are some examples of São Paulo's first modernist houses, from the 1920s and '30s.

▶ For more, see pp85-88.

Time Out São Paulo

Editorial
Editor Anna Katsnelson
Managing Editor Mark Rebindaine
Copy Editors Jeremy Helligar, Patrick Welch
Listings Editor Eric Rosenbaum
Proofreaders Emma Clifton, Simon Cropper, John Watson
Editorial Assistant Amanda Guerrero
Indexer Anna Norman

Managing Director Peter Fiennes
Editorial Director Ruth Jarvis
Series Editor Will Fulford-Jones
Business Manager Dan Allen
Editorial Manager Holly Pick
Assistant Management Accountant Ija Krasnikova

Design
Art Director (Buenos Aires office) Gonzalo Gil
Designer (Buenos Aires office) Javier Beresiarte
Art Director Scott Moore
Art Editor Pinelope Kourmouzoglou
Senior Designer Henry Elphick
Graphic Designers Kei Ishimaru, Nicola Wilson
Advertising Designer Jodi Sher

Picture Desk
Picture Editor Jael Marschner
Deputy Picture Editor Lynn Chambers
Picture Researcher Gemma Walters
Picture Librarian Christina Theisen

Advertising
Commercial Director Mark Phillips
International Advertising Manager Kasimir Berger
International Sales Executive Charlie Sokol
Advertising Sales (São Paulo) Silvio Giannini

Marketing
Marketing Manager Yvonne Poon
Sales & Marketing Director, North America & Latin America Lisa Levinson
Senior Publishing Brand Manager Luthfa Begum
Art Director Anthony Huggins

Production
Group Production Director Mark Lamond
Production Manager Brendan McKeown
Production Controller Damian Bennett

Time Out Group
Chairman Tony Elliott
Chief Executive Officer David King
Group General Manager/Director Nichola Coulthard
Time Out Communications Ltd MD David Pepper
Time Out International Ltd MD Cathy Runciman
Time Out Magazine Ltd Publisher/MD Mark Elliott
Group IT Director Simon Chappell
Marketing & Circulation Director Catherine Demajo

Contributors
Introduction Anna Katsnelson. **History** Eric Rosenbaum. **São Paulo Today** Eric Rosenbaum. **Architecture** Anna Katsnelson. **Brazil's Boomtown** Eric Rosenbaum. **Centro** Nico Oved. **Luz & Other Districts** Juliana Guarany. **Bela Vista & Liberdade** Karim Alexander Khan. **Consolação & Higienopolis** Karim Alexander Khan. **Jardins & Avenida Paulista** Camila Belchior. **Parque Ibirapuera** Jennifer Prado. **Pinheiros & Vila Madalena** Camila Belchior. **Itaim Bibi & Vila Olimpia** Camila Belchior. **Brooklin, Butantã & Morumbi** Richard Lomas. **South of the City** Kim Beecheno (*The Immigrant's Canvas* Anna Katsnelson). **Hotels** Kim Beecheno, Camila Belchior, Juliana Guarany, Anna Katsnelson, Eve Richer. **Restaurants** Kim Beecheno, Camila Belchior, Silvio Giannini, Juliana Guarany, Karim Alexander Khan, Anna Katsnelson, Eve Richer (*Berry Controversial*). **Bars, Cafés & Botequins** Juliana Guarany, Mose Hayward, Anna Katsnelson, Karim Alexander Khan, Nico Oved (*Cachaça's Shot at the Top*, *The Big Freeze* Eric Rosenbaum). **Shops & Services** Camila Belchior, Juliana Guarany, Karim Alexander Khan (*Profile* Anna Katsnelson). **Calendar** Camilo Rocha. **Carnival** Juliana Guarany, Mose Hayward. **Children** Meieli Sawyer Detoni. **Film** Camilo Rocha, Eric Rosenbaum. **Galleries** Camila Belchior. **Gay & Lesbian** Ricardo Bairos. **Music** Mose Hayward, Anna Katsnelson. **Nightlife** Karim Alexander Khan, Camilo Rocha. **Performing Arts** Mose Hayward (*Subversive Plays* Anna Katsnelson). **Sports & Fitness** Juliana Guarany, Jennifer Prado (*King of the Road* Eric Rosenbaum). **Escapes & Excursions** Kim Beecheno, Juliana Guarany, Mose Hayward, Eric Rosenbaum. **Directory** Eve Richer.

Maps E-cartografia Luis Maria Benitez (www.e-cartografia.com), except: page 239 courtesy of Metrô São Paulo.

Photography Anna Katsnelson, except: pages 11 (photo 4) and 166 courtesy of Grand Hyatt; pages 11 (photo 5), 205 (photo 2) and 206 Sylvia Masini; page 16 Navio de Emigrantes; page 19 Militão Augusto de Azevedo/Arquivo Agência Estado; pages 21, 25, 171, 173, 197 Arquivo Agência Estado; pages 80, 82, 87, 165, 169, 209 Wanderlei Celestino-SP Turis; page 83 Richard Lomas; page 87 André Stéfano-SPTuris; page 88 courtesy of Acervo Museu Lasar Segall; pages 133, 135 Carol Quintanilha/Cartaz Comunicação; page 165 Alexandre Diniz-SPTuris; page 170 Antonio Aguilar/Agência Estado; page 174 Epitácio Pessoa/Agência Estado; page 178 Mariana Maltoni/Cartaz Comunicação; pages 179, 198 Felipe Lopez courtesy of Cartaz Comunicação; pages 164, 208 Jefferson Pancieri-SPTuris; page 181 Camila Belchior; pages 182, 184 Gabriel Victal; 187 Alan Rodrigo; pages 183, 199, 200, 201 Nico Oved; page 211 courtesy of Instituto Ayrton Senna; pages 215, 216 courtesy of Guarujá Convention & Visitors Bureau; page 220 Kim Beecheno. The following images were supplied by the featured establishments/artists: pages 36, 86, 90, 91, 92, 93, 95, 96, 100, 103, 104, 119, 122, 128, 175, 176, 177, 180.

The Editor would like to thank Juliana Carrasco, Luciane Leite, Marisa Marrocos and Carol Negri at SPTuris; Christine Caterina at SPFW; Federico Gilardi; Juliana Guarany; Marine Guyot; Matias Claret; Claire Rigby; Adriana Rinaldi; Eric Rosenbaum; Grand Hyatt; L'Hotel.

About the Guide

GETTING AROUND
The back of the book contains street maps of São Paulo, as well as overview maps of the city and its surroundings. The maps begin on page 239; the locations of hotels (**❶**), restaurants (**❶**), and bars, cafés and *boteqins* (**❶**) are marked on them. The majority of businesses in this guide are located in the areas we've mapped; the grid-square references at the end of each listing refers to these maps.

THE ESSENTIALS
For practical information, including visas, disabled access, emergency phone numbers, lost property, useful websites and local transport, please see the Directory. It begins on page 223.

THE LISTINGS
Addresses, phone numbers, websites, transport information, hours and prices are all included in our listings. All were checked and current at press time. However, business owners can alter their arrangements at any time, and fluctuating economic conditions can cause prices to change rapidly.

The best venues in the city, the must-sees and must-dos, have all been marked with a red star (★). In the Sights chapters, we've also marked venues that do not charge admission with a **FREE** symbol.

PHONE NUMBERS
The area code for São Paulo is 011. You don't need to use the code when calling within São Paulo: simply dial the eight-digit number as listed in this guide.

To reach numbers in this guide from outside Brazil, first dial your country's international access code (011 from the US, 00 from the UK) or a plus symbol, then the Brazilian country code (54), then 11 for São Paulo (omitting the initial '0') and finally the eight-digit number as listed in the guide. For more on phones, including information on calling abroad from Brazil and local mobile phone access, *see p231*.

FEEDBACK
We welcome feedback on this guide, both on the venues we've included and on any other places that you'd like to see featured in future editions. Please email us at guides@timeout.com.

Time Out Guides

Founded in 1968, Time Out has grown from humble beginnings into the leading resource for anyone wanting to know what's happening in the world's greatest cities. Alongside our influential weeklies in London, New York and Chicago, we publish more than 20 magazines in cities as varied as Beijing and Beirut; a range of travel books, with the City Guides now joined by the newer Shortlist series; and an information-packed website. The company remains proudly independent, still owned by Tony Elliott four decades after he launched *Time Out London*.

Written by local experts and illustrated with original photography, our books also retain their independence. No business has been featured because it has advertised, and all restaurants and bars are visited and reviewed anonymously.

ABOUT THE EDITOR
Anna Katsnelson is a former Fulbright scholar to Brazil. She is currently writing her doctoral dissertation in Comparative Literature at the University of Texas at Austin.

A full list of the book's contributors can be found on the opposite page. However, we've also included details of individual writers in selected chapters throughout the guide.

Time Out

timeout.com/travel
Get the local experience

Dream deli counter at Franchi, in the Prati district, **Rome**

© Gianluca Moggi

In Context

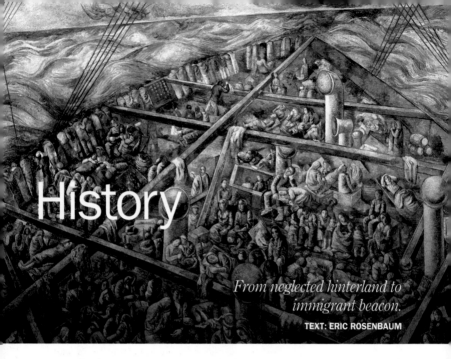

History

From neglected hinterland to immigrant beacon.

São Paulo's official motto is the Latin phrase 'Non ducor, duco' ('I am not led, I lead'). Yet the city began its life as a minor dot on the Portuguese colonial map of Brazil, close to the coastal ports for both commercial and strategic reasons. It played the part of poor colonial relation to the historic Brazilian capitals of Salvador da Bahia and Rio de Janeiro for much of its 455-year history. But once given the opportunity, São Paulo worked faster and more feverishly than its rival cities, eventually surpassing them.

The city's colonial roots – a typical New World story of exploration and exploitation – have been largely overshadowed by its more recent history. The transition from a plantation economy to industrial powerhouse, large-scale immigration, the fits and starts of early republicanism, and the development of an advanced capitalist state all played a crucial role in São Paulo's history. And the figures who propelled the development of Brazil as a whole – Jesuits and pioneers, slaves, immigrants and coffee barons, power-tussling generals and statesmen, captains of industry and striking workers, student revolutionaries and dictators – all played specific roles in the development of São Paulo. It may be relatively young in megacity terms, but it has been busy over the past century, becoming Brazil's largest city (in fact, one of the world's largest), and the financial and cultural capital.

Eric Rosenbaum is a North American journalist who has lived and worked in various Brazilian cities.

'Gold made Rio de Janeiro, as surely as sugar made Salvador and Recife, and as coffee made São Paulo.'

EARLY HISTORY

The original settlement was distinctive for one reason, its inland location – a rarity in colonial Brazil. Founded by two Jesuits in 1554 (on the day of the Feast of Saint Paul) as the settlement of São Paulo de Piratininga, it was, at least theoretically, to be a stopping point between the coast and the unexplored interior of the country.

The founding Jesuits, missionaries Manuel da Nóbrega and José de Anchieta, established the Colégio de São Paulo de Piratininga with the goal of converting the Tupi-Guarani tribes in the area. Other arrivals in the area, the trailblazing *bandeirantes* (flag bearers) – colonialists who set out on forays of exploration in search of slaves, precious metals and gems – were less religiously inspired and often at odds with the missionaries, sometimes employing violence. These early explorers spread out across the interior of the country in the 17th century to make their fortunes far from the established sugar and cattle industries that dominated the country (*see p18* **The Wild, Wild West of São Paulo**).

Even with the gains made by the *bandeirantes*, São Paulo would remain one of the poorest and most isolated colonial areas in Brazil for the first 200 years of its history. The only connection the outpost had to the rest of the colonial world before the 19th century was through the port of Santos. But the journey between the two was not easy. The road from Santos, over the coastal mountains, was so treacherous that in 1765 – after delaying the trip for a full year – Governor Luiz Antonio de Souza finally decided to climb the road on foot rather than risk death by being carried up the *caminho do mar* (road to the sea) in a sedan chair.

EVE OF TRANSFORMATION

Towards the end of the 18th century, an immigrant merchant class was merging with the original patriarchs, forming the first São Paulo elite; it was buoyed by mineral riches discovered in Minas Gerais. As a result, a proper road over the mountains was finally constructed in 1780. Brazil was declared independent of Portugal in 1822, as the Brazilian Empire, and this change precipitated important events in the making of São Paulo, the city. Officials appointed by the Rio court appeared, the city's first newspaper was printed, and an imperial law of 1827 established one of the first law schools in Brazil. Now known as the Faculdade de Direito USP (University of São Paulo School of Law), it defined São Paulo as a university town. However, despite these developments, in 1872 the city's population remained just 31,000.

THE PLANTATION ECONOMY

In Brazil, it is often said that 'Gold made Rio de Janeiro, as surely as sugar made Salvador and Recife, and coffee made São Paulo'. As the mining industry led to greater regional wealth and regional markets for goods opened, Paulistas (people from São Paulo state) began to introduce African slaves instead of rely on indigenous slaves. What had been a relatively stable population exploded in the early 19th century, with the import of thousands of male slaves to work on the coffee plantations. It was the coffee-growing economy that was responsible for the fact that most of Brazil's slave population lived in São Paulo state. By the 1830s, among a population of 282,000, 81,000 were slaves.

The Wild, Wild West of São Paulo

Bandeirantes, pioneers of the Brazilian interior.

Brazilian history probably has more than its fair share of folkloric figures and legendary tales, but the truth about the *bandeirantes* is more complicated than the myth of heroic explorers in an undiscovered country. *Bandeirantes* were, indeed, explorers, encountering, enslaving and interbreeding with indigenous people, mixing languages and cultures, searching for mineral riches, all the while claiming interior land for the Portuguese flag.

Miscegenation and social democracy were part of the *bandeirante* pioneer experience, but these men were far from political idealists. Their morals encompassed extremes: one *bandeirante*, Fernão Dias Pais, never returned from a expedition in search of emeralds that he undertook at the age of 66. His mission failed when, among other events, he refused to sanction the enslavement of natives by some members of his party. *Bandeirante* leaders including Manoel Preto and Antonio Raposo Tavares destroyed Jesuit missions and enslaved thousands of natives during the first half of the 17th century in countless vicious raids that kept the Jesuits and natives scurrying for refuge.

Due to the actions of the roaming *bandeirantes*, the peace-loving Jesuits were forced to function as de facto weapons dealers, arming natives, who imposed some crushing defeats on the explorers between 1628 and 1641.

The *bandeirantes* were the original Paulistas, paving the way for the 18th-century mineral exploration of neighbouring state Minas Gerais, along with the search for gold and diamonds elsewhere. They laid the groundwork for the development of the plantation economy of São Paulo state. They also helped Portugal fight off territorial challenges from other European colonisers in the 1600s.

Cassiano Ricardo, an early 20th-century journalist and poet, wrote that within every contemporary Brazilian can be found 'a heavy dose' of the wandering *bandeirante*, and that the two aspects of the Brazilian self would finally converge 'like waves along a single stretch of beach'. Perhaps to remind Paulistanos of this mystical adage, **Parque Ibirapuera** (pictured; *see p74*) features a stone sculpture tribute to the explorers.

Poetry doesn't represent literal truth, but the *bandeirantes*' imprint was undeniable: as a result of their inland forays, by 1720 the captaincy of São Paulo included the present-day states of Minas Gerais, Mato Grosso, Parana, Goias, Santa Catarina, and parts of Rio de Janeiro and Rio Grande do Sul.

19th-century São Paulo.

Although the end of slavery in Brazil in 1888 was considered a 'bloodless miracle', countless bloody altercations and massacres actually occurred in São Paulo state in the period leading up to abolition. The region had been singled out by abolitionists, including José do Patrocínio, as 'the strong fortress of heinous slavism' in Brazil. They distributed abolitionist literature to slaves who could read, and organised sensational public displays of slave torture instruments. Administrative political positions to fight for abolition were also created, known as the *caifazes*. Such was the determination of those whose interests lay in preserving slavery that some of those who became *caifazes* were murdered. In the final years before abolition, runaway slaves were hunted by vigilante police on their way to the port of Santos, and insurrections were common on the *fazendas* (plantations). Anarchy reigned, and the *fazendeiros* were well aware of it.

NEW LABOUR: IMMIGRATION

In some respects, it was the end of slavery rather than its existence that was the most important event in São Paulo's history. When slavery was finally abolished in 1888 there was a huge demand for new labour to do the work previously done by slaves. A huge effort to attract immigrants to do that work began. It coincided with the greatest boom period for coffee: production doubled between 1886 and 1894; it doubled again by 1900 and once more by 1929. São Paulo had become the most important coffee-producing region in the world. 'Braços para a lavoura' or 'manpower for agriculture', was the cry, and that meant manipulation of immigration policy by the coffee barons. The most important development in São Paulo's immigration policy was the creation of the Sociedade Promotora da Imigração in 1886. This non-profit organisation was established by the coffee barons and political leaders to assist the new provincial government in its efforts. Between 1886 and 1904, Promotora expenditures, dominated by travel subsidies of 80 per cent for immigrants, were fully funded by the provincial government. The first president of the Promotora, Martinho Prado Junior, was a coffee baron. He personally went to northern Italy to publicise the programme and set up a recruiting office in Genoa.

In the half century before the Great Depression, Brazil ranked third in the western hemisphere (behind the US and Argentina) in numbers of immigrants entering the country, and many arrived in São Paulo. Between 1886 and 1930, more than two million immigrants arrived in the city. In 1886 the population of the state was 1.2 million. By 1920, it was 3.7 million; of these, 800,000 people, or 22 per cent of the population, were foreign-born. By 1905, 65 per cent of the more than 338,000 agricultural workers in the coffee zone were foreign-born.

IN CONTEXT

THE COFFEE GRINDER

A huge hostel built by the government to house 4,000 often held upwards of 10,000 foreign immigrants in its early years. Between 1910 and 1928, approximately 684,000 immigrants went from the hostel to the coffee zone. When the transport subsidies finally ended in 1928, the coffee bubble was about to burst. Total immigration in 1929 was over 100,000; in 1930, it was down to 39,644. By this time, however, São Paulo was already a dense ethnic weave. Government registries listed immigrants from most major eastern and western European countries, as well as Lebanon, Syria and Japan. Brazil now has the largest expat Japanese population in the world – 1.4 million – most of whom are concentrated in São Paulo, with many in Liberdade.

Foreign immigrants were not the only new faces in this industrial centre: beginning in 1923, one of the greatest migration movements began arriving in São Paulo from north-east Brazil. Many *nordestinos* came to escape the drought, sickness and poverty prevalent in the interior of the semi-arid north-east area. They served as construction workers in many of the city's neighbourhoods, and were also among the first to live in *cortiços* (tenement buildings) that later gave way to *favelas*.

THE NEW OLD REPUBLIC

The end of the Brazilian empire in 1889 led to a period of uncertainty in country, during which the Paulistano elite wielded a considerable amount of power. São Paulo was the first state after Rio to form a republican party, the Partido Republicano Paulista (Republican Party of São Paulo, PRP), and most of the country's early presidents were educated at USP, until Getulio Vargas, who took power in 1930. São Paulo itself provided four of Brazil's nine elected presidents between 1891 and 1930. All but one of the remaining early presidents came from the neighbouring state of Minas Gerais, and this was no coincidence. The need for political pragmatism had led São Paulo and Minas Gerais to cobble together an agreement at the Convention of Taubate in 1906 to shuttle the presidency back and forth, an agreement helped by voting laws that favoured literacy and wealth, which remained in place until the 1930s.

SAO PAULO AND THE TENENTES

During the formative years of the Brazilian republic, the Brazilian military rebel *tenentes* (lieutenants) provided a colourful opposition to the São Paulo establishment. The *tenentes* launched successive guerrilla campaigns under the direction of Luis Carlos Prestes, and led the failed revolutions of 1922 and 1924. In 1924, the *tenentes* actually seized control of São Paulo. Revolutionary activity was coordinated to break out in multiple states, but Paulistanos were the only Brazilians to awake to a revolution in their streets. A *tenente* force of 1,500 rebels seized federal buildings over a period of three days and fought troops and police loyal to the government. By 27 July, the *tenentes* had to flee São Paulo on a long trek that would ultimately lead them to Foz de Iguaçu, in February 1925. Only in Rio Grande do Sul, home state of Luís Carlos Prestes, did the *tenentes* succeed and create what is known as the Prestes Column. By April of 1925, the Prestes Column had broken through loyalists' troops to reunite with the São Paulo rebels at Iguaçu.

Among the São Paulo leaders of *tenentismo*, only Miguel Costa stayed with Prestes to fight against the government campaign being led by General Rondon, who had been US President Theodore Roosevelt's guide in the Amazon in 1913-14. The Prestes Column wandered from state to Brazilian state fighting the federal army until February of 1927. Later Prestes became the head of the Partido Comunista do Brasil, with a direct line to Moscow.

Japanese immigrants on a coffee plantation in the late 1800s.

A REPUBLIC AT WAR WITH ITSELF

When Getulio Vargas took power in 1930, he had wrestled the presidency from yet another São Paulo native, former governor Julio Prestes (no relation to Luís Carlos Prestes). Prestes had been elected but never took office, and Vargas's ascendancy marked the abrupt death of Brazil's first modern democracy, known as A Velha República (The Old Republic).

São Paulo would never again dominate national politics like it did in the pre-1930 period. The Revolução Constitucionalista of 1932 in São Paulo, which came two years after Vargas's successful coup, was a last-ditch effort by the Paulista elite to assert its authority on the national scene. The struggle hinged on Vargas's increasingly authoritarian control and his use of *interventors* – federal officials, often military men – as regionally placed governors. João Alberto, a *tenente*, arrived in São Paulo to take the place of the elected state governor in 1932. That power play by Vargas, combined with the shooting of four students protesting federal policy on the streets of São Paulo in May 1932, triggered a short civil war. São Paulo armed 30,000 men, while leading industrialists manufactured grenades and gas masks. The Revolução was crushed within a matter of months, after support from the states of Minas Gerais and Rio Grande do Sul failed to materialise in support of the Paulista rebels.

STRIKE!

Official political theatre largely excluded the masses of immigrant and Brazilian workers who had flocked to São Paulo, but these groups did not hold back from expressing their presence in the streets and neighbourhoods of São Paulo during the city's period of industrialisation, a period during which the city's population continued to expand, reaching 600,000 by 1920.

Working-class districts emerged from São Paulo's run-down central slums, such as the Italian enclave of Bixiga and the Japanese community of Liberdade, as well as nearby industrial areas, such as Ipiranga, Mooca, Bras, Lapa and Vila Madalena. It was the beginning of an urban-development trend that would last for decades. During a World War II-era visit to São Paulo, New York City Mayor Fiorello LaGuardia observed the city from the top of its tallest building at the time, the Martinelli Building. He is reported to have said: 'I understand, in that part [pointing to the area encompassing Bras and Mooca] people work; in this part [pointing to the city centre, Consolação and Paulista] they eat'. As early as 1902, local journalist José Americano noted that of the 30 to 40 industrial chimneys emitting black smoke from English coal, most were in Brás and Mooca. By 1917, children in Mooca were entering factories at seven in the evening and not leaving until six in the morning. Labour-sympathising newspapers began to publish works like Maxim Gorky's *Mother*, in serial form. The bad conditions imposed on workers by the capitalist elite led to the Greve Geral (General Strike) in June and July of 1917, a landmark in the history of the São Paulo and wider Brazilian workers' movement. It began in the largest factories, including the Brazilian beer manufacturer Companhia Antarctica and textile giant Cotifinicio Crespi in Mooca, controlled by Rodolfo Crespi, where women weavers were among the first to strike. On 9 July, police shot and killed Antonio Inequez Martinez, a young shoemaker in Brás, leading to a public march and funeral that brought more support for the strike. By 14 July, the city was a war zone, with 40,000 striking workers and military personnel roaming the neighbourhoods.

Eloi Chaves, State Secretary of Justice and Public Security, commandeered the leaders of the São Paulo Centre for Commerce and Industry, including Crespi, Francisco Matarazzo and textile industrialist Jorge Street. They agreed to a 20 per cent wage increase, amnesty for the strikers, union freedom, and improvement of living and working conditions. By 18 July, the strike was over, and modern industrial relations in São Paulo had been created.

THE AVANT-GARDE

The artistic movement in São Paulo was also challenging the Paulista establishment. Mario de Andrade, one of the most important Paulistano writers of the modernist period, said that it was in 1916 that 'the conviction of a new art' came to 'a little group of Paulista intellectuals'. An exhibit of young artist Anita Malfatti's expressionist paintings, after she had just returned from Europe, stimulated Emiliano Di Cavalcanti, the poet Guilherme de Almeida and the novelist Oswald de Andrade to begin an artistic salon at the O Livro bookstore.

The idea for the Paulistano artistic manifesto of February 1922 known as the Semana de Arte Moderna had its beginning in this group. Most of these artists, writers and musicians were born after 1890 and experienced the explosion of São Paulo as a city. They sought to reconnect art with the rapidly changing contemporary Paulistano society.

The modernist explosion also showcased the growing wealth of São Paulo. Paulo Prado hosted *modernistas* in his mansion on Avenida Higienopolis and funded the avant-garde magazine *Knock-out*. The aristocratic Paulistano Penteado family was the first to purchase a painting from di Cavalcanti. It was the beginning of a long patronage of the arts by elite families: Yolanda Penteado would later marry Ciccillo Matarazzo of the Matarazzo clan, who was the founder of the Museu de Arte de São Paulo (MASP). Publisher and editor Monteiro Lobato was probably the most important arts patron to the modernists. In 1920, he founded Monteiro Lobato & Cia, with the mission of creating a Brazilian reading public. He edited such famous writers as Oswald de Andrade, Ribeiro Couto, Lima Barreto and Guilherme de Almeida. Lobato's company lasted only five years, but it gave birth to the São Paulo publishing industry. In 1926, only 173,000 books were printed in São Paulo state, a figure that increased to 2,300,000 in 1937 and 6,700,000 by 1946. By that time, São Paulo state was buying 40 per cent of the books printed in Brazil.

POST-WAR SAO PAULO

As early as 1930, the power and importance of São Paulo's working class was apparent at the highest levels of national politics: during the Depression, Vargas even ordered that the production of coffee and the shipping of the 60-pound sacks to the port of Santos continue, even if the sacks had to be stockpiled as export markets had collapsed during the crash, just to keep workers in employment. In 1945, post-war populism resulted in the first popularly elected São Paulo state governor, Adhemar de Barros of the Partido Socialista Progresiva (PSP). The rise of Adhemarismo, which had the support of the newly re-legalised Partido Comunista Brasileiro (PCB) of Luis Carlos Prestes, and its sudden claim to São Paulo's

Paulistano Fascism

From modernism to right-wing militarism.

A powerful but short-lived political movement born in São Paulo was the fascist integralist philosophy of Plinio Salgado and his **Açao Integralista Brasileira** (AIB, Brazilian Integralist Action) party. Salgado had been a literary figure during the modernist Semana de Arte Moderna (*see p34* **Semana 22**). He may not have written odes to Mussolini like Ezra Pound, but the *integralistas* were an influential force. There were at their height of power between 1932 and 1938, coinciding with the transition of the government to Vargas' Estado Novo (a mix of Mussolini-style fascism and the authoritarian regime of Portugal's Antonio de Oliveira Salazar).

With green-shirt uniforms and the Greek sigma as a symbol, Salgado carried the banner of 'God, Country and Family' throughout Brazil, from the birth of the first *integralista* cell in São Paulo in 1932. In 1934, the party counted 170,000 members, and by 1936, the AIB had elected 20 mayors and 3,000 city council members across Brazil. According to Salgado, it was Vargas's top army officer, General Pedro de Goes Monteiro (an avid fan of Salgado's early writing), who went so far as to suggest uniform design for the AIB. When a communist revolt began in Brazil in 1935, Salgado offered Vargas an army of 100,000 men.

By 1937, anxious *integralistas*, frustrated by Vargas's lack of power sharing, were planning coups. Salgado kept negotiating, but the AIB history effectively ended in a coup attempt on 11 May 1938. Vargas and his family holed-up in Rio's Guanabara Palace for one day until the army arrived to snuff out the threat. Vargas kept the AIB close at hand long enough to benefit from the national fervour it had raised; it was the first truly national party in Brazil. In the end, the Estado Novo reassembled, but it couldn't make room for a national paramilitary organisation that had begun life as a tiny fascist group in São Paulo.

IN CONTEXT

political sceptre, surprised both the capitalist elite and conservative Vargas elements. The PCB candidate for president in 1945, Yedo Fuiza, carried large sections of the São Paulo metropolitan area in the national elections. At the time of the Adhemarismo electoral victories in 1947 and São Paulo's May Day celebrations of the same year, General Pedro de Goes Monteiro said that there was 'an imminent danger for democracy in Brazil'.

Numerous political movements were active during this transformational period for São Paulo, not only Adhemarismo and Communists, but also the Queremismo movement of those still loyal to Vargas – know by their slogan 'Queremos Getulio' (We Want Getulio [Vargas]) – as well as other populist groups such as the *trabalhista* movement of Hugo Borghi. All made major overtures to labour and for good reason: though strike waves were to remain an important factor in capitalist-labour relations throughout the period, the rise of Adhemar de Barros's PSP reflected the more mature organisation of the labour movement in the country's most developed economic state. São Paulo's working class had definitively arrived as a mass electorate.

In the period between the end of World War II and the military *golpe* (coup) of 1964, São Paulo reflected the common motifs of the jubilant post-war period, despite its fragmented politics. Urban renewal, the redrawing of the city map because of car use, industrial and retail development, and suburbanisation replaced pre-war growing pains. In 1940, the Rodovia Anhangüera (SP-330) linking São Paulo to the growing industrial areas of the state, became the first four-lane, asphalt-paved road in the country. Volkswagen set up its first full-scale assembly plant in the São Paulo suburb of São Bernardo do Campo in 1953.

The selection of Brasília as the new federal capital sparked an identity crisis for backward looking Rio, but economic dynamism had become São Paulo's reason for being. In 1940, Rio was still the larger of the two cities, with a population of 1.8 million versus São Paulo's 1.3 million. By 1960, São Paulo had finally eclipsed Rio, with a population of 3.8 million to Rio's 3.3 million.

THE 1964 COUP

Adhemar de Barros's period in power in São Paulo ended in 1966 when he was ousted by the military dictatorship. He died in exile in Paris in 1969. After the military *golpe* of 1964, São Paulo became a terrorised police state. The Açao Libertadora Nacional (ALN), a radical offshoot of the Communist Party centred in São Paulo, was responsible for creating an urban guerrilla movement in Brazil. It played a leading role in two of the defining moments of São Paulo's response to the military regime. First, ALN founder Carlos Marighela was ambushed and killed by São Paulo police in late 1969, after the group had participated in the abduction of the US ambassador to Brazil; Marighela's successor would be tortured to death in 1970.

The second major event was the 1973 killing of USP student Alexandre Vannucchi Leme. It shocked the city and is now considered the pivotal event in triggering large-scale resistance to the regime. Leme was a key student leader said to be affiliated with ALN, but there was not much hard evidence linking him to the group. For two days, on 16 and 17 March, two squads of interrogators brutalised Leme; when they went to retrieve him from his cell for another beating, they discovered him dead. The authorities told the media that Leme had been hit by a truck while attempting to flee. For those inside the maximum security prison where Leme was killed, false documents listed the cause of his death as suicide. In fact, after his death his neck was cut from ear to ear.

Leme's death turned the archbishop of São Paulo, Dom Paulo Evaristo Arns, into a leading figure against the regime. Dom Paulo had previously spoken out against torture but had not taken direct action against the government. He convinced students to attend a mass at the Catedral Metropolitana, the city's largest church, on the eve of the ninth anniversary of the coup, instead of carrying out their threats of a 10,000-student riot on the campus. The combination of secular Paulistano society and the powerful church in resistance to the military regime was a major factor in the eventual return of civil rule to Brazil in 1985.

GOD'S CIA: THE CHURCH INTELLIGENCE AGENCY

During the early 1980s, the Catholic Church's Archdiocese of São Paulo worked as an effective covert intelligence operation. The church created a secret team of lawyers and researchers who gathered and photocopied the records of 707 cases of political trials against 7,367 defendants. The church was able to keep its efforts under wraps for five years; the result was one of the most comprehensive records of dictatorial repression in the 20th century. The archive, *Brasil: Nunca Mais* (*Brazil: Never Again*), contained over one million pages detailing how the regime had monitored, investigated, arrested, tortured and prosecuted citizens. More than 300 forms of torture are documented in its pages. The book was released just as the church's intelligence team completed its research in 1985 and during the transfer from military to civilian rule. It immediately became a bestseller in Brazil, but it would take another ten years for the military to finally admit to its widespread use of torture.

IN CONTEXT

Library books being burnt in 1964, during the military dictatorship.

Sadly, the end of the military regime did not mean the end of all military violence. The killing of 111 prisoners by the military police at the city's Carandiru prison on 2 October 1992 was a high-profile human rights tragedy.

SAO PAULO HITS THE WALL

A seminal 1933 article written by geographer Preston James declared that São Paulo was at the vortex of modern urbanity. Metropolitan São Paulo was once confidently projected to reach 24 million inhabitants by the year 2000. But the 20th-century surge turned into a lurch at the century's end, and the 1990s were a period of declining demographic significance for the city.

Most of São Paulo's recent growth has been on the periphery of the city, in the poorer areas, where 41 per cent of the city's population now lives alongside raw sewage canals. Decentralisation has also been caused by the affluent, however, as more middle-class Paulistanos are choosing to live in gated communities far from the centre of town or public transport.

The city is now a 'greater São Paulo metropolitan region': a post-industrial polycentric metropolis. Urban transport problems highlight the fragmentation of the city in terms of wealth and place. Mayor Luiza Erundina, former president of the Partido dos Trabalhadores (1989-91), proposed a controversial policy of free bus transport during his time in power. The measure, which was to have been funded by taxes, was defeated. Erundina's successor, conservative Partido Progressista populist Paulo Maluf (1992-1996), focused instead on cars, building expensive traffic tunnels in a period in which the state was excessively overspending and the state bank, the Banespa, was in danger of bankruptcy. São Paulo authorities recently adopted a similar approach in dealing with traffic to Mexico City's, with vehicles restricted in the days of the week they can be driven; yet congestion still chokes the city.

While the days of anarchists, workers and student protestors seem distant, São Paulo has experienced civil unrest in the 21st century, although its motives were anything but lofty. In 2006, a prison-organised mafia, the Primeiro Comando da Capital (PCC), led attacks at 64 prisons in São Paulo state.

The days of rapid industrial growth may be over for São Paulo, but that doesn't mean the city isn't continuing to develop, but economically and culturally. And the city's complicated ethnic, political and economic weave means that its development will continue to hold global interest. It's worth remembering that only 200 years ago São Paulo was barely a stitch of thread on the Brazilian fabric.

IN CONTEXT

São Paulo Today

A city on the verge of breaking out, or apart?

TEXT: ERIC ROSENBAUM

São Paulo's reputation tends toward extremes. Enormous wealth coexists with appalling poverty; gleaming skyscrapers loom over crumbling edifices; newspaper headlines are devoted to an uneasy mix of glitzy celebrity parties and violent crime. It's a town with a super-sized identity crisis, and the truth about its character is wrapped in an enormous city-of-contrasts cliché.

São Paulo's jumble of self-contained worlds reflects the ongoing tussle between youthful progress and decaying chaos. But despite problems with the infrastructure, and despite a level of social inequality that means safety and security remain major concerns, visitors from other large cities may find that São Paulo feels surprisingly familiar. Between the helicopters of the mega-rich and the shacks of the *favelados*, large working- and middle-class communities exist and, in some cases, thrive. There's normality here, in other words. It just may take a little longer to find.

Museu de Arte de São Paulo (MASP).

THE ATLAS OF AVENIDA PAULISTA

The best symbol of the city's potential is located on the famous Avenida Paulista at a high point in the city, with massive urban sprawl stretching out on both sides below and far beyond it. A massive concrete box wrapped in red, the Museu de Arte de São Paulo (MASP; *see p158*) seems to levitate a full storey above Avenida Paulista atop ingenious and seemingly fragile concrete pillars. The MASP is the Atlas of São Paulo, shouldering the city's metaphorical burden. It's a striking sight. But if you stand directly beneath the hovering geometric behemoth, you'll see delicate cracks in the concrete. Is the clever construction floating confidently on the potential of São Paulo to become one of the world's top-tier metropolises? Or will those cracks lengthen and deepen, a metaphor of sorts for the difficulties facing the town?

KASSAB ON THE JOB

The human Atlas bearing the weight of São Paulo may be the 48-year-old mayor Gilberto Kassab, a descendant of Lebanese immigrants. With degrees in civil engineering and economics, Kassab is well versed in the themes and difficulties that sit at the core of São Paulo's promise. The city may be an economic powerhouse, but the city fathers aren't necessarily doing all they can for their residents. And São Paulo's position as a huge construction site doesn't help. Massive malls, hotels and condo buildings are on the rise, but the array of drab, derelict concrete boxes point to a larger history of failed urban experiments that at one time may have seemed inspired.

Kassab, a mayor in the technocratic can-do spirit of New York's Michael Bloomberg, won't admit to this two-steps-forward, one-step-back dilemma. Although he's seen by some as little more than a puppet of the country's most prominent conservative politician, São Paulo state governor José Serra, Kassab is a progressive politician, and some of the accomplishments made during his tenure are impressive.

In 1999, the homicide rate in São Paulo had reached 35.7 per 100,000 residents, and had been increasing since the 1980s. By 2006, though, the murder rate had fallen to 15.1, and has decreased even further since then. For a city where the residents' worries about violence border on obsession (a significant, and, up to a point, understandable quirk of the Paulistano psyche), a drop of around 50 per cent in the

IN CONTEXT

Whose Art Is It, Anyway?

Beauty is in the eye of the cleaner.

So, which is the better art jury: London's Tate Modern, or the clean-up crew of São Paulo's mayor Gilberto Kassab's *Cidade Limpa* initiative?

In 2008, Otavio and Gustavo Pandolfo were in London. São Paulo's most famous graffiti artists, the brothers had been invited by Tate Modern to work on adorning the building's exterior. But while they were away, officials in their home town removed one of their most famous street murals as part of Kassab's controversial plan for urban renewal.

Still high on the positive public response to *Cidade Limpa*, the city government quickly went into response mode when it realised that it had painted over such a valuable work. Commonly referred to as Os Gêmeos (the twins), the Pandolfos are world-renowned artists that have long used São Paulo as their canvas. By way of apology to graffiti-loving Paulistanos, Kassab and his office created a registry of street art, balancing out what had become a public relations nightmare.

The particular Os Gêmeos work at the centre of the street art scandal was a 680-metre mural on the 23 de Maio highway, which had been approved by the city of São Paulo in 2002. However, it wasn't the only victim. Many street artists in São Paulo, including Os Gêmeos, say that the virtual graffiti genocide was an indirect by-product of *Cidade Limpa*. The twins still contend that hundreds of their works are gone as a result of the city's energetic, monotone paint roller that works with unceasing bureaucratic fury.

The question of street art ownership and maintenance can be a tricky one. After the city's *mea culpa* and the restoration of the offending piece on 23 de Maio, the Os Gêmeos mural was once again the victim of an assault. This time, though, it wasn't the city at fault, but graffiti 'tags' that were sprayed on t he mural in early 2009 by street artists who were less inspired than the famous brothers. Os Gêmeos had to head back to paint over what had been painted over their piece.

It seems that any wall is fair game to the city's graffiti painters, regardless of whether it has international gallery-calibre work on it. The twins could be as busy brushing up their impressive work as the Louvre staff is guarding the Mona Lisa. And although their work could make them wealthy, their full career's worth of street art was available to all for free.

• For more on street art, visit the **Choque Cultural** gallery (*see p179*).

homicide rate in such a short space of time gets a big thumbs up. (Kassab can't take all the credit; the fall in the murder rate started under the tenure of Jose Serra.) The improvement bucks the overall trend in Brazilian cities. Yet, while the homicide rate plummets in comparison with Rio's – and any Paulistano will humbly defer to *Cariocas,* as Rio's residents are known, when it comes to claiming to live in the more violent metropolis – the bulletproofing of cars in São Paulo continues to be a boom business.

CLEAN SLATE

The other high-profile campaign overseen by Kassab is the more controversial *Cidade Limpa* (Clean City) initiative. The law requires any public billboard or sign ten metres or greater in size to be removed; they're all classified as visual pollution. After a spirited but losing battle fought by the Brazilian advertising industry, even the venerable golden arches of McDonald's were brought down. The campaign, a bid to change the city's reputation as one of the world's ugliest urban centres, has proven popular with many Paulistanos. However, critics say that it may be diverting attention from much larger issues about the city's aesthetics. Not for nothing was São Paulo the city chosen by Brazilian director Fernando Mereilles as the location for exterior shots for his 2008 film *Blindness*, based on the José Saramago novel that depicts a bleak vision of a near-future hell on earth.

Supporters of the campaign say that the removal of the billboards has uncovered the city's unique architecture. Detractors say that the missing billboards hid unsightly signs of ageing on too many of the town's buildings. And an effort to revitalise the Centro neighbourhood, which was linked to the *Cidade Limpa* initiative, is still a work in progress. Although a few chic bars and night spots have opened in historic Centro locations, the area can still feel like an abandoned post-apocalyptic nightmare later in the evening. And despite appearances, Kassab is not opposed to advertising in general: in early 2008, the city launched an ad campaign for itself as a tourist destination on CNN International.

IN CONTEXT

Centro. *See p44.*

The *Cidade Limpa* initiative treads delicately on the issue about which image of São Paulo the mayor is working to promote. Even crediting Kassab for the uniqueness of the programme, there's the hint of a collective cognitive dissonance at work among a populace and press that responded with more energy to the removal of advertisements than they do to efforts aimed at more basic and critical elements of urban renewal. The same social vision and relentless municipal drive could seek higher aims, such as improving the lives of São Paulo's population of children living on the streets.

The *Cidade Limpa* campaign came amid a major effort to relocate residents of various *favelas*. In the Morumbi neighbourhood, for instance, business campuses and luxury shopping centres loom over the vestiges of what was once a sprawling *favela* but which is now just a blip of poverty amid the construction cranes and hotels such as the Hilton, where George W Bush once stayed. Apartment buildings constructed for relocated residents are adequate, but stipends that residents have been paid to relocate haven't ensured the creation of viable communities.

Some critics argue that efforts to move communities from former rainforest hillsides border on abuse of environmental rhetoric in their stated aim of 'reclaiming green space'. Pushing the poor to the unseen perimeters of the city with a quick cash incentive, or uprooting an 80-year-old resident from a neighbourhood that has been his or her only home in order to replenish the palm frond, are not the same as solving the problem of poverty in an urban-planning context. Too many migrants coming to São Paulo still land in the *favelas*, extending the sprawl and setting it in contrast to the suburban enclaves in which increasing numbers of São Paulo's professional set live.

Nevertheless, Kassab's achievements resulted in his re-election in 2008. He waged a hard-fought and downright nasty campaign against his main rival, former national tourism minister and ex-São Paulo mayor Marta Suplicy, who went so far as to question Kassab's sexuality. Regardless, Kassab won in a run-off with almost double the votes of Suplicy, raising São Paulo's profile ahead of the national elections of 2010. While Kassab was supported by Serra, Suplicy had the support of President Luiz Inácio Lula da Silva. When the popular Lula's second term comes to an end in 2010, Serra is expected to be a main challenger for the presidency. Winning the support of Kassab's São Paulo electorate is key to the national elections, with more than eight million votes up for grabs.

THE SAO PAULO PSYCHE

The Paulistano populace, so diverse in ethnicity, ideals and opportunities, can tell you more about the São Paulo experience than Kassab's 30 seconds of city marketing on CNN. Yet Paulistanos can can be their own worst enemy. Locals often feel tempted to demonise their city, stoked by a fear of violence that's often irrational. It's a situation not helped by elements of the press that revel in sensationalising violent crime, or by the world's largest private security industry, which does particularly well out of people's safety concerns.

But it's not all bad. For all the complaints, it's not an accident that Brazilians of all stripes flock to São Paulo. A common Paulistano boast is that the city represents the best of rest of the world: during São Paulo Fashion Week, it dresses as Milan; through its most innovative restaurants, it cooks up dishes you'd only find in the likes of New York and London; palm-lined boulevards with iron-gated colonial mansions sit next to luxury SUV dealerships in suburbs that evoke Los Angeles. Sometimes it seems as if Paulistanos would almost prefer their city to be any city but the city it is.

The persistent inferiority complex about falling short compared to the world's 'true' capitals of cosmopolitan life may be understandable, but it doesn't do justice to São Paulo's uniqueness. The city doesn't need to lean on any other place, or any other history. After all, as you'll see for yourself if you stand on Avenida Paulista and admire the bright red box of the MASP, São Paulo has the ability to rise above the chaos. Whether or not it actually *will* remains to be seen.

IN CONTEXT

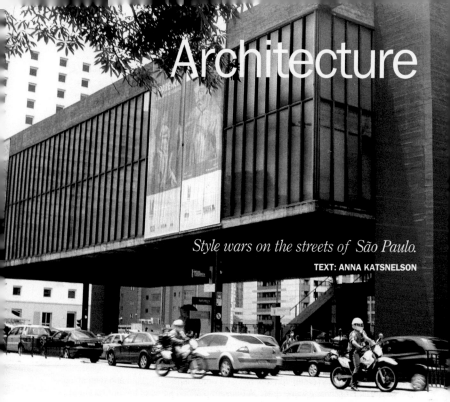

Architecture

Style wars on the streets of São Paulo.

TEXT: ANNA KATSNELSON

It used to be that only expletives and curses hailed down on the heads of the architects and urban planners of this modern megalopolis. That's no longer the case. Thanks to a flood of domestic investment, foreign capital and increased attention from the international architectural community (including recent Pritzker and *Architectural Review* awards that went to Brazilians), São Paulo is experiencing a building boom. The signs are that a fully fledged contemporary architectural renaissance – bold designs, preservation projects and socially responsible engineering – is unfolding.

São Paulo may not be the world's prettiest city, but few towns of its size have such distinctive architecture: the red concrete and dark glass of the MASP and the concrete undulations of the COPAN building are prominent examples of daring 20th-century design. And the new century has been picking up where the last one left off. Ennobling the face of the city is the illuminated Ponte Estaiada Octavio Frias de Oliveira in the Brooklin neighbourhood, while Ruy Ohtake's upside-down arc of copper, the Hotel Unique, has not been out of the spotlight – or the style mags – since it opened in 2003.

'The end of World War II brought the razing of the mansions on Avenida Paulista, which was replanned as the new financial district.'

COLONIAL, NEOCOLONIAL AND NEOCLASSICAL

The pre-20th century period of the city's architectural history is as short as the 20th century's flurry of activity is impressive and long. Prior to the late 19th century, Brazilian colonial motifs were standard: churches varied from severe 16th- and 17th-century rectangular edifices to 18th-century Baroque and rococo structures with rounded steeples, pulpits and elegant, flowery interior decorations. The majority of houses were two storeys, in pink, yellow and white tones, the *chacaras* (country houses) were larger, and the *sobrados* (homes of the wealthy) were made of flattened earth (*taipa*).

Only in the late 19th century did the city depart from its colonial foundations. Francisco de Paulo Ramos de Azevedo constructed the first academic buildings in the city in the late 1890s. His most important work, the **Teatro Municipal** (1911; *see p204*) was modelled on the Paris Opera House. He also began to work with Ricardo Severo, a Portuguese engineer, in championing Brazil's historical identity by using the neocolonial style – an architectural approach that harked back to the colonial buildings of the 18th century, with their Baroque embellishments.

Many significant innovations in early 20th-century Brazilian architecture came directly from Europeans who were eager to ply their trade on new ground as undeveloped as São Paulo. The **Estação da Luz** train station (1901; *see p54*) was designed by Englishman Henry Driver. The ornamented iron roof trellises were made in England and then shipped over to Brazil. French landscape artist JA Bouvard planned some of the pivotal green spaces in the urban fabric: the **Dom Pedro** and **Anhangabaú** parks. These projects, as well as the **Trianon Park** (*see p68*) on Avenida Paulista and **Parque de Buenos Aires** in Higienópolis, give a slight European feel to the city.

Frenchman Victor Dubugras and Swede Carl Eckman brought art nouveau to São Paulo at the turn of the century. Eckman's **Vila Penteado** (1902; Rua Maranhão) and its decorative mouldings, constructed for coffee baron Antônio Penteado, is typical of this style. Dubugras' transformative work, the Mairinque Railway Station (1907) in the state of São Paulo, was one of the first European modernist buildings in the country.

In the second half of the 20th century, prominent architects continued working in the neocolonial idiom. Oswaldo Bratke built a great number of houses in the California mission and Spanish Renaissance styles. His work can still be seen in the residential construction on **Rua Avanhadava** in the city centre.

URBAN PLANNING

The historic centre of the city was reconstructed in the 1910s, and the new city plan replaced the old colonial structures with a commercial centre. A number of concentric neighbourhoods for the working classes were planned around it and the growing factories. Meanwhile, **Avenida Paulista** (*see p67*) was laid out with fashionable mansions by leading lights on the Paulistano architecture scene, such as Azevedo and Dubugras (some of his mansions were in the neocolonial style). This was the first of several reconfigurations of the city centre. The end of World War II brought the razing of the mansions on Avenida Paulista, which was replanned as the new financial district. The neighbouring areas of **Jardim América**, **Jardim Europa** and **Jardim Paulista** were used to relocate the elite; many houses have now been supplanted by high-rise condominiums, and the mansions have once more relocated, this time to Morumbi.

COMMUNISM, LE CORBUSIER AND ESCOLA PAULISTA

It can be said that all roads in 20th-century Brazilian architectural history lead to Communism and Le Corbusier. This Swiss modernist master, who visited Brazil in the 1930s, had a profound influence on his southern-hemisphere counterparts through his use of mass-produced building units (a technique that, for a time, made him popular in the Soviet Union, although he was never a Communist).

The Brazilian Communist party had a huge following among the liberal left, and a number of famous Brazilian artists and prominent architects were Communist Party members. This membership influenced, to no small extent, the types of projects and constructions undertaken in Brazil during the 1940s, '50s and '60s, up to the military coup of 1964. The dictatorship that followed made it increasingly difficult for Communist architects to hold important posts or practise their profession.

One such important figure was **João Vilanova Artigas**, who was influenced by Frank Lloyd Wright (who visited Brazil in 1933) and Le Corbusier. Artigas wanted to create housing for the ever-expanding population of São Paulo. One example of his work is the **Parque Cecap** (1967; Avenida Monteiro Lobato 320, Guarulhos), a construction of 10,000 affordable utility apartments. Artigas directly suffered for his Communist Party association under the military regime, which took away his post as a professor at the Universidade de São Paulo (USP) in 1969. His **Faculdade de Arquitetura e Urbanismo** at USP (1969) is one of the most important concrete constructions completed during the dictatorship. Its style of construction, known as brutalism, originates from the French word for concrete – *béton* – and the word for raw – *brut* – and refers to the domination of concrete on the landscape in its naked and unadorned form. In the Escola Paulista architecture movement that emerged under the leadership of Artigas, the designs of the 1960s and 1970s were characterised by raw materials, airy spaces and large building blocks.

If Le Corbusier was the spiritual father of Brazilian 20th-century architecture, then **Oscar Niemeyer** is its most famous, prolific and beloved son. A Communist Party member, he developed his famous curved style on a number of residential high-rise buildings: one example is the **Edificio COPAN** (1953; *see p45*), located in the centre of the city. The building reflected Niemeyer's belief in integrating rich and poor by offering apartments in the building to the Paulistano elite as well as to blue-collar workers. His other works in the city include the museum complexes in Ibirapuera Park – the **Pavilhão Ciccillo Matarazzo** and the **Memorial da America Latina** (*see p58*).

Another controversial architect working in Brazil at the time was the creator of the **MASP** (1957-68; *see p68*). A surrealist, Communist and brutalist, **Lina Bo Bardi** (1914-92) had been a member of the Italian resistance during World War II,

IN CONTEXT

Pavilhão Ciccillo Matarazzo.

Semana 22

Swept up in the modernist current.

In 1922, a wave of European modernism swept Brazil; Paulistano artists, writers and musicians, having inhaled the contagious air of European Futurism, expressionism and Dadaism, organised the Semana de Arte Moderna, which became known as the 'Semana 22', at the Teatro Municipal. Assembling the greatest Brazilian minds, it gave birth to the first Brazilian artistic 'ismo': *Antropofagismo*. Brazilian modernists saw themselves as New World cannibals, ingesting European influences in order to bring their own profound vision to the world and leave classicism in the dust.

In architecture, the movement took off in the work of **Flavio de Carvalho**, who drew (unbuilt) futuristic designs for the Palacio do Governo, influenced by German expressionism and English modernism. This modernism reflected a reaffirmation of clean lines, simplicity and the rejection of Baroque flourishes used by classicists in Brazil.

The schools of architecture in Brazil at the time were engaged in a 'battle of styles' between young modernist architects (supported by the avant gardists of the Semana 22), and a Brazilian neocolonial school of academic architects.

The anti-establishment camp rose to prominence after the Semana 22, and the work of modernist architects like **Gregori Warchavchik** and **Rino Levi** became especially lucrative. Warchavchik, a Russian-Jewish émigré, designed the **Casa** and **Parque Modernista** (1927; *see p85*), a Cubist masterpiece, which drew 20,000 visitors in the year it opened. He also designed the house and studio for his brother-in-law, the expressionist painter Lasar Segall. Rino Levi, who studied in Italy, built the **Columbus Building** (1932, now demolished), the first group of modernist flats in the city, and the **Galeria FIESP** (1979; *see p69*), which was built using his plans.

At the same time, under the direction of modernist **Lúcio Costa**, the architecture department at the National School of Fine Arts in Rio de Janeiro hired modernists such as Warchavchik, and exposed a wave of young students to its precepts. Among them were **Oscar Niemeyer**, the biggest name in 20th century Brazilian architecture, and **Roberto Burle Marx**, the father of tropical landscape art. Marx was born in São Paulo, and his work can be seen at **Parque Burle Marx**. You'll have to leave town, however, for Marx, Costa and Niemeyer's most spectacular work: **Brasília** (1960). The nation's UNESCO-listed capital, in all its *Buck Rogers*-esque glory, was built in a little over four years.

but somehow she had fallen in love with an ex-fascist and migrated to Brazil in 1946. Bo Bardi's main influence was Mies van der Rohe, and she worked on projects that reflected her interests in social equality; she kept the factory surroundings in the **SESC Pompéa Center** (1977; *see p205*) so that its working-class origins could always remind the visitors of the reality and history of the recreation centre.

BRAZILIAN NAMES IN THE PRESS

In December 2007, Oscar Niemeyer celebrated his 100th birthday, and his centenary is a convenient date to mark the end of what has been an incredible century of building in São Paulo. He continues to be an active presence in the country's architecture, yet there are numerous other names that have joined his in the Brazilian and foreign press.

Firmly in the international spotlight is **Paulo Mendes da Rocha**, a Marxist and the 2006 winner of the prestigious Pritzker prize. A protégé of Le Corbusier, da Rocha taught at USP until the 1960s, when he lost his post. He is responsible for the **Paulistano Athletics Club** (1957; Rua Honduras 1400, Jardim America), the **Museu Brasileiro da Escultura** (1986-95; see p71) and the restoration of the **Pinacoteca do Estado** (1993), originally built by Ramos de Azevedo, which he converted into a brutalist work. Da Rocha incorporates both concrete and the natural environment – for example, roofs with pools of water – in his work. He created a number of projects with renowned architect Fernando Brandão, the man responsible for **Livraria Cultura** (see p147), a unique book store whose brilliant realisation of art as public space made Portuguese Nobel Prize winner José Saramago cry.

Paulistano blockbuster architect **Isay Weinfeld** received a Future Projects Award from *Architectural Review* in 2008 for the **Edifício 360°** (Rua Camburiú, Lapa), a design for a residential high-rise with private gardens in every apartment. Weinfeld is responsible for some of the nicest commercial properties in the city: **Espaço Havaiana** (see p155), **Clube Chocolate** (see p149), **Hotel Fasano** (see p99) and **Livraria da Vila** (see p147). His structures feature uniform lines of clean concrete and the use of wood for the façades. Weinfeld worked on the Fasano hotel with another famous Paulistano architect, **Marcio Kogan**, whose work tends to highlight natural materials such as bamboo and other types of wood, as well as outdoor pools.

Finally, **Ruy Ohtake** is São Paulo's well-known contemporary architect. His best-known works include the **Hotel Unique** (see p99), **Hotel Renaissance** (see p101) and the **Tomie Ohtake** (see p77) and Crianças e O Mar (Child and Sea orphanage in the coastal town of Ubatuba) institutes. Ohtake's other designs pay homage to and reinvent Niemeyer's curves for the 21st century.

DEGRADATION AND DECAY

Cranes and new construction sites are everywhere, yet only a few real-estate investors willingly fund the city's past. A great problem of Paulistano architecture, and Brazilian architecture in general, is the lack of sponsorship for restoration projects and the lack of effective laws to enforce renovation. In the late 1980s, the city government passed a law that established the protection of buildings with historic or architectural significance. More than 60 per cent of these *edificios tombados* have been restored, but the other 40 per cent are still at risk of complete degradation. The law's purpose was to fine owners if they did not repair the property, yet only in 2006 did the city work out a way to enforce the fines. Many owners exploited the legal weaknesses: if a building is left to degrade, the city eventually has to deem it unsalvageable and demolish it, despite its protected status. And although Brazilian law does not allow for a building to be demolished or altered without the authorisation of the mayor's office, this law is almost impossible to enforce. There are currently around 1,800 buildings under government protection in the city of São Paulo; two-thirds of these are in the centre.

TENEMENTS AND SLUMS

The housing boom for the rich in the 1970s and '80s was itself the cause of some of the most expansive favela-building in the city. Paraisopolis, the second largest favela in São Paulo (after Heliopolis), sits in one of the city's wealthiest neighbourhoods, Morumbi. It grew out of a need for worker housing close to the sites of construction in Morumbi, and now houses 80,000. Typically, these

Hotel Unique. *See p35.*

slums were patched together with a number of discarded materials: boards, metals and tubes, as well as the ubiquitous brown bricks and tin roofs.

The city government has two distinct ways of addressing the often problematic and troubling issue of slums. The first is to recognise favelas as city neighbourhoods and use city funding to make them more liveable. The city government has been pouring a great deal of money into Paraisopolis, by paving streets, providing sources of clean water and plumbing, as well as constructing new units of housing. In addition, it has constructed a health centre, and is now building a new football field. The second way of dealing with favelas caters to the demand of the middle and upper classes for more building land, and includes razing the favelas closer to the city centre.

The government is trying to reclaim favelas it deems to be at risk, or that pose a 'significant threat' to the environment. The not-so-new government plan removes favelas and repays the *favelados* a portion of their property's value either as a lump sum or in monthly installments. Favela Aldeinha and Favela da Paz, both located on the banks of the River Tietê, are two of the vanishing favelas.

SUSTAINABLE ARCHITECTURE AND THE FUTURE

The newly constructed and undoubtably stunning **Ponte Estaiada Octavio Frias de Oliveira**, a cable-stayed bridge designed by architect João Valente, finally opened in May 2008 after three years in construction. The suspension cables attached to the top of a two-legged concrete sling support the double road tracks underneath. The construction took place on the former location of several major favelas, the remnants of which still can be seen from the major hotel and business complex in Morumbi, the **World Trade Center** (Avenida das Naçoes Unidas).

However, if São Paulo's architects really want to redefine their city for the 21st century, they will have to incorporate careful city planning as well as beautiful designs to remake this boomtown. With an average commuting time of two hours and 47 minutes, getting around this city is a major problem affecting both quality of life and the local economy.

The USP is constructing the first sustainable building for Ciências Atmosféricas (Centre of Studies for Atmospheric Climate) in the city. It will run completely on the energy produced by its solar panels, and is set to be completed in 2010/2011. São Paulo's first eco-park was recently built on what had been the site of a rubbish incinerator; the park has solar panels, and reclaimed wood is being used for the amphitheatre and decks (on Praça Victor Civita, at Rua Sumidouro). Meanwhile, São Paulo is pledging its allegiance to architecture by sponsoring one of the largest architecture gatherings in the world: the **Bienal Internacional de Arquitetura de São Paulo** (*see p162*) is going into its eighth session in 2009.

The bulls, bears and billionaires behind São Paulo's rise.

TEXT: ERIC ROSENBAUM

Brazil's Boomtown

São Paulo may not have the distinction of being Brazil's capital city, or even its most beloved – those two honours go to Brasília and Rio respectively. But, with the city's stock exchange, the BOVESPA, now the fourth largest in the world, Mexico City's status as Latin America's financial powerhouse has been usurped – the region's Wall Street has moved south of the equator.

The city's financial might is now global: São Paulo is the de facto home of the Mercosur alliance that links South America's biggest powers in one regional voice on economic and trade issues, and it stands centre stage for Brazil in the BRIC (Brazil, Russia, India and China), the fantastic four of emerging economic powers. Its service industry continues to churn out a mini-metropolis of business-themed neighbourhoods, turning it into the flashy host for globetrotting business elites. Meanwhile, its homegrown captains of industry represent all sectors of the world economy, from banking to aircraft manufacturing to beer-brewing. And the city's financial ascendance has been mirrored in its rise as a cosmopolitan metropolis: what started with 19th-century sacks of coffee has turned into a century-long coming-out party to remember.

Blue Business

Profiting from porn in the city of Saint Paul.

Moviemaking is big business, and Brazil has become a location-filming favourite. But it's not just car commercials and big-budget films like *The Incredible Hulk 2* that have decamped south. São Paulo has become the base for what is considered to be – by some admittedly unscientific estimates – the second largest pornographic film industry in the world, second only to the moviemaking empire based in the San Fernando valley of California.

The clichéd saying relating to Brazil – 'no sin south of the equator', or in other words, 'anything goes' – can bring Brazilians to boiling point, and rightfully so. For when it comes to the business of filming behind closed bedroom doors in São Paulo, it is the puritanical North Americans and sophisticated Europeans who were among the big, bad adult entertainment names to make Brazil's financial capital a porn empire in the early 2000s, when the Brazilian currency reached a low against the dollar.

Anglo-American John Gilbert Bowen, also known as director John T Bone and actor Harry Horndog, best known for making such 'classics' as *World's Biggest Gang Bang* and its imaginatively named sequel, *World's Biggest Gang Bang II*, set up a production studio in São Paulo in 2004.

In the same year, however, the Brazilian porn industry gained column inches for the case of US adult film star Darren James, who returned from a shoot in Brazil infected with HIV, and who subsequently went on to infect several co-stars. At least 30 adult film companies in the US halted production, bringing California's porn empire to its knees. The fault was not necessarily Brazilian in terms of production standards, as condom use in Brazilian porn has typically been obligatory – unlike in the US. But American critics cited the lack of HIV testing in the country as a key factor.

While the São Paulo porn industry is still burgeoning, and it's hard to pass a street corner without being assaulted by smutty magazine and DVD covers on kiosk shelves, it's not a given that the city will become the world's blue-movie Hollywood, as some have predicted.

Even with its massive porn production, Brazil doesn't figure in the ranking of the top countries that generate revenues from adult entertainment. Brazilian production companies may keep pumping out DVDs and magazines to satisfy their loyal patrons, but these flicks remain unattainable for a large percentage of the domestic market. And the worldwide trend of porn moving online isn't so strongly felt in Brazil, a country where access to computers (and credit cards) remains a distant dream for the large numbers of poor citizens. Yet another inequality in a country rife with them – though one not quite serious enough to merit a UN task force, perhaps.

Centro. *See p44.*

THE BEAN BOOM

São Paulo's neighbouring state Minas Gerais developed the largest-ever gold industry in the western hemisphere in the 18th century; indeed, historians argue that the construction of modern day Lisbon and London post-Great Fire were more or less financed by slave labour in the precious metals mines of Brazil. São Paulo's early economy reflected the same Brazilian colonial model as Minas Gerais. In São Paulo, though, the financial gemstone was the coffee bean.

A favourable climate and fertile soil helped the crop thrive, and the need to move the 60-pound sacks of coffee to the export docks led to the development of São Paulo's first transport infrastructure, finally breaking Rio de Janeiro's stranglehold on export. British investment spurred the development of a rail system that was the vital link in moving coffee from the interior plantations to the port of Santos and out across the globe. Historian Warren Dean, an expert on Brazilian socio-economic matters, remarked that São Paulo is unique as 'one of the few places in the underdeveloped world where an advanced industrial system has grown out of a tropical raw-material-exporting economy'.

Coffee export did more than caffeinate the masses. It provided foreign credit and exchange, which helped to finance the equipment of a modern economic engine: raw industrial materials needed for the coffee industry, such as bricks and cement, were prohibitively expensive to import, so a homegrown industry was started. Tax revenue from coffee exports – by far the largest part of the state's coffers until the Great Depression – allowed young industries to be taxed at minimal rates, removing a potential growth impediment. The sustained workforce recruitment from abroad and from poor Brazilian states by the Paulistano oligarchy resulted in labour gluts and a nomadic working class that not only moved from plantation to plantation, but back towards the city as well. São Paulo ballooned from a 19th-century university town to a city of 240,000 by 1900.

Worldwide markets evaporated overnight in 1930, but as a financial capital São Paulo was already well on its way to global stature. One core link to this early period in the city's modern economic history is drink-based, but not tied to coffee. AmBev, the \$27 billion beverage company, is the fifth largest public company in Brazil. It now brews a huge quantity of beer, but its progenitor company came to life as a single brewery in the working class city centre. In the first decades of the 20th century, Companhia Antarctica brewed all of the bottled beer in Brazil. The Antarctica plant

The Count of São Paulo

The clan behind Brazil's first great industrial empire.

Some kingdoms are built in a day; others build enough factories for every day of the year. Such was the case of **Industrias Reunidas F Matarazzo (IRFM)**. By 1952, when *Time* magazine was writing profiles of Count Francisco Matarazzo Junior (the title was first bestowed on founder Francisco Senior by Italy in 1917 for his charitable endeavours during World War I), IRFM had 367 plants ranging from textiles to foodstuffs, and at that time was breaking into plastics.

Francisco Matarazzo Senior had arrived in the port of Santos in 1881 without his first batch of products – the cans of lard and cheese he had planned to sell had been lost in a shipwreck, forcing him to start his Brazilian enterprise in the red. He opened a commercial house in the interior of São Paulo state, and sold so much pork lard that he eventually opened his own lard factory. In 1890, the Matarazzo clan moved to São Paulo city, and the IRFM empire began.

Early on, Matarazzo zeroed in on two important elements of modern capitalism: convince people they need something (marketing), and fabricate that something yourself, from raw material to shelf product (vertical integration). Soon it wasn't just pork lard that was being flogged; sugar, wheat and salt were made, oils, soaps and paper were produced, alcohol and petrol distilleries sprung up – and even train building got a look in. And for a time, the products of IRFM were on the table of every house in the city. For husbands keen to save cash, a common domestic refrain emerged: 'Who do you think I am, a Matarazzo?'.

was also the site for some of the first major labour strikes in São Paulo, a signal that São Paulo's industrialisation trends had become global in scope. A century after its beginnings, AmBev made a fortune by merging with Belgian beer giant InBev in 2007. In 2008, the merged company went on to acquire US brewery Anheuser-Busch, creating the largest brewery in the world (a move that stirred up political controversy among US senators angered at the acquisition of Anheuser-Busch – the brewery behind the all-American Budweiser brand – by a European and, gasp!, Brazilian confederation).

GIVE AND TAKE

Multinational corporations were also creating beachheads in São Paulo during the first wave of industrialisation. Initially, plants located in Brazil were often designed to do little more than assemble import kits shipped from car capitals like Detroit. The Ford Motor Company, for example, had been in Brazil since the 1920s, but sales, not industrial production, were the original goal for its Brazilian operation.

In the 1950s, free-trade policy had gone too far, allowing foreign companies to penetrate the Brazilian market without spurring domestic production. Strict import laws were implemented, setting off a long battle between the government and firms like Ford, General Motors and Volkswagen; it was a struggle begun by Getulio Vargas and expanded by the democratic administration of Juscelino Kubitschek.

The give and take between the government and the multinationals, balancing rigorous and sometimes regressive import laws with incentives for domestic production, would forever change the original São Paulo industrial model. A strong national government and a mix of domestic and foreign companies would shape an industrial centre that more closely resembled the typical model of developed world capitalism.

SAME STAGE, DIFFERENT PRODUCTION

The Kubitschek-era domestic production agenda spread the industrial base of Brazil far beyond São Paulo. São Paulo state is still home to Embraer, one of the largest aircraft manufacturers in the world, but its plants are far from the city centre. Finance and the service sector have become much more important to the city as industrial production moved away from the city to provincial areas within and beyond São Paulo state.

The largest bank in Brazil, Banco Itaú, was created in 1945 in São Paulo as the Banco Central de Credito. Beginning life with $513,000 of capital, the smallest amount allowed by law, it rose to prominence as one of Brazil's most important private-sector financiers in the period between 1945 and 1960, when industrialisation on a large scale across the country was tied to massive urbanisation and the state-supported relocation of rural citizens. Itaú became one of the largest banks in Brazil within 15 years. By 2008, 63 years after its creation, Banco Itaú had become the largest bank in Latin America, after a merger with Unibanco.

Famous São Paulo families also served as chief agents in the city's rise to become Latin America's financial services capital (*see left* **The Count of São Paulo**). The Moreira Salles family was a founding member of the Brazilian private banking industry. Banco Moreira Salles was established in 1926 and later changed its name to União de Bancos Brasileiros (aka Unibanco), at present the third-largest privately owned bank in Brazil. The Moreira Salles fortune has not limited itself to the forefront of Brazilian finance. Long-time Unibanco chairman Walter Moreira Salles has four sons, one of whom, Walter Salles, is the filmmaker who directed the 2004 Che Guevara biopic *The Motorcycle Diaries* (a rather anti-capitalistic turn for a son of Brazil's most legendary banker).

THE BILLIONAIRE PAULISTAS

São Paulo has become one of the world's playgrounds for the wealthy. Nowhere is this better reflected than in the annual Forbes rich list. The 2009 list featured 12 billionaires from Brazil (as opposed to nine in Mexico), and some of the biggest names, and families, are based in São Paulo.

IN CONTEXT

Silver Bullet?

The worldwide recession has hit São Paulo, but one business sector seems immune to the crunch: the bulletproofing of cars.

6.4 million: The number of cars in São Paulo.

1,728: The number of civilian cars that were armoured in Brazil in 1998.

7,000: The number of civilian cars that were armoured in Brazil in 2008.

120 bulletproofing companies in Brazil.

Six per cent: The percentage decrease in armed robberies since 1999.

$22,000: The cost to bulletproof a car in São Paulo; less than half the price charged a decade ago.

181: The weight in kilograms added to a car by bulletproof armour.

.44 magnum revolver and nine millimeter submachine gun: The main weapons against which bullet-proofing seeks protection.

Centro. *See p44.*

BOVESPA stock exchange.

Among the São Paulo finance celebrities to make the list of the world's wealthiest were brothers Joseph and Moise Safra, the banking kings behind São Paulo-based Banco Safra. The press is constantly trailing the Safras, whether detailing their attempts to avoid the violence of São Paulo by helicopter travel and the hiring of Israeli agents to train their bodyguards, or covering sensational family tragedy. Joseph and Moise's father Edmond died under bizarre circumstances in December 1999, far from the violence of São Paulo. An ex-Green Beret, Ted Maher, had been hired to care for the Parkinson's-afflicted mogul. Maher set fire to Edmond's penthouse, hoping a fake rescue would gain him stature. He lost control of the fire and was sentenced on a charge of arson, before breaking out of jail and making it all the way to Nice, where the police caught up with him. He served eight years before his 2007 release.

Also making the Forbes list were Guilherme Peirão Leal, the self-made cosmetics king of Brazil's version of Avon, Cochairs Natura Cosmeticos; Marcel Herrmann Telles and Jorge Paulo Lehman, controlling shareholders in Anheuser-Busch Inbev; and Dorothea Steinbruch, who controls one of Brazil's largest steelmakers, Companhia Siderurgica Nacional, and is the only woman among the billionaire Brazilians.

GROWING PAINS, GROWING LINKS

The era when there wasn't even a decent road or section of railroad track linking São Paulo to the rest of the world now seems like a distant memory. But recent economic history hasn't all been positive: just as the country finally proved it deserves a place among the big, investment-worthy nations (and just after the huge 2008 financial services mergers involving BOVESPA and Mercadoria e Futuros, and Banco Itaú and Unibanco), the global recession hit.

Moderate growth is the forecast now, and for a go-go financial capital like São Paulo, that may be hard to accept. However, pushing its image as simply a tropical coffee exporter to a distant past has also meant hitching itself to the global themes of boom and bust. When early 20th-century radicals were striking around the globe, they were also striking in São Paulo; when the Great Depression hit, São Paulo's economy had to reinvent itself; and when the postwar boom led to a global surge, São Paulo was pushing beyond its early industrial limits. Whether the market is up or down, one thing is certain: after a century-long burst, São Paulo is the biggest business in Latin America.

Sightseeing

Pinacoteca do Estado. *See p56.*

Centro

The historic heart of the city.

In a 455-year-old city that has demolished and rebuilt most of its neighbourhoods many times over, Centro retains a link to the past. Here colonial churches and neoclassical buildings compete for space with gargantuan skyscrapers. The area is split down the middle by the verdant **Vale do Anhangabaú** and the **Avenida 9 de Julho**, and can loosely be organised into **República**, the area west of the park, and **Sé**, east of the park. The former has some of São Paulo's most famous modern architectural landmarks: Edifício Itália, Edifício Copan and the Old

Map p243   **Bars** p131, p132
Hotels p92, p95

Hilton building; the latter is the city's original banking district, filled with cobblestone streets and ornately detailed old office blocks. Around the edge of these two areas you'll encounter budget shopping on **Rua 25 de Março**, the geographic centre of the city in **Praça da Sé** and the city's most famous intersection at **Avenida Ipiranga** and **Avenida São João**.

REPUBLICA
Metrô República

Once a neighbourhood of lavish mansions housing the first coffee barons in the 1870s, this area was annexed into the commercial centre and came to be known as Centro Novo when the **Viaduto do Chá** spanning Vale do Anhangabaú opened in 1892. The mansions were quickly demolished, and the barons and their families fled to apparently more hygienic Higienópolis and the newly inaugurated Avenida Paulista. Like many world financial centres, República remains quiet (and gritty) at night and weekends, but during daylight hours it is as safe and as loud as Jardins. The businessmen along Avenida Ipiranga and Avenida São Luís and the tattooed hipsters and hippie vendors along Avenida São João bring a pulsating energy to the city streets and a reminder that the term 'traffic' in São Paulo can refer just as easily to *calor humano* (human heat) as to carbon dioxide-producing vehicles.

About the author
Nico Oved *is a Canadian freelance writer and photographer based in São Paulo (www.nicooved.com).*

Praça da República is a lush green oasis in the middle of a desert of grey buildings – the arguably successful result of 2007's Cidade Limpa law (*see pp26-30*). In the 19th century, República was a centre of community activity, hosting rodeos and bullfights; in modern times, the square has been a natural home to political protests and free concerts. Recently restored, it contains small lakes crossed by iron footbridges, where turtles sun themselves on rocks.

One entire side of the square is taken up by the yellow **Prédio do Caetano de Campos**. Designed by architect Ramos de Azevedo in 1894, the building housed an exclusive school whose alumni include Mário de Andrade (a modernist writer) and Sérgio Buarque de Holanda (a historian, and father of musician Chico Buarque). In 1978, the building was almost demolished during the construction of the new subway, but a last-minute campaign by local architects was successful, and it found a new life as the Ministério da Educação.

Running south from Praça da República, Avenida Ipiranga is the address of three of the city's modern architectural gems. Just across the street from the square itself is the **Edifício Itália** (Avenida Ipiranga 344, www.edificio italia.com.br). Inaugurated in 1965, the project

Vale do Anhangabaú.

was spearheaded by the Circolo Italiano, an association of Italian immigrants, to commemorate their economic contribution to the city and their newly solidified standing in Paulistano society. Reminiscent of the Ferrari logo, the rearing, bronze stallion that overlooks the street from the building's mezzanine is called the Cavalo Rampante de Pericle Fazzini, and was a gift from the Italian government in 1974. However, the building's main attraction is its rooftop restaurant and bar, the **Terraço Itália** (*see p132*).

INSIDE TRACK
NIGHTLIFE IN CENTRO

The strip along Rua Martinho Prado now houses a number of independent theatres and reasonably priced bars with fantastic patios that cater to the late-night crowd. Often open much later than anywhere else and without a cover charge, bars like **Papo**, **Pinga e Petisco** (Praça Roosevelt 118, 3257 4106, closed Sun) can be a welcome reprieve from the hipsters on Rua Augusta or the high-rollers in Vila Olímpia. It was in this bar, previously called Djalma's, that Elis Regina (a legendary brilliant Brazilian songstress) first played in São Paulo.

Oscar Niemeyer's 1961 landmark social experiment **Edifício Copan** (Avenida Ipiranga 200, www.copansp.com.br) is famous for its undulating wave form. It's home to more than 2,000 people, who live in apartments ranging from inexpensive studios to luxurious four-bedroom flats. The building's most famous one-time resident was the Pretenders' Chrissie Hynde, who bought a condo in 2004 when she collaborated on a disc with Caetano Veloso's son, Moreno. The building once offered everything a resident could need, and although the original cinema has since been converted into an evangelical church, much of the modest ground-floor mall remains. Stop at **Café Floresta** (Avenida Ipiranga 200, loja 21), visible from the street, for an espresso at the counter, and imagine a time when this was the city's most coveted address.

Across the street is the iconic, cylindrical **Old Hilton** building (Avenida Ipiranga 165). Due to its street-level pedestal, it's easy to miss if you aren't looking up. When the business centre of São Paulo relocated first to Avenida Paulista and then to Avenida Brigadeiro Faria Lima, the Hilton found its business in decline. In 2004, it moved from this modernist concrete icon to a new steel-and-glass building on Rio Pinheiros. The state court of São Paulo is set to occupy the building by the end of 2009 (ending five years of disuse).

A block further west, where Avenida Ipiranga meets Rua Consolação, is **Praça Roosevelt**;

this cement monstrosity built atop a sunken highway has one of the worst reputations in the city. During the past ten years, performers and theatre students slowly reclaimed the area from drug dealers and prostitutes by providing free entertainment on the street. Stop at the local stalwart theatre and bar **Espaço dos Satyros** (Praça Roosevelt 214, 3258 6345, www.satyros.com.br) and meet some of the staff working the tables. You can also see them act in the company's independent productions.

Three blocks north of Praça da República is **Largo do Arouche**, a serene square and daily flower market; it's pleasant for a sit-down coffee or drink in the afternoon. Try the traditional French restaurant **La Casserole**, a mainstay from 1954, with small portions and hefty price tags (Largo do Arouche 346, 3331 6283, www. la casserole.com.br, closed Mon). Beyond the boundaries of the square the area is renowned for its gay clubs and slightly daring nightlife.

Back in the nitty-gritty of Avenida São João is the rough and tumble **Largo do Paiçandú**, a square that is thick with card-playing homeless people and prostitutes. The mustard-yellow **Nossa Senhora do Rosário dos Homens Pretos** church is the main attraction on the square (*see p49* **Walk**). Beside the church is the polemical **Monumento à Mãe Preta** (1953), a statue by Júlio Guerra that depicts an African slave breastfeeding a white baby – a common practice during the era of slavery in Brazil. Across the street, **Ponto Chic** (Largo do Paiçandú 27, 3222 6528, www.pontochic.com.br, closed Sun) is a traditional *lanchonete* run since 1925 by a family from Bauru, São Paulo state; the place is famed for inventing the omnipresent *bauru* sandwich. This Rolls Royce of *baurus* is, at R$16, pricier than most deli sandwiches, but with roast beef, pickles and a mixture of four cheeses, it's also the real deal.

Directly across Avenida São João from Largo do Paiçandú is São Paulo's hub of youth culture and rebellion via consumption, **Galeria do Rock** (*see p159*); look for the 'Shopping Center

Grandes Galerias' sign. Further down Avenida São João is **Galeria Olido**, home to a free cultural centre incorporating a gallery, cinema and concert theatre.

East on Avenida São João, where it crosses the valley, is the ornate Ramos de Azevedo building **Palácio dos Correios** (*see p53* **Preservation Projects***)*. Walk north to the pedestrian valley crossing known as **Viaduto Santa Ifigênia**. The beautiful, yellow cast-iron bridge was fabricated entirely in Belgium before being shipped over and assembled on site in 1913; originally trolley tracks ran across it in both directions. You may see one of the many Baianas (women from Bahia) dressed in white, tossing sea shells called *búzios* over the side, reading the fortunes of the passersby.

From here, there's a majestic view of the **Vale do Anhangabaú** (bad spirits in the native Tupi-Guarani language). Until the late 1980s, it was just an ugly concrete thoroughfare for Avenida 9 de Julho. The city government remade the valley by sinking the street into a tunnel that passes underneath, and devoting the space to greenery and pedestrians. Just north of the Viaduto Santa Ifigênia is the **Mirante do Vale**, São Paulo's tallest building. Looking south you can see the **Teatro Municipal** (*see 204*) and Praça Ramos de Azevedo, the **Viaduto do Chá** and the **Sede da Prefeitura** (city hall) housed in the green-roofed **Edifício Matarazzo** (*see p40* **The Count of São Paulo***)*.

At the western end of the Viaduto do Chá is the **Prédio Alexandre Mackenzie**, which originally housed the headquarters of the old Light São Paulo (as the electricity company was known even in Portuguese). Constructed in 1929 it was converted into a mall known as **Shopping Light** (Rua Colonel Xavier de Toledo 23, 3154 2299, www.shoppinglight.com.br) in 1999.

Just south, off Rua 7 de Abril, is São Paulo's oldest monument, the obelisk that sits in front of the **Ladeira da Memória** fountain. Erected in 1814 along with the original fountain, it marks the place where mule trains, on their way to the interior of the state, would stop for water. The fountain was reconstructed in 1919 with Portuguese *azulejos* (blue tiles) by Guilherme de Almeida and Wasth Rodrigues. Down the street, on the shady Praça Dom José Gaspar is the **Biblioteca Mário de Andrade (BMA)** (*see p53* **Preservation Projects**), housed in a minimalist art deco building; it will be the second-largest library in Brazil when it reopens.

FREE Galeria Olido

Avenida São João 473 (3331 8399/www.galeria olido.blogspot.com). Metrô República. **Open** 10am-9pm Mon-Sun. **Admission** free. **Map** p243 N5. This community hub offers a cinema, dance school, theatre, library and free internet services. A special

---

Praça Ramos de Azevedo.

space is devoted to the memory of Brazil's rich circus and clown history. The glassed-in interior faces the street; it is used every day for events ranging from free rock shows to dance performances and author readings. Check the website for cinema listings.

SE
Metrô Sé or São Bento

Sé is Centro. In fact, in the square of the same name in front of the massive **Catedral**

INSIDE TRACK
THE REAL RIO

You might not think it, given its concrete façade, but São Paulo is a city of rivers and canals. Founded at the crossing of two rivers, Pinheiros and Tietê, it's encircled on its eastern side by the Rio Tamanduateí and its tributary Rio de Anhangabaú. Most of São Paulo's centre lies on top of what was the Rio de Anhangabaú. The viaducts around the city serve as reminders of the river. The Viaduto do Chá, built in 1892 by Jules Martin, connected a tea plantation called the Morro do Cha with Rua Direita.

Metropolitana (sometimes referred to as the Catedral da Sé), you'll find the *marco zero* (ground zero marker), from which all distances in São Paulo are measured in concentric circles. The square itself was occupied by elaborate office buildings until the construction of the subway in the late 1970s. It is nevertheless always humming with activity; preachers, magicians and clowns have a ready pulpit here, surrounded by attentive and often participatory audiences, as well as teams of pickpockets. Much of the surrounding area (especially the **Triângulo**, which runs north to **Largo São Bento** and west to **Parque Anhangabaú**), is cut off to vehicle traffic and consists of tightly packed cobblestone pedestrian streets filled with crowds, mediocre shopping and the best of São Paulo's old architecture. Not only a window into the past, Sé is still the financial heart of São Paulo and a mecca of cultural attractions.

Praça da Sé is one of the nicest public plazas in the city: the two parallel lines of giant palm trees that lead to the front steps of the **Catedral Metropolitana** (*see p49* **Walk**), along with a number of newly painted public sculptures and concrete fountains, make it an oasis (of sorts) in the heart of Centro.

On the southern side of the plaza is the art deco **Edíficio Sé**. With its distinctive giant black pillars and cast-bronze grates, it houses both the galleries and museum of the **Caixa**

Catedral Metropolitana. *See p47.*

SIGHTS

Cultural (*see p52*). Just around the corner you'll find the sumptuously salmon **Solar da Marquesa de Santos** (Centro's last remaining 18th-century residential building), currently under restoration, though it usually serves as a venue of the **Museu da Cidade**.

Continuing north, you'll arrive at the spot where São Paulo was founded in 1554, the blue and white neocolonial **Pátio do Colégio**, which was inaugurated by the Jesuits. Commemorating the occasion is a smallish pillar topped by a bronze angel, the hyperbolically named **Glória Imortal aos Fundadores de São Paulo** monument. Erected in 1925 by the sculptor Amadeu Zani, the monument depicts the three groups responsible for the founding of the city: the natives, the Jesuit priests and the Portuguese. The buildings, which were reconstructed and whitewashed in 1979, contain a functioning Jesuit church known as the **Igreja do Beato Anchieta** (*see p49* **Walk**). Adjacent is the **Museu Padre Anchieta** (*see p52*); it contains a modest collection of church artefacts that date back more than 450 years. The preserved foundations of the so-called **Terceira Igreja** (1585) surround a pleasant café and a nice courtyard: a perfect place for contemplation, reflection and refreshments. Beside the museum's

entrance is the **Marco da Paz** (www.marcoda paz.org.br) peace bell. A private initiative started by the Commercial Association of São Paulo has erected identical peace bells throughout the state and country, and as far away as Mexico, Spain, Italy and China. Go ahead, give it a ring. Next to both the Pátio do Colégio and Praça da Sé is one of São Paulo's few remaining colonial churches, the recently restored **Igreja do Carmo** (*see p49* **Walk**).

The cobbled Rua 15 de Novembro, in Triângulo proper, leads into the heart of the city's original financial district. Cut over Rua Quitanda and you'll find the **Centro Cultural Banco do Brasil** (**CCBB**) (*see p52*). In front of the building is a good example of public art, currently in vogue around the city: a bronze sculpture of a thin and elongated bed propped up on books which functions as a bench.

BOVESPA (Rua 15 de Novembro 275, 3233 2178, www.bovespa.com.br, closed Sun) is Brazil's stock exchange and the heart of one of the world's fastest growing economies. The original trading floor is open to visitors during business hours, but other than the electronic boards and a small display about its history (in Portuguese), there isn't much to see. As with most of the world's major exchanges, all trading

Walk Historic Churches

São Paulo's churches and cathedrals span the 16th to 20th centuries.

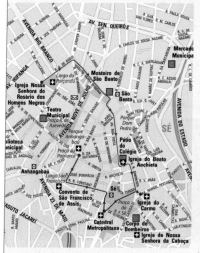

Not surprisingly, São Paulo's oldest churches are concentrated in its oldest neighbourhood. Start your walk from Largo do Paiçandú on Avenida São João. The deep yellow **Nossa Senhora do Rosário dos Homens Pretos** (Largo do Paiçandú s/n, 3223 3611) was built by a volunteer force of black labourers in 1906. It sits on a site where rites of the Afro-Brazilian religions Candomblé and Umbanda were once performed. Its interior is painted floor-to-ceiling in a near-rainbow of vibrant colours.

Walk north along Rua Antônio de Godói, which runs alongside the square, until you come to Rua Santa Ifigênia, and then turn right, crossing the Vale do Anhangabaú on the Viaduto Santa Ifigênia. On the other side of the valley you'll reach Largo São Bento, the **Mosteiro de São Bento** (Largo São Bento s/n, 3328 8799, www.mosteiro. org.br). This complex includes a school, a university, monastery and the original Basilica from 1598. It hosts Gregorian chants from the Benedictine monks early every morning. The monks operate a kitchen where they sell home-made bread, cakes, chocolates and jams.

Leaving the monastery, turn left and follow Rua Boa Vista along the edge of the ridge that forms the natural boundary of the Triângulo. In a few blocks you'll reach the city's founding site: Pátio do Colégio. Immediately beside it is the **Igreja do Beato Anchieta** (Patío do Colégio 2, 3105 6899, www.pateocollegio.com.br, closed Mon). With bare walls and a humble altar, it often hosts choral concerts. (There are three different spellings in use for Pátio do Colégio; this is the accepted spelling.)

At the southern end of the square, make a left in front of the Palácio da Justícia and then an immediate right on Rua Roberto Simonsen. Turn left on Avenida Rangel Pestana, where you'll see the **Igreja do Carmo** (Rua Rangel Pestana 230) facing you, right across the street. Dating from 1632, it retains its original gilded Baroque high altar, and the small church is cluttered with paintings, sculptures and artefacts.

Exiting the church, turn left and return the way you came, back to Praça da Sé. There, you can't miss the **Catedral Metropolitana** (Praça da Sé s/n, 3106 2709), which is surprisingly new. It was constructed in its most recent incarnation between 1913 and 1967, and is one of the largest Gothic churches in the world, seating a staggering 8,000 worshippers. The cathedral's completion was delayed considerably by the two World Wars, since its organ, all its mosaics, sculptures and furniture were imported from Italy by ship. Nevertheless, the cathedral was inaugurated, without its two towers, in 1954.

From the front steps of the cathedral, exit the square to the left along Rua Benjamin Constant. After two blocks it will open up into Largo São Francisco, where there are two 18th-century colonial churches filled with extravagant religious paintings and frescos: the **Convento de São Francisco de Assis** (Largo de São Francisco 133) and the unfortunately condemned **Igreja da Ordem Terceira** da Penitência (*see p53* **Preservation Projects**).

From there, leave the square walking straight ahead along the cobbled Rua São Bento until you reach Praça do Patriarca. Saving the best for last, the **Igreja de Santo Antônio** (Praça do Patriarca s/n) is the oldest church in the city, dating from 1592. It survived two fires, and its unique wooden roof is a highlight, while the frescoes and glassed-in wooden sculptures are worth a quiet peek into its dark interior.

SIGHTS

Get the local experience

Over 50 of the world's top destinations available.

Banespa.

is now electronic. When the original BOVESPA opened in 1891, trading was done on big stone blackboards, a quaint historical footnote to consider in the age of trades executed in milliseconds. For the real action, one of the few live trading floors left in the world is just down the street at the **BM&F** (Praça Antônio Prado 48, 3119 2000, www.bmf.com.br, closed Sun). Though not one of São Paulo's most visited attractions, the viewing gallery has detailed descriptions in English of everything related to the scrum of brokers down in the pit, including the detailed hand signals they use to stop trading from descending into chaos. It's a fascinating sight to behold, as scruffy brokers throw paper at each other and perform calisthenics to get noticed. Take your passport and don't be fooled into thinking this is small-time capitalism by the old-school approach on the floor; when BOVESPA and BM&F merged in 2008, they created the third-largest exchange in the world.

Nearby is the **Edifício Altino Arantes**, commonly called the **Banespa** building (Rua João Bricola 24, 3249 7466, closed Sat & Sun). Inaugurated in 1947 and modelled on the Empire State Building, it was São Paulo's (and Brazil's) tallest building until 1960. The highlight is a trip up to the viewing tower, where you get a 360-degree view of the city and on a (very rare) clear day, it's claimed that you can see up to 40 kilometres. It's free to go up as long as you take your passport, but on busy days there is a five-minute limit before the next group is ushered up. Also of note is the Banespa museum, with its collection of Brazilian art from the likes of famous modernist painter Di Cavalcanti and documents relating to the bank's history. The library has an extensive collection of old newspapers, and the lobby has a

spectacular 13-metre-high chandelier made with 10,000 crystals.

Across the square, towards the valley is São Paulo's first skyscraper, the **Prédio Martinelli** (Rua São Bento 397, www.predio martinelli.com.br). Built between 1922 and 1934, the building was designed by its owner, Italian immigrant Giuseppe Martinelli, to be the tallest on the continent and the first to break the so-called 100-metre height barrier. Though closed to the public, visits can be arranged in advance through the building's website. Stop at the **Café Martinelli-Midi** (Rua Libero Badaró 508, 3104 6825, closed Sat & Sun), a recent addition to the building that features furniture and decorations from the 1920s and 1930s, as well as great coffee.

North on Rua São Bento you'll find the **Largo São Bento**, a square with the notorious distinction of being the starting point for *bandeirante* (*see p18* **The Wild, Wild West of São Paulo**) expeditions into the interior of Brazil. The imposing **Mosteiro de São Bento** resides on this square (*see p49* **Walk**). From here walk a few blocks north and east to **Rua 25 de Março** (*see p44*) for shopping and the **Mercado Municipal** (*see p127 and p156*) for food.

Praça do Patriarca (on the Sé side of the Viaduto do Chá) was given a modern facelift by Paulo Mendes da Rocha in 2002. Da Rocha suspended a massive floating white roof over the entrance to the **Galeria Prestes Maia**, an underground passage. It was originally a cultural space that fell into disarray in the 1970s; after a number of failed attempts at restoration, it will finally house rotating exhibitions from the Pinacoteca do Estado. Don't

---

**INSIDE TRACK
PUBLIC ART CONTROVERSY**

The intellectual establishment of Brazil tends to be left-leaning, and discussions about public art can get quite polemical. In front of the **Igreja da Ordem Terceira da Penitência** on Largo São Francisco is William Zadig's *Idilio ou o Beijo Eterno*. The Swiss artist depicts a seated, masculine Frenchman in a passionate embrace with a small native girl reaching up to him from below. In this case, the statue was unpopular not because it was perceived as a symbol of European superiority, but because the usually liberal denizens objected to its nudity and overly sexual content.

miss modernist sculptor Victor Brecheret's twin bronze nudes, *Graça I* and *Graça II* (1940). Almost hidden on the square is the oldest church in the city, the **Igreja de Santo Antônio** (*see p49* **Walk**). On the opposite side is the **Museu de Arte Brasileiro (MAB) Fundação Armando Alvares Penteado (FAAP) – Centro** (Praça do Patriarca 78, 3101 1776, www.mbafaap.net/museu/index.htm, closed Mon), opened in 1992 in a restored Ramos de Azevedo building. The second floor is an exhibition space, while the first floor hosts artists' studios.

About half way between Praça do Patriarca and Praça da Sé is Largo do São Francisco, a square that houses the USP law school. Founded in 1827, it is the oldest university in the country and has bestowed law degrees on a Who's Who of São Paulo's famous names. Directly adjacent are two colonial churches filled with extravagant religious paintings and frescoes: the **Convento de São Francisco de Assis** (*see p49* **Walk**) and the unfortunately condemned **Igreja da Ordem Terceira da Penitência** (*see p53* **Preservations Projects**).

Pátio do Colégio. *See p48.*

FREE Caixa Cultural

Praça da Sé 111 (3321 4400/www.caixa cultural.com.br). Metrô Sé. **Open** 9am-9pm Tue-Sun. **Admission** free. **Map** p243 O6.

Filled with old mechanical counting and lottery machines, maps of the city from a century ago, examples of Brazilian currency notes from throughout history as well as the first credit cards that arrived in the 1980s, this museum is the Praça da Sé centre's highlight. Unfortunately, texts are all in Portuguese only. Nevertheless, the creepy 1930s medical office transcends language barriers. High-quality galleries outside the museum focus on historical photography and document Amazonian tribes.

FREE Centro Cultural Banco do Brasil

Rua Álvares Penteado 112 (3113 3651/ www.bb. com.br/cultura). Metrô São Bento or Sé. **Open** 10am-8pm Tue-Sun. **Admission** free. **Map** p243 O5.

The edgiest of the Paulistano cultural centres for visual art, the CCBB is housed in a building from 1901. Considered one of the best examples of turn-of-the-century architecture, it became the first Banco do Brasil in 1923 and was restored in 2001. Beyond a couple of galleries and a quality theatre schedule, it offers numerous live music shows, panels, discussions and guided tours of the exhibitions (the latter available in English). There is also a cinema and video-art viewing room.

FREE Museu Padre Anchieta

Pátio do Colégio 2 (3105 6899/www.pateo collegio. com.br). Metrô Sé. **Open** 9am-5.45pm Tue-Fri; 9am-5.30pm Sat, Sun. **Admission** R$5; free under-7s, seniors. **No credit cards.** **Map** p243 O5.

The foundation of this structure was made from an odd mixture of manure, cows' blood, earth, sand and vegetation – a fact discovered in 1979, when the mission was rebuilt after the construction of the city's metrô system. It was named after one of the two founding Jesuits, and is packed with innumerable examples of mediocre religious art. The standout sights are the oldest: the first holy-water sink from 1554 and the original 'Terceira Igreja' foundations from 1585, which are visible from both the museum's pleasant café as well as underground in its crypt.

Preservation Projects

Closed for renovation. Opening soon?

The lack of a world-renowned reputation for tourism, and a city-wide philosophy of destroying the old to usher in the new, have led São Paulo to allow many of its few remaining historic sites slide into decay throughout the past century. But, spurred by the city's new-found cachet as both a business and cultural hotspot, the municipal and state governments have, to their credit, poured a lot of money into sprucing up the city's neglected gems in the past few years. As with most urban regeneration in Brazil, though, when the work will be completed is anybody's guess.

Likely to reopen first will be the **Biblioteca Mário de Andrade** (Rua da Consolação 94, 3256 5270), which will add to its collection of 3.3 million by absorbing another library and opening an annex just down the street. It's named after the city's great modernist poet, whose monumental work is a 1922 homage to São Paulo called *Paulicéia Desvairada* (translated in English as *Hallucinated City*). Among the treasures to be found inside are the nine *incunabulas* (books printed before the 1500s) and the *Vocabulário na Língua Brasílica* (printed in 1621) – without doubt one of the most precious documents in existence relating to the indigenous Tupi tribes of Brazil. On an artistic note, the library also holds the 'Jazz' series by Henri Matisse. Originally opened in 1926 with a meagre collection of 15,000 books, the library was abandoned and left to fend against weather and decay, then covered in ugly black *pixação* (*see p52*) before its restoration (the reopening is set for mid 2009, although nobody can say for sure).

A 1922 project from Ramos de Azevedo's office, **Palácio dos Correios** (Praça dos Correios s/n), has had its interior gutted numerous times, and sat empty for many years before its latest renovation. It reopened as a functioning post office in 2008, but there is still no date for when the future **Centro Cultural dos Correios** will begin to function.

The oldest residential building in Centro, and last remaining example of 18th-century architecture, the **Solar da Marquesa de Santos** (Rua Roberto Simonsen 136, 3396 6407, www.museu dacidade.sp.gov.br) belonged to the Marquesa de Santos or Domitília de Castro Canto e Mello, the favourite mistress of Emperor Dom Pedro I. They were lovers from 1822 to 1829 and had four children; he gave her the palace in the centre of São Paulo as a token gift. Marquesa de Santos had a reputation for meddling in a number of state matters, and the emperor even fired a couple of ministers at her request. The torrid affair ended when Dom Pedro found a European bride after his first wife died. The palace housed one of the collections of the historical **Museu da Cidade**. It's due to reopen at the end of 2009.

On Largo São Francisco, the second of the two colonial churches, the **Igreja da Ordem Terceira da Penitência**, was inaugurated in 1774 and used as a crypt for various illustrious citizens of the city. It was condemned by the municipal government in early 2008, as the roof was leaking and had become structurally unsound, electrical wiring was exposed and there was no sprinkler system. The church is the responsibility of the order of Franciscan monks next door and will remain closed until they can raise the necessary money for repairs through public contributions.

SIGHTS

Luz & Other Districts

Immigration saturation in the industrial heart of Brazil.

Going north in São Paulo is like turning back the clock, as the area hasn't changed or innovated like its southern neighbours. Some of its older enclaves might seem like a collection of the city's cultural pariahs, but an intrepid tourist can find hidden gold here, from neoclassical architecture via tropical forests to some of the world's best DJs. The history of immigration in São Paulo is on display north and east of the centre, and it's a history that's still being made.

The neighbourhood of **Luz** is remarkable for its colonial and neoclassical architecture. Its namesake train station received all the immigrants who arrived in São Paulo; currently, though, it's the commuter hub for the bridge-and-tunnel Paulistanos. The **Bom Retiro** area flourished at the turn of the century as a garment district founded by Jewish immigrants. It's now home to a burgeoning Korean population, and Korean barbecue (including non-kosher pork) can be found on many corners.

SIGHTS

LUZ
Metrô Estação da Luz

One of the oldest neighbourhoods in the city, Luz is home to a number of early 20th-century landmarks. Up until the mid-20th century, it was considered a desirable address, but that changed as the area industrialised and as its *luz* (light) descended into the dark era in the 1970s and '80s of drug dealers, prostitutes and homelessness. The resurrection of the area in the late '80s and '90s was tied to government investment in local landmarks, including two gorgeous train stations from the early 1900s. It is impeccably clean, well lit and policed around the clock, but it retains a liberal sprinkling of seediness.

Walking north from Centro to Luz along Rua Santa Ifigenia, you will come across a number of electronic and musical stores where Paulistano musicians buy their instruments; it's a good place in which to purchase your first *cavaquinho* (uekelele) and *pandeiro* (tambourine), and begin your career as a gringo *sambista*. Stop at the

About the author
Juliana Guarany, *entertainment and travel reporter for* Universo Online *and* Viagem e Turismo, *was born and raised in São Paulo.*

store **Contemporânea** (Rua General Osório 46, 3221 8477), where João Nogueira and Zeca Pagodinho (famous *sambistas*) are just some of the musical patrons. Open since 1946, it hosts regular Saturday *choro* concerts from 10am to 2pm. Around the corner is the **Escola de Música do Estado de São Paulo – Tom Jobim** (Largo General Osório 147, 3362 1692). With over 1,600 students all enrolled for free, it is central to the neighbourhood's revitalisation efforts, but the location makes it a target for vandalism and crime.

The first cultural landmark you will encounter is the **Estação Pinacoteca** (*see p56*), the contemporary art annex of the **Pinacoteca do Estado** (*see p56*). Art and authoritarianism may seem a strange mix, but this beautifully restored brick building is also home to the **Memorial da Resistencia** (*see p56*), a museum documenting the atrocities committed by the military dictatorship. To the west is the neoclassical train station **Estação Julio Prestes** (Rua Mauá 51, 3351 8000). Designed by Cristiano Stockler das Neves (from 1925-1936), it serves as one of the main interurban train stations of the city. A renovated space inside the station is home to the **Sala São Paulo** (*see p203*), the city's premier classical music venue.

Walk directly east, until you reach the **Estação da Luz** (Praça da Luz), which

Estação da Luz.

could be a little London architectural theme park in the historic heart of São Paulo – the station is adorned with a clocktower copy of Big Ben. Built by the British-owned São Paulo Railway, the station opened in 1901, and for many years it was São Paulo's first stop for the wealthy, the civil servants and the foreigners arriving from the port city of Santos. The money to build it came from the coffee industry, and its heyday lasted until World War II: in 1946, a fire burned down most of the structure. As part of the state's more recent attention to its faded icons, the old structure was rebuilt and painted in 1996.

For a more intriguing paint job, however, pay attention in the passage leading from the metro to the trains, where there is a 73x3-metre work of art called *Epopeia Paulista* (1973) by Maria Bonomi, one of Brazil's most famous contemporary artists. The concrete panel tells the story of north-eastern migrants to São Paulo.

If you need some Portuguese words in praise or criticism of art after viewing Bonomi's mural, head to Luz's **Museu da Lingua Portuguesa** (*see p56*), dedicated to the native tongue of Brazil. Currently, Luz functions as a suburban train station and is set to become the busiest metro station in the city when the projected yellow subway line begins to operate. It is also the setting for government-sponsored free concerts that attract commuters.

Facing Luz from the north is the sculpture garden **Parque da Luz** (Praça da Luz s/n). The first botanical garden in São Paulo, this 113,000-square-metre area was conceived in the 18th century, but didn't open to the public until

1825 as Jardim Botânico da Luz. It served as the main social venue for the rich until the end of the 19th century, and since then has mirrored the larger ups and downs of the area's history. As the neighbourhood industrialised and degraded in the 1950s, the park became quite dangerous, and in the '70s and '80s it was virtually abandoned. In 1999, a complete reconstruction of the park restored its former foliage glory, and it now showcases nearly 50 of the Pinacoteca do Estado's best sculptures: works by Victor Brecheret, Lasar Segall and Amilcar de Castro are displayed along its green lanes. The Pinacoteca do Estado, which is inside the park with an entrance facing Luz, was the first Paulistano museum.

INSIDE TRACK
SAO PAULO'S GIBRALTAR

To the east of Estação da Luz and across the pedestrian overpass is Sao Paulo's only authentic English neighbourhood. From 1915 to 1919, a small village consisting of 28 English-style houses was built for the British engineers from São Paulo Railway. The **Vila dos Ingleses** (Rua Mauá 836) was used by the English until 1932, when houses in the area were burned during the revolution. In 1986, the founder's grandson began a revitalisation project, and the village gained landmark status from the city government.

SIGHTS

From the Pinacoteca, continue north along Avenida Tiradentes, on your way to a bit of religious devotion and sacred creativity after having worshipped at the secular art altar of the Pinacoteca. The colonial complex **Convento da Luz** includes a monastery, museum, cemetery and church. The **Museu de Arte Sacra** is a great introduction to colonial-church art in Brazil, and the small park outside features fantastic replicas of the sculptures *Os Profetas* by Aleijadinho (often referred to as the Michelangelo of Brazil). The original 12 prophets are actually located in the colonial city of Congonhas in Minas Gerais state. Around the corner from the museum, you'll find the **Museu de Policia Militar** (Rua Jorge Miranda 308, 3311 9955, closed Mon). Designed by Ramos de Azevedo and built from 1890 to 1916, it is a fine example of neo-Renaissance style. Further east and to the right is the **Liceu de Artes e Oficios** (Rua Cantareira 1351, 2155 3300, closed Sat & Sun). If you're tiring of Brazilian art, you're in luck, as the art school houses a cultural centre with reproductions of famous European sculptures. Across the river Tietê and to the north is the **Museu dos Transportes Públicos Gaetano Ferolla** (Avenida Cruzeiro do Sul 780, 3315 8884, closed Mon). After so much walking, a museum detailing the history of public transport, with documents, photos and an example of the first trolley bus to circulate in the city, in 1872, may be as refreshing as a cold pint in stifling summer heat.

Estação Pinacoteca
Largo General Osório 66 (3337 0185/ www.pinacoteca.org.br). Metrô Estação da Luz. **Open** 10am-6pm Tue-Sun. **Admission** R$4 (incl same-day admission to Pinacoteca do Estado); free under-11s, over-65s. Free to all Sat. **No credit cards.**
This 1914 building now houses the visiting exhibits of the Pinacoteca do Estado, as well as the free museum – the Memorial da Resistencia. The military dictatorship (1964-85) established the Departamento de Ordem Politico e Social (DOPS) housing political prisoners here who were interrogated and tortured on site. This dark page of Brazilian history is well documented on its walls. In 1997, the state transformed it into a museum, and the cells used as torture chambers were spruced up and painted, a move that was criticised by the authorities and ex-prisoners, but the ugly and fascinating history on display can't be whitewashed.

Museu da Língua Portuguesa
Praça da Luz (3326 0775/www.museudalingua portuguesa.org.br). Metrô Estação da Luz. **Open** 10am-6pm Tue-Sun. **Admission** R$4; free under-10s, over-60s. Free to all Sat. **No credit cards.**

For an introduction to the countries and territories that use Portuguese as their first language – Goa in India, Macau in China, Angola and Capo Verde in Africa, and Brazil, of course, whose population makes Portuguese one of the most spoken languages in the world – there is a short film on the top floor. The second floor shows a permanent collection of images and a language timeline, as well as the adaptation of foreign words from sources as diverse as English, Indian *tupi* and African tongues; the first floor hosts a temporary exhibition that changes every three months. The exhibits are visually striking, although there are no signs in English.

★ Museu de Arte Sacra
Avenida Tiradentes 676 (3326 1373/ www.museuartesacra.org.br). Metrô Tiradentes. **Open** 11am-7pm Tue-Sun. **Admission** R$4; R$1 with subway ticket; free under-7s, over-65s. Free parking at Rua Jorge Miranda 43. **No credit cards.**
Frei Galvão, the first Brazilian to be canonised (in 2007), founded this monastery in 1774. The museum houses a fantastic collection of over 4,000 pieces of art, of which about 800 are on display. Most of the sculptures are made of clay and wood. A special room exhibits *Nossa Senhora da Luz*, a painting brought from Portugal in 1603 that gave its name to the neighbourhood. A separate wing houses a folk art tour of nativity scenes from around the world, and Brazil's own signature nativity scene by Mestre Vitalino, one of the most important Brazilian figurine sculptors.

★ Pinacoteca do Estado
Praça da Luz s/n (3324 1000/www.pinacoteca. org.br). Metrô Estação da Luz. **Open** 10am-6pm Tue-Sun **Admission** R$4 (incl same-day admission to Estação Pinacoteca); free under-11s, over-65s. Free to all Sat. **No credit cards.**
Like the MASP (*see p158*), the Pinacoteca reflects the theory that an art space must be worthy of the art it exhibits. Designed in 1897 by Ramos de Azevedo, it housed the first art school of the city, Liceu de Artes e Oficios. In 1997, Paulo Mendes da Rocha renovated the eclectic neoclassical building by stripping it of the stucco that covered it and leaving a stunning columned palace in exposed

---

**INSIDE TRACK
GOD'S FERTILITY CLINIC?**

The small church at the entrance to the Convento da Luz is busy throughout the week, but especially on Sundays, when the seven cloistered nuns prepare 'Frei Galvão pills' – pregnancy aids that are distributed to the public daily. The pills are wrapped in pieces of paper with a prayer to the Virgin.

Parque da Luz. *See p55.*

brick. The most important Brazilian modernists are on display inside: Cândido Portinari, Anita Malfatti, Victor Brecheret, Tarsila do Amaral and Di Cavalcanti are just some of the star attractions.

BOM RETIRO
Metrô Tiradentes

Prior to the 1980s, Bom Retiro was a microcosm of the Mediterranean, with a population of Italians, Jews, Greeks, Syrians and Lebanese. In 1912, newly arrived Jewish immigrants erected the first synagogue in the neighbourhood; at the height of Jewish immigration between the world wars and until Getulio Vargas stemmed the flow by imposing quotas on Jewish immigrants, the *bairro* had ten synagogues. It would be tough to do a synagogue crawl these days, but one of the few functioning is the **Beth Itzchak El Chonon synagogue** (Rua Prates 706; contact the Federação Israelita do Estado de São Paulo 3088 0111, www.fisesp.org.br). For some eastern European food, try the **Adi Shoshi Delishop** (Rua Correia de Melo 206, 3228 4774, no credit cards, 9.30am-3.30pm Mon-Sat, closed Sun). In the 1980s, Jews began to leave the area in large numbers and move to Higienopolis. The majority of the current businesses are owned by Korean immigrants, who began to arrive in the '60s and successfully took over the garment industry from their Jewish neighbours.

The **Oficina Cultural Oswald de Andrade** (Rua Três Rios 363, 3222 2662), which opened in 1905 as the Escola Livre de Farmácia, is now the neighbourhood's leading cultural centre. It features rotating expositions, theatre presentations and free community classes. Further into the neighbourhood is the city's best Greek restaurant, **Acrópoles** (Rua da Graça 364, 3223 4386).

BRAS E MOOCA

The first neighbourhood to be settled east of the Tamanduateí River, Brás was founded during the 19th century around the local church Nossa Senhora do Brás. Mooca, on the other hand, was an ancient site that Indian tribes settled before the Europeans arrived, and to this day its streets use native names. In the 19th century Brás and Mooca were the industrial centres of the city, and it was here that anarchists and Communists waged battles and strikes that had repercussions for the country's entire labour force. The Italians as well as Greeks and Armenians arrived in the late 1800s; now Bolivian and Korean immigrants reside here.

Memorial do Imigrante
Rua Visconde de Parnaíba 1316, Mooca (2692 1866/www.memorialdoimigrante.sp.gov.br). *Metrô Bresser-Mooca.* **Open** 10am-5pm Tue-Sun. **Admission** $4; free under-7s, over-60s. Free to all last Sat of mth. **No credit cards**. More than 2.5 million people came to São Paulo between 1870 and 1939. This museum, commemorating the history of Sao Paulo's immigrants, occupies the old lodging-house complex that from 1887 received up to 1,000 people a day from Italy, Germany, Japan, Russia, Spain and Portugal. The immigrants were housed for eight days and had access to all the facilities for free.

SIGHTS

Park Life

Hike and bike in São Paulo's green spaces.

Above the Tietê river, you will find several parks and forests, a pleasant retreat from the intense urban experience. Paulistano authorities claim that **Parque da Cantareira** is the world's largest native urban forest, with almost 8,000 hectares of land. The huge four-park complex was one of the main stops for *tropeiros* (travelling salesmen in the 16th and 17th centuries). Águas Claras park has easy trails through the forest, and a lake full of carp; the trails connect it to another park, Pedra Branca. There are three main trails here, and a half-hour walk takes you to the viewing point, where on a cloudless day you can see the Serra do Mar Mountains across town.

The most popular park in the north, the **Horto Florestal**, is smaller than Ibirapuera but just as beautiful. The Palácio do Horto (known also as the government's summer palace) is a building built in the 1930s, and contains pieces of art from Oscar Pereira da Silva, Margaret Mee, Collete Pujol and other important contemporary artists. The **Museu Florestal Octávio Vecchi** (Rua do Horto 931, 2231 8555) holds an impressive collection of woodcrafts.

BARRA FUNDA

Metrô Barra Funda.

The industrial region of Barra Funda was formed during the 19th century when an old plantation was subdivided into several properties. By the 1900s, the area had become home to numerous Italian immigrants, who worked on the two railroads that crossed the region. The Italian connection can still be found in the Várzea football stadium, which is owned by Palmeiras, a traditional Italian football team. To tourists, Barra Funda is known mostly as an up-and-coming district that brings a certain cachet of frontier-land danger to its nightlife. People from far and wide trek out here for some of the best clubs in São Paulo, if not South America. Visitors with an interest in partying should check out D-Edge and Berlin (*see p201*).

The most iconic city designs can be found at the Fundação Memorial da América Latina (Avenida Auro Soares de Moura Andrade 664, 3283 4600, www.memorial.sp.gov.br), Oscar Niemeyer's futuristic complex of buildings right outside Metrô Barra Funda. The 84,000-square-metre conglomeration was built in 1989 with the goal of bringing together all Latin American nations. The foundation is home to a great number of the city's cultural centres, including the Pavilhão da Criatividade, which holds a great collection of popular art from all over Latin America, and the Galeria Marta Traba de Arte Latino-Americana, another venue for art. The Simón Bolivar Auditorium is a performance venue for many Brazilian artists, and the Biblioteca Victor Civita (closed Sun) is a library devoted to Latin American work.

HORTO

Bus 177H-10.

Horto Florestal

Rua do Horto 931 (2193 8282/www.horto florestal.com.br). Bus 177H-10. **Open** 9am-3pm daily. **Admission** free.

Parque da Cantareira

Rua do Horto 1799. Bus177H-10. **Open** 8am-4pm Sat, Sun. **Admission** $2; free under-10s and over+60s. **No credit cards**.

INSIDE TRACK
FRANGO

North of Barra Funda, in the Freguesia do Ó neighbourhood, you'll find **Frangó** (Largo da Matriz Nossa Senhora do Ó 168, 3932 4818, www.frangobar.com.br, closed Mon), a 20-year-old bar filled with the charm of an old-school drinking joint. Simple wooden tables complement the inside of this 19th century house, while beer bottles gleam on wooden shelves. The ambrosias that wait inside are worth the Herculean effort of arriving at this *boteco* (take buses 178T-10, 847P-42, 8199-10). An extensive and half-decent selection of European beers (such as Kronenberg 1664) makes a good match for the bar's *salgados*, including the chicken *coxinha*, which were recently voted the best in the city – an impressive feat in a country obsessed with its fried finger foods.

Bela Vista
& Liberdade

Superlative sushi and perfect pizzas.

Immediately south of Centro are two of São Paulo's most famous immigrant neighbourhoods: **Bela Vista**, an Italian stronghold, and **Liberdade**, the formerly Japanese enclave. Although the latter is marketed to tourists as 'Japantown', many of Liberdade's inhabitants are, in fact, increasingly of Chinese or Korean descent; among the plethora of traditional Japanese restaurants and shops selling knick-knacks, there is now a noticeably higher number of Chinese and Korean amenities, such as road signs, restaurants and bookshops.

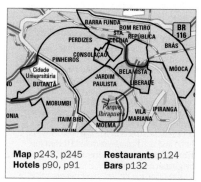

Map p243, p245	**Restaurants** p124
Hotels p90, p91	**Bars** p132

BELA VISTA

Metrô São Joaquim or Trianon-MASP. Bus 475M-10, 475R-10, 967A-10.

This antique, colourful part of town was – and continues to be – the home of Italian immigrants arriving en masse in Brazil as part of an organised campaign in the late 19th century (*see p16*). The most notable of these was Francesco Matarazzo (1854-1937), the founder of what was to become the largest industrial empire in Latin America at the start of the 20th century (*see p40* **The Count of São Paulo**). The Italians assimilated more easily into Brazilian culture than the Japanese, owing to their European descent and the religious and linguistic similarities between the two countries. Nonetheless, the conditions for the first immigrants in Bela Vista were extremely difficult: several families would cram into single houses to keep living costs down, and children would be sent to work in the local factories. However, as the Italians imprinted

their culture more firmly on to the borough, it became recognised for containing some of the best theatres, bakeries and restaurants in the city. For this reason, Bela Vista, despite its relatively poor transport links (few buses run here, and it's a long walk from the closest metro station), has risen to become one of the most important visitor destinations in São Paulo.

On Sunday, the **Praça Dom Orione** is home to the wonderful **Feira das Antiguidades** or **Feira do Bixiga** (*see p158*). Keep an eye (or rather, an ear) out for the group of elderly gentlemen playing a 130-year-old style of popular Brazilian music called *chorinho* and also look out for a granite statue of Adoniran Barbosa (*see p197* **The Troubadour of Bixiga**) in hat and bow-tie by Luis Morrone. From the plaza, turn towards Rua 13 de Maio and you'll see an ornate staircase made of stone, flanked by traditional streetlamps. At the top of the staircase you'll come to Rua dos Ingleses, a street marked by its unusual houses and a liberal number of statues and mosaics. In the evening you can stop at **Bar Drops** (*see p199*), situated in an Italianate house from the 1930s, where DJs play most nights.

Nearby, the **Teatro Ruth Escobar** (Rua dos Ingleses 209, 3289 2358, www.ruthescobar. apetesp.org.br), inaugurated in 1963, puts on

About the author
Karim Alexander Khan *is a freelance journalist and has worked for* Time Out London.

INSIDE TRACK
VAI VAI

One of the first samba schools in São Paulo, **Vai Vai**, was created when its two founders were kicked out of Cai-Cai, a carnivalesque troupe and football team from Bixiga. Parading for the first time in 1930, Vai Vai established itself with its colours of black and white. It has since won 13 of the city's Carnival championships. For more info on samba school hours and rehearsals, *see p166*.

plays for both adults and children on its three stages. A block east is Rua dos Franceses and close by is the tiny Rua Veloso Guerra, notable for its picturesque houses and balconies. It's one of the rare examples of a quiet, house-lined street, without the ubiquitous presence of huge security walls, and, Rua 13 de Maio aside, it's perhaps one of the most authentic Italian scenes in the city. The area of Bela Vista between the streets of Rui Barbosa, Nove de Julho and dos Frances is called **Bixiga** (or **Bexiga**), the popular name used in neighbourhood folklore.

The principle Italian street in Bela Vista, Rua 13 de Maio, begins at Avenida Paulista and stretches to Centro. Near the **Praça Dom Orione** is the lovely **Ludus** (Rua 13 de Maio 972, 3253 8452, www.ludusluderia.com.br), a café that's also a board gamer's paradise. Check out the quasi-*Alice in Wonderland* chess set-up, and come on a Thursday or Friday to take part in a board game or a poker tournament. For a perspective on Italian-Brazilian cuisine, stop at **Pizzeria Speranza** (*see p116*). This restaurant is considered one of the most traditional Italian eateries in all of São Paulo; the original proprietor, Dona Speranza, began making pizzas here in the 1950s. **Basilicata** (Rua 13 de Maio 614, 3289 3111) is a beautiful bakery that has left its Italian bread-making process unchanged for over 90 years. It also stocks great novelties like vintage soft drinks and delicious home-made sandwich fillings like aubergine in truffle oil.

Igreja da Nossa Senhora Achiropita (Rua 13 de Maio 478, 3105 2789) is a delightful light blue church built by Italian immigrants in 1926. Its delicate gates and numerous statues make it one of the street's standout buildings, while its huge golden dome is visible on a clear day from as far away as Avenida Paulista. At the end of Rua 13 de Maio closest to Centro are a number of bars, the most famous of which is **Piu Piu** (*see p190*), a 21-year-old establishment that's a reference point for live music in São Paulo. Several blocks east of Rua 13 de Maio, on Rua Major Diogo, one of the old moneyed streets in the city, is the **Casa da Dona Yayá** (Rua Major Diogo 353, 3106 3562, www.usp.br/cpc, closed Sat), a 19th-century mansion. One of the few remaining urban estates in São Paulo, the mansion last belonged to Sebastiana de Melo Freire, who suffered from dementia from the early 1920s, and was house-bound until her death in 1961. The family's assets were given over to the University of São Paulo in 1969, which transformed it into the **Centro de Preservação Cultural** (Cultural Preservation Centre) and restored the building to its former glory. The Centro regularly puts on children's plays, circus and musical performances – sometimes in the beautiful garden behind the house.

South of here is one of the city's most beautiful theatres, **Teatro Abril** (Avenida Brigadeiro Luis Antonio 411, 2846 6232, www.teatroabril.com.br). This art nouveau building from 1929 was once called Teatro Paramount, and it was here that Gilberto Gil and Caetano Veloso sang 'Domingo no Parque', the song that launched Tropicalismo (Brazil's second greatest cultural movement after Brazilian Modernism).

LIBERDADE
Metrô Liberdade or São Joaquim

The Japanese community of São Paulo makes up the largest Japanese 'city' outside of Japan, a distinction it had already claimed by 1960. The Nikkei (Brazilians of Japanese descent, also spelled 'Nikkey') first came to São Paulo state as part of the immigrant labour force for the

Liberdade.

Liberdade.

coffee economy (*see p16; photo p21*). In 1912, four years after the ship *Kasato Maru* landed in Santos (bringing with it the first 165 Japanese families to Brazil), the first Nikkei settled in Liberdade, on Rua Conde de Sarzedas. They began moving into Brazil's largest city as the coffee economy stagnated in the late 1920s.

Throughout the 20th century, second and subsequent Nikkei generations served as both emblem of the clichéd 'urban melting pot' of São Paulo and symbol of the difficulties experienced by different groups in defining their own ethnicity within a nationalistic country. In 1938, the Vargas regime began its 'whitening' campaign; under the oppressive nationalism of the Estado Novo government, further Japanese immigration as well as the public use of the Japanese language and expression of the culture were banned. In 1942, when Brazil entered World War II on the side of the Allies, Nikkei became targets of discrimination. And during the military dictatorship of the 1960s and 1970s, as the Nikkei population peaked, their 'Brazilianness' was again questioned. In the 1990s, many Nikkei moved to Japan to seek better jobs and salaries. Recently, the Japanese government announced that because of the credit crisis and high rate of unemployment, it would pay the Nikkei (who are often considered foreign in Japan, despite being of Japanese descent) to return to Brazil.

The Praça da Liberdade is the starting point for any ramble around Liberdade, and not all of its sights are specific to Asian culture. The humble-looking **Igreja Santa Cruz da Almas dos Enforcados** (Praça da Liberdade 238) dates back to 1821 and is one of the most popular churches in São Paulo. Its plain exterior masks intricate gold-leaf detailing in the interior, which has an altar that was the only relic to survive a fire in 2000 (a result of the overwhelming number of prayer candles) and walls replete with colourful paintings of cherubs. Candles can be bought from R$1, but visitors should be aware that this church offers prayer for departed souls only. If you're here on a Sunday, the Praça hosts what is arguably the city's yummiest fair – **Feira de Arte, Artesanato e Cultura da Liberdade** (*see p145*), an ongoing event since 1975, with hundreds of stalls – including excellent tempura – to entertain the meandering visitors.

The founder of **Livraria Sol** (Praça da Liberdade 153, 3208 6588, www.livrariasol. com.br), Yoshiro Fujita, was a worker at an import company during World War II who lost his job and became a door-to-door salesman. He received a few Japanese books from the old country, which sold so rapidly that he opened an entirely Japanese bookshop. Open since 1949, it's now the oldest Japanese book importer in the city.

Further down Avenida da Liberdade is the **Casa de Portugal** (Avenida da Liberdade 602, 3209 5534, www.casadeportugalsp.com.br), a beautifully restored colonial building. It houses a large library and archives on the Luso-Brasilian experience, as well as a Portuguese restaurant, bar and gallery.

★ Museu Histórico da Imigração Japonesa no Brasil

Rua São Joaquim 381, Liberdade (3208 1755/ www. bunkyo.org.br). Metrô São Joaquim. **Open** 1.30-5.30pm Tue-Sun. **Admission** R$5; R$1-$2.50 reductions; free under-5s and over+65s. **No credit cards. Map** p245 O8.
This museum specialises in the history of Japanese immigration with photos, documents and archives that span the 100-year history of Japanese immigration to Brazil.

INSIDE TRACK
FESTAS IN LIBERDADE

Various festivals of Japanese culture bring Eastern colour and noise to Liberdade. The **Festa das Estrelas** (Festival of Stars), for instance, is based on the yearly mythological meeting of star-crossed lovers Orihime and Kengyu. On 7 July, the Japanese celebrate the lovers' reconciliation with parades and festivities. And every February, **Chinese New Year** draws a huge, enthusiastic crowd to watch free public shows and exhibitions put on by the growing Chinese population.

SIGHTS

Walk Temples, Treats and Sweets

The Japanese and Chinese sub-cultures of Liberdade.

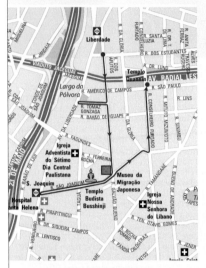

From **Praça da Liberdade**, head south down Rua Galvão Bueno, which during the last decade has become, increasingly, a Chinese neighbourhood – note the Chinese street signs, and restaurants offering a Chinese take on local cuisine. On your left, you'll come across a small, picturesque Japanese garden (open July and December only), filled with seven stone lanterns and a bust of Hachiro Miyasaki, one of the first Japanese immigrants to come to Liberdade in 1913. He helped popularise the prospect of living in Brazil among other Japanese natives.

Stop at the excellent Japanese restaurant **Lamen Aska** (*see p124*). Move on to the artisanal snack shop **Kanazawa** (Rua Galvão Bueno 379, 3207 1801), which produces handmade sweets. The *sakura moti*, made of red kidney bean paste, rice and cherry leaves, is perhaps the most popular sweet, but the *yokan*, a solid marmalade square, is a traditional treat for sweet tooths.

Next, turn left on to Rua Tomáz Gonzaga until you reach the **Largo da Pólvora**, where another traditional garden can be found – this can be enjoyed all year round. Turn back onto Rua Galvão

Bueno and onward south to Rua São Joaquim, where you'll find some of the most important Japanese buildings in Liberdade. The **Templo Budista Busshinji** (Rua São Joaquim 285, 3208 4515, www.sotozen.org.br, closed Sat & Sun), was built in 1994 by Japanese immigrants to the Soto-Zen Buddhist persuasion. Busshinji translates as 'Heart of the Buddha', and in the true spirit of conviviality, the temple is open to anyone for meditation. Arrival, though, must be punctual and formal wear is advised: no jeans, shorts or skirts.

For an interesting comparison after your visit to the Japanese Buddhist temple, head to its Chinese counterpart, the **Templo Quannin** (Viaduto da Rua Conselheiro Furtado), located close by. It's also devoted to the Buddha, and the sculptures here are especially vivid, if a little surreal.

Another stop on Rua São Joaquim is the **Bunkyo** or **Sociedade Brasileira de Cultura Japonesa e de Assistência Social** (Rua São Joaquim 381, www.bunkyo.org, closed Mon), an epicentre of the Japanese community. It houses the **Museu de Arte Nipo-Brasileiro** on the first floor (temporarily closed), the **Associação Brasileira de Taikô** (second floor), **Escola de Bailado Clássico Fujima** (fourth floor) and the **Museu da Immigração Japonesa**. The building is also home to the **Centro de Chadô Urasenke do Brasil** – with specific rooms that offer cultural classes and cover traditional topics like flower arranging and traditional tea ceremonies. The inauguration of the Bunkyo was so important that it was attended by the Prince and Princess of Japan in 1978.

Another stop on this tour that should soon be open to the public is **Museu de Arte Moderna Nipo-Brasileira Manabu Mabe** (Rua São Joaquim 288, Liberdade, 5011 5869, www.institutomanabumabe.org.br). Named after one of São Paulo's best-loved Japanese artists, the self-taught abstract painter Manabu Mabe, the gallery was designed by Victor Hugo Mori in 1992. It documents every phase of Mabe's career until his death in 1997 (he was awarded the Painter Laureate in 1939).

SIGHTS

Consolação & Higienópolis

Beyond Jardins, vibrant bairros beckon.

The area immediately west of Centro might not be a top tourist attraction like neighbouring Jardim Paulista, but it is home to a great array of verdant parks, cemeteries, historic mansions and some iconic Paulistano architecture. The neighbourhoods' feel changes after dark. Wander around **Consolação** when the sun is out, and you'll be surprised by how bohemian it is: graffiti, appealing New Age stores and art galleries mix with trendy restaurants. Walk through the red-light district of **Rua Augusta** at night, and you'll come face to face with São Paulo's seedy side as well as one of its nightlife hotspots. Meanwhile, the old-money enclave of **Higienópolis** is always family-friendly, and full of greenery, great dining and good shopping.

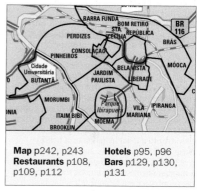

Map p242, p243	**Hotels** p95, p96
Restaurants p108, p109, p112	**Bars** p129, p130, p131

CONSOLACAO & HIGIENÓPOLIS

Metrô Clinicas, Bus 177H-10, 508L-10, 877T-10

The district of Consolação is best known for its historical and cultural heritage. It was the site preferred by Brazilian coffee growers who, rich from the boom in coffee production during the 19th century, settled in Higienópolis and Pacaembu. However, Consolação is perhaps most remembered for the student battle that took place on Rua Maria Antônia on 2 October 1968. It was among the first acts of public resistance against the right-wing military dictatorship and prompted a nationwide military siege by the government. The battle was fought between anti-Communist members of the **Universidade Mackenzie** and the left-wing students of the **Universidade de São Paulo**, resulting in the death of one student. These days, the only acts of aggression you're likely to encounter around Consolação come in the form of car horns blaring – perhaps the only form of catharsis available from the traffic that congests Avenida Paulista.

On Rua da Consolação, the pleasant cinema **HSBC Belas Artes** (*see p173*) hosts a movie marathon every second Friday of the month, from midnight until around 7am, when it serves a complimentary breakfast. An underground passage to the other side of the street doubles as a contemporary book market, with its entrance marked by black and white posters.

Northwest of Avenida Paulista on Rua da Consolação you will unearth the city's premier necropolis; it's no Paris's Père Lachaise or Buenos Aires' Recoleta, but the **Cemitério da Consolação** (Rua da Consolação 1660, 3396 3815) is the resting place for a number of the country's artistic and cultural greats. Modernist artist Tarsila do Amaral, poets Oswald de Andrade and Mário de Andrade (no relation to each other), and celebrated children's author and publisher Monteiro Lobato, are all buried here. The cemetery dates back to 1858 and the rise of the bourgeoisie (those coffee growers again). The elite commissioned renowned sculptors such as Victor Brecheret, Celso Antônio Silveira de Menezes and Galileo Emendabili to create large-scale works to honour the dead. Bruno Giorgi's famous abstract *Prece* sculpture (1970), made from Carrara marble, is now one of around 80 historically valuable pieces in the cemetery (it sits in quadrant 17-9).

Take the Rua Mato Grosso exit out of the cemetery and head north into Higienópolis, known for its large Jewish community. **AK Delicatessen** (Rua Mato Grosso 450, 3231 4497, www.akdelicatessen.com.br) and **Casa Zilanna** (Rua Itambe 506, 3256 5053, closed Sun) are the community's better-known culinary outposts. Head to the latter for Passover products. North-east on Rua Maria Antonia are the cultural institutions **Centro Universitário Maria Antônia** (*see p65*) and **Instituto de Arte Contemporânea** (*see p65*). There arc mansions and modernist buildings on Avenida Higienópolis, as well as the **Pátio Higienópolis** shopping mall (*see p145*), and at the end of this bairro, the charming Praça Esther Mesquito is perched on a city overlook. Head here if you can't afford the prices at Brazilian gyms, as the tiny plaza offers free exercise machines (during the day, they are often used by patients of nearby Hospital Samaritano, but at night they are free to all). The nearby buildings are home to a number of celebrities, among them Jô Soares, the country's most famous talk show host.

Rua Alagoas is a quintessentially upper-middle-class Brazilian street – with the Universidade Mackenzie at its heart. The leafy, shaded road is filled with delicate paving and quaint apartment blocks, ubiquitous *padarias* (bakeries), *lanchonete*s (snack bars) and convenience stores that become more ornate as you head to the centre of Higienópolis.

Parque Buenos Aires, on Rua Angélica, with its fountains, sculptures, benches and swings, is quite popular with the elderly, kids and their carers. Designed in the manner of a European garden in 1916 by the French architect Brouvard, it boasts a number of excellent sculptures, including the looming 24-tonne *Mãe*, created by national prize-winning sculptor Caetano Fraccaroli, Roberto Vivas' *Homage a Tango* and the mildly nightmarish bust of the first Argentinian president, Bernadino Rivadavia.

Stop in at **Instituto Moreira Salles** (Rua Piaui 844, 3825 2560, www.ims.uol.com.br). Founded by banking tycoon Walther Moreira Salles in 1990, the institute develops cultural programmes nationwide in the areas of photography, literature, modern art and Brazilian music. Its corresponding art gallery in São Paulo can be found on the third floor of **Shopping Frei Caneca** (Rua Frei Caneca 569, 3472 2000, www.freicanecashopping.com). The institute coordinates its activities with the various **Espaços Unibanco de Cinema/ Arteplex**, and together they constitute the biggest private company dedicated to arts and culture in Brazil.

Straight ahead is the **Higienópolis Dining Triangle**, with a tiny island of green at its centre known as the **Praça Vilaboim**. Look for the Villanova Artigas building, **Louveira** (Praça Vilaboim 144), on the same street. The Dining Triangle is so called on account of the multitude of cafés, restaurants and boutiques around it. The colourful art space **Artesanato Oui** (Praça Vilaboim 41-A, 3825 2206, closed Sun) specialises in national artists like Eduardo Iglesias and the Silva brothers, João and Conseição. A pleasant place to have lunch nearby is the **Le Vin Bistro** (Rua Armando Penteado 25, 3668 7400), which serves a mouth-watering steak sandwich and green salad for R$32. South is the **Museu de Arte Brasileira** (*see p65*), one of the top art venues in the city, with an entrance that boasts beautiful statues carved by the 18th-century sculptor Aleijadinho.

Nearby is the **Estádio do Pacaembu** (*see p207*), the city's famous football field, and the **Museu do Futebol** (*see p85*), dedicated to Brazil's favourite national pastime. South of the football stadium are winding streets; one in particular, the Rua Minas Gerais, is famed for its mix of old and new, intriguing houses from the heyday of the neighbourhood facing modern condos. Close by is a great new gallery inside an old mansion: **Galeria Pontes** (*see p176*) is filled with contemporary art from the interior of the country and large, voluptuous sculptures. **Galeria Vermelho** (*see p178*) is one of

Cemitério da Consolação. *See p63*.

the newest galleries on the scene, dealing exclusively in art of the new media variety – video and installations. A good restaurant, **Sal Gastronomia** (*see p109*), is located on the premises should you find yourself getting a little peckish after so much food for thought.

West is the **Cemitério do Araçá** (Avenida Doutor Arnaldo 666, Consolação, 3256 6486). This sprawling, second-oldest cemetery in the city is a bit of a walk from Rua da Consolação, but it contains important sculptural works, like Victor Brecheret's early work, *A Musa Impasivel*. The piece was made for the renowned poet and author Francisca Júlia, who committed suicide after the death of her husband in 1920. Other sites of interest are the Muslim tomb and a monument to the fallen Italian soldiers of both world wars. Daily tours are given by Osmair Camargo (enquire at the office). **Avenida Doutor Arnaldo**, which borders the cemetery, has interesting graffiti close to Avenida Paulista.

FREE Centro Universitário Maria Antônia

Rua Maria Antônia 294, Higienópolis (3255 7182/www.usp.br/mariantonia). Bus 408A-10, 7703-10, 778R-10. **Open** 9am-7pm Mon-Fri; 10am-10pm Sat, Sun. **Admission** free. **Map** p242 L5.

This 1930s building is part of the USP university campus and was one of the founding homes of its Philosophy, Humanities and Letters department – for a time, the centre of intellectual life in the city. The department gained cult status as a spearhead for the resistance against the dictatorship that began in 1964, culminating in a clash with the students of the largely pro-military Universidade Mackenzie in 1968. It continues as a hub of art exhibitions, musical concerts and educational arts programmes.

FREE Instituto de Arte Contemporânea

Rua Maria Antônia 258, Higienópolis (3255 2009/www.iacbrasil.org.br). Bus 408A-10, 778R-10. **Open** 10am-7pm Tue-Sat; noon-5pm Sun. **Admission** free. **Map** p242 L5.

The geometric and constructivist works of four artists – Sergio Camargo, Mira Schendel, Willys de Castro and Amilcar de Castro – are deemed fundamentally influential to modern-day Brazilian art. The Instituto de Arte Contemporânea (founded in 1997) is a non-profit, cultural organisation that publicly displays their works and promotes cultural exchange programmes and exhibitions. The space is as interesting for its linear architecture as it is for its contents.

★ FREE Museu de Arte Brasileira (FAAP)

Rua Alagoas 903 (3662 7198/www.faap.br/museu). Bus 408A-10, 177H-10, 719P-10. **Open** 10am-8pm Tue-Fri; 1-5pm Sat, Sun. **Admission** free. **Map** p242 J5.

Inaugurated in 1961, the museum inside the Fundação Armando Álvares Penteado (FAAP) building has a superlative collection of works by Tarsila do Amaral, Anita Malfatti, Victor Brecheret, Cândido Portinari, Di Cavalcanti, Lasar Segall and Ernesto De Fiori, as well as modern-day notables such as Sandra Cinto, Anatol Wladyslaw and Cláudio Mubarac. The museum occasionally hosts international exhibitions from countries including France, China and Russia.

Museu do Futebol

Estádio do Pacaembu, Praça Charles Miller s/n, Pacaembu (3663 3848/www.museudofutebol.org.br). Bus 408A-10. **Open** 10am-6pm Tue-Sun. **Admission** R$6; R$2 reductions; free under-7s. Free to all Thur. **Map** p242 J5.

In a land where Pelé and Ronaldo are kings, it's no wonder that finally someone has erected a temple to the national sport. The Museu do Futebol does just that by treating football as a manifestation of Brazilian culture. On display are documents, photos and video footage, as well as numerous other archival items.

RUA AUGUSTA

Rua Augusta, a road associated with frivolity and fun since the 1960s, is now all about conspicuous consumption. On the Cerquera César side of Paulista, it was the smartest street in 1970s São Paulo and although it's less glamorous today, it's being spruced up and there are a few highlights. It makes a nice

Avenida Doutor Arnaldo.

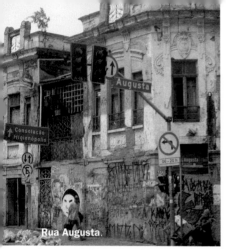

Rua Augusta.

on the lives of the Guarani and Kayapo tribes.

At night, this part of the street turns into red-light central. The strip bars hire both men and women to get in punters from the street; you'll see this going on any time after dark if you're coming from Jardins towards Centro or vice versa. Friday nights on this side of Augusta, however, are the preserve of 15- to 17-year-old Emo kids. Watching tribes of them amble down the sidewalk and cluster around alternative bars such as **Ibotirama** (Rua Augusta 1230, 3205 2247) is akin to watching a David Attenborough documentary. The sheer proximity and overlapping of these very different worlds makes Rua Augusta an important and interesting part of São Paulo's urban culture.

Follow Rua Augusta down towards Centro, and on the other side of the pedestrian overpass (over Avenida 9 de Julho) you'll see beautiful **Sinagoga Israelita Paulista** (Rua Augusta 259, 3120 5094). Around the corner from it and opposite the large Braston Hotel is a tiny street called **Rua Avanhandava**. Marked by the many potted plants dotted all over the street and little wooden parrots peeping out from the trees, it makes a pleasant retreat: the mosaic fountain that sits outside the **Central 22** café (Rua Avanhandava 22, 3258 4243) is the perfect antidote to the noise of the street. Avanhandava was built in 1929 using neocolonial designs reminiscent of the California Mission style. It is dominated by restaurants and bars run by the Mancini family. Their main restaurant, **Famiglia Mancini** (Rua Avanhadava 81, 3256 4320) was founded in 1980 and serves good traditional pasta dishes and pizza.

change from the sometimes clinical, *Truman Show*-like sensation of the Oscar Freire – Haddock Lobo axis in Jardins (*see p71*). Exhibition space and trendy contemporary art school **Escola São Paulo** (Rua Augusta 2239, 3060 3636, www.escolasaopaulo.org, closed Sun) fills with Paulistano in-the-know fashion and art elites on opening nights. It offers talks and lectures from leading lights in fashion, cinema, art and gastronomy. The library is one of the highlights, offering DVDs, journals and magazines. There's a café too.

Galeria Ouro Fino (Rua Augusta 2690, 3082 7860, www.galeriaourofino.com.br, closed Sun), was the city's first shopping complex (1962). Today it offers hip boutiques, music shops, tattoo parlours and a salon that specialises in dreadlocks. **Livraria Gaudi** (Rua Augusta 2872, 3081 1010, www.gaudi. com.br, closed Sat & Sun) specialises in art books. **Cine Sesc** (*see p174*) screens mainly art house films and has a bar with a glass panel that allows you to enjoy a drink while watching the movie.

This part of Rua Augusta is also home to chichi skate shop **Maze** (*see p151*) and **Eastpak** (Rua Augusta 2685, 3081 1979). From the junction of Rua Augusta and Avenida Paulista, and towards Centro, the area offers an eclectic mix of vintage hamburger bars like **Frevo** (Rua Augusta 1563, 3284 7622, www. frevinho.com.br) and cultural spaces like the **Espaço Unibanco** (*see p172*), which combines arthouse cinema with a bookstore and café.

Stop at **Iandé** (Rua Augusta 1371, 3283 4924, www.iande.art.br) in **Galeria Ouro Velho**, arguably the best place in the city to find indigenous Brazilian tribal arts and crafts. The name Iandé itself means 'head dress' – but although the shop does stock interesting masks and handicrafts, it also offers literature and DVDs

Rua Avanhandava.

Avenida Paulista & Jardins

São Paulo's neighbourhood extraordinaire.

Avenida Paulista is São Paulo's most emblematic thoroughfare. Once lined with coffee-baron mansions, the road is now 2.8 kilometres of skyscraper-lined avenue – symbolic of Latin America's 20th-century business aspirations and home to some of the continent's most expensive real estate. Museums and restaurants, antiques markets and parks, beggars and bankers, cinemas and street stalls all coexist here and blend into an organised chaos typical of the city. Down the hill to the Rio Pinheiros and one of the city's main roads (**Avenida Faria Lima**), are several of São Paulo's most exclusive addresses and venues, in

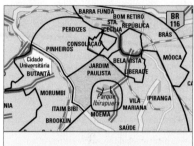

Map p244,	Hotels p99, p100,
p245, p249	p101, p103, p104,
Restaurants p117,	p105
p119, p120, p121,	**Bars** p133, p135,
p122, p123, p124	p137

Jardins. The collective Jardins area refers to the wealthy and leafy neighbourhoods including **Jardim Paulista**, **Jardim Europa**, **Jardim America** and **Cerqueira César**, which are home to diverse residential, commercial and cultural enclaves, as well as to some of the city's best shopping.

AVENIDA PAULISTA

Metrô to Brigadeiro, Consolação, Paraiso, Trianon-MASP

In the 18th century, Avenida Paulista was just a *caaguaçú* (native Tupi for 'large forest'). Situated on one of the highest points in the city, this vast stretch of rainforest became a strip of wealthy coffee barons' homes in the 19th century and one of the country's most vibrant and valuable real estate hubs in the 20th century. The development of Avenida Paulista was led by Joquim Eugenia de Lima and it was inaugurated on 8 December 1891. Since the popular residential areas of the time – Higienópolis and Praça República – were rapidly becoming over-populated, farmland around the area was parcelled up into lots and promoted as a new residential option. Avenida Paulista was the most important road in the newest, most desirable area of town, and was therefore the first to be paved, in 1909. It was

not until the 1950s that its transformation architecturally and socially into the financial and business hub of the city began.

Thousands stomp Avenida Paulista's iconic black and white stone pavements and cross at its traffic lights every day. Periodically, the crowds also stop its erratic flow. In the 1950s, Nat King Cole and Marlene Dietrich performed in the Fasano Restaurant, originally located in the **Conjunto Nacional** (*see p68*). In the 1990s, Avenida Paulista witnessed enormous protests in favour of impeaching President Fernando Collor de Mello on corruption charges (in 1992 he was impeached and resigned from office). The street is also home to the biggest gay pride celebrations in the world at the annual **Parada** (*see p187* **Profile**). Athletes zoom through the street during the **São Silvestre** (*see p162*) half-marathon and denizens decked out in white welcome New Year's Eve: in fact, most things of note in São Paulo happen on Avenida Paulista, which always exudes a festive joie de vivre.

Avenida Paulista.

Avenida Paulista is an ideal place to explore on foot. People-watching, soaking up a little history and a little art, and blending in by grabbing a drink at a corner bar, or a *pão de queijo* (cheese bread) and *cafezinho* (espresso), easily combine to fill a day.

The **Pasteur Institute** (Avenida Paulista 393, Cerqueira César, 3145 3145, www.pasteur.saude.sp.gov.br) is one of a handful of buildings on Avenida Paulista that tells the city's pre-skyscraper story. Founded in 1903 to provide healthcare and conduct rabies research, and designed by the iconic Ramos de Azevedo architecture firm, it still functions today.

A few metres along is another of Ramos de Azevedo's landmarks, **Grupo Escolar Rodrigues Alves** (Avenida Paulista 227, Cerqueira Cesar). Dated 1919 and listed in 1985, this is the only state school on Avenida Paulista. When it was restored in 2003 and 2005, paint had to be brought from Italy as the local yellow wasn't close to the tone Ramos had originally selected for it.

Dwarfed by the high-rises and closed for refurbishing for years now is coffee magnate **Joaquim Franco de Melo**'s house (Avenida Paulista 1919, Cerqueira Cesar). Built in 1905 by Antonio Fernandes Pinto, it is one of Azevedo's grandest homes, and the only one standing on Avenida Paulista from the period of the coffee barons. It is not far from **Trianon Park**, and is almost in abandon: part of the grounds have now been taken over by a parking lot. The 1930s **Casa das Rosas** (Avenida Paulista 37, Cerqueira Cesar, 3285 6986, www.casadasrosas.sp.gov.br, closed Mon) may be the most appealing of the Azevedo buildings along Avenida Paulista – mainly because you can spend time in it. Inspired by Versailles and built originally for Azevedo's daughter, it's famous for its roses. It houses the **Espaço Haroldo de Campos de Poesia e Literatura**, where exhibitions and seminars take place. This is a grand old house, and the clash between its sculpted exterior, marble and crystal interior and the shiny glass tower behind it, is picture-perfect then-and-now Avenida Paulista.

The neighbour of Casa das Rosas is home to **Fundação Japão** (Avenida Paulista 37, 1st & 2nd floors, 3141 0110, www.fjsp.org.br, closed Sat & Sun). A hub for everything Japanese, Fundação Japão was established in 1972 as a cultural exchange between Brazil and Japan and to promote Japanese culture in the city.

The convent-like, vaulted building diagonally across several lanes of Avenida Paulista is **Hospital Santa Catarina** (Avenida Paulista 200, 3016 4133, www.hsc.org.br). Often referred to as São Paulo's first private hospital, Hospital Santa Catarina was inaugurated in 1906 in a building designed by Maximilian Hehl (who also designed **Catedral Metropolitana**; *see p49*). It was at first a psychiatric hospital run by nuns. In 1974, a new wing was inaugurated from which you can see the original building and chapel today. Across the Rua 13 de Maio, which heads down into Bixiga, São Paulo's 'little Italy', is Avenida Paulista's only shopping mall, **Shopping Paulista** (*see p145*).

The impressive dome of the **Catedral Ortodoxa** (Rua Vergueiro 1515, 5579 0019, www.catedralortodoxa.com.br) stands out a mile from the otherwise uninspired surroundings; it is open Wednesday at 11am and Sunday at 10.30am. It opened in 1954 to accommodate the growing community of Orthodox Christians, mostly of Syrian and Lebanese origin. Inside, the Byzantine-style building has stained-glass windows and the iconostasis (the structure that separates the altar from the nave) is made of Carrara marble with frescoed icons.

A little further down Rua Vergueiro is **Centro Cultural São Paulo** (Rua Vergueiro 1000, 3397 4000, www.centrocultural.sp.gov.br, closed Mon), one of São Paulo's most important entertainment venues and architectural sites. This vast 1970s cement, iron and glass complex is interlinked by flowing ramps and walkways, offering sweeping views of the multi-lane 23 de Maio motorway below. It is home to libraries, music halls and theatres, and hosts exhibitions and film screenings. Although disappointingly not as vibrant as it should be on an average day, it's worth a visit for its unique structure, especially if there's an event of interest on.

A few metres from Casa das Rosas, towards Consolação, is the exhibition centre and important archive of Brazilian culture, **Itaú Cultural** (Avenida Paulista 149, 2168 1700, www.itaucultural.org.br, closed Mon). Lodged in a typical Avenida Paulista glass building and run by one of the country's largest banks, Banco Itaú, the institute holds temporary, contemporary art exhibitions. The initial goal of the centre was to set up a computer database storing information on Brazilian arts and culture. In 2000, a large collection of online works was made available to the wider public through Enciclopédia Itaú Cultural. In 2002, the institute moved into its current building, from which it supports and stimulates the development of digital/media art and interdisciplinary productions.

Nearby, a pleasant whitewashed house is home to **Associação Palas Athena** (Rua Leôncio de Carvalho 99, 3266 6188, www.palasathena.org, closed Sat & Sun),

Caixeiro Viajante. See p72.

a traditional centre for short courses and workshops (mainly on modern and classical philosophy), t'ai chi and yoga. Famous for its sloping façade, the 1966 **Gazeta** building (Avenida Paulista 900, 3170 5757, www.fcl.com.br), serves as a well-known meeting point on Avenida Paulista. It is home to the media hub, **Fundação Casper Líbero**, and atop the building is one of the many famous antennae that define Avenida Paulista's skyline – the 85-metre (280-foot) TV Gazeta antenna. Across the *avenida* is the French megastore chain FNAC. It competes with the other bookstore on Avenida Paulista, the traditional and local **Livraria Cultura** (*see p147*) inside the landmark, **Conjunto Nacional** (*see below*), down at the other end of the avenue. Another local option for books is **Livraria Martins Fontes** (Avenida Paulista 509, 2167 9900, www.martinsfontes paulista.com.br).

The sloping façade of the **Federação das Indústrias do Estado de São Paulo** (FIESP), or State Industries Federation (Centro Cultural Sesi, Galeria & Teatro Sesi, Avenida Paulista 1313, 3146 7405, www.sesisp.org.br), is another of Avenida Paulista's many architectural and cultural landmarks. Designed by Luis Roberto de Carvalho Franco and Roberto Cerqueira César in the late 1960s, the FIESP building houses **Centro Cultural Fiesp**, inside of which are the **Galeria and Teatro do Sesi**. Revamped by architect Paulo Mendes da Rocha, they hold exhibitions and theatre productions at affordable prices.

Parque Trianon (Rua Peixoto Gomide 949, 3289 2160), was inaugurated in 1892, a year after Avenida Paulista. Its original landscaping was done by French landscape architect Paul Villon and later added to by Englishman Barry Parker. A hangout for the Avenida Paulista elite in the 1920s and '30s, the park went into steady decline when its administration was handed over to the city in the early 1930s. During this period, it gained its official yet little used name – **Parque Tenente Siqueira Campos**. It was only in 1968, when Brazil's landscaper icon Burle Marx and architect Clovis Olga revamped it, that its slow re-gentrification began. During the day, it welcomes joggers, toddlers and pensioners, and towards the evening, it fills up with prostitutes and the homeless. It closes at 6pm. The lanes of the park are filled with sculptures, while the endemic species of flora and fauna (with a few added species) are all that remain of the original Mata Atlântica forest. Opposite the park is the **Museu de Arte Moderna de São Paulo** (*see p70* **Unmasking the MASP**).

One of Avenida Paulista's most famous landmarks is the **Conjunto Nacional** complex (Avenida Paulista 2073, 3179 0000, www.ccn.com.br). It is said that 30,000 people

SIGHTS

Profile Museu de Arte de São Paulo

Works of art within a work of art.

The cutting-edge design of the **Museu de Arte de São Paulo (MASP)** has been a hot topic since its inauguration in 1968 (building started in 1956). There's also been a lot said about its poor administration over the last few decades. But regardless, inside you'll find the best collection of 20th-century European and Brazilian art in South America. The dream of communications tycoon Assis Chateaubriand and Italian art critic and dealer Pietro Maria Bardi, it's a museum that lives up to the standard of its counterparts abroad.

After World War II, with many European countries hard up, a lot of important European artworks became readily available to international buyers. Beginning in 1947, a large collection was acquired for the new museum. In 1968, the collection moved into the landmark building, designed by Lina Bo Bardi, an Italian modernist architect who was also Pietro Maria Bardi's wife.

The building (which, inevitably, critics called a concrete monstrosity) has its main body suspended by four red columns with a 74-metre (243-foot) space below. A children's park was part of the original plan for the area beneath the glass and concrete box, but it never materialised. Opinion has always been divided on the building – especially the exhibition easels, which were removed in 2000 when the building was refurbished. Seen as outrageous, these fixed glass and concrete structures were central to Lina Bo Bardi's concept of one fluid exhibition space. The uniquely designed easels appear in the museum every now and again. Works by important French Impressionists like Manet, Renoir, Toulouse-Lautrec, and the complete collection of Degas bronzes (there are 73 of them) can be seen in the permanent collection. There are old Spanish masters here such as Velázquez and Goya, Renaissance icons like Titian, Tintoretto and Raphael, and the Brazilian modernists Portinari, Di Cavalcanti and Anita Malfatti. However, only about 500 of the museum's 7,000 works are on show at any given time.

Poor management has led to many scandals: one of them was the robbery of two priceless (and uninsured) works in December 2007 – Picasso's *Portrait of Suzanne Bloch* and Cândido Portinari's *O Lavrador de Café*, both of which were eventually retrieved in January 2008.

The museum café makes a good pitstop after a few hours browsing. On Sundays, an antiques market installs itself beneath the MASP (*see p158*).

Jardim Paulista

pass through the complex everyday.
This David Libeskind project from 1958 is innovative in its housing of businesses, flats and shops. Revamped after a fire broke out in 1978, the complex is home to the bookshop founded by Kurt and Eva Herz, Livraria Cultura (*see p148*), and to one of São Paulo's best cinemas, **Cine Bombril** (*see p172*). The digital clock and thermometer that crown the building are a landmark and reference for many Paulistanos daily.

At the corner with Rua Bela Cintra, just metres from the lively stretch that houses some of the city's hippest bars, is the 1932 **São Luiz Gonzaga** church (Avenida Paulista 2378, 3231 5954, www.saoluis.org.br). This Romanesque building with towering 11-metre pink marble columns and bronze capitals, designed by Luis de Anhaia Mello, opened its doors to the community in 1935. The silence inside is astounding, considering its surroundings. Nine stained-glass windows at either side of the building filter the light through Christian scenes.

★ Museu de Arte Moderna de São Paulo (MASP)

Avenida Paulista 1578, Cerqueira Cesar (3251 5644/www.masp.art.br). Metrô Trianon-MASP. **Open** 11am-6pm Tue, Wed, Fri-Sun; 11am-8pm Thur. **Admission** R$15; R$7 reductions; free under-10s and over-60s. Free to all Tue. **Map** p244 K8.
See left Unmasking the MASP.

JARDIM PAULISTA & CERQUEIRA CESAR

Metrô to Brigadeiro, Consolação, Paraiso, Trianon-MASP.

Jardim Paulista and Cerqueira Cesar are the most entertaining and vibrant of the neighbourhoods in Jardins. These sections, above Avenida

Estados Unidos, bordering Avenida Rebouças and Avenida Brigadeiro Luis Antonio, are filled with shops and residential blocks, and English is widely spoken. Neighbourhood folklore has it that local fashionista residents have nominated a smaller section as 'baixo Jardins' (lower Jardins) to separate the truly hip from the merely hip. 'Baixo Jardins' is between Alameda Jaú, Rua 9 de Julho, Rua Augusta and Avenida Estados Unidos. Don't come looking for history and important architectural sites; come to enjoy the shopping and the quirky holes in the wall, and to have a good old gawp at the beautiful people.

One of the few architecturally relevant stops is the mews on Alameda Jaú, a dead-end street with cute houses on both sides, designed by architect Flávio de Carvalho. Some of the originally blue-collar homes have been taken over by the likes of **Adriana Barra** (Rua Peixoto Gomide 1801, casa 05, 3062 0387, www.adriana barra.com.br, closed Sun), who sells trendy floral print clothes, and **Pelú** (*see p151*). The **Fasano Hotel** (*see p99*) and its clock tower designed by hip architect Isay Weinfeld sits on a one-block-long street in the company of trendy **Cris Barros** (*see p149*), a women's wear shop.

The city's most cosmopolitan and exclusive shopping and dining addresses are on Rua Haddock Lobo and Rua Oscar Freire. These streets are so fancy that here the overhead cables visible everywhere else in the city have been put underground. Haddock Lobo boasts luxury brands: Tiffany, Cartier, Louis Vuitton, Dior and Marc Jacobs, as well as some of São Paulo's flashiest restaurants, including **Figueira Rubaiyat** (*see p121*). Oscar Freire is home to national fashion heroes, including the **Havaianas** flagship shop (*see p155*), the surf-cum-streetwear brand **Osklen**, and **Galeria Melissa** (*see p155*), with its vibrant, frequently changing atrium designs and crazy jelly shoes.

Rua Doutor Melo Alves provides an interesting stroll up a steep hill – you will find a rich blend of colours, venues, shops and hangouts. There are unusual (and pricey) presents at **Loja do Bispo** (*see p156*); fusion dishes at **Obá** (Rua Melo Alves 205, 3086 4774), hamburgers served in large iceberg lettuce leaves at **A Chapa** (Rua Dr Melo Alves 238, 3085 0521) and traditional *padaria* (bakery) delights at **Dengosa** (Rua Dr Melo Alves 281, 3061 2919).

Two popular watering holes are near the top. **Bar Balcão** (*see p133*) has a winding, uninterrupted counter (*balcão*), and everyone sits at one long communal table. **Bar da Dida** (*see p186*), popular with lesbians, serves fancy toasties at outdoor tables. One street over, on the smarter strip of Consolação, gay customers keep things buzzy into the night. Rua Bela Cintra is home to glam Brazilian brands and swanky

SIGHTS

eateries. You'll find jeweller Antonio Bernardo, São Paulo fashion icons Gloria Coelho, Reinaldo Lourenço and Lino Villaventura, as well as international Versace and Armani. Argentinian café Havanna sells great *alfajores*.

JARDIM EUROPA, JARDIM PAULISTANO & JARDIM AMERICA
Bus 702P-42, 477A-10.

On the corner of Estados Unidos, right at the bottom of the hill next to Haddock Lobo, is **Galeria dos Paes** (Rua Estados Unidos 1645, 3064 5900, www.galeriadospaes.com.br), a 24-hour food hall crammed late at night with partied-out clubbers pit-stopping for hearty sandwiches before heading home. The gorgeous, colonial **Nossa Senhora do Brasil** church at the crossing of Avenida Estados Unidos with Avenida Brasil is one of the most exclusive churches in the city. Dozens of eligible Brazilian girls spend a year on the waiting list to get married here.

Further down are the **Museu da Imagem e Som** (MIS or Museum of the Moving Image), and the **Museu Brasileiro da Escultura** (MUBE). Recently refurbished and under new administration, MIS has adopted a vibrant exhibition programme. Above the MUBE there is a weekend market with a mixture of craftworks and bric-a-brac. The nearby **Fundação Ema Gordon Klabin** has fantastic art. Stop at **Caixeiro Viajante** (Rua Joaquim Antunes 223, 3062 3535); this soulful and colourful gift shop has everything from household goods to quirky mementos, clothes and jewellery.

Around Faria Lima and Alameda Gabriel Monteiro da Silva is where you will find the most expensive real estate in the city today. Commercial for the most part, Avenida Faria Lima is home to **Museu da Casa Brasileira**, a beautiful mansion with a great permanent collection and a garden that's a perfect place to visit on a sunny afternoon.

Intersecting Faria Lima is São Paulo's most exclusive design and furniture street: Alameda Gabriel Monteiro da Silva. Towards Avenida Brasil, it diagonally runs through Jardim Paulistano and Jardim América. It's pleasant to explore on foot (especially in January and February when the sales are on).

Rua Joaquim Antunes crosses Alameda Gabriel Monteiro da Silva almost at Avenida Brasil. The memorable **Mercearia do Conde** (Rua Joaquim Antunes 217, 3081 7204, www.merceariadoconde.com.br) attempts to reinvent the past with its beautiful and colourful decorations. **Ravioli Cucina Casalinga** (Rua Joaquim Antunes 197, 3082 3383) is more sober

than its neighbours but the food is tasty, while **Toro** (Rua Joaquim Antunes 224, 3085 8485, www.tororestaurante.com.br, closed Mon) specialises in Spanish cuisine.

★ Fundação Ema Gordon Klabin
Rua Portugal 43, Jardim Europa (3062 5245/ www.emaklabin.org.br). Bus 702P-42. **Open** 2-4pm Tue, Thur-Fri; 10am-2pm Sat, public holidays. **Admission** R$10; R$5 reductions. **No credit cards**. Map p249 H11.
An eclectic, personal mix reflects the collector Klabin's interests over four decades. There is pre-Columbian, European, Asian and African art, decorative arts, and silverware in this beautiful house. Booking a guided tour is worthwhile.

FREE Museu Brasileiro da Escultura (MUBE)
Avenida Europa 218, Jardim Europa (2594 2601/ www.mube.art.br). Bus 702P-42. **Open** 10am-7pm Tue-Sun. **Admission** free. Map p249 G11.
Designed by Paulo Mendes da Rocha, with landscaping by Burle Marx, the MUBE building is worth a visit if you are interested in architecture. Otherwise, it's rather glum. With exhibition halls below street level and made mainly of cement and iron (a Mendes da Rocha signature), the building is impressive inside and out. On the weekend, you'll find a market stall on the upper level; it gets in the way of the experience, but it is pleasant nonetheless.

★ Museu da Casa Brasileira
Avenida Brigadeiro Faria Lima 2705, Jardim Paulistano (3032 3727/www.mcb.sp.gov.br). Bus 477A-10. **Open** 10am-6pm Tue-Sun. **Admission** R$4; reductions R$2; free Sun. **No credit cards**. Map p249 F12.
Previously owned by the Prado family, this beautiful building houses a museum specialising in interior design. The permanent collection includes furniture from the 17th to 21st centuries, but the museum also hosts temporary exhibitions, as well as the annual design awards. There's a great restaurant here too – Quinta do Museu, and, on Sundays, there is music performances in the garden.

Museu da Imagem e do Som (MIS)
Avenida Europa 158, Jardim Europa (2117 4777/www.mis-sp.org.br). Bus 702P-42. **Open** noon-10pm Tue-Sat; 11am-9pm Sun. **Admission** R$4; reductions R$2; seniors free. Free to all Sun. **No credit cards**. Map p249 H11.
The recent change in administration has helped pull MIS out of the dark ages, it now puts on diverse and interesting exhibitions: it's home to an important collection of 30,000 items, with photos, films and records. There are recorded statements by modernist artist Tarsila do Amaral and Tom Jobim (the father of bossa nova). Fresh, innovative temporary exhibitions and retrospectives are often on display.

Parque do Ibirapuera

São Paulo's Central Park.

Perhaps the hardest name for a foreigner to say in Portuguese after 'Jardins', **Parque Ibirapuera** is where Paulistanos head to for some fresh air, exercise and culture. It's home to a number of museums and institutions, and its popularity has turned it into a lively slice of the city surrounded by greenery. You'll find in-line skaters and skateboarders cruising around and doing tricks under the cement overpass near the Museu Afro Brasil, urban dance enthusiasts practising routines, students holding theatre rehearsals, possibly a yoga or t'ai chi class or two, dog walkers, comedians, and even an occasional accordion player.

Map p244, p246
Restaurants p116

Bus 5164-10, 5175-10, 5178-10, 5194-10.

It's hard to believe that the name of this gorgeous, popular city park means 'rotten tree' in the native language of Tupi-Guarani. Maybe the Brazilian Indians thought some bad press would delay the government's development plans for the park. It may have worked.

Although an ambitious blueprint for the park was first drafted as early as the 1920s, taking cues from the bois de Boulogne in Paris, Hyde Park in London and Central Park in New York, only in 1951 did the dream become a reality. A team was invited to help execute the plans: the globally acclaimed Brazilian architect Oscar Niemeyer, and landscape designer Roberto Burle Marx, were involved. The park officially opened in 1954, supported by both public and private funding, as well as a generous donation from Japan of a replica of the Katsura Palace, now called the **Pavilhão Japonês** (Japanese Pavilion).

Visitors should pick up a free map of the park from the guard booths at the park's entrances. Inside the gates there are two running tracks: one in the middle of the park on asphalt (Rua Antonio de Quieroga), and the second around its perimeter (a dirt trail that is shaded by trees). There is also a cycle path, marked by faded red paint, that runs alongside the asphalt running track (runners and walkers should note that cyclists are likely to run you over if you stray into their lane). Bicycles are available to rent inside the park at reasonable prices. Other leisure areas include: soccer pitches, basketball courts, two children's playgrounds, a carp pond, a duck pond and picnic spaces.

Early-rising fitness enthusiasts begin congregating in the park as early as 5.30am. Be prepared to see some sexy work-out gear and washboard abs: this is where normally buttoned-up Paulistanos take their shirts off. To cool off after your run or walk, try one of the *frescão* panels: these cover park visitors in a refreshing mist when a button is pushed. For food and beverages check out the **Prêt no MAM** (*see p116*) buffet and café. There are also numerous vendors with push carts selling *agua de coco*: chilled green coconut water, a good natural alternative to branded sports drinks.

INSIDE TRACK
NO PAIN, NO GAIN

Feeling a little wobbly with all those buff Brazilian bodies jogging past? Make like a local and get yourself a personal trainer in the park. Try www.pntreinamento.com.br.

About the author
*US born author **Jennifer Prado** (www.jenniferprado.com) resides in São Paulo.*

SIGHTS

MAM.

Occasionally, the park management sponsors a film on a large outdoor screen or hosts rock concerts, and the **Pavilhão Japonês**, located on the eastern side of the lake, sometimes has free origami workshops. Near the pavilion is the **Planetário Professor Aristóteles Orsini**. The planetarium, like many things in the park, is a futuristic construction, and is quite popular on the weekends with families.

Parque Ibirapuera is also home to some of the city's major museums. Oscar Niemeyer created a number of buildings for the museum complex in the park, including the Palácio das Indústrias, otherwise known as the **Pavilhão Ciccillo Matarazzo** (*see below* **Fundação Bienal**). This pavilion is an exhibition space and also houses part of the large collection of the **Museu de Arte Contemporânea (MAC)**. One of the most interesting architectural achievements in the park is the Grande Marquise, popular with in-line skaters and skateboarders for its wide, smooth concrete surface. This construction links a number of buildings, including the **Museu de Arte Moderna (MAM)**, by a concrete walkway that has a floor and a ceiling, but no walls. The other side of the walkway connects the MAM to the **Auditório Ibirapuera**, a major venue for music performances in the city. Nearby is the Oca exhibition space, also designed by Niemeyer, and the **Museu Afro Brasil**, a great resource about Brazil's African heritage and the history of its African population.

Located in the green space in front of MAM, the **Jardim de Esculturas** (sculpture garden) is a permanent sculpture display that combines art with a public space. The garden covers an area of 6,000 square metres (64,500 square feet) and showcases the vision of Roberto Burle Marx (who, along with Niemeyer, designed Brasília, the nation's capital). The sculpture garden was created in 1993 and features the work of 30 contemporary Brazilian sculptors, including Amilcar de Castro, Carlos Alberto Fajardo and Emanoel Araújo.

Auditório Ibirapuera

Rua Pedro Álvares Cabral s/n, Parque Ibirapuera (5908 4290/www.auditorioibirapuera.com.br). Bus 5506. **Open** 9am-midnight Mon-Fri. **Admission** varies. **Credit** MC , V. **Map** p244 K12.

The Ibirapuera Auditorium features a performance space designed by Niemeyer. It holds weekly classical and contemporary concerts in both open-air and indoor theatres. Check the website for schedules, box office hours and prices. Tickets are also available from Ticketmaster (2846 6000, www.ticketmaster.com.br).

Fundação Bienal

Rua Pedro Álvares Cabral s/n, Parque Ibirapuera, (5576 7600/http://bienalsaopaulo.globo.com). Bus 5006. **Open** varies; see website for details. **Admission** varies. **Credit** MC, V. **Map** p244 J12.

The Bienal building was designed by Oscar Niemeyer to hold large exhibitions and events. The first Bienal exhibition in São Paulo was held by the Museu de Arte Moderna in 1951, when some of the first paintings by Picasso to arrive in Brazil were displayed here. By 1962, the Bienal and MAM had become separate exhibition centres and the Bienal was converted into a foundation. Most recently, it has become known for hosting the Bienal de Arquitetura, one of the largest architectural events in the world, São Paulo Fashion Week (*see p152* **Profile**), and the Bienal de Arte (*see p181* **Profile**). Until recently the book festival, Bienal do Livro, was celebrated in the same location, however now the events for the literary festival take place in the Parque do Anhembi in the neighbourhood of Santana.

Museu Afro Brasil

Rua Pedro Álvares Cabral s/n, Parque Ibirapuera (4004 5006/www.museuafrobrasil.com.br). Bus 5006. **Open** 10am-6pm Tue-Sun. **Admission** R$5. Free Sun. **Credit** MC, V. **Map** p244 K12.

The Afro-Brazilian museum is the most authentically Brazilian of all the museums in the park. Its collection features an impressive array of paintings by Afro-Brazilians. There's an interesting wall display of the folkloric Saçi, a one-legged mythical creature, as he appeared over the years in advertising. The displays also showcase colourful photography, African-themed clothing, the hull of a slave ship and a helpful timeline of Brazilian historical events.

Museu de Arte Contemporânea (MAC)

Pavilhão Ciccillo Matarazzo, 3rd floor, Rua Pedro Álvares Cabral s/n (5573 9932/www.mac.usp.br). Bus 5006. **Open** varies; see website for details. **Admission** varies. **Map** p244 K12.

The Museum of Contemporary Art contains over 10,000 works by Picasso, Matisse, Modigliani, Tarsila do Amaral, Portinari and Di Cavalcanti, spread across three sites. Its largest exhibition space is on the campus of USP in Cidade Universitaria (*see p82*). This smaller space in the park has rotating displays, and the schedule depends on the events taking place in the rest of the building. The museum also showcases contemporary Brazilian artists and offers courses, guided tours, a library and a gift shop.

Museu de Arte Moderna (MAM)

Rua Pedro Álvares Cabral s/n, Parque Ibirapuera (5085 1300/www.mam.org.br). Bus 5506. **Open** 10am-6pm Tue-Sun. **Admission** R$5.50; free under-10s and over-65s. Free to all Sun. **Credit** MC, V. **Map** p244 K12.

MAM was the first museum of its kind in Latin America. Founded in 1948, it based itself on the model of the Museum of Modern Art (MOMA) in New York. In fact, MAM's founders lead a lengthy correspondence with Nelson Rockefeller, who ended up donating 13 works of art to the museum. In the 1960s, one of the founders, Ciccillo Matarazzo (*see p40* **The Count of São Paulo**), decided to break away from the museum and in 1963 he donated his entire collection of modern art to the MAC (*see above*). Nevertheless, the MAM continues as a historically and culturally relevant institution. It contains over 5,000 works of art representing both internationally acclaimed and Brazilian artists like Regina Silveira, Cildo Meireles and Leonilson. The museum is known for highlighting the work of contemporary artists in frequently changing exhibitions. It also contains a cinema, library, auditorium, gift shop, restaurant and café.

Oca

Rua Pedro Álvares Cabral s/n. Bus 5506. **Open** 9am-5pm Mon-Fri. **Admission** varies. **Map** p244 K12.

The curving saucer-like building looks like a UFO that has just landed. Oca was designed by Oscar Niemeyer to hold temporary exhibitions and events. Since 2005, it has been managed by the Ministerio de Ambiente (Ministry for the Environment).

Pavilhão Japonês

Avenida República do Líbano (3208 1755). Bus 5116. **Open** 10am-noon, 1-5pm Wed, Sat, Sun. **Admission** R$3. **No credit cards**. **Map** p244 K12.

The Japanese Pavilion is a replica of the Katsura Palace in Kyoto, and was actually constructed in Japan and assembled in Brazil. The building contains a dining hall for tea ceremonies and a workshop space that occasionally offers instruction in Japanese crafts, such as a make-your-own kimono class. On display is a collection that includes some pieces dating back to the 11th-century, as well as contemporary Japanese art. The grounds include a small fish pond and a traditional Japanese garden.

Planetário Professor Aristóteles Orsini

Avenida República do Líbano (3208 1755/ www.prefeitura.sp.gov.br/planetarios). Bus 5516. **Open** 9am-6pm Sat, Sun. **Admission** R$5. **Credit** MC, V. **Map** p244 J12.

The planetarium is your chance to be transported back to a primary-school science trip and offers a rare opportunity to learn about the southern hemisphere's constellations. Features include high-tech equipment, soothing classical music and a video presentation (in Portuguese).

Parque Ibirapuera.

The Grande Marquise.

Pinheiros & Vila Madalena

Samba, shop and snack in São Paulo's bohemia.

The neighbouring districts of **Pinheiros** and **Vila Madalena**, west of the centre but east of the Pinheiros River, are two of the liveliest in São Paulo. Yet, for all their fine restaurants, popular bars, bohemian shopping streets and antiques markets, and specialist galleries and music venues, these areas still manage to retain their original vibes as out-of-the-way destinations. Most of the houses here are just one or two storeys high, and this is also one of the rare places in town where residents live in houses rather than apartment blocks, and where you can head to a host of decent eating and drinking joints on foot. As a result, these neighbourhoods are popular with both families and party animals.

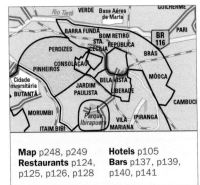

Map p248, p249	**Hotels** p105
Restaurants p124, p125, p126, p128	**Bars** p137, p139, p140, p141

SIGHTS

PINHEIROS

Metrô Sumaré or Clínicas

Pinheiros was originally an indigenous settlement. The *aldeia* (village) of Pinheiros was one of a number of villages that the Portuguese created over 400 years ago to organise natives for the purposes of labour as well as security. These villages were sources of revenue for the Portuguese crown. The neighbourhood burgeoned in the 1930s as a residential and commercial district, and continues to thrive today as a nightlife hotspot. This large area is bordered by Jardim Paulistano, Vila Madalena and the Pinheiros River, the latter extending into Alto de Pinheiros, the leafier and more residential part of the district.

The **SESC Pinheiros** (*see p205*) arts complex has an auditorium for 100 people, exhibition spaces, a restaurant, reading rooms and sports facilities (including heated swimming pools), although the latter are only accessible to members. The exterior of the **Instituto Tomie Ohtake** (*see p77*)

building, meanwhile, provokes a range of opinions; steel waves of maroon and purple intertwine around its base, while a dark glass skyscraper juts into the sky. The modern geometric tower has completely changed the Pinheiros skyline. Not far away is the **Centro Brasileiro Britânico** (*see p77*), inside of which is the British Consulate and headquarters of the British Council.

On a Saturday, make your way to the market at **Praça Benedito Calixto** (*see p158*), where hundreds of people gather to hear live *chorinho* music and to eat at the well-known restaurant **Consulado Mineiro** (*see p124*), which is normally heaving. Vendors' stalls are up early and stand until the end of the afternoon. Above the square, at the top of a hill, is the **Igreja do Calvário** (Rua Cardeal Arcoverde 950, 3085 1307, www.paroquiadocalvario.org.br), a church dating back to 1923. At night, the blue neon lights of its façade spruce up the surroundings, including the parking lot that once housed a convent, but which was demolished in 1990. The church is open for mass only; call to check the schedule.

Praça Benedito Calixto.

Rua Teodoro Sampaio, on the southern side of the plaza, is well known for its specialist musical instrument shops. Its equivalent for antiques (some of them fake, however) is Rua Cardeal Arcoverde. At night, local couples congregate at **Teta Bar** (*see p141*), a tiny, quaint jazz bar. Most of São Paulo's music venues, and in particular its samba clubs, are concentrated in Pinheiros and Vila Madalena (*see pp188-197*).

At the extreme end of Rua Oscar Freire is the **Centro da Cultura Judaica** (*see below*). It promotes cultural activities, such as theatre productions, and exhibits work by well-known artists. Very close by is one of the city's best Italian eateries, **Pasquale** (*see p126*), where pasta is made fresh and with care.

There are a couple of pleasant grassy patches in the region, visited mainly by locals on bikes, kids on skateboards and dog-lovers. **Praça Pôr do Sol** (Rua Desembargador Ferreira Franca 1) is on a hill, so the view over the western part of the city is sublime, especially at sunset. **Praça Horácio Sabino** stands between Rua João Moura and Cristiano Viana and has a similar vibe. However, if you're looking for a serious park in the region, **Parque Villa Lobos** (Avenida Professor Fonseca Rodrigues 1655, Alto de Pinheiros, 3023 2229) is your only real choice. A fairly recent venture – it opened in 1994 – this park is just about starting to stand on its own. Its oldest trees are now fully grown, but in some of the more open stretches it's wise to wear a hat for protection from the glaring sun. The sporting facilities are great here: a bike path and jogging track run around the park, and there are decent football pitches.

Pinheiros is also home to several of the city's most established galleries (*see pp179-180*).

FREE Centro Brasileiro Britânico (CBB)

Rua Ferreira de Araújo 741, Pinheiros (3039 0508/www.cbb.org.br). Bus 117Y-10. **Open** 10am-7pm Mon-Fri; 10am-6pm Sat. **Admission** free. **Credit** AmEx, DC, MC, V. **Map** p248 D9.
The official British Headquarters in town also hosts lively art shows and nightlife. The exhibition centre often holds temporary expositions that promote links between the UK and Brazil. Panoramic views can be had from the rooftop restaurant, the Bridge. Downstairs, Drake's Bar (*see p125*) is popular with expats as well as locals, journalists working for the nearby Abril publishing house and Guinness-lovers.

FREE Centro da Cultura Judaica

Rua Oscar Freire 2500, Sumaré (3065 4333/ http://culturajudaica.uol.com.br). Metrô Sumaré. **Open** noon-9pm Tue-Sat; 11am-7pm Sun. **Admission** free. **Map** p249 G1.
This Torah-shaped building was designed by well-known architect Roberto Loeb and is set behind high gates. (Since the bombing of two Jewish institutions in Argentina in the 1990s, many South American Jewish cultural centres and synagogues have stepped up their security.) The impressive edifice has a bookstore and puts on film festivals and plays. Works by major artists are on loan from cultural institutions around the world – a recent exhibition featured works by Marc Chagall. The Gerstein Café offers a pleasant lunchtime buffet from R$25 to R$35 and a Shabbos dinner for R$35. *Photo p78.*

FREE Instituto Tomie Ohtake

Avenida Faria Lima 201, Pinheiros (2245 1900/www.institutotomieohtake.org.br).

Bus 748F-31. **Open** 11am-8pm Tue-Sun.
Admission free. **Map** p248 D9.

Tomie Ohtake was born in Kyoto, Japan, and came to Brazil at the age 23 in 1936. She became a revered artist, specialising in geometric forms in her painting and sculptures; she exhibited both in Brazil as well as outside of the country. The Complexo Ohtake Cultural, designed by Tomie's son, architect Ruy Ohtake, comprises two buildings and includes the cultural institute, an office building and a convention centre.

VILA MADALENA
Metrô Vila Madalena

Local word-of-mouth history has it that this area was originally owned by a prosperous Portuguese businessman who divided his land and named the plots after his three daughters, thus giving the neighbourhoods their names: Vila Ida, Vila Beatriz and Vila Madalena. Vila Madalena, or Vila, as it's endearingly known, takes the Pinheiros buzz and ups it a few notches in style and vibe (and real-estate prices). It was a bohemian neighbourhood in the 1970s and '80s, when the residents were mainly writers, immigrants and students at USP (São Paulo State University). Today, the area has become very gentrified, but it retains an alternative edge. Although quite hilly, it's best explored on foot – stumbling across cute little bars and stores is half the fun here.

Parts of the district have been taken over by swanky real-estate developments, but for the most part, it's the small houses, cul-de-sacs and simple but charming apartment blocks that dictate the neighbourhood's residential feel. Walking around, you'll find that some of the streets are lined with some of the most vibrant grafitti in the city, so keep your eyes peeled if you appreciate this type of art. Home to small advertising agencies and film studios, Vila Madalena has restaurants and bars that are busy at lunchtime and even busier at night – especially at the weekend, when traffic jams line the hills.

Residents of this neighbourhood are very loyal to it. If you are staying in the area, you may want to venture to the local grocery warehouse,

Sacolão da Vila (Rua Medeiros de Albuquerque 352), for fresh produce, cut flowers and to sample the atmosphere. It's not a particularly beautiful place in terms of aesthetics, but it's perfect for travellers interested in local authenticity.

You won't come across many chain shops or megastores in Vila (apart from FNAC). Shops tend to be independently run businesses, ranging from design studios (**Atelier Carlos Motta** and **Marcenaria Trancoso**; *see p159*) and small boutiques to unique establishments like **Tchayka – A Casa da Rússia** (Rua Aspicuelta 300, 3032 0332, www.tchayka.com.br, closed Sun), a gem of a shop specialising in Russian mementoes. Matryoshka dolls, amber jewellery, Communist posters and hand-painted ornaments are all for sale here, and the space also serves as a centre for Russian studies and has a specialised travel agency.

Another politically charged doll shop can be found nearby in the form of **Preta Pretinha** (Rua Aspicuelta 474, 3812 6066, www.pretapretinha.com.br, closed Sun). It was founded by three Brazilian sisters, Joyce, Lucia and Cristina, who, with their darker skins, couldn't identify with the white European-looking dolls that were sold everywhere when they were growing up. Their grandmother, worried about the effect of this on their self-esteem, began to make dolls for them out of brown and black silk socks. The dolls sold here today are more sophisticated versions of these originals, and make great gifts.

Some of the best bars, very popular with local residents and Paulistanos at large, are **Filial** (*see p140*), **Astor** (*see p137*) on Rua Delfina and **São Cristóvão** (*see p141*), a small watering hole lined with football memorabilia that offers great music and caipirinhas to die for. Ruas Mourato Coelho and Aspicuelta are additional streets to head down for live music joints and bars with tables spilling out onto the pavements.

Like most hip neighbourhoods, Vila is also a good spot for art galleries. One of the top contemporary art galleries in the country, **Galeria Fortes Vilaça** (*see p180*), is to be found just a few metres away from another favourite, **Galeria Millan** (*see p180*).

Centro da Cultura Judaica. *See p77.*

Itaim Bibi &
Vila Olímpia

Bustling streets, malls for billionaires and burger bistros call this home.

For the city's wealthy twentysomething party mavens and thirtysomething businessmen, this is *the* place to be; full of clubs, bars and fine dining, **Itaim Biba** is, at least as far as they're concerned, the hippest and most glamorous of São Paulo's neighbourhoods. Forget the bohemia of Vila Madalena and the swankiness of Jardins: for the seriously moneyed, it's all about Itaim Bibi.

Over in the vaguely village-like **Vila Olímpia**, a previously dreaded industrial wasteland has morphed into a playground for the new rich. You might struggle to fit in here if you don't travel by helicopter or shop at the super-exclusive Daslu mall.

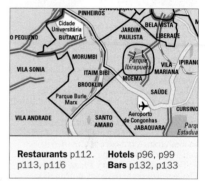

Restaurants p112. **Hotels** p96, p99
p113, p116   **Bars** p132, p133

SIGHTS

ITAIM BIBI
Bus 637P-10, 106A-10, 5118-10.

In the late 19th century, the area that now comprises the popular middle-class neighbourhood of Itaim Bibi was a large farm called the Chácara do Itahy (little rock). Since then the flat farming area has undergone a complete transformation: gone is the plantation green; now, concrete and glass are king in this commercial and residential area.

While the middle class continues to thrive in the many residential buildings east of Rio Pinheiros, on Ruas Itacema and Jesuino Arruda, the working classes that set up home here in the 1960s and '70s have largely moved on. The area is known for swanky lofts, popular with young and successful businessmen who'd rather not have to commute to work. However, elderly residents who have lived here for generations, for the most part in old-fashioned, tall apartment blocks, help to maintain the community feel.

Rua Amauri is the restaurant strip of the area, offering fancy dining options like the eateries owned by the Fasano group, Forneria

San Paolo and Parigi. For a late-night snack head to Rua Joaquim Floriano to try the burgers at **Joaquin's** (*see p121* **The United States of Brazil**), or at **New Dog** (Rua Joaquim Floriano 254, 3168 7899); both are popular with the party crowd. **The Fifties** (Rue Tabapuã 1100, 3078 4858) is another popular spot that offers classic American fare, while the well-to-do head to **General Prime Burger** (Rua Joaquim Floriano 541, 3168 0833) and **Hambugueria Nacional** (Rua Leopoldo Couto de Magalhães Júnior 822, 3073 0428).

The main streets are lined with tiny hole-in-the-wall services like key cutters, cobblers and repairs shops, which coexist with glossier boutiques, wine shops, galleries and quirky vintage furniture shops such as **Herrero** (Rua João Cachoeira 159, 3168 4469, closed Sun). The latter looks intriguingly shambolic from the outside, with piles of furniture that can be seen through the window, but although it is bursting at the seams it manages to be a one-of-a-kind store and does a great job of restoring vintage furniture pieces.

If you're looking for some tradition in the midst of modernity, head to the **Botequim de Hugo** (Rua Pedroso Alvarenga 1014, 3079 6090,

Rio Pinheiros. *See p79*

www.botequimdohugo.com.br, closed Sat & Sun). This place is a must if you're around at the end of the week. The seating is outdoors in the small patio area that belongs to the main house; the owners live in the back. The front room is small and lined with an endless array of bric-a-brac and booze. Hugo himself is always there serving up cold beers and different blends of cachaça. The famous *buraco quente* (hot hole) snack is a white flour roll stuffed with juicy minced meat and cheese – which sounds strange, but once you've tried it, you'll come back wanting more.

The **Brascan Century Plaza** (Rua Joaquim Floriano 466) sits at the heart of Itaim Bibi. Bounded by Ruas Bandeira Paulista and Joaquim Floriano, it is popular with lunching office workers. The spacious open-air plaza has a good variety of fast food restaurants, a large Artiplex cinema complex, gift shops, ATMs, a travel agency and a money exchange bureau.

Rua João Cachoeira was revamped a few years ago with the addition of benches and wider pavements, and is now an open-air shopping area. It offers an odd mixture of everything from wigs and underwear to sports gear. Beyond Avenida Presidente Juscelino Kubitschek, towards Vila Olimpia, Rua João Cachoeira is lined with fabric shops and gala dress retailers. Not far from The Fifties (*see p79*), lies **Casa Triângulo** (*see p176*), offering contemporary art in a two-storey white cube-like gallery. **Galeria Baró Cruz** on Clodomiro Amazonas (*see p176*) is another gallery housed in a contemporary building with national and international household names for sale.

MOEMA
Bus 647C-10

Moema, in the central-south zone of the city, developed as a region of large farmsteads during the 19th and 20th centuries. Bordered by Ibirapuera Park (*see pp73-75*), the more commercial Indianópolis side of the area, to the east of Avenida Ibirapuera, has streets named

after indigenous tribes. To the west of the avenida is Moema proper, where the streets have native bird names. The upmarket residential Vila Nova Conceição lies to the south-east.

Aside from its famous park, Moema has a number of charming squares, most notably **Praça Pereira Coutinho** (located between Rua Domingos Fernandes and Rua Baltazar Veiga) in Vila Nova Conceição. With its children's playgrounds and dog-friendly area, this plaza provides a tranquil retreat in the middle of the affluent high-rise neighbourhood.

The nearby **Parque das Bicicletas** (Alameda Iraé 35) provides a smaller, sportier alternative to Parque do Ibirapuera. If cycling, rollerblading or jogging is your thing, head to the 20,000 square metres (215,300 square feet) of greenery a couple of blocks south of Ibirapuera Park, which has facilities for all three activities. Nearby is the Praça Nossa Senhora Aparecida, just off Avenida Ibirapuera. This shady square in the heart of commercial Moema is home to the neo-Roman **Igreja Senhora Aparecida** (Praça Nossa Senhora Aparecida, 5052 4919). The church is named after Brazil's patron saint, and houses a portrait of her that was once paraded through the streets as part of the 1932 Constitutional Revolution (*see pp16-25*).

VILA OLIMPIA
CPTM Vila Olímpia

Vila Olimpia was an industrial neighbourhood until a decade ago, when its nightlife scene started to flourish. Since then it has been taken over by restaurants, offices and **Daslu** (*see p143*), the most exclusive shopping complex in Brazil, and the epitomy of flashy, preened Brazilian money (complete with helipad). Design studio **Ovo** (*see p159*) is one of the 'must-visits', as is **Galeria Luciana Brito** (*see p177*). **Via Funchal** (Rua Funchal 65, 2198 7718, www.via funchal.com.br) is one of the city's most vibrant festival halls. A typically generic events venue, it hosts concerts, ballets and other performances.

Brooklin, Butantã & Morumbi

Stunning forest trails and architectural wonders in the Zona Sul.

Straddling the Rio Pinheiros in the southern zone of the city, these three neighbourhoods epitomise São Paulo's variety: the seat of state government and palatial homes sit alongside shanty towns in **Morumbi**, there are glass corporate skyscrapers galore in **Brooklin**, and over in **Butantã** you'll find renowned academic and scientific centres. While they're a little out of the way if you are only visiting the city for a day or two, there are plenty of reasons to come here, whether it's for arts, culture, a slice of history, or simply to escape the mayhem of the centre.

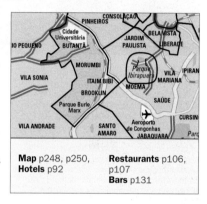

Map p248, p250,	**Restaurants** p106,
Hotels p92	p107
	Bars p131

Navigation might be something of a challenge. The CPTM train line runs north–south along the east side of the river, but only accesses the edge of each area. Buses leave from Jardins and Centro, however, unless you speak some Portuguese and/or are good with maps, a taxi is likely to be your best option.

BROOKLIN
CPTM Berrini

Named after the New York district of the same name (give or take a letter) in the early 20th century by the then tram operator, Light, Brooklin occupies the area between the Pinheiros River, Avenida dos Bandeirantes, Rua Roque Petroni Junior and Avenida Washington Luis.

Although best known for its vibrant nightlife, clubs, bars and restaurants, Brooklin contains a combination of luxury high-rise apartment buildings and the Brazilian headquarters of various multinationals. As one of the financial centres of the city, it is typically congested during weekday rush hour, especially

---

About the author
Richard Lomas *is a writer and adman who moved from London to São Paulo five years ago after getting hooked on the city.*

around Avenida Engenheiro Luis Carlos Berrini, although down time and weekends are much quieter and more navigable.

The newest and arguably most impressive sight in Brooklin is the suspension bridge, **Ponte Estaiada Octávio Frias de Oliveira**, which links Brooklin and Itaim Bibi with Morumbi. Shopping Morumbi (*see p144*) is also located here (rather than on the Morumbi side of the river).

BUTANTA
Bus 577T-10, 702C-10, 7598-10

Beyond the Institute Butantan (*see p83*) and the commercial district around Avenida Vital Brasil, Butantã comprises a mostly residential neighbourhood on the west bank of the Rio Pinheiros. Sightseeing highlights include the **Jockey Club** (*see p208*), which provides a panoramic view of the east side of the river, from Pinheiros to Itaim. For a more historical and cultural experience, head towards the

SIGHTS

Estádio do Morumbi. See p207.

Cidade Universitária (University City), by way of the **Casa do Bandeirante**.

The Cidade Universitária (Avenida Prof Almeida Prado 1280, 3091 4700, ww.usp.br, closed Sun) is a nearly self-contained city within a city, housing the USP (University of São Paulo) campus. It provides a large expanse of green, sparsely populated terrain near the centre of the city, and is very popular with weekend joggers or anyone wishing to get away from traffic without travelling too far. It also houses several museums like such as the **Museu do Crime** and **Museu de Arte Contemporânea**, and galleries which are free.

FREE Casa do Bandeirante
Praça Monteiro Lobato (3031 0920/ www.museudacidade.sp.gov.br). Bus 701T-10. **Open** 9am-5pm Tue-Sun. **Admission** free. **Map** p248 B9.
This rural colonial dwelling has been converted into a museum recreating a residence of the first explorers (Bandeirantes – flag carriers, or Brazil's equivalent of the American frontiersmen). It showcases early farming and cooking techniques.

★ Instituto Butantan
Avenida Dr Vital Brasil 1500 (3726 7222/ www.butantan.gov.br). Bus 577T-10. **Open** 9am-4.30pm Tue-Sun. **Admission** R$6 adults; R$2.50 reductions; free under-7s, over 60s. Free to all Thur. **No credit cards**. **Map** p248 A10. *See p83* **The Serpents' Den**.

★ FREE Museu de Arte Contemporânea
Cidade Universitária, Rua da Reitoria 160 (3091 3039/www.mac.usp.br). Bus 701T-10. **Open** 10am-6pm Tue-Fri; 10am-4pm Sat, Sun. **Admission** free. **Map** p248 A9.
The MAC is one of Brazil's most famous cultural institutions; it houses an impressive collection of works by world-renowned artists (including Picasso,

Modigliani and Matisse) as well as stars of Brazilian painting (such as Di Cavalcanti, Alfredo Volpi and Tarsila do Amaral). The exhibits are divided into a number of areas, including modernism, abstract art and contemporary art.

FREE Museu do Crime
Cidade Universitária, Praça Professor Reinaldo Porchat 219 (3039 3460). Bus 701T-10. **Open** 1-5pm Tue-Fri. **Admission** free. **Map** p248 B9.
This homage to notorious crimes and crime-fighting paraphernalia is situated in the heart of the Civil Police training school, literally at the end of a corridor of lecture theatres. Be warned: some of the photos are truly gruesome – even those not in the over-16s-only section.

MORUMBI
CPTM Morumbi

Morumbi, or 'green hills' in the native Indian (Tupi) language, grew out of a former tea farm. Its rapid development during the last century was largely due to the efforts of engineer Oscar Americano in dividing up and populating the land. The transfer of the state government's headquarters to the Palacio dos Bandeirantes further accelerated immigration into the area. In the 1920s, the bourgeoisie of São Paulo moved in a southwestern direction from Paulista to Jardins, as well as to Morumbi and Santo Amaro, which made up the furthest reach of what is now considered the Zona Sul.

Although separated from the centre of São Paulo by the Rio Pinheiros, Morumbi is worth a visit if you're in town for more than a few days. Aside from the architectural botanical and cultural highlights listed below, its hilly, tree-lined avenues house some of the most luxurious private houses and apartment buildings in the city. Conversely,the area is also home to the favela of Paraisópolis (*see p84*).

SIGHTS

The Serpents' Den

Welcome to the largest serpentarium in the country.

Founded in 1901 by Brazilian physician and biomedical scientist Vital Brazil, the **Instituto Butantan** (*see left*) was originally involved in fighting outbreaks of bubonic plague before evolving into its current guise: a research facility that specialises in venomous animals and produces around 80 per cent of Brazil's vaccines.

Highlights include the largest serpentarium in the country and the Biological Museum. The former is a sunken outside area, surrounded by glass walls, where you can watch rattlesnakes, pythons and pit vipers basking in the sun (or hiding in their shelters) from a safe distance.

The Biological Museum houses a wider selection of native and imported snakes, as well as spiders, scorpions and fish. Highlights include anacondas, a white Burmese python, potentially deadly coral snakes, as well as tarantulas.

The place has an endearingly low-tech, low-budget feel – don't worry though, those scary critters are safe behind substantial glass barriers. The museum is popular with children; it has colourful, cartoon-style signage in the Biological Museum and a selection of cuddly snakes in the gift shop. The monkey house, closed for refurbishment until further notice, is also, unsurprisingly, very child-friendly.

On a dry day, the extensive, leafy grounds make for a pleasant stroll among local flora and period buildings. A portion of the museum (the Museu da Rua, or Street Museum) is located in the gardens – there's a walkway of illustrated posters in Portuguese and English that take you through key episodes in the Institute's history.

Also noteworthy are the Historical Museum, with an array of antique equipment used in anti-venom research and production, and the Museum of Microbiology, which combines interactive multimedia, microscopes and models to appeal to a wide cross section of visitors.

If all those pesky kids tapping on the glass just a little too vigorously bring you out in a cold sweat, take comfort in the fact that should the ultimate Hollywood-style snake breakout occur, those unfortunate enough to fall prey to one of the Institute's many dangerous species can pop into the on-site hospital for a shot of anti-venom. Convenient, that.

SIGHTS

SIGHTS

On Avenida Morumbi, between numbers 4077 and 5594, you'll find the **Palacio dos Bandeirantes**, **Fundação Maria Luisa E Oscar Americano**, **Casa da Fazenda** and **Capela do Morumbi**. North-east of the palace is the well maintained, open parkland of **Praça Vinicius de Moraes** (between Avenida Giovanni Gronchi and Rua Barão de Pirapama), a popular weekend strolling destination for Morumbi residents in the form of a landscaped, sloping garden. Within walking distance is the **Estadio Cicero Pompeu de Toledo** (Morumbi Stadium; see p207).

If you are in search of greenery, highlights of Morumbi's park life are the forested **Parque Alfredo Volpi** and, further afield, the landscaped **Parque Burle Marx**. The **Parque Alfredo Volpi** (Rua Eng Oscar Americano 480, 3031 7052, www.prefeitura.sp. gov.br), named after the Brazilian modernist painter, is an expanse of dense rainforest, through which you can follow a meandering footpath (but not by bike). It contains 142 species of trees and 73 types of birds, plus lakes, picnic areas and a children's playground. Tread quietly and look carefully, and you might be lucky and see a sloth in the canopy.

Finally, tempting though it might be, venturing off into a favela alone is ill-advised. A guided visit to the awe-inspiring **Casa das Pedras** (see below) in **Paraisópolis** can be arranged without compromising your safety, and as well as the house, you'll also get to see views out over the whole favela.

FREE Capela do Morumbi
Avenida Morumbi 5387 (3106 2218/ 3772 4301/www.prefeitura.sp.gov.br). Bus 6267-10. **Open** 9am-5pm Tue-Sun. **Admission** free.
Originally part of a 19th-century tea farm, this former slave chapel was restored from its ruins in the 1940s. The current structure combines new brickwork with the original adobe construction. A fresco depicting Christ being baptised, flanked by angels of native Indian appearance, was also added during the refurbishment.

FREE Casa da Fazenda
Avenida Morumbi 5594 (3742 2810/ www.casadafazenda.com.br). Bus 6267-10. **Open** noon-3pm, 7pm-midnight Tue-Fri; noon-5pm Sat, Sun. **Admission** free.
Casa da Fazenda is a 19th-century mansion, restored and run by the Brazilian Academy of Art, Culture and History. It features reconstructed slave quarters and gardens. A bar and restaurant with a large outside terrace has a menu serving contemporised local 'farmhouse' dishes and traditional afternoon tea.

★ Casa das Pedras
Rua Herbert Spencer 38, Paraisópolis. **Open** 10am-5pm daily. **Admission** R$10. **No credit cards.**
This is the 'Gaudi House' of Paraisópolis, the fruit of over 20 years of labour by its owner, Estevão. It includes a labyrinth of arches and tunnels, with every surface covered in a mosaic of everyday bric-a-brac, from tiles and crockery to clocks, coins, toys and electronics. The roof-terrace offers a panoramic view of the favela. It's truly impressive and inspirational. A recommended guide who can also arrange transport is Flávia Liz Di Paolo at Unique in São Paulo (8119 3903, www.uniqueinsp.com).

★ Fundação Maria Luisa e Oscar Americano
Avenida Morumbi 4077 (3742 0077/ www. fundacaooscaramericano.org.br). Bus 6267-10. **Open** 10am-5.30pm Tue-Sun. **Admission** R$10; R$6 reductions. Free 1st Tue of the month. **No credit cards.**
Opposite the palace and set within 75,000sq m of parkland, the Fundação Maria Luisa e Oscar Americano has an outstanding collection of paintings, furniture, porcelain, fans and weaponry from imperial times onwards. The gallery is Oscar and Maria Luisa's former home, underneath which you'll find a charming, if pricey, tearoom.

FREE Palacio dos Bandeirantes
Avenida Morumbi 4500, Portão 2 (2193 8282/ www.saopaulo.sp.gov.br). Bus 6267-10. **Open** 10am-5pm Tue-Fri; 11am-4pm Sat, Sun. **Admission** free.
The Palacio and its grounds house a vast collection of artwork that reflects the history of the state, including paintings by Candido Portinari and Manabu Mabe, as well as Chico Stokinger and Felicia Leiner sculptures. Artefacts are organised into temporary exhibitions within the palace. There is also a separate tour of the gardens.

★ FREE Parque Burle Marx
Avenida Dona Helena Pereira de Morais 200 (3746 7631/www.prodam.sp.gov.br). Bus 6291-10. **Open** 7am-7pm daily. **Admission** free.
Concrete sculptures and artistic fountains characterise these beautiful gardens, designed by the world-renowned landscape artist of the 20th century, Roberto Burle Marx (1904-94) and inaugurated in 1995. He carefully weaved the natural flora of the Atlantic Forest with imported imperial palms and other plants and flowers, creating an oasis among the concrete. It's not the place to spend a day lounging around with a picnic and playing Frisbee (they are not allowed in the park); also banned are bikes, balls, skates and dogs. Bring water as there won't be anyone selling cold drinks or snacks here and be prepared to climb trails in the forest because this park is for the pure contemplation of nature.

South of the City

Where parks, palaces and playgrounds dominate the landscape.

One of the largest and most populous parts of the city, **Zona Sul** (the southern zone) incorporates some of São Paulo's most affluent areas, where the rich and the super-rich hang out in high-class shopping centres and armoured cars. It also, conversely, contains the biggest favela in São Paulo: **Heliópolis**, near Ipiranga, where the poor make do in cramped squalor.

In the last few years, the area has gone through a process of 'verticalisation', with the construction of innumerable skyscrapers to create more homes. This has led to problems in air circulation and quality. Yet with numerous parks, Zona Sul is still the greenest region in São Paulo, in part through the concerted effort of local authorities to plant trees on the sidewalks.

Map p246, p247
Hotels p105
Restaurants p128

THE SOUTH IN BRIEF

This is the area in which to enjoy beautiful views of the city at the **Museu de Ipiranga** and historic **Parque da Independência**, where Dom Pedro I famously declared Brazil's Independence in 1822. You can also quench your architectural thirst here in Brazil's first modernist house, the **Casa Modernista**, or satisfy your love for art at **Museu Lasar Segall**. Escape the hustle and and bustle of central São Paulo by stretching your legs in the **Parque Estadual das Fontes do Ipiranga**, also known as the **Parque do Estado**. This huge area of rainforest is protected, and you can catch a glimpse of exotic animals here at the **Zoo Foundation** and **Zoo Safari**, or disconnect from the city completely in the **Jardim Botanico**, one of the most beautiful natural areas of the city. Or stare up at the stars in **Parque Cientec**, São Paulo's science park and observatory, which houses a giant telescope for star-gazing.

FREE **Casa Modernista**
Rua Santa Cruz 325, Vila Mariana

About the author
Kim Beecheno *is a writer from London who lives in São Paulo.*

(5083 3232/www.museudacidade.sp.gov.br).
Metrô Santa Cruz. **Open** 9am-5pm Tue-Sun.
Admission free. **Map** p247 O14.
Recently refurbished and reopened to the public in 2008, Casa Modernista was the first modernist building to be constructed in Brazil. It was built by Russian-born Gregori Warchavchik in 1928, who is considered the pioneer of Brazilian modernist architecture. The house had a groundbreaking impact when it was erected – devoid of ornamentation and constructed with giant concrete, white walls. It's said that to obtain a building permit, Warchavchik initially submitted a plan for a traditional house and, when he had finished, claimed lack of funds to continue the outlined project. Inside is an exhibition on modern architecture and on Sundays there are sometimes classical music and jazz concerts. The garden, planned by his wife Mina Klabin, daughter of an elite Paulista industrialist, was also considered pioneering at the time due to her use and combination of tropical plants. Guided visits are available and some guides also speak English.

★ **Fundação Parque Zoológico de São Paulo**
Avenida Miguel Estefano 4241, Água Funda (5073 0811/www.zoologico.com.br). Metrô Jabaquara, shuttle from Metropolitan Terminal

Fundação Parque Zoológico. *See p85.*

(EMTU). **Open** 9am-5pm Tue-Sun. **Admission** R$13; R$3.50-$6.50 reductions. **Credit** V.

Opened in 1958, the Fundação Parque Zoológico de São Paulo is the largest zoo in Brazil and the fourth largest in the world. It receives over 1.5 million visitors a year and participates in many Brazilian endangered species programmes. Actively participating in protection for wild animals, the zoo boasts over 3,200 creatures, including the rare white rhinoceros, the golden marmoset, the golden-headed lion tamarind and several types of macaw that are native to the Amazon. Be sure to swing by the cold-blooded animal house (Casa do Sangue Frio) and check out the zoo's 98 species of reptile.

FREE Jardim Botânico

Avenida Miguel Estéfano 3031, Agua Funda (5073 6300 ext 229/www.ibot.sp.gov.br). Metrô São Judas/4742 bus. **Open** 9am-5pm Wed-Sun. **Admission** free.

Next to the Zoo and also inside the Parque do Estado is the Jardim Botânico, one of the nicest tourist attrac-

Volunteering in a Favela

Schemes to help the less fortunate abound in São Paulo.

Volunteering can be a very rewarding way to immerse yourself in the local culture and increase your understanding of the trials and tribulations that many Brazilians experience on a daily basis. From the country's population of 186 million, 40 million live below the poverty line, and Brazil has some of the widest divisions between rich and poor in the world. Many affluent areas of São Paulo, like Morumbi and other neighbourhoods in the south, are also home to some of the biggest favelas (shanty towns) in Brazil.

As Brazil moved from being an agricultural country to an industrialised one in the 1970s, there was a large migration of the rural population to the towns and cities, in search of jobs and a better life. The lack of housing and low wages drove many to live in temporary, self-constructed shelters where they didn't have to pay rent or bills. But a lack of governmental organisation and forethought, and a rapid expansion of urban areas, created the shanty towns you see today. São Paulo and Rio have the highest concentration of favelas in Brazil, and they continue to grow.

Favelas were originally areas that were illegally taken over by people who could not afford rents in traditional properties. The most basic had no electricity, running water

or rudimentary sanitation. Many modern favelas have comparatively good infrastructures, with access to electricity, and with a series of constructed stairways and passageways. However, as many favelas are built into hillsides, landslides are often common. And favela-dwellers tend, not surprisingly, to be trapped in the poverty cycle, with high unemployment, poor access to education, high levels of gang- and drug-related crime, and lack of police protection common features.

For visitors interested in volunteering, there are many opportunities for teaching English, taking part in youth outreach programmes or helping out in orphanages and cultural centres. Some organisations allow you to study Portuguese and volunteer at the same time. Check out www.volunteer abroad.com for details.

If you're staying in São Paulo for an extended period of time and are interested in volunteering, check out Children at Risk Foundation (CARF; www.carf web.net), which runs several programmes in Diadema, on the periphery of São Paulo. Some foreign organisations, such as the American Society of São Paulo (www. americansociety.com.br), also support various outreach programmes. Those who speak Portuguese should also visit www.voluntariado.org.br.

SIGHTS

Museu Ipiranga & Parque da Independência.

tions in São Paulo and a real paradise away from the concrete jungle of the city centre. A long, palm-fringed entrance leads to the Lineu Garden, inspired by the Uppsala Garden in Sweden, with two giant green-houses, one used for temporary exhibitions and the other housing exotic, tropical plants. Further in, a lake with water nymphs and aquatic plants inspires peace and tranquillity. This beautiful nature reserve is home to wild animals such as monkeys, sloths, tucans and herons among many others. The 360,000 square metres of protected rainforest is also home to the source of the Ipiranga River, which the government has protected since 1893. The Botanical Institute was created in 1938 when the Botanical Gardens were made official; botanical research is carried out here. Visitors can enter the Museu Botânico to learn about the evolution of plants and Brazilian flora. The gar-dens also contain a children's play area, a bamboo tunnel and many trails through the vegetation.

It's set in a state reserve of over 800,000 square metres of coastal rainforest inside São Paulo's giant 526 hectare Parque Estadual das Fontes do Ipiranga,

also known as the Parque do Estado (state park). As temperatures in São Paulo never fall below zero degrees, the animals live largely in outdoor enclosures and open paddocks, shaded by the trees of the forest. Guided tours (including night tours) are offered, with English-speaking guides availabe on request.

★ Museu Ipiranga & Parque da Independência

Parque da Independência, Ipiranga (2065 8000/ www.mp.usp.br/). Metrô Vila Mariana/374T-10 bus. **Open** 9am-5pm Tue-Sun. **Admission** *Museum* R$4; reductions R$2. *Park* free.
Set on a hill overlooking a small replica of the gar-dens of the Chateau de Versailles, the Parque da Independência, the Museu Ipiranga was built in commemoration of Dom Pedro I, who declared Brazil's independence in 1822. The impressive Renaissance-style building took ten years to com-plete and dates from 1895. Inside it traces the his-tory of Brazil, from the early settlers to the 1950s, highlighting the role played by the people of São

Paulo. The museum and the gardens offer great views of the city of São Paulo and Parque Independência (free) is a great place to kick off your shoes and lounge around in the shade on a hot day.

★ Museu Lasar Segall
Rua Berta 111, Vila Mariana (5574 7422/ www.museusegall.org.br). Metrô Vila Mariana or Santa Cruz. **Open** 2-7pm Tue-Sat; 2-6pm Sun. **Admission** free. **Map** 247 O13.
See below **The Immigrant's Canvas**.

FREE USP Cientec (Science & Technology Park)
Avenida Miguel Stéfano 4200, Água Funda (5077 6312/www.cientec.usp.br). Metrô São Judas, bus 4742. **Open** by appointment Tue-Fri. **Admission** free.

Also inside the Parque do Estado is the University of São Paulo (USP) Science & Technology Park, which was created in 2001 and houses the São Paulo Observatory. Originally built on Avenida Paulista in 1912, the observatory moved to its current location in the 1930s. The Parque Cientec aims to promote science and technology, with visits possible, though they must be booked in advance. On certain evenings and Saturdays each month visitors can use the giant telescope in the observatory. The art deco buildings feature a beautiful sculpture in the fountain in the main entrance by Eugenio Prati, evoking Urania, the Greek goddess of astronomy and geometry. Call to arrange a tour; some guides speak English.

Zoo Safari
Avenida do Cursino 6338, Vila Moraes (2336 2131/www.zoologico.sp.gov.br/zoosafari). Metrô São Judas to bus 4742-10. **Open** 9.30am-5pm Tue-Sun. **Admission** R$13; R$6.50 reductions. **Credit** DC, MC, V.

Inside the Parque do Estado and next to the Zoo Foundation is the Zoo Safari. Inaugurated in 2001, it consists of a 4km trail that takes about an hour to traverse inside a vehicle. This can be done in a private car or in a van provided by the Zoo Safari. The zoo contains 380 animals of 42 different species including lions, tigers, lamas, ostriches, and zebras, as well as reptiles and birds that roam freely throughout the park in 18 different territories. From 10am to 4pm you can access the Zoo Safari from the Zoo Foundation for R$11 via the entrance at the lion sanctuary. Be aware of marauding monkeys who like to get their hands on anything they can from the tourists.

The Immigrant's Canvas
Lasar Segall's influence on the Paulistano art scene.

Lasar Segall was one of the most influential Brazilian modernists until his death in 1957. Born into an orthodox Jewish family in Vilnius, Lithuania, Segall immersed himself in the world of art and travelled to Berlin to study at the tender age of 15. Even

before he turned 20, he was putting on solo shows and working with artists like Otto Dix and Georg Grosz. Together they laid the foundation for German Expressionism.

Finding his hometown destroyed after World War I, a restless and homeless Segall moved to Brazil in 1923. In São Paulo, Segall's artistic focus changed. He painted fellow immigrants (*see p16* for a photo of his painting *Navio de Imigrantes* (*Ship of Immigrants*)) as well as Afro-Brazilians, and would depict himself as a mulatto – a controversial move in a European-obsessed country.

Segall came to join the ranks of Brazil's leading artists and the Brazilian modernist movement. Yet, even in Brazil he couldn't escape the stigma of being Jewish. The Nazis exhibited his work in the 1937 show of 'degenerate art', and his retrospective at the Museu de Bellas Artes in Rio in 1943 incited protests from right-wing intellectuals.

Segall's São Paulo home was turned into the non-profit **Museu Lasar Segall** (*see above*) in 1967, where his most famous works are on display. The organisation also runs a variety of art classes and courses.

Consume

Feira da Liberdade. *See p145.*

Hotels

A plethora of luxury pads – for those on luxury budgets.

São Paulo is remaking itself as a city of the architectural-landmark hotel. The luxury accomodation scene is defined by beautifully designed, chic hotels like the Fasano and Unique. Although top-end tourists and business travellers will have no problem finding great stylised rooms, those with more modest means will have to search harder for decent, wallet-friendly sleeping quarters. When it comes to inexpensive hotels or budget hostels, São Paulo is still redefining itself as a tourist destination, and although the number of hostels seems to be growing, bargain lodging options are still meagre.

NEIGHBOURHOODS & PRICES

The most popular and chi-chi areas for fancy hotels are around Avenida Paulista, Jardins and Higienópolis. Most of the hotels in these districts are located close to bars, restaurants and tourist attractions. For the visitor who wants to get to know the city by walking, these areas are highly recommended. In the south of the city, swish new hotels are going up in the neighbourhoods of Morumbi and Brooklin, including the **Grand Hyatt** and the **Hilton**, as well as **Blue Tree Towers**. These hotels tend to offer higher-quality service, fantastic rooms and better views than at comparable hotels in the centre. That said, unless you have access to a car, you will spend a lot of time and money commuting from the deep south to downtown. Taxis from here to Jardins start at R$30. Buses and the CPTM (commuter rail line) are also available, but these options can be quite time consuming and are less viable at night.

São Paulo is a business capital, and most of the hotels in the city are orientated specifically towards this kind of traveller. Tourists will find that many hotels have business centres and concierges. On the weekend, prices often go down, as most of the hotels are booked throughout the week. Usually prices in the centre go up in June around the Parada (Gay Pride Parade).

Our hotel listings are organised by area and price category. We have divided the listings into four categories: Luxury (R$500 and above);

Expensive (R$300-$500); Moderate (R$100-$300); Budget (below R$100).

BELA VISTA & LIBERDADE
Expensive

Maksoud Plaza
Alameda Campinas 150, Bela Vista (3145 8000/ www.maksoud.com.br). Metrô Trianon-MASP. **Rates** R$280-$550. **Rooms** 416. **Credit** AmEx, DC, MC, V. **Map** p244 L8 ➊
This 31-year-old hotel was São Paulo's best hotel during the 1990s. Today, it's lost some of its glamour and is, in fact, reminiscent of a somewhat weary Las Vegas casino. Nevertheless, it has enough entertainment to keep a tourist inside all week long: three restaurants, a theatre, a convention centre, a well-equipped gym and an internal atrium that goes all the way to the top floor. Rooms have carpets, somewhat dated furniture and heavy fabrics.
Bars (5). Business centre. Concierge. Disabled-adapted rooms. Gym. Internet (R$30/day wireless, high-speed). Non-smoking rooms. Parking (R$25). Pool. Restaurants (5). Room service. TV.

Moderate

Ibis Paulista
Avenida Paulista 2355, Bela Vista (3523 3000/ www.ibis.com.br). Metrô Consolação. **Rates** R$159. **Rooms** 236. **Credit** AmEx, DC, MC, V. **Map** p244 J7 ➋
This branch of the Ibis chain caters to Brazilian tourists as much as to foreigners. A mix of

small-business and holiday travellers love the location, which is a good base from which to explore the city. Getting to the centre of town or any of the major tourist attractions is easy by taxi, bus or metrô, and there is great nightlife close by on Rua Bela Cintra and in Jardins. All of the rooms have modern double beds and contemporary furnishings that could have come from IKEA. Breakfast is an extra R$10.
Bar. Business centre. Disabled-adapted rooms. Internet (R$12 high-speed, wireless). No smoking rooms. Parking (R$14). Restaurant. TV.

Nikkey Palace Hotel

Rua Galvão Bueno 425, Liberdade (3207 8511/ www.nikkeyhotel.com.br). Metrô Liberdade or São Joaquim. **Rates** R$325. **Rooms** 95.
Credit AmEx, DC, MC, V. **Map** p245 O7 ❸
If it's Japanese-Brazilian culture you're looking to discover on this trip, then this place is for you. Located in the heart of the Japanese quarter on one of the most well-known streets in Liberdade, this hotel brings the best of both the Japanese and Brazilian worlds. The rooms are pleasant, with cream and brown tones, and can come with traditional Japanese 'Ofuro' baths on request. The hotel caters to a predominantly Japanese clientele, with a sauna (for men only), a barber shop, and Japanese breakfasts. There are discounts for guests staying four days or more.
Bar. Business centre. Disabled-adapted room (1). Internet (free wireless). Restaurant. Room service. Parking (R$10). TV: DVD.

Budget

Akasaka Hotel

Praça da Liberdade 149, Liberdade (3207 1500/www.akasakahotel.com.br). Metrô

Liberdade. **Rates** R$99. **Rooms** 50.
No credit cards. Map p245 O7 ❹
This inexpensive hotel is aimed mostly at Japanese businessmen, meaning that it's always busier during the week than on weekends. Simple and clean, the no-frills rooms are decorated with traditional cream fabrics, and have white walls and Japanese decorations. Kitchenettes are also available to rent on a monthly basis. The breakfast is not included in the price, although it is available for only R$10 per person. The plethora of Asian restaurants in the area means that you definately won't go hungry when staying at the Akasaka.
Business centre. Internet (R$15 wireless in business centre only). Restaurant. TV.

★ Pousada dos Franceses

Rua dos Franceses 100, Bela Vista (3288 1592/www.pousadadosfranceses.com.br). Metrô Brigadeiro. **Rates** R$88-$98; R$36 dorm bed. **Rooms** 13. **No credit cards. Map** p245 M7 ❺
Tucked away in a calm residential section of Bela Vista, the sweet Pousada dos Franceses is a typical metropolitan hostel installed in a house with a garden and filled with foreign travellers. The members of the young, friendly staff are eager to show proficiency in their second languages (English and French) and interact with guests, making them feel right at home. Rooms vary from group to single and are basic, with bunk or full-size beds, and multi-coloured walls. If you have laundry, do it here; the washing machine is set on a terrace that looks out onto a typically Paulistano view – a mass of buildings and antennas. There's also a barbeque area at the back.
Internet. TV.

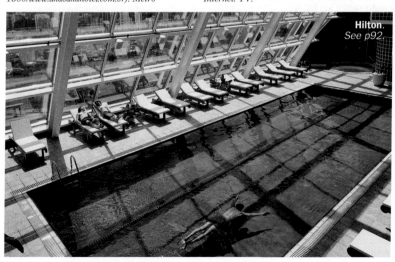

Hilton.
See p92.

CONSUME

Tryp Jesuíno Arruda.
See p99.

Bars (5). Business centre. Concierge. Disabled-adapted rooms. Gym. Internet (free high-speed). Non-smoking rooms. Parking (R$35). Pools (1 indoor, 1 outdoor). Restaurants (3). Room service. Spa. TV: DVD.

Hilton
Avenida das Nações Unidas 12901, Centro Empresarial Nações Unidas (6845 0000/ www.hilton.co.uk/saopaulo). CPTM Berrini, bus 609F-10. **Rates** R$429-$15,000. **Rooms** 487. **Credit** AmEx, DC, MC, V.
The Hilton is high-tech central. Ideal for the business traveller, it is walking distance from the Centro Empresarial Naçoes Unidas, the new business hub of São Paulo. This contemporary skyscraper has 28 floors, an enormous lobby and a 24-hour spa. The rooms come in beige and cream tones, with king-size beds and fully equipped work-stations; there's no Wi-Fi signal on the beds, though, in order to preserve their sanctity. The deluxe package includes buffet breakfast, executive lounge access (happy hour included), and express check in and check out. *Photo p91.*
Bar. Business centre. Gym. Internet (free high-speed). Parking (R30). Pool (outdoor). Restaurant. Spa. TV: DVD.

CENTRO
Expensive

São Paulo Bourbon
Avenida Dr Vieira de Carvalho 99, Vila Buarque (3337 2000/www.bourbon.com.br). Metrô República. **Rates** R$184-$440. **Rooms** 127. **Credit** AmEx, DC, MC, V. **Map** p243 M4 ❻
The location – at Rua Vieira de Carvalho – makes Bourbon one of the favourite hotels for gay travellers. If you want to stay there during the Parada (Gay Pride Parade), it's best to book well in advance; the parade ends right on República, a block away from the hotel. During the rest of the year, the hotel is popular with business travellers. There are great restaurants around this area and good nightlife on Avenida Dr Vieira de Carvalho and on Largo do Arouche. The hotel is quite charming, with a reading room, a pleasant lobby with paintings and large rooms with desks and love seats.
Bar. Business centre. Concierge. Gym. Internet (free high-speed, wireless). Parking (R$14). Pool (indoor). Restaurant. Room service. TV.

Moderate

Hotel Excelsior
Avenida Ipiranga 770, Centro (3331 0377/ www.hotel excelsiorsp.com.br). Metrô República. **Rates** R$165-$183. **Rooms** 183. **Credit** AmEx, DC, MC, V. **Map** p243 N5 ❼
In the heart of downtown, the Hotel Excelsior is something of a convention mecca. Its huge meeting

BROOKLIN
Luxury

★ Grand Hyatt
Avenida das Naçoes Unidas 13301 (2838 1234/ www.saopaulo.grand.hyatt.com). CPTM Morumbi. **Rates** R$575-$715. **Rooms** 458. **Credit** AmEx, DC, MC, V.
The movers and shakers of the international art and political scenes stay here. The penthouse is always hosting either a music star or a commander in chief: recent residents have included Madonna and Elton John, but every guest receives star treatment here. This hotel gets it right: for its size, the number and prominence of guests that it hosts, the Grand Hyatt offers attentive and engaging service that normally would be expected only from the best family-run bed and breakfasts or spas. The beautiful rooms are large and airy, with marble bathrooms and floor-to-ceiling windows. The breakfast buffet includes an enormous spread of fruit and pastries, while there's a complimentary cocktail hour at 6pm. São Paulo's environs may not immediately bring wine country to mind, but the Hyatt's Wine Library, a floor-to-ceiling glass-enclosed collection of more than 2,500 European and new-world *vinhos*, offers a robust gateway on your way into the hotel's upscale restaurant complex. (It has three of the best eateries in town.) Although the hotel is most accessible by car, the minor inconvenience of the location is offset by the attention and pampering that is lavished on the guest. *Photo p104.*

Profile Hotel Unique

Ruy Ohtake's hotel really is one of a kind.

Hotel Unique (*see p99*) is an architectural landmark first, and a hip venue for beautiful trendies second: its role as a mere hotel comes in a poor third. The greenish copper-plated half sphere (hence the 'watermelon' nickname) dotted with giant porthole windows is 25 metres high and stands alone in an otherwise low-rise area, with residences to one side and services to the other, making it hard to miss.

The Unique's success is down not just to architect Ruy Ohtake, but to designer João Armentano and landscape artist Gilberto Erkis, who take its noteworthiness beyond just the brick and mortar structure. Armentano took Ohtake's watermelon concept and made it work for the 85 rooms and ten suites in the interior, where hardwood floors can suddenly bend upwards, mirroring a ship's curve. From their porthole windows, landscape artist Gilberto Erkis's serpentine water channels can be viewed (from the ground floor the steel-lined watercourse is just visible snaking through the agaves).

In the vast lobby, opposite the seven-metre-high doorway, is the colourful 15-metre-high bar, the Wall – supposedly inspired by the Pink Floyd song. At one end is a cosy reading corner stocked with design and architecture books.

You'll want to hit the rooftop bar, **Skye** (*see p137*), before you do anything else. It's by far the best thing Unique has to offer, not only for its own assets but for the panoramic views it offers, particularly impressive at sunset. The sweeping vistas extend uphill to the coloured antenna-lined horizon of Avenida Paulista above the Jardins neighbourhoods, and, to the other side, towards Parque do Ibirapuera. In fact, the view from the Unique's bar and pool is arguably one of the world's most spectacular sights and an attraction in its own right.

The 95 rooms and suites vary hugely in size, starting at 36 square metres and running up to 312 square metres. In an ultra-cool design touch, the curve of the exterior, lined in pale wood, serves as one of the walls in the rooms. The furniture is as modern and sleek as the staff's uniforms (which come courtesy of São Paulo designer Alexandre Herchcovitch). Unique indeed.

Also pictured on p100.

CONSUME

GRAND STYLE

EXPERIENCE BRAZILIAN FLAIR AT GRAND HYATT SÃO PAULO

470 luxurious and spacious guestrooms and suites · Three signature restaurants: Italian, Japanese and Contemporary French, including sumptuous Sunday Brunch Bar with live music and a Wine Library · Urban Spa with private treatment rooms Flexible and unique events space · Executive floors in the exclusive Grand Club®

FEEL THE HYATT TOUCH®

Av. das Nações Unidas, 13.301, São Paulo, SP
TEL + 55 11 2838 1234 FAX + 55 11 2838 1235 saopaulo.grand.hyatt.com

Fasano. *See p99.*

rooms fit about 2,000 people. There's a retro mood throughout, in the multicoloured bedspreads and in the timber wood flooring. Meanwhile, the well-cared-for bathtubs take guests back to the 1940s. Just beyond the heavy curtains covering the windows is a great view of Praça da República.
Bar. Business centre. Concierge. Disabled-adapted rooms (2). Gym. Internet (free wireless). Parking (R$15). Restaurant. Room service. Spa. TV: DVD.

★ Normandie Design
Avenida Ipiranga 1187, Santa Ifigênia (3311 9855/www.normandiedesign.com.br). Metrô São Bento. **Rates** R$180. **Rooms** 180. **Credit** AmEx, DC, MC, V. **Map** p243 N4 **8**
This hotel, one of the best boutique hotels in town, was recently updated and gained a clean design, with modern furniture in black and white on the walls. The discreet service takes good care of the rooms, which have great natural ventilation and older, wide bathrooms. Located on the corner of Avenida Ipiranga and electronics mecca Rua Santa Ifigênia, it is not a particularly peaceful spot during the day, when Santa Ifigênia's walking crowd gets out of control. At night it's quieter and great for a night of heavy sleeping, but should you decide to walk alone in the area after 11pm, proceed with extra caution.
Bar. Business centre. Concierge. Disabled-adapted rooms. Internet (free wireless). No smoking rooms. Parking (R$15). Restaurant. Room service. TV.

Novotel Jaraguá
Rua Martins Fontes 71 (2802 7000/www.novotel. com.br). Metrô Anhangabaú. **Rates** R$196-$226. **Rooms** 415. **Credit** AmEx, DC, MC, V. **Map** p243 M6 **9**

A find for the history buffs, this hotel occupies a building with a past. In this spot once stood the headquarters of *O Estado de São Paulo*, one of the most important newspapers in Brazil. A mosaic from the Brazilian modernist artist Di Cavalcanti has been on the outside area of the building since the newspaper era. The well-lit rooms are decorated in pleasant pastels and have large beds and modern wood furniture. Some quarters are carpetted while all have locked windows.
Bar. Business centre. Concierge. Disabled-adapted rooms. Gym. Internet (R$10 wireless). No smoking rooms. Parking (R$18). Restaurants (2). Room service. Spa. TV.

Budget

★ São Paulo Hostel
Rua Barão de Campinas 94 (3333 0844/ www.hostelsp.com.br). Metrô República. **Rates** R$87; R$40-$42 dorm bed. **Rooms** 45. **Credit** DC, MC, V. **Map** p243 M4 **10**
Being so close to Largo do Arouche is a plus for those who want to party all night long. Culture vultures can revel in the plethora of museums and historic sights around the neighbourhood. This 80-year-old building gets refitted constantly, and its private rooms are well preserved. The dorm rooms have old showers and are a bit dark, but they are otherwise clean and spacious. The matresses are a bit thin, and the single beds are a little small. The building has a games room and kitchen, making it good for socialising and meeting people.
Bar. Concierge. Internet (R$3 high-speed). No smoking rooms. TV (in private rooms).

CONSOLAÇÃO
Moderate

★ Augusta Park Suite Hotel
Rua Augusta 922, Paulista Centre, Consolação (3124 4400/www.augustapark.com.br). Metrô Consolação. **Rates** R$116-$132. **Rooms** 56. **Credit** AmEx, DC, MC, V. **Map** p242 L6 **11**
Located in an attractive building on the not-so-upmarket side of Rua Augusta, this pleasant hotel has small white rooms with red curtains, although most come with French windows that make them light and airy. They are all fitted with kitchenettes. This is a good option for business travellers or for those intending to stay for a while, as it is well situated and more reasonably priced than other hotels closer to Avenida Paulista.
Business centre. Gym. Internet (R$8/day wireless). No smoking rooms. Parking (free). Pool (outdoor). Restaurant. Room service. TV.

Paulista Center Hotel
Rua Consolação 2567, Consolação (3062 0421/ www.paulistacenterhotel.com.br). Metrô

CONSUME

Consolação. **Rates** R$139. **Rooms** 50.
Credit AmEx, DC, MC, V. **Map** p244 J7 ⑫
It may be on Consolaçao, facing five lanes of traffic and some rather run-down buildings, but at least the owners of this hotel can boast about being close to Avenida Paulista. The rooms are functional and, with very small windows, a little airless. The lighting isn't particularly atmospheric and the colour combination – peach and white walls with dark blue chairs – don't boost the relaxation factor. Ask for group and low- season discounts.
Bar. Business centre. Internet (R$5/day high-speed, wireless). No smoking floors. Parking (R$24). Restaurant. TV.

Budget

Formula 1 Paulista
Rua da Consolação 2303 (3123 7755/ www.formule1.com.br). Metrô Consolação. **Rates** R$99. **Rooms** 399. **Credit** DC, MC, V. **Map** p244 J7 ⑬
Bright, bizzare and somewhat tacky, this huge building resides on the very busy intersection of Rua Consolaçao and Avenida Paulista. The lobby looks a lot like an airport check-in desk, decorated in attention-grabbing orange and blue, and the place is as busy as an airport too, with a steady throng of people pushing trolleys piled high with luggage. It is very functional: all rooms sleep up to three people. The walls are white with blaring flowery bedcovers. Scary colours aside it's a great budget option; here you know what you're getting and what to expect. The buffet breakfast is an extra R$6 and free to students on presentation of an ISIC card at check-in.

**INSIDE TRACK
STAY FOR FREE**

For those who are tired of staying in impersonal hotels, the era of the internet has brought an alternative. Two websites – **www.couchsurfing.com** and **www.hospitalityclub.com** – offer weary travellers a respite from hotels. Become a member and within a click of a mouse (or perhaps several clicks) you can gain a new friend and find a bed to sleep in at the same time. Couch Surfing counts more than 2,000 Paulistanos as members, many of whom have already offered their beds and sofas to visitors who are looking to meet locals and travel on the cheap. If you want to really scratch beneath the surface of São Paulo and find out what makes the city tick, then these services could certainly assist you in your quest.

Disabled-adapted rooms. Internet (R$12 wireless; R$10 shared terminal). No smoking floors. Parking (R$9). Restaurant. TV.

HIGIENOPOLIS
Moderate

Tryp Higienópolis
Rua Maranhão 371, Higienópolis (3665 8200/ www.solmelia.com.br). Metrô Marechal Deodoro. **Rates** R$201-$292. **Credit** AmEx, DC, MC, V. **Map** p242 K5 ⑭
Leafy plazas and hilly streets surround this lovely hotel. In the heart of the wealthy area of Higienópolis, Tryp is part of the Melia chain and keeps a high level of service. The furniture should soon be changed as the room decorations were updated recently. Two blocks away is Patio Higienópolis, a charming mall that is usually full on Sundays. Nice restaurants can be found at Praça Vilaboim, which is great for happy hours and dinner. Breakfast is an extra R$18.
Bar. Business centre. Concierge. Disabled-adapted rooms. Gym. Internet (free wireless). No smoking rooms. Parking (R$10). Pool (outdoor). Restaurant. Room service. TV.

ITAIM BIBI & VILA OLIMPIA
Expensive

★ Blue Tree Towers Faria Lima
Avenida Brigadeiro Faria Lima 3989, Vila Olimpia (3896 7544/www.bluetree.com.br). Bus 958P-10. **Rates** R$293-$490. **Rooms** 282. **Credit** AmEx, DC, MC, V.
Stylish, sleek and trendy the chain hotel focuses on businessmen who appreciate the hotel's proximity to Berrini, the business area. Close by is Rua Atilio Innocenti, with more than 15 options for bars, many of them with live music. Basic clear wood furniture and carpeted rooms with beds that can be folded, leaving the space free for work, are standard.
Bar. Business centre. Concierge. Disabled-adapted rooms. Gym. Internet (R$22/day wireless). No smoking rooms. Parking (R$14). Pool (1 indoor, 1 outdoor). Restaurant. Room service. TV.

★ Radisson Hotel Faria Lima
Avenida Cidade Jardim 625 (2133 5960/ www.radisson.com/hotels/brasaop). Bus 609F-10, CPTM Cidade Jardim. **Rates** R$374-$419. **Rooms** 200. **Credit** AmEx, DC, MC, V. **Map** p249 F12 ⑮
The Radisson features a 'Women's Executive Floor' with extra flowers and toiletries. There is also a 'Royal Floor', where the rooms have attractive wood panelling, with CDs and DVDs among other extras. Part of the upmarket Radisson chain, the Faria Lima hotel doesn't disappoint. Located in the heart of the city's business and entertainment

L'Hotel. *See p100.*

CONSUME

Bags packed, milk cancelled, house raised on stilts.

You've packed the suntan lotion, the snorkel set, the stay-pressed shirts. Just one more thing left to do – your bit for climate change. In some of the world's poorest countries, changing weather patterns are destroying lives.

You can help people to deal with the extreme effects of climate change. Raising houses in flood-prone regions is just one life-saving solution.

**Climate change costs lives.
Give £5 and let's sort it *Here & Now***

www.oxfam.org.uk/climate-change

Be Humankind Oxfam

district, it is just steps away from the Iguatemi shopping mall and São Paulo Jockey club. The luxury rooms are decorated in relaxing and neutral tones of brown and cream. They are furnished with classic wooden furniture and extra large desks for business travellers. Quite rare for a Brazilian hotel, it is 100 per cent non-smoking, and the rooms are light and airy, with balconies and superb views across the city.

Bar. Business centre. Gym. Internet (free high-speed). No smoking floors. Parking (free). Pool. (indoor) Restaurant. Room service. Spa. TV.

Moderate

Mercure Apartments The Executive One
Rua Santa Justina 210, Vila Olimpia (3089 6222/ www.mercure.com.br). Bus 637P-10. **Rates** R$241. **Rooms** 210. **Credit** AmEx, D, MC, V.
Get away from the rush of the centre. Mercure is located in a residential area, which keeps it quiet at night-time; the hotel is three blocks away from the bus line of Avenida Santo Amaro. It is also just a block away from Rua João Cachoeira and its decent clothing stores, restaurants and authentic jazz bar, All of Jazz (Rua João Cachoeira 1366). The nice pool on the first floor gets very busy in the morning. The rooms have lots of natural light. Breakfast is an added R$15.
Bar. Business centre. Concierge. Disabled-adapted rooms. Gym. Internet (R$12/day wireless). No smoking rooms. Parking (R$7). Pool (outdoor). Restaurant. Room service. TV.

Tryp Jesuíno Arruda
Rua Jesuino Arruda 806, Itaim Bibi (3704 4400/ www.solmelia.com). Bus 106A-10. **Rates** R$212-$271. **Rooms** 139. **Credit** AmEx, MC, V. **Map** p249 H12 ⑯
Giant rooms, king-size beds and panoramic views can be found at this perfectly priced option. Tryp hotels are among the most popular in their range for travellers from Brazil and abroad. This one is in the heart of the Itaim Bibi district, close to shops, cinemas and restaurants that you can explore locally on foot. It is not, however, so conveniently located for visiting iconic tourist sites, for which you will have to take a bus or taxi. Although lacking in character, the rooms are spacious enough for two, and if you are high up, you'll have a great view at night. *Photo p92.*
Bar. Business centre. Gym. Internet (free high-speed; R$20-$30 wireless). No smoking rooms. Parking (free). Restaurant. TV.

JARDINS
Luxury

★ Emiliano
Rua Oscar Freire 384, Jardins (3068 4399/ www.emiliano.com.br). Metrô Consolação/
bus 702P-42. **Rates** R$1,100. **Rooms** 47. **Credit** AmEx, DC, MC, V. **Map** p244 J9 ⑰
Standing tall and golden on the city's most exclusive shopping address, this slick tower's exterior is all glass and cream tones. Inside, the lobby is full of Campana brothers' chairs, floating orchids and a cool, carefully manicured vibe. The helipad on the roof is used by the country's richest citizens. The rooms have high-tech bathrooms with Japanese toilets, and good reading chairs, and the location is ideal for anyone who enjoys good cafés, high-end shops, leisurely strolls and people-watching. A balanced blend of business and holiday travellers can be found here, and the staff is young and eager to please. As an extra bonus, a bottle of wine, fruit, a 15-minute massage and the ironing of two items of clothing are all on the house. *Photo p103.*
Bar. Business centre. Gym. Internet (free wireless). No smoking rooms. Pool (indoor). Restaurant. Spa. TV: DVD.

★ Fasano
Rua Vittorio Fasano 88, Jardins (3896 4000/ www.fasano.com.br). Metrô Consolação. **Rates** R$1,350. **Rooms** 60. **Credit** AmEx, DC, MC, V. **Map** p244 I8 ⑱
Architects Isay Weinfeld and Marcelo Kogan's great achievement is an English brown brick-and-wood model of simple refinement and elegance. The decor unites the old-school, clubby charm of hefty leather armchairs in the foyer with chic, contemporary twists and a sunken lobby bar. The rooms are luxuriously large and well lit through a combination of windows and gleaming wooden floors. Great views of the city complement the restrained colour scheme. The Fasano fulfils all the expectations of a luxury hotel, from impeccable service to perfect location. Its Baretto Bar (*see p133*) is an award-winning restaurant and well-known musical destination. Breakfast is an extra R$50 per person. *Photo p95.*
Bars (2). Business centre. Concierge. Gym. Internet (R$45/day wireless). Pool (indoor). Restaurants (2). Room service. Spa. TV: DVD.

★ Hotel Unique
Avenida Brigadeiro Luis Antônio 4700, Jardins (3055 4710/www.hotelunique.com.br). Bus 477U-10. **Rates** R$1,100-2,250. **Rooms** 95. **Credit** AmEx, DC, MC, V. **Map** p244 J11 ⑲
See p93 **Profile**.
Bar. Disabled-adapted rooms. Gym. Internet (free wireless). Pool (1 indoor, 1 outdoor). Restaurant.

Tivoli São Paulo Mofarrej
Alameda Santos 1437, Cerqueira César (3146 5900/www.tivolihotels.com.br). Metrô Trianon-MASP. **Rates** R$1,000-$1,467. **Rooms** 220. **Credit** AmEx, DC, MC, V. **Map** p244 K8 ⑳
The privileged location made this one of the most important hotels in the 1990s. Right across the street from Trianon park and the MASP, the old Mofarrej

CONSUME

was completely retro-fitted and has two different decoration styles. The classic, which keeps the old hotel's figure, and the new-concept decor, filling the contemporary rooms with up-to-date furniture and black marble in the bathrooms. The views of Avenida Nove de Julho are superb. Breakfast is an adicional R$40 per person. *Photo p92.*
Bar. Business centre. Concierge. Disabled-adapted rooms. Gym. Internet (free wireless). No smoking rooms. Parking (R$25). Pool (outdoor). Restaurant. Room service. Spa. TV.

Expensive

★ George V Casa Branca
Alameda Casa Branca 909, Jardins (3067 6000/ www.georgev.com.br). Metrô Trianon-MASP. **Rates** R$600-$800. **Rooms** 58. **Credit** AmEx, DC, MC, V. **Map** p244 J9 ㉑
The royal name guarantees royal treatment at this fancy accommodation option. The George V has modern wood furniture, enormous beds with light white fabrics and wide balconies. All the rooms are equipped with a kitchen and living room. The location is great for daytime walks to Oscar Freire and Rua Augusta, and the Nove de Julho bus corridor is a block away.

Business centre. Gym. Internet (R$28/day wireless). No smoking rooms. Parking (free). Pool (indoor). Restaurant. Room service. Spa. TV.

★ L'Hotel
Alameda Campinas 266, Jardim Paulista (2183 0500/www.lhw.com). Metrô Trianon-MASP or Brigadeiro. **Rates** R$300-$477. **Rooms** 75. **Credit** AmEx, DC, MC, V. **Map** p244 L8 ㉒
This beautiful boutique hotel, conceived in the best European style, is one of the few accomodations in São Paulo that was designed with a theme. Once inside you can imagine you're staying right on the Champs-Elyseés. The decor in the rooms and throughout is light pink and salmon, with velvet fabrics and sandalwood furniture. The beds are enormous, with luxury sheets, and there are two bathrooms per room. This is São Paulo's most romantic hotel and perfect for a honeymoon. The concierge welcomes you with a glass of champagne, and the breakfast is an enormous spread of Brazilian breakfast foods. The hotel offers good discounts, and the highest double-room rate of R$477 is rarely paid. There are also relaxation/meditation rooms, but in a place like L'Hotel, that might seem redundant to the overall experience. *Photo p97.*

Hotel Unique. *See p99.*

Bar. Business centre. Disabled-adapted rooms.
Gym. Internet (free wireless). Parking (free).
Restaurant. Room service. Sauna. TV: DVD.

Meliá Jardim Europa

Rua João Cachoeira 107, Itaim Bibi (3702 9600/
www.meliajardimeuropa.com). Bus 477A-10.
Rates R$298. **Rooms** 320. **Credit** AmEX, DC,
MC, V. **Map** p249 G12 ㉓
Don't be overwhelmed by the monstrosity of the
building – it's huge, but a considerable number of
floors contain residential apartments. A clean and
efficient chain hotel, the Meliá is a safe choice if
you're dying to be in Itaim Bibi. As an added
bonus, it's just metres from Avenida 9 de Julho,
where you can easily find taxis and buses for your
ventures further afield, and it's surrounded by good
restaurants and cafés. In addition to a pool with an
excellent view, the hotel includes a green floor:
everything in the rooms and social areas is eco-
friendly. Breakfast is an extra R$28 per person.
Bar. Business centre. Disabled-adapted rooms.
Gym. Internet (free wireless). Parking (R$12).
Pool (outdoor). Restaurant. Room service. TV.

Quality Jardins

Alameda Campinas 540, Jardim Paulista
(2182 0400/www.atlanticahotels.com.br). Metrô
Trianon-MASP. **Rates** R$308-$408. **Rooms** 222.
Credit AmEx, DC, MC, V. **Map** p244 L9 ㉔
Quality Jardins benefits from its prime location –
otherwise, it is a run-of-the-mill mid-range chain
hotel for business people. The rooms are small, carpetted and comfortable, with low beds and wooden
headboards. The location is just one block away
from Avenida Paulista, and its proximity to fantastic bars, restaurants and shops certainly makes up
for the deficit of charm. Just try not to think that
you would probably pay a quarter of the price for
a similarly decorated motel room in the US. The
swimming pool is a bonus in the summer.
Bar. Business centre. Disabled-adapted room (1).
Gym. Internet (free high-speed, wireless).
No smoking floors. Parking. Pool (outdoor).
Restaurant. TV.

Quality Suites Imperial Hall

Rua da Consolação 3555, Jardim Paulista
(2137 4555/www.atlanticahotels.com.br).
Metrô Consolação. **Rates** R$285. **Rooms** 194.
Credit AmEx, DC, MC,V. Map p244 I8 ㉕
The tall building has a number of price ranges,
depending on the view you want – the higher you
go, the higher the price and the nicer the rooms and
the view. All the guest quarters are comfortable and
come with a kitchenette, which is thoroughly unnecessary, considering the amazing array of restaurants
on your doorstep (it's just a block away from Rua
Oscar Freire). The rooms are spacious with light
wood panelling, soft lighting and warm colours that
give a welcoming air of warmth.

Bar. Business centre. Disabled-adapted rooms.
Gym. No smoking rooms. Internet (free wireless,
high-speed). Parking (free). Pool (indoor).
Restaurants (2). Room service. TV: DVD.

★ Renaissance

Alameda Santos 2233, Jardim Paulista (3069
2233/www.marriott.com.br). Metrô Consolação.
Rates R$450-$500. **Rooms** 445. **Credit** AmEx,
DC, MC, V. **Map** p244 J7 ㉖
Part of the Marriott group, this 25-storey high-rise
hotel designed by star Paulista architect Ruy
Ohtake is popular with business travellers and
families. The exterior looks like a regular skyscraper, except for the wavy lines, which point to
Ohtake's lifelong homage to his teacher, Oscar
Niemeyer. The interior is stylishly minimalist,
with warm light colours and plenty of windows.
The rooms are huge, with enormous king-size
beds, fabulous down comforters and pleasant furniture, while the overall design of the suites is old-
world charm meets 21st-century cool. The location
can't be beat, as its one block from Avenida
Paulista and within walking distance to the rest of
the Jardins hot spots.
Bars (2). Business centre. Concierge. Gym.
Internet (free high-speed). Parking (R$25
standard rooms, free premium rooms). Pool
(outdoor). Restaurants (3). Room service. Spa.
TV: DVD.

★ Sofitel São Paulo

Rua Sena Madureira 1355, Ibirapuera
(3201 0800/www.sofitel.com). Metrô Santa Cruz
or Vila Mariana. **Rates** R$410-$525. **Rooms** 218.
Credit AmEX, DC, MC, V. **Map** p247 M13 ㉗
Beautiful Sofitel is attracting more clients than many
other hotels in its price range: for its edgy designs, fantastic breakfasts and gorgeous rooms. Steering away
from the soulless business hotel model, Sofitel prizes
itself on being French (as do all the Sofitels worldwide), and its walls are covered with tasteful works of
art. One of the three restaurants is dedicated to photographer Pierre Verger, and there's an 'art gallery' in
situ. Poorly located for anyone who wants to walk
anywhere, the hotel looks out over Ibirapuera Park,
which is a blessing in concrete São Paulo, but don't
forget to request a room at the front. Sofitel is an ideal
spot for company events and businessmen.
Bar. Business centre. Internet (R$35/day
wireless). Parking (R$27). Pool. Restaurants (3).

Moderate

Blair House

Alameda Franca 1645, Jardins (3083 5988/
www.blairhouse.com.br). Metrô Consolação.
Rates R$172-$224. **Rooms** 42. **Credit** DC, MC,
V. **Map** p244 I7 ㉓
Another high-rise in Jardins, Blair House is so simi-
lar to the apartment buildings in the area that you

CONSUME

Discover the city from your back pocket

Essential for your weekend break, 25 top cities available.

Emiliano. See p99.

could almost imagine being a Paulistano here. If you don't mind the impersonality of a clean serviced flat in light of good location, this might be for you. Blair House could really do with a revamp, however; the rooms are a little old with coloured bedspreads and wooden panels – but on the plus side, they have separate living rooms and, if you'd rather eat in, a kitchen. The rooftop pool is small and serves more for visual effect than swimming.

Internet. Parking (limited). Pool (indoor). TV.

Central Park Jardins

Alameda Ministro Rocha Azevedo 523, Jardins (3087 0100/www.cpark.com.br). Metrô Trianon-MASP. **Rooms** 64. **Credit** AmEx, DC, MC, V. **Map** p244 K8 ㉘

This hotel offers a great cost-benefit option: it's three blocks from the Trianon-MASP metrô and two blocks from Avenida Paulista. Ask for a top floor and enjoy the seemingly neverending skyline. If you can't see it from your room, just go to the restaurant, or even better, the pool. Both are located on the top floor. All the rooms have wooden floors and new furniture.

Bar. Business centre. Gym. Internet (free high-speed). No smoking rooms. Parking (free). Pool (indoor). Restaurant. Room service. TV.

★ Estanplaza Paulista

Alameda Jaú 497, Cerqueira César (3016 0000/ www.estanplaza.com.br). Metrô Trianon-MASP. **Rooms** 120. **Rates** R$129. **Credit** AmEx, DC, MC, V. **Map** p244 K9 ㉚

The decor in the restaurant has colonial and indigenous influences, while the rooms delight with their simplicity and cleanliness. For an unbeatable price and an ideal location this is a great option if you are in town for a short period. In comparison to other hotels in its category, Estanplaza Paulista is a pleasant place to stay, and breakfast is included in the rate. The staff are not very attentive, however.

Business centre. Gym. Internet (R$10 high-speed). No smoking floors. Parking (free). Pool (indoor). Restaurant. TV.

★ Le Premier Othon Flat

Rua Guarará 511, Jardins (3884 0514/ www.hoteis-othon.com.br). Metrô Trianon-MASP. **Rates** R$180-$200. **Rooms** 230. **Credit** AmEx, DC, MC, V. **Map** p244 K10 ㉛

This hotel is a great deal for anyone looking to stay in Jardins on a budget. Situated in the centre of Jardins, with a small fountain outside, it has a pleasant lobby and a large dining room with a grand piano. The breakfast features typical Brazilian cheeses, juices, breads and a generous portion of fruit – papaya, mango, bananas and anything else that is in season. The rooms are clean and have a pleasant view of the neighbourhood. Non-smoking rooms should be requested if you want to be sure of a room without a stale smell. All rooms feature a sofa and a writing desk. This hotel is almost always offered on discount websites for roughly one-third less than the advertised rates.

Bar. Business centre. Internet (R$10/hr). Gym. Pool (indoor). No smoking rooms. Parking (free). Restaurant. TV.

Massis Five Stars

Rua Luis Coelho 80, Consolação (3141 4400/ www.massisfivestars.com.br). Metrô Consolação. **Rates** R$215. **Rooms** 80. **Credit** AmEx, DC, MC, V. **Map** p244 K7 ㉜

On a quiet road parallel to Avenida Paulista and behind Shopping Centre 3, this modern skyscraper towers above many around it. The chic, well-designed

THE BEST HOTEL POOLS

For superb views
Massis Five Stars. *See p103.*

For fancy architectural design
Fasano. *See p99.*

For swimming laps and tanning
Grand Hyatt. *See p92.*

CONSUME

rooms come with an American-style kitchen, two flat-screen televisions and a balcony. Most have a separate bedroom and living room, giving a sense of space and comfort. If you don't suffer from vertigo, the views from the top are fantastic, especially in the top-floor pool area, which has a retractable roof.
Bar. Business centre. Gym. Internet (R$5.25 high-speed, wireless). No smoking floors. Parking (free). Pool (indoor). Restaurant. Room service. TV.

Mercure São Paulo Jardins

Alameda Itu 1151, Cerqueira Cesar (3089 7555/ www.mercure.com.br). Metrô Consolação. **Rates** R$248-$298. **Rooms** 126. **Credit** AmEx, DC, MC, V. **Map** p244 J8 **33**
The high rise's glassed-in exterior transforms the otherwise forgettable decor into what you would expect from a top-range chain hotel, while the views from the higher floors are spectacular. Ideally located in the Jardins and not far from Avenida Paulista, this is a great hotel for the business traveller. The rooms are clean with lots of light, while the furniture and furnishings come mostly in greys and maroons. The pool, however, is small and leaves a lot to be desired.
Business centre. Disabled-adapted room (1). Gym. Internet (free high-speed, wireless). No smoking floors. Parking (R$11). Pool (indoor). Restaurant. Room service. TV.

★ Pousada Dona Zilah

Alameda Franca 1621, Jardins (3062 1444/www.zilah.com). Metrô Consolação.

Rates R$168-$180. **Rooms** 15. **Credit** AmEx, DC, MC, V. **Map** p244 I7 **34**
This charming guesthouse just metres down from Blair house is worthy of your investment. Rooms are scattered throughout the house all the way to the back, and many look out onto a cute internal quad. The feeling it creates is of a homely bed and breakfast. Rooms towards the front are noisier, but all are small, clean and well cared for. The highlight is the restaurant, which also attracts locals. Staff are friendly and solicitous, and breakfast is included.
Bar. Internet (free wireless; R$6/hr shared terminal). No smoking rooms. Restaurant. TV.

Regent Park Hotel

Rua Oscar Freire 533, Jardins (3065 5555/ www.regent.com.br). **Rates** R$272-$304. **Rooms** 70. **Credit** AmEx, DC, MC, V. **Map** p244 I8 **35**
If location is everything, it can't get much better than the Regent Park Hotel. Situated on the most stylish street in São Paulo's most à la mode neighbourhood, this apartment-hotel is just a stone's throw from some of the city's best restaurants and designer stores. All suites and apartments are equipped with a kitchen, while the rooftop solarium has a sauna.
Bar. Business centre. Concierge. Gym. Internet (free high-speed). Parking (free). Pool (outdoor). Restaurant. Room service. TV.

Transamerica Flat Opera Five Stars

Alameda Lorena 1748, Jardim Paulista (3062 2666/www.transamericaflats.com.br).

Grand Hyatt. *See p92.*

Metrô Consolação. **Rates** R$270. **Rooms** 55. **Credit** AmEx, DC, MC, V. **Map** p244 I8 ⬤
Located in the heart of Jardins, Transamerica Opera is surrounded by the best – and most expensive – restaurants in town as well as the nicest couture stores at Rua Oscar Freire and Rua Alameda Lorena. The furniture appears a bit worn, but the rooms have a microwave, and it's an overall good option for those who want to be in Jardins without blowing the entire holiday budget on a hotel.
Bar. Business centre. Concierge. Gym. Internet (free wireless). No smoking rooms. Parking (free). Pool (indoor). Restaurant. Room service. TV

Budget

Paulista Garden Hotel
Alameda Lorena 21, Cerqueira César (3885 8498/www.paulistagardenhotel.com.br). Metrô Brigadeiro. **Rates** R$110. **Rooms** 27.
Credit MC, V. **Map** p244 K10 ⬤
Close to Ibirapuera Park, this very simple hotel has limited service. The rooms have wood furniture and colourful bedspreads, while the vintage bathrooms still use electric showers. From this spot, on the corner of Avenida Brigadeiro Luis Antonio, you can walk 1km uphill to Avenida Paulista.
Gym. Internet (free wireless). Parking (free). TV.

Pousada Hostel São Paulo
Avenida Rebouças 1015 (2841 1115/ www.pousadaehostelsaopaulo.com.br) Metrô Consolação. **Rates** R$83; R$35-68 for dorm bed.
Rooms 15. **No credit cards. Map** p244 I8 ⬤
This purple house on one of the city's most important thoroughfares is in a noisy spot, but it's well located if you want to explore the Jardins neighbourhood and Avenida Paulista on foot. It's somewhat lacking in charm, so if you are in town for a night, this will satisfy your needs but not your yearning for cosiness away from home. The rooms are small and basic, and there are no on-site amenities to invite you to spend time there other than to sleep.
Internet (free high-speed, wireless). Parking.

★ Residenza Mantovani
Rua Desembargador Eliseu Guilherme 269, Paraíso (3889 8624/www.residenzamantovani. com.br). Metrô Paraíso. **Rates** R$105. **Rooms** 23. **No credit cards. Map** p245 M10 ⬤
This quintessential family-run guesthouse is typically Brazilian and has been going for decades. It's popular with Brazilian travellers who come from other parts of the country to spend time in São Paulo and who have been staying here for years, so foreigners are a minority. The highlight is the free Wi-Fi, so freelance (travel) writers can be found here periodically. Rooms 38 and 39 open onto a mini terrace which adds oomph to those otherwise small and basic rooms. Although it's not hugely cosmopolitan, you should feel safe

and welcome here, plus it's strategically located – you guessed it – by Avenida Paulista.
Internet (free wireless). TV.

SOUTH OF THE CENTRE

★ Albergue Praça da Árvore
Rua Pajeú 266, Chácara Inglesa (5071 5148/ www.spalbergue.com.br). Metrô Praça da Árvore.
Rates R$88; R$28-$42 dorm bed. **Rooms** 9.
Credit MC. **Map** p247 O15 ⬤
This huge house, like many in this residential region, was completely adapted to receive backpackers. The southern neighbourhood of Chacara Inglesa is not a district that receives many tourists, but it's a nice place to understand how the city really works. The average traveller will find the family environment very pleasant. The big kitchen is perfect for being used by many guests at once. The hostel is two blocks away from the metrô, but the area is a little steeply.
Internet (R$4/hr high-speed; R$5/day wireless).

VILA MADALENA
Budget

★ Casa Club Hostel
Rua Mourato Coelho 973, Vila Madalena (3798 0051/www.casaclub.com.br). Metrô Vila Madalena/bus 701A-10. **Rates** R$35-$40.
Rooms 4. **Credit cards** AmEx, DC, MC, V.
Map p249 E8 ⬤
One of its kind in the city, Casa Club is ideal for travellers between the ages of 18 and 30 who are happy to share communal rooms (mixed gender and one female room). Shared rooms can also be converted into private rooms for R$120. It's perfect for meeting young travellers and located in walking distance from bars, restaurants and shops. All rooms have bunks, and each guest has a lockable cupboard for valuables. Casa Club started as a bar which still functions today with frequent lock-ins for guests, who also pay no cover charge. This is a good choice if you are looking for an interesting place to stay.
Bar. Internet (free wireless, shared terminal). Restaurant.

> **INSIDE TRACK**
> **SMOKE-FREE SAO PAULO**
>
> A smoking ban is scheduled to take effect in São Paulo from August 2009. While many hotels will maintain smoking floors, others like the Fasano (*see p99*) are planning to become completely smoke-free. In summer 2009, most hotels were still hammering out the details of their policies on the matter.

CONSUME

Restaurants

Creativity transforms peasant food into a gastronomical delicacy.

The São Paulo culinary scene has never had it so good. Paulistano chefs are creating hitherto unknown flavours and tastes by using ingredients from the Amazon as well as the rest of the country. Many of the city's best kitchens are now championing dishes that once were the mainstay of the Brazilian poor but now, served up in designer spaces, they're topping the city's restaurant price lists. Brazil's strength – its astounding variety of fruit and vegetables, as well its history of immigration and migration, has made it possible to borrow from outside cuisines but also to come up with a style of cooking and indeed eating that's entirely Brazilian. And as aficionados of Brazilian cooking wait to export this new wave of gastronomy, one thing's for sure: whether it's all-you-can-eat meat fests or snacking on *salgados* on the street, Brazilians love their food – you can expect a lot more converts around the world – and soon.

CONSUME

THE LOCAL SCENE

For the crème de la crème of Paulistano society, the place to eat is **D.O.M.**, chef Alex Atala's temple to Brazilian gastronomy. The name (Deo optimo maximo) is Latin for 'God is best and greatest', but in Attala's version, the Latin word for 'home' replaces God in the acronym.

Eating out on a daily basis is a regular activity for Paulistanos. It's no surprise, then, that **Dalva e Dito** (*see p120*), a joint venture of Atala and chef Alain Poletto, was awaited by the foodie establishment like the culinary second coming. Expectations fizzled after the early 2009 opening, but its owners are still hoping that Dalva e Dito will conquer.

Many restaurants present the best of traditional regional foods, from the dried meats of the north-east (*carne seca* and *carne sol*, for instance) to Bahian *moqueca* stew and Mineiran *tutú* (mashed beans). Many local chefs have studied in Asia, Europe and the US, but their experience with international haute cuisine tends to be just a means of enlightening the food from their own back yard.

> ❶ Blue numbers given in this chapter correspond to the location of each restaurant on the street maps.
> See pp242-249.

Working alongside the celeb chefs in São Paulo, albeit in considerably less snazzy kitchens, numerous cooks bring Brazilian home-cooking to the masses on a daily basis. There are thousands of cheap eateries and *lanchonetes* in São Paulo that can be just as good as the more expensive options in offering the best of Brazilian dining, not to mention more authentic. Their affordability is also an asset; note that we've marked the best-value restaurants in this section with the symbol **R$**.

BROOKLIN

Govinda

Rua Princesa Isabel 379, Brooklin (5092 4816/ www.govindarestaurante.com.br). Bus 669A-10. **Open** noon-3pm, 7pm-midnight Mon-Fri; noon-4.30pm, 7pm-midnight Sat; noon-4.30pm Sun. **Main course** R$25-$97. **Credit** AmEx, MC, V. **Indian**
It's Krishna by way of Lisboa at this classic dining spot, situated snugly in the middle of a residential area. The 30-year-old Govinda, recently energized by a makeover, represents an interesting mixture of Luso-Brazilian architecture and Indian decor. The ceiling is supported by open wooden beams (in a former 19th-century life, the house was a grease-processing factory), while sumptuous sub-continent furniture occupies the various rooms. Reflecting the novelty of Indian food in Brazil

Prêt no MAM. See p116.

(Govinda was the first such restaurant in the city), a shop in the entrance sells gifts and clothing from the sub-continent. The couvert is a great start for the meal; taste eight different sauces with the house bread. You can't miss with classic Indian dishes either. The lamb or chicken curries as well as the tandoori specials will result in gastronomic bliss. **Other location** Ganesh, Morumbi Shopping, Avenida Roque Petroni Jr. 1089, piso Lazer, Morumbi (5181 4748).

Kinoshita
Rua Jacques Félix 405, Vila Nova Conceição (3849 6940/www.restaurantekinoshita.com.br). Bus 6418-10. **Open** noon-3pm, 7pm-midnight Mon-Sat. **Main course** R$49-$90. **Tasting menu** R$230. **Credit** AmEx, DC, MC. **Map** p246 I13 ❶ **Japanese**
Improvisation is the key at this Japanese sensation. Kinoshita practises a concept called Kappo cuisine: immaculately presented, unique creations prepared spontaneously by master sushi chef Tsuyoshi Murakami and his team. After a hearty welcome, the (incredible) maître directs you to menu gems such as mini Nameko mushrooms caramelized in a lemon and Shoyu conserve, delicately served in a hollowed lime. Culinary innovations such as scallops and cod roe served in a lime and orange juice, downed in a martini glass, are joys to sample – with the accompanying steep price, of course.

Recanto Vegetariano
Rua Flórida 1442, Brooklin (5506 8944/ www.recantovegetariano.com.br). Bus 7245-10. **Open** 11.30am-3pm Mon-Fri; noon-3.30pm Sun. **Main course** R$19. **No credit cards**.
Vegetarian
Vegetarianism isn't exactly the norm in a country seemingly obsessed with meat and organic garden-ing hasn't yet swept through Brazil, but the owners of this all-inclusive vegetarian buffet have staked their reputation on it. Overshadowed by skyscrapers along Avenida Berrini, this pleasant corner eaterie serves the best organic food in town, and you will be hard-pressed to find another restaurant that grows all its own ingredients. Recanto Vegetariano exemplifies the energy of natural food lovers the world over: frustrated by the lack of fresh ingredients, these enterprising locals decided not only to open their own restaurant but to supply it with the biggest organic vegetables ever to be seen. The owners even provide photo proof of their agricultural prowess. Recanto Vegetariano is a healthy eating experience that far surpasses a garden-variety meal.

Tiger
Rua Jacques Félix 694, Vila Nova Conceição (3045 2200/www.tigerrestaurante.com.br). Bus 6418-10. **Open** noon-3.30pm, 7-11.30pm Tue-Fri; noon-midnight Sat, Sun. **Main course** R$23-R$60. **Tasting menu** R$69. **Credit** AmEx, DC, MC, V.
Thai-Japanese
The stripes on this tiger belong to two distinct cultures and three different chefs: one prepares Thai dishes, while two experts in hot and cold Japanese cuisine complete the culinary triumvirate. The result? A best-of-both-worlds dining experience. Where else is it possible to taste a Thai noodle with a selection of sushi on the side? The à la carte menu offers traditional dishes like pad thai for R$39 as well as a variety of sushi, maki and tempura. The restaurant recently started serving alcohol – a change of policy for the venue. The decor too is a hit with wooden furniture and sparkling white walls reflecting the place's adherence to simplicity as well as good taste.

CONSUME

Brasil a Gosto. *See p119.*

CONSOLACAO & HIGIENOPOLIS

Arabia Café
Praça Vilaboim 73, Higienópolis (3476 2201/ www.arabia.com.br). Bus 805L-10. **Open** 11am-midnight Mon-Thu, Sun; 11am-1am Fri, Sat. **Main course** R$15-$45. **Credit** AmEx, DC, MC, V. **Map** p242 K5 ❷ **Middle Eastern**
An offshoot of the expensive and highly acclaimed Arabia restaurant in Jardins, the Arabia Café is a small and stylish eaterie in the middle of the Higienópolis Dining Triangle. The café is light and airy, and a very popular spot thanks to its reasonable lunch menu. Try the meat shawarma or the excellent falafel. The salad Chanclich is quite small but very appetizing, with spicy Arabian cheese, tomato, onion and cilantro. A must is the delicious tamarind juice, rarely served in restaurants and found more often in *lanchonettes* in the centre where it is made from pulp. For R$28.90 you can make your own lunch; it includes a main course and two accompanying dishes. In between meals, Arabia is also a great spot to relax in, with Wi-Fi and a comfortable coffee- drinking area at the front. *Photo p120.*
Other locations Arábia, Rua Haddock Lobo 1397, Jardim Paulista (3061 2203/www.arabia. com.br); Shopping Iguatemi food court.

★ R$ Athenas
Rua Augusta 1449, Consolação (3262 1945). Metrô Consolação. **Open** 11.30am-3.30pm Mon-Fri. **Main course** R$15-$20. **Credit** DC, MC, V. **Map** p244 K7 ❸ **Traditional Brazilian**
For the average Brazilian, there's nothing better than sitting down to a meal, usually lunch, at a restaurant that serves all the wide-ranging delicacies of the country's cuisine. Athenas is such a place. While the restaurant is split into two distinct areas, with an a la carte place next door, the excellent buffet, with its varied selection of salads,

grilled meats and stews, all cooked well and with care, is the best option here. Choose what you want to eat and pay for the weight of your plate. A healthy and filling meal will normally set you back around R$18.

Avenida Angélica Grill
Avenida Angélica 430, Santa Cecilia (3664 0070 /www.angelicagrill.com). Metrô Marechal Deodoro, bus 805L-10, 874T-10, 7701-10. **Open** 11.30am-midnight Mon-Sat; 11.30am-11pm Sun. **Set meal** R$25 Mon-Fri; R$35 Sat, Sun. **Credit** AmEx, DC, MC, V. **Map** p242 K3 **Barbecue** ❹
Make sure you are feeling carnivorous when you visit this large *rodízio* – it's all-you-can-eat meat, fresh off the grill. Waiters here circle the brightly lit dining room with any of 24 types of *carne* (meat) and fill your plate until you surrender. Supplement your meal with side dishes from the extensive salad bar (sushi, bread, veggies and more), but be careful not to overload here, or you will not be able to take full advantage of the meat bonanza. *Rodizio* plate management is a practiced art. If you are vying for the title of World's Biggest Glutton, servers will tempt your sweet tooth with a rolling dessert cart or cook up delicious banana flambé while you watch. Desserts and beverages are charged separately.

Benjamin Abrahão
Rua Maranhão 220, Higienópolis (3258 1855/ www.benjaminabrahao.com.br). Metrô Santa Cecilia. Bus 669A-10, 805L-10, 874T-10. **Open** 6am-8.30pm daily. **Main course** R$2-$30. **Credit** AmEx, DC, MC, V. **Map** p242 K5 ❺ **Bakery**
Paulistanos adore their *padarias*, and by many accounts, Benjamin Abrahão is the best bakery in the city (even visited by Brazil's former president Fernando Henrique Cardoso). French-born baker Benjamin Abrahão started the business in 1987, and his family maintains his legacy today, creating exceptional pastries, sandwiches and savoury snacks. Stop

The desserts deserve equal praise, especially the icy profiteroles and the signature *pan perdu* – a heavenly slice of caramelized French toast served with a dollop of pear compote bathed in double cream.

by for a breakfast of coffee, juice and mini-*pães de queijo* (cheese breads), or surprise that special someone with a selection of succulent chocolate truffles.

★ Carlota

Rua Sergipe 753, Higienópolis (3661 8670/ www.carlota.com.br). Bus 805L-10, 874T-10, 877T-10. **Open** 7pm-midnight Mon; noon-4pm, 7pm-midnight Tue-Thu; noon-4pm, 7pm-1am Fri; 7pm-1am Sat; noon-6pm Sun. **Main course** R$70-$120. **Credit** AmEx, DC, MC, V. **Map** p242 K5 ❻ **Eclectic**

The chef Carla Pernambuco (of gaucho origin, from the south of Brazil) has an enviable creative spirit. In her multicultural kitchen, international cuisine is fused with typical Brazilian gastronomy and delivers surprising results. The amazing sole filet with golden goat's cheese sauce, fresh palm hearts and mushroom fettuccine is one example of why Carlota has legions of foodie fans. The recreation of the classic Brazilian dessert known as Romeo and Juliet elevates a simple dessert to an exquisite guava soufflé in a *queijo catupiry* (Brazilian cream cheese) sauce.

ICI Bistro

Rua Para 36, Higienópolis (3257 4064/ www.icibistro.com.br). Metrô Consolação. **Open** noon-3pm, 7pm-midnight Mon-Sat; 12.30-5pm Sun. **Main course** R$38-$65. **Credit** AmEx, DC, MC, V. **Map** p242 K6 ❼ **French**

The Brazilian remake of the popular American TV show *Desperate Housewives (Donas de Casa Desesperadas)*, should probably feature some scenes at this bistro, frequented as it is by the spiritual and physical doubles of the Wisteria Lane girls. This chic yet classically French restaurant has won considerable acclaim since its 2002 opening. The appetiser list includes the *duo de lula panée*, crisp and wonderfully spicy squid, although the modest portion is an appetite-whetting trick (long in use by the purveyors of haute-French cuisine). The sesame seed-encrusted tuna steak is supremely tender and well flavoured.

Mestiço

Rua Fernando de Albuquerque 277, Consolação (3256 3165/www.mestico.com.br). Metrô Consolação. **Open** 11.45am-midnight Mon, Sun; 11.45am-1am Tue-Thu; 11.45am-2am Fri, Sat. **Main course** R$25-$58. **Credit** AmEx, DC, MC, V. **Map** p242 K6 ❽ **International**

From musicians like Caetano Veloso and Gilberto Gil to Jorge Amado, Brazil's beloved author, the state of Bahia has produced some of the country's greatest talents. And some of São Paulo's best chefs, like Ina de Abreu, also hail from the north-east. De Abreu founded this restaurant 11 years ago after travelling the world and studying Thai cooking in order to combine it with her native Bahian cuisine. With as eclectic a menu as any in São Paulo, Mestiço isn't limited to Asian and Brazilian fare. The menu also offers American and Italian specialties like hamburgers and pastas. The dining room reflects the philosophy of the food, and the sunny interior is accented with a painted wall of characters straight out of a Benetton ad. Reservations strongly suggested.

R$ Monarca

Rua Augusta 1599, Consolação (3289 2899). Metrô Consolação. **Open** 7am-11pm Mon-Sun. **Main course** R$15-$30. **No credit cards.** **Map** p244 K7 ❾ **Brazilian**

Monarca is a royal among countless peasant *botecos*. Marble floors, sparkling mirrors and a visible display of exotic fruit enhance the atmosphere of this Consolação favourite. It's tucked into the corner of one of the busiest streets in São Paulo, and hearty meals and budget prices mean a constant bustle of the starving lunch masses. Daily specials are surprisingly varied and inventive: cannelloni, marinated fried chicken and beef stews served with rice and kidney beans are all superior to the usual *boteco* menu fare and prepared with loving care. The famous coffee and toasted buttered bread, called *pão na chapa*, complement the meal perfectly. It's a good idea to arrive early, but if it's too crowded, the *boteco* next door, BH Lanches (1533 Rua Augusta, Cerqueira César, 3283 3653), is also great value, though without the regal ambiance.

Sal Gastronomia

Rua Minas Gerais 350, Higienópolis (3151 3085/ www.salgastronomia.com.br). Bus 719P-10. **Open** noon-3pm Mon; noon-3pm, 8pm-midnight Tue-Fri; noon-6pm Sat. **Main course** R$35-$60. **Credit** AmEx, DC, MC, V. **Map** p244 J7 ❿ **Eclectic**

Sal is nestled in the courtyard of Galeria Vermelho (*see p176*), one of São Paulo's contemporary art galleries. It grew from a simple café to a hip fusion

CONSUME

Whatever your carbon footprint, we can reduce it

For over a decade we've been leading the way in carbon offsetting and carbon management.

In that time we've purchased carbon credits from over 200 projects spread across 6 continents. We work with over 300 major commercial clients and thousands of small and medium sized businesses, which rely upon our market-leading quality assurance programme, our experience and absolute commitment to deliver the right solution for each client.

Why not give us a call?

T: London (020) 7833 6000

A Moveable Feast

São Paulo's on-the-go street eats.

São Paulo's street fare should not be overlooked. In fact, if your stomach were Odysseus, the cheap, tasty, and sometimes even healthy snacking that abounds might be a tougher gastronomic siren to resist than some of the city's most desired evening dining spots. The go-go attitude of Paulistanos and the lack of spare time for an actual meal has made Brazilian finger food a way of life.

For just R$1 or R$2, you can eat buttery, salty sweetcorn fresh from the cob, or buy a cup of creamy, sweetcorn juice. Slices of pineapple, watermelon and other tropical fruit are found on many street corners. For drinks on the move, there is freshly squeezed orange juice, *agua de coco* (coconut water) still in the coconut and accessed by straw, and for those with a very sweet tooth, *caldo de cana* – pressed sugar cane juice which you can watch being grinded into your cup by a cross between a juice machine and wood shredder.

Brazilians love their *salgadinhos* (appetisers), and with good reason. Little plastic stools by the food stands allow you to sit briefly as you devour the famous *pastel* – a crispy, thin, deep-fried pastry with a variety of fillings, such as cheese,

chicken, palm hearts, minced meat or the Brazilian *catupiry* (soft cheese).

The *coxinha* may have the finest of all *salgadinhos*. Made from minced chicken and seasonings, and enclosed in a deep-fried, wheat batter, it is roughly shaped to resemble a chicken drumstick, or sometimes a tear drop. The *bolinho de bacalhau*, a delicious, deep-fried cod croquette, and the kibbeh *de carne*, based on the Lebanese favourite and made from ground beef, wheat, onions and herbs, are also near impossible to resist. Arab immigration has had a strong influence on Brazilian eating, and open or closed *esfihas*, a sort of mini-pizza made with soft dough, filled with meat, cheese and vegetables, are very popular too.

Pão de queijo (cheese bread) is a staple for breakfast, and many street vendors set up in the early morning selling it alongside homemade chunks of cake plus *café puro* (black coffee) or *café com leite* (coffee with milk) for the hungry morning work commuters.

Brazilians have a very sweet tooth, and you will find plenty of street vendors selling *cocada*, grated coconut cooked in syrup of white or brown sugar, and *brigadeiros*, a chocolate fudge made with condensed milk. Sickly but superb.

CONSUME

restaurant popular with artists, journalists and trendy Paulistanos. Outdoor tables are inviting on a sunny Saturday, while inside the sleek environment reflects the contemporary menu. The dishes are always doused with exotic spices or served with typical Brazilian sides. The highlights are the ceviche starter, the lamb with *jabuticaba* sauce (made from the tasty Brazilian berry) and the two-cheese purée. On a hot day, the tangerine sorbet hits the spot.

★ Sujinho

Rua da Consolação 2068, Consolação (3231 5207/www.sujinho.com.br). Metrô Consolação. **Open** 11.30am-4am daily. **Main course** R$25-$70. **No credit cards.** **Map** p242 K6 ⓫ **Traditional Brazilian**

Sujinho (literally 'the dirty little bar') is one of São Paulo's favourite serving sons – no frills, just good food and plenty of it. Most of the plates listed for one easily serve two, which is especially true of the *frango a milanesa* (chicken fried in breadcrumbs). Its simple fried goodness has been known to seduce even the most die-hard, discriminating foodies. Similar encomiums are reserved for the filet mignon *a parmesana* – steak smothered in tomatoes and melted cheese. With such delicious and abundant food, this place is a must for the budget-conscious.

Tappo Trattoria

Rua Consolação 2967, Consolação (3063 4864). Metrô Consolação. **Open** noon-3pm, 7.30pm-midnight Tue-Fri; 12.30-4pm, 7.30pm-midnight Sat; 12.30-5pm Sun **Main course** R$32-$59. **Credit** AmEx, DC, MC, V. **Map** p244 J7 ⓬ **Italian**

This claustrophobia-defying corridor of a restaurant, only ten tables long, serves fantastic Italian food. The layout is surprisingly romantic and cosy, and the cooking matches this superior ambience. The carpaccio of filet mignon is succulent, while the ricotta balls cooked in a rich tomato sauce are tasty without overloading the palate. Mains of lasagne bolognese and spaghetti *a la amatriciana* (bacon, tomato and onion) surprise, like the space itself, with a lightness that defies the typical idea of carb-heavy Italian cooking. The homemade pasta is the key to the dishes' light touch.

Vira Lata

Rua Minas Gerais 112, Higienópolis (3258 6093/www.restauranteviralata.com.br). Metrô Consolação. **Open** noon-4pm Tue, Wed; noon-4pm, 7pm-midnight Thur-Sat; noon-5pm Sun. **Main course** R$30-$70. **Credit** AmEx, DC, MC, V. **Map** p242 J6 ⓭ **International**

Situated in a beautiful olive-coloured house that dates from the turn of the century, this charming and unpretentious restaurant is a popular choice with Paulistanos. Soft, twinkling lights, artsy lampshades and warm tones contribute to the boutique-

like atmosphere. The prices are reasonable, while the menu's range is interesting. The kitchen uses local ingredients to make European-influenced dishes. The main courses include the fillet of St Peter fish in coconut- cream sauce, with rice and banana-flavoured *farofa* (manioc meal). The Sicilian lemon risotto topped with dry pork is another interesting option.

ITAIM BIBI, MOEMA & VILA OLÍMPIA

R$ Beth Cozinha de Estar

Rua Pedroso Alvarenga 1061, Itaim Bibi (3073 0354). Bus 6401-10. **Open** noon-3.30pm Mon-Fri; noon-4.30pm Sat. **Main course** R$35-$41. **Credit** AmEx, DC, MC, V. **Map** p249 G12 ⓮ **Brazilian**

Beth is in her fifties and always behind the self-service counter helping you decide on the best home-cooked option. Catering to suits who work in Itaim Bibi, this buffet joint offers a selection of salads and dressings, fish, chicken and beef creations, and comforting sides such as spinach or corn in white sauce, kale, or grilled vegetables and bananas. Wednesdays and Saturdays feature the traditional *feijoada*, and a light version with the pork and black beans served separately. If you have room for dessert, go for the flan or crème caramel.

R$ Cachoeira Tropical

Rua João Cachoeira 275, Itaim Bibi (3167 5211/www.cachoeiratropical.com.br). Bus 6401-10. **Open** 11am-3pm Mon-Fri; 11.30am-4pm Sat, Sun **Main course** R$16-$19. **Credit** AmEx, DC MC, V. **Map** p249 G12 ⓯ **Vegetarian**

Nostalgic for your college dining experience? This restaurant offers great vegetarian food at a set price in a cafeteria environment. Sample all you want for less than R$20, or pick the three-course option. Don't plan to eat, or move, for a while afterwards. **Other location** Avenida São Gabriel 300 (3884 8868). This branch also has meat dishes.

Due Cuochi Cucina

Rua Manoel Guedes 93, Itaim Bibi (3078 8092/www.duecuochi.com.br). Bus 609F-10. **Open** noon-3pm, 7.30pm-midnight Mon-Thur; noon-3pm, 7.30pm-1am Fri; noon-4pm, 7.30pm-1am Sat; noon-5pm Sun. **Main course** R$33-$68. **Set lunch** R$44. **Credit** AmEx, DC, MC, V. **Map** p249 G12 ⓰ **Italian**

Positively buzzing with energy, this Itaim Bibi mainstay is arguably the finest Italian restaurant in town. The restaurant's name refers to the two chefs who first opened this institution, Ida Maria Frank and Paulo Barros. The dining area is lined with dozens of windows, and is popular with both families and business people. The most affordable way to try this eaterie is to come for the delicious prix fixe lunch Monday to Friday, which, at R$44, is one of the best values in town; this includes a light snack, an appe-

Prêt no MAM. *See p116.*

tiser, a main course and a dessert. If you're choosing from the a la carte menu, try the tagliolini ao sugo with shrimp – all the pastas are home-made. While the restaurant highly recommends its beefsteak florentine, the meat can be a bit chewy. The wine selection is extensive and is a good mix of Argentine, Chilean and Italian wines. Lunch reservations are not accepted, so come early, around 12.30 at the latest, to get a seat. *Photo p124.*

Other location Shopping Cidade Jardim, Avenida Magalhaes de Castro 12,000, 3rd floor (3758 2731/www.duecuochi.com.br).

▶ *Also in the running for best Italian food in town is the fancy Restaurante Fasano (Rua Vittorio Fasano 88, Jardins, 3062 4000).*

★ E.A.T.

Rua Pedroso Alvarenga 1026, Itaim Bibi (3017 3492/www.eatcasualfood.com.br). Bus 609F-10. **Open** noon-3pm, 7pm-1am Mon-Fri; 1pm-1am Sat. **Main course** R$18-$40. **Credit** AmEx, DC, MC, V. **Map** p249 G12 ⑰ **Mediterranean**

A relative newcomer on the scene, having opened its doors in 2008, E.A.T. is a small, busy place full of garrulous businessmen for lunch and smart-set couples for dinner. Its recipe for success is two parts classic Mediterranean with a generous dash of the contemporary: classic mousakka and couscous dishes can be found, as well as more experimental plates including empanadas in a sauce of the Amazonian jabuticaba fruit. The menu of chef Fernando Corsi Eiger (who grew up in the US) is equally divided between salads, sandwiches, signature plates, and core grilled entrées accompanied by a wide sides list. The colour scheme is black, white and grey, but the mood is bright. Young waiters in 'Just do E.A.T.' t-shirts circulate and, due to its fresh and delicately designed dishes, it's recently been

out-performing its bigger and more established competitors also located in the heart of Itaim Bibi. Service can be a little slow, especially during busy hours. Great as most of the menu is, unfortunately dessert tends to be nothing special.

KAÁ

Avenida Pres. Juscelino Kubitschek 279, Vila Olímpia (3045 0043/www.kaarestaurante.com.br). Bus 677A-10. **Open** noon-3pm, 7pm-midnight Mon-Fri; noon-5pm, 7pm-1am Sat; noon-5.30pm Sun. **Main course** R$45-$70. **Credit** AmEx, DC, MC, V. **French-Italian**

The newest French-Italian addition to the scene from celebrated chef Pascal Valero is another of São Paulo's exquisite Amazonian retreats, designed by architect Arthur Casas. The outside seating (with a retractable roof) is overshadowed by a monumental wall covered by 7,000 tropical plants. (Kaá means forest in the native language of Tupi.) Valero, who came to Brazil in 2002 from France, has already headed two of the city's finest establishments: Le Coq Hardy and the Eau restaurant at the Grand Hyatt Hotel. His signature dish is *peixe do momento* (fish of the moment), with mushrooms and truffle oil. For dessert, the chocolate fondue with coconut cream and bananas is a must. To get the full experience of rainforest elegance, a table outside must be reserved in advance. Be warned that the service still doesn't live up to the standard set by the food.

PJ Clarke's

Rua Dr. Mário Ferraz 568, Itaim Bibi (3078 2965/www.pjclarkes.com.br). Bus 702P-42, 7040-10. **Open** noon-midnight Mon-Thur, Sun; noon-1am Fri, Sat. **Main course** R$27-$65. **Credit** AmEx, DC, MC, V. **American**

www.treesforcities.org

Trees for Cities
Charity registration number 1032154

Travelling creates so
many lasting memories.

Make your trip mean
something for years to
come - not just for you
but for the environment
and for people living in
deprived urban areas.

Anyone can offset their
flights, but when you
plant trees with Trees for
Cities, you'll help create
a green space for an
urban community that
really needs it.

Leave
Your
Mark

Create a green future for cities.

Berry Controversial

From internet spam to juice bar chic, the 'cure-all' açai seeds suspicion.

You no longer need a magic pill: one diminutive purple berry from the Amazon can cure all your ills. Once limited to the Brazilian market (the berry perishes rapidly, an impediment to exporting it), **açai** has left the rainforest and become a world celebrity. The little berry that could has joined the ranks of the web's most notorious junk emails and chills in the refrigerated sections of high-end supermarkets; designer juice bars can't get enough of it (though outside Brazil, it's often a pre-mixed version of the real stuff).

Loaded with biological buzz – antioxidants and essential amino acids – açai is nature-made for an age in which medical and food marketing are increasingly interlaced. In the past five years, product wizards have utilised açai for products that go beyond standard food and drink: detox agents, anti-wrinkle creams, diet remedies – even for life-extension products. Is there nothing this rainforest berry can't do? The age of exploration may be over, but we are still searching for fountains of youth in legendary locations.

Steering clear of controversy about its miracle-making ability is also an issue. One thing that açai certainly can do is make people a lot of money. While a scant number of studies have stopped short of verifying medical claims, entrepreneurs have found personal El Dorados in açai regardless.

In the US, sales of more than 50 açai-related products surpassed $100 million in 2008. There is now a 60-proof liqueur, VeeV, made with açai so you can get sloshed in a pseudo-healthy manner. US-based açai juggernaut Sambazon has brought açai marketing to its berry zenith, with 20 products that range from energy drinks and slushy juices to supplements. Its açai empire even features the bandwagon message of sustainable rainforest production: becoming immortal by eating a berry also helps support indigenous farming.

The most unfortunate part of the açai saga is not that it has so far failed to conquer fat or wrinkles. What has been neglected amid the public furore for and against açai is its most magical, and also most fundamental, property. Foodies of the world decry the lengths to which we have taken 'food' out of the eating equation, turning our bodies into anti-epicurean vessels nourished by a perfect algorithm of ingestible chemicals. Açai (with a hefty calorie total in a typical helping) is to be savoured for a far simpler reason than dreams of tea at the Ritz on the occasion of your 150th birthday.

Everywhere you wander in São Paulo, you'll find a *lanchonete* prominently displaying a poster of açai. The poster won't claim that a *tigela* (bowl) piled high with icy açai will make anabolic steroids seem second-fiddle in the potency department, or that you will be able to defeat an army of would-be pickpockets with one açai-infused fist. Brazilians have been spooning this berry for many years (most often as a breakfast, blended with banana or strawberry, and with granola sprinkled atop the purple summit) for the right reason, and the only verifiable one too: the riches of the Amazon aren't to be discovered in laboratory analysis, but on your palate, where açai simply tastes so good.

CONSUME

Temakeria e Cia. *See p122.*

Longing for the Big Apple? You can track down a karaoke bar in Liberdade and butcher a few stanzas of 'New York, New York', or hit this São Paulo clone of the famous Manhattan establishment once frequented by Frank Sinatra. The NYC original created the 'Cadillac' burger and was not only a favourite of the Chairman of the Board but also of Marilyn Monroe. PJ Clarke's attempts to recreate (quite successfully) the post-war glory years's sanctum of American authenticity with tables draped in red-checked cloth; the old-style diner even had its chandeliers shipped over from New York. The overall ambience is fitting for the home fries and the delicate onion rings. For dessert, the strawberry and raspberry cheesecake is exceptional, and short of flying 11 hours to Juniors in Brooklyn, you won't find anything quite like it.

Prêt no MAM

Parque Ibirapuera, MAM s/n, Ibirapuera (5574 1250/www.mam.org.br). Bus 5164-10, 5175-10, 5178-10, 5194-10. **Open** *Buffet* noon-4pm Mon-Fri; 12.30-5pm Sat, Sun. *Café* 10am-6pm daily. **Set menu** R$35-$40. **Credit** DC, MC, V. **Map** p244 K12 ⑬ **Buffet**
Hobnob with designers, artists, or just regular old fashionistas dressed to kill at this stunning architectural gem, offering a fantastic lunch buffet inside the Museu de Arte Moderna in Parque Ibirapuera. The bright and gorgeous modern dining room is half-moon shaped, with fantastic views of the sculpture garden designed by Roberto Burle Marx. The dishes might range from ocean-fresh salmon to mouth watering meatloaf (the restaurant boasts that its menu features daily picks from 1,600 international recipes). This is your best bet for quality food if you are spending the entire day at either São Paulo Fashion Week, the Art Biennale or at the myriad other cultural activities that take place in the park. *Photos p107 and p113.*

Speranza

Avenida Sabiá 786, Moema (5051 1229/ www.pizzaria.com.br). Bus 2290-10, 5300-10. **Open** noon-3.30pm, 6pm-1am Mon-Fri; noon-3.30pm, 6pm-2am Sat; noon-midnight Sun. **Main course** R$35-$60. **Credit** DC, MC, V. **Map** p246 J15 ⑲ **Pizza**
The large village hall, with shelves stacked with cans of Italian tomatoes and walls lined with olive oils, makes for a wonderfully rustic setting. This Italian classic, which harks back to the European working-class immigrant roots of the city, is actually the newest branch of a São Paulo institution. The good news is that while the Moema location is huge, it sacrifices none of the charm that makes the original (in Bixiga) such a family favourite. The waiters itch to tell you about the entrées, but it may take everything they've got to entice you away from the flawless R$43 pizza margarita. They are also, somewhat dangerously, always on hand to top up your draught beer.
Other location Rua 13 de Maio 1004, Bixiga (3288 8502).

Tantra

Rua Chilon 364, Vila Olímpia (3846 7112/ www.tantrarestaurante.com.br). Bus 847P-42. **Open** noon-3pm, 6pm-midnight Mon-Fri; 1-6pm, 7pm-2am Sat; 1-5pm Sun. **Main course** R$35-$57. **Credit** AmEx, DC, MC, V.
Pan-Asian
Although the nightly entertainment here can't be beaten – a belly dancer with an albino snake and a sword – we recommend coming here for lunch. This large warehouse, isolated in the heart of Vila Olímpia, has a fantastic Mongolian grill (R$56); pick your ingredients wisely and hope that your choices mix well. If you prefer a safer choice, the limited menu offers a selection of Asian and Pacific inspired dishes – a pricier option.

Yucatán

Avenida Pres. Juscelino Kubitschek 393,
Itaim Bibi (3846 3505/www.yucatan.com.br).
Bus 677A-10. **Open** noon-3pm, 6pm-midnight
Tue-Thur; noon-3pm, 6pm-2am Fri; noon-2am
Sat; noon-midnight Sun. **Main course**
R$26-$29. **Credit** AmEx, DC, MC, V.
Mexican

Mexican food, or in this case Tex-Mex, may seem out of place this far south in the Americas, but if comfort Mexican food strikes you as a welcome respite from the manic energy of South America's land-locked megalopolis, this traditional restaurant is the place to come. It serves a complete all-you-can-eat lunchtime meal for a great set price of R$26-R$29 and what you expect is what you get: the guacamole, salsa and sour cream are always on the table, and tacos, burritos and quesadillas are served with chicken, meat or vegetables. Order the chilli first, so you can use it as an extra sauce with your meal; otherwise it tends to be brought out to your table last. Informal wooden folding tables and chairs dominate the interior. Drinks are inventive, but the creative flair raises their price as well.

▶ *You can also try Viva México (Rua Fradique Coutinho 1122/1124, Vila Madalena, 3032 0901).*

JARDINS

Adega Santiago

Rua Sampaio Vidal 1072, Jardim Paulistano
(3081 5211/www.adegasantiago.com.br).
Bus 6401-10. **Open** noon-3pm, 6-11pm
Mon; noon-3pm, 6pm-midnight Tue-Fri;
12.30pm-midnight Sat; 12.30pm-11pm Sun.
Main course R$25-$116. **Credit** AmEx, DC,
MC, V. **Map** p249 E10 ⑳ **Iberian**

A cosy tavern with dishes inspired by Iberian cuisine, Adega (as it's referred to by habitués) is one of São Paulo's most popular restaurants. Good food and a great atmosphere are the secret to its success, but the wine list helps as well. Lovers of seafood will be in heaven and vouch for the *polvo a lagareira* (char-grilled octopus) – a must, especially with a side of buttered vegetables, for a simple but mouth watering duo. If you prefer something more solid, the pork is highly recommended. The more expensive fish dishes like the cod (R$116) serve two.

★ Amadeus

Rua Haddock Lobo 807, Cerqueira César
(3061 2859/www.restauranteamadeus.com.br).
Bus 702P-42. **Open** noon-3pm, 6pm-midnight
Mon-Thu; noon-3pm, 6pm-1am Fri; noon-4.30pm,
7pm-1am Sat; noon-4.30pm, 7-11pm Sun.
Main course R$70-$120. **Credit** AmEx, V.
Map p244 J7 ㉑ **Seafood**

The passion of the Masano family for fish and seafood has reached the second generation. Young chef Bella Masana practically grew up in the dining room of the restaurant and completed her studies at Le Cordon Bleu. For an unforgettable experience, experiment with the marvellous Moqueca Amadeus, Bahian-style fish stew made with palm oil, fish and shrimp, and cooked in a clay dish. Another excellent option is the *camarão 'rosso e nero'* (shrimp in a tomato sauce with basil, served with rice and black olives). Another great option is the dessert with banana and tamarind sauce, while the chocolate ice-cream and coffee liquor will leave you longing for more.

America

Avenida Paulista 2295, Cerqueira César
(3067 4424/www.americaburger.com.br).
Metrô Consolação. **Open** 11.45am-midnight
Mon-Thur, Sun; 11.45am-1am Fri, Sat. **Main course** R$15-$49. **Credit** AmEx, DC, MC, V.
Map p244 J7 ㉒ **American**

Flipping fancy burgers since its inauguration in 1985, this upscale chain was one of the first casual dinner restaurants in town and a pioneer in the Paulistano craze for the American all-beef patty. It remains a particularly good place for families. Your tough-to-please kids will be conquered by creative meals and desserts, especially the Yogurt Farofino, a fancy frozen-yogurt sundae with chocolate syrup, nuts and whipped cream. Since the arrival of the 'age of obesity', pasta and salad options have been added to the menu, but don't kid yourself or your kid: the hamburger is still very much king at this Jardins joint.

Other locations throughout the city.

INSIDE TRACK
COOK'S TOUR

The lyric 'Quem quiser vatapá, ô' (oh, who wants vatapá) begins Gal Costa's celebrated foodie tune. It's possible that Morena Leite, the young and impressive owner of **Capim Santo** (*see p120*), may be the only chef in this culinary mecca to appreciate the Brazilian connection between food and music. Several times a week, Leite teaches cooking classes on the second floor of the Capim Santo restaurant; don't miss it, the haut monde of São Paulo and enough Louis Vuitton bags to fill Barneys are to be found there. Lessons are arranged according to Morena's theory of cooking with music, and a guitarist accompanies the class with favourite Brazilian food songs. If you can't afford to splurge on the class, Morena's book on Bahian food can be found in English, Portuguese and French in many of São Paulo's book stores, and it includes a CD.

CONSUME

© 2006 Marcus Bleasdale/VII

WHEREVER CRIMES AGAINST HUMANITY ARE PERPETRATED.

Across borders and above politics.
Against the most heinous abuses
and the most dangerous oppressors.
From conduct in wartime
to economic, social, and cultural rights.
Everywhere we go,
we build an unimpeachable case
for change and advocate action
at the highest levels.

HUMAN RIGHTS WATCH TYRANNY HAS A WITNESS

WWW.HRW.ORG

HUMAN
RIGHTS
WATCH

Chef Morena Leite at **Capim Santo**. See p120.

★ Bio Alternativa
*Alameda Santos 2214, Jardim Europa
(3898 2971/www.bioalternativa.com.br). Metrô
Consolação.* **Open** 11.30am-3.30pm Mon-Fri.
Set menu R$26. **Credit** AmEx, MC, V.
Map p244 J7 ❷❸ **Vegetarian**
This little green health food spot is as cool as a
cucumber. A buffet on the second floor offers an all-
you-can-eat meal with fresh salads and inventive
dishes for lacto-vegetarians. A mixture of Oriental
and Brazilian cuisine appeals to the executive lunch
crowd: Indian rice (with vegetables, nuts and dried
fruit) and Moroccan sweet-and-sour stew are so popular they regularly disappear from the pans as soon
as the kitchen delivers them. If you're vegetarian,
don't miss the *feijoada* black bean stew, and if you're
a vegan, end your meal with the ice-cream.
Other location Rua Maranhão 812, Higienópolis,
(3825 8499/www.bioalternativa.com.br).

Bolinha
*Avenida Cidade Jardim 53, Jardim Europa
(3061 2010/www.bolinha.com.br). Bus 6262-10,
967A-10.* **Open** 11am-1am daily. **Main course**
R$38-$81. **Credit** AmEx, DC, MC, V. **Map** p249
G12 ❷❹ **Traditional Brazilian**
Bolinha proudly holds the title as *the* place in São
Paulo to eat *feijoada*, Brazil's beloved national dish.
Be warned, this hearty stew of black beans and
pork requires the appetite of a giant, and that's not
even taking into account the gamut of traditional
sides with which it is served: rice, kale, fried
bananas and manioc flour. Service is top notch (as
one would expect given the hefty prices) and when
prompted, the waiters will happily tell you more
about the history of the humble origins of this
special Brazilian meal. *Feijoada* was invented by

Afro-Brazilian slaves, who devised the dish
through using a variety of different food scraps
in the cauldron of black beans. There is a menu
replete with entrees beyond the traditional
and 'light' *feijoada*, but experiencing the *feijoada*
is a must while in Brazil, and in Bolinha, they get
it just right.

★ Brasil a Gosto
*Rua Professor Azevedo do Amaral 70, Jardim
Paulista (3086 3565/www.brasilagosto.com.br).
Metrô Trianon-MASP.* **Open** noon-4pm, 7pm-
midnight Tue-Fri; noon-5pm, 7pm-1am Sat;
noon-6pm Sun. **Main course** R$32-$64.
Credit AmEx, DC, MC, V. **Map** p244 J9
❷❺ **Modern Brazilian**
Ready for a taste of the Amazon? Chef Ana Luiza
Trajano floats the finest ingredients of the jungle
river to your table. Start your adventure by ordering the lovely jabuticaba and caju caipirinha, artfully decorated with the head of the caju fruit (the
unfamiliar, inedible cover of the cashew nut). The
optional couvert is R$9.50, but there are too many
tropical treats to waste your hunger on breadsticks.
Instead, order the mini *acarajé* appetiser, which
allows the diner to assemble shrimp, avocado,
pumpkin and the amazing hot sauce and onion
vinaigrette into a brilliant, self-made recreation of
this classic Bahian sandwich. For your starter, try
the *abadejo grelhado com crosta de baru* (grilled
haddock with a crust of Brazilian baru nut), or the
grilled *pararucu* – the largest freshwater fish in the
world. Finish the dinner off with a tasting of the
plum or banana cachaça; the sugar cane tipple here
reaches the level of fine cognac. Reservations are
recommended if you want to secure a spot in the
lovely upstairs dining room. *Photo p108.*

CONSUME

★ Capim Santo

Alameda Ministro Rocha Azevedo 471, Jardim Paulista (3068 8486/www.capimsanto.com.br). Metrô Consolação. **Open** noon-3pm, 7.30pm-midnight Tue-Thur; noon-3pm, 7.30pm-1am Fri; 12.30-5pm, 8pm-1am Sat; 12.30-5pm Sun. **Main course** R$35-$65. **Credit** AmEx, DC, MC, V. **Map** p244 K8 **㉖ Modern Brazilian**

Morena Leite's *Jungle Book* restaurant features two gardens. The front bar patio is reminiscent of Bahian beaches, with wooden benches and throw pillows, and the stunning back garden is fit for Amazonian royalty (to sit here, reservations are a must). For the appetiser have a *pastelzinho* of duck with *pitanga* sauce (a small fried pastry covered with a tangy fruit juice from Brazil's northeast). The couvert comes with specialty crackers and *vatapá* (fish paste with pumpkin and *dende* oil). Try the escalope of fillet mignon with the three-pepper sauce, served with broccoli, or the other favourite, the Badejo (sea bass) rolled in a couve leaf and filled with farofa, served on top of grilled jaca fruit. Last but not least, the waiters are attentive, warm, and entirely tuned in to the needs of the diners – they round out a perfectly divine dining experience. *Photos p119 and p128.*

Dalva e Dito

Rua Padre João Manuel 1115, Cerqueira César (3064 6183/www.dalvaedito.com.br). Metrô Consolação. **Open** noon-3pm, 7pm-midnight Mon-Thur; noon-3pm, 7pm-1am Fri; noon-4.30pm, 7pm-1am Sat; noon-5pm Sun. **Main course** R$35-$145. **Credit** AmEx, DC, MC, V. **Map** p244 J9 **㉗ Modern Brazilian**

Keen to see how the other half live? Head to Dalva e Dito. Owner Alex Attala struck gold with D.O.M.

(*see below*), which elevated Brazilian cooking to high art. Here, Chef Alain Poletto attempts the same for Brazilian street food, with mixed results: a rotisserie chicken cooked on the world's most expensive spit is still a rotisserie chicken, even if you pay R$65 for it. Street snacks that have been reworked, like *pasteis* (fried snacks), *bolinhos de mandioca* and *carne seca* (fried balls of mandioca and dry meat), are among the highlights. The design is striking, but the beautiful wooden tables can be too wide for conversation. The basement level has an elegant bar, if you don't feel like a full meal – which at these prices might be a wise decision.

★ D.O.M.

Rua Barão de Capanema 549, Jardim Paulista (3088 0761/www.domrestaurante.com.br). Metrô Consolação. **Open** noon-3pm, 7pm-midnight Mon-Thur; noon-3pm, 7pm-1am Fri; 7pm-1am Sat. **Main course** R$80-$195. **Credit** AmEx, DC, MC, V. **Map** p244 I9 **㉘ Modern Brazilian**

The waiters at D.O.M., one of the top 50 restaurants in the world according to the UK's *Restaurant* magazine, don't shy away from embracing the place's self-importance, carefully explaining that you are about to go on a 'culinary voyage'. Relax in a Ruy Ohtake chair while enjoying the seemingly endless procession of wondrous food, created using many ingredients from the Paraense region of the Amazon: delicate oysters fried in brioche batter, foie gras served with an ice-cream made from the Cambuci flower, and more. Food this exotic needs a calm backdrop, and the sophisticated design is punctuated with huge striped walls and a wooden door by artist Ricky Castro, combining flashes of dark colour with the otherwise neutral decor.

Arabia Café. *See p108.*

CONSUME

The United States of Brazil

Where's the beef?

The American burger arrived in the city right after World War II, when the first burger restaurants opened. Later, Brazilians started adapting it to their tastes, and the salad cheeseburger became the big hit. The medium-rare meat with melting cheese, fresh tomatoes and lettuce and homemade mayonnaise can be combined with up to ten different ingredients: mushrooms, glazed onions, tartar sauce and corn cream are Paulistano favourites.

There are great restaurants all over town, but on Rua Joaquim Floriano, in Itaim Bibi, you'll find some of the best burger places, including **Joakin's** (Rua Joaquim Floriano 163, 3168 0030, www.joakins.com.br) and **Rockets** (Alameda Lorena 2090, 3081 9466, www.rockets.com.br). Another great thing about these places: they usually close after 5am, making them perfect for an after-hours snack following a night on the tiles.

Eñe
Rua Dr. Mário Ferraz 213, Jardim Europa (3816 4333/www.enerestaurante.com.br). Bus 609F-10. **Open** noon-3pm, 7pm-midnight Mon-Thur; noon-3pm, 7pm-1am Fri; 1-4pm, 8pm-1am Sat. **Main course** R$25-$50. **Credit** AmEx, DC, MC, V. **Map** p249 F12 ㉙ **Spanish**

The Brazilian capital of gastronomy was still aching for a signature Spanish addition as recently as two years ago, when the twin brothers Sergio and Javier Torres Martinez from Barcelona eased the pain, stepping up to the culinary scene with this small, high-quality, Catalan-influenced restaurant. Eñe immediately became a reference point. It is architecturally unique on the exterior, a mix of concrete and dark wood, as well as inviting on the inside, with sleek lines and smooth surfaces. Eñe's preoccupation with beauty extends to food and raises the bar for aesthetically pleasing culinary concoctions. For mains, selections of fish and vibrant vegetables with bold Spanish spices are great options. The twins' imprint is all over the menu, but the restaurant is managed by a trained team of local chefs, headed by a Japanese-Brazilian, Flávio Miyama, who is extremely faithful to the restaurant's Catalan origins and dramatic tastes. For dessert, try the pecan pie, a great example of the robust flavours extending all the way to the end of the meal.

★ A Figueira Rubaiyat
Rua Haddock Lobo 1738, Jardim Paulista (3087 1399/www.rubaiyat.com.br). Metrô Consolação. **Open** noon-12.30am Mon-Thur; noon-1am Fri, Sat; noon-midnight Sun. **Main course** R$70-$180. **Credit** V. **Map** p244 I8 ㉚ **Steakhouse**

The number of architecturally significant and gastronomically superb restaurants in São Paulo is astounding. Still, finding gentrified country dining a block away from the Bond Street of Brazil (Rua Oscar Freire) is surprising. A huge 130-year-old fig tree dominates the eating area of Figueira Rubaiyat, an enchanting detail that lends the restaurant an intimate, romantic air. The restaurant is famed for serving the best beef in the city and for catering to Paulistano power couples and the financial elite. The appetiser of *carpaccio di funghi* in truffle oil is a must, as are the *paes de queijo*. A main course mainstay is the sumptuous premium master beef. There is an extensive wine list with over 850 bottles, and the Chateau Haut-Badon Bordeaux '05 is an excellent, if hefty addition, at just over R$200. **Other locations** throughout the city.

★ Maní
Rua Joaquim Antunes 210, Jardim Paulista (3085 4148/www.restaurantemani.com.br). Bus 795P-10, 577T-10, 724P-10. **Open** noon-3pm, 7-11.30pm Tue, Wed; 7pm-midnight Thur; noon-3pm Fri; 1-4pm, 7pm-12.30am Sat; 1-4:30pm Sun. **Main course** R$40-$60. **Credit** AmEx, DC, MC, V. **Map** p249 G10 ㉛ **International**

Tucked away on a classy, quiet street in the Jardins district, Maní manages to be contemporary and sophisticated yet artfully unpretentious. Whether you choose a table inside or out, you're sure to enjoy an exquisite meal amid the natural, earthy ambience of one of São Paulo's most popular and innovative restaurants. Modern cuisine is served here with flair, and chefs Daniel Redondo and Helena Rizzo deserve all the praise they've received for their creative, wide-ranging menu. Try their award-winning fish entree served with Tucupi (cassava sauce) and bananas. Reservations strongly recommended.

Margherita
Alameda Tietê 255, Jardim Paulista (2714 3000/www.margherita.com.br). Metrô Consolação. **Open** 6.30pm-1am Mon-Thur; 6.30pm-1.30am Fri-Sun. **Main course** R$35-$45. **Credit** AmEx, DC, MC, V. **Map** p244 J8 ㉜ **Pizza**

Brazilians like to claim that the world's best pizza is not found in Naples but rather in São Paulo. Italians may beg to differ, but why not visit this classic

CONSUME

pizzeria and join the debate? A creative assortment of pizza pies are served up here, topped with cheese, veggies, meats and more. The namesake pizza is a must, while mildly more adventurous diners might like to try the Campesina, featuring eggplant, parmesan and olives.

Ráscal

Alameda Santos 870, Jardim Paulista (3078 3351/www.rascal.com.br). Metrô Brigadeiro. **Open** noon-3pm, 7-10.45pm Mon-Thur; noon-3pm, 7-11.45pm Fri; noon-5pm, 7-11.45pm Sat; noon-5pm, 7-10.45pm Sun. **Main course** R$20-$35. **Credit** AmEx, DC, MC, V. **Map** p244 L9 ㉝ **Vegetarian**

Ráscal offers six branches throughout the city (four of them inside malls) and spoils vegetarians silly with arguably the best salad bar in town. Quiches, marinated vegetables, cheeses galore, breads and green salads can be found among the 40 different items. Speciality hams are also among the salad bar offerings. If the salad bar simply presents too many healthy options, the pizza corner is generous, as are the pasta and grill sections. For a delicate and colourful meal try the grilled trout with green ravioli and fresh tomato sauce.

Other locations throughout the city.

Ritz

Alameda Franca 1088, Jardim Paulista (3062 5830). Metrô Consolação. **Open** noon-3pm, 8pm-1am Mon-Fri; 1pm-1.30am Sat; 1pm-midnight Sun. **Main course** R$19-$45. **Credit** AmEx, DC, MC, V. **Map** p244 J8 ㉞ **Burgers**

Ritz has a hard time determining what city it's in, and providing you can get in you'll also have a hard time believing that you're still in São Paulo and not in Paris or the East Village. It has the look of a French bistro with mirrors and red leather banquettes; and is popular with gay folk and trust fund bohemians. As for the food, it's known for its great hamburgers (witness the odd spectacle of Brazilians delicately cutting up burgers with a knife and fork) and delicious pastas. For an appetiser, try the portion of *pasteis* or the *bolinhos de arroz* (fried rice balls), a speciality you're not likely to find outside of São Paulo. The portions are generous, and if you're not too hungry, feel free to share your entrée – the penne mediterraneo is a great for-two option. Although the tunes lean towards indie rock, the drinks are far from dive bar prices (a caipirinha will set you back R$14).

Other location Rua Jerônimo da Veiga 141, Itaim Bibi (3079 2725).

★ R$ Temakeria e Cia

Rua Oscar Freire 507, Jardim Paulista (3062 3920/www.temakeriaecia.com.br). Metrô Consolação. **Open** noon-midnight Mon-Fri; noon-1am Sat; noon-11pm Sun. **Main course** R$7-$43. **Credit** AmEx, DC, MC, V. **Map** p244 I8 ㉟ **Japanese**

You certainly *can* order sushi at this tiny Japanese eaterie devoted to *temaki* (seaweed wrapped cones of fresh fish, rice and other ingredients), but it would be an unwise move. Instead order two of the *temaki* (all under R$10) that are the darling creations of Eduardo Inoue, the owner/sushi chef, who is always hanging around the second restaurant in Itaim Bibi. Try a temaki hot roll, filled with deep-fried salmon, cream cheese and crabsticks. Indulge in the *empanado da casa* hot roll with salmon, crabstick, onion, cream teriyaki sauce and sesame seeds. Although the *temakes* appear small, they deliver the perfect serving of fish and not too much rice. Plus,

Arturito. *See p124.*

CONSUME

Temakeria e Cia. *See p122.*

despite having been approached various times to franchise his popular restaurant, Inoue has refused – as such, other than the other branch, you're unlikely to find a better sushi cone this far from the Pacific. *Photo p116.*
Other location Rua Joaquim Floriano 307, Itaim Bibi (3073 0905/www.temakeriaecia.com.br).

★ Tordesilhas
Rua Bela Cintra 465, Cerqueira César (3107 7444/www.tordesilhas.com). Metrô Consolação. **Open** noon-3pm, 7pm-midnight Tue-Fri; noon-5pm, 7pm-midnight Sat; noon-5pm Sun. **Main course** R$32-$80. **Credit** AmEx, DC, MC, V. **Map** p242 K6 ❸❻ **Traditional Brazilian**
Fans of Brazilian high-gastronomy will not be disappointed by this rare example of a famous chef making truly traditional dishes. Mara Salles was inspired by her Pernambucan roots (a state on the north-eastern coast) to work mostly with local ingredients and to highlight regional dishes. Salles's origins and culinary wizardry though, are best tested in the *guisado de carne seca* (dried meat served on top of mandioca.) For dessert, try the ice-cream of *cupuaçu*, a mind-blowingly tangy Amazonian fruit. If the variety on the menu makes choosing too difficult, you can opt for the delectable tasting menu for around R$110.

Trebbiano
L'Hotel, Alameda Campinas 266, Cerqueira César (2183 0500/www.lhotel.com.br). Metrô Trianon-MASP. **Open** noon-3pm, 7.30-11pm daily. **Main course** R$39-$61. **Credit** AmEx, DC, MC, V. **Map** p244 L8 ❸❼ **Mediterranean**
Classy, elegant and refined. The neoclassical dining room of the L'Hotel, in pink and salmon hues, sandal-wood and velvet, is slightly reminiscent of 19th-century Europe. Overlooking Alameda Campinas, it is popular with smart and middle-aged businesspeople for lunch and dinner. The prix fixe lunch at R$65 includes a green salad, an entrée of either fish (grilled linguado) or meat, and an interesting dessert. Pleasant but cool service adds to the appeal.

Wraps
Rua Oscar Freire 206, Jardim Paulista/Cerqueira César (3063 4329/www.wraps.com.br). Metrô Trianon-MASP. **Open** noon-3.30pm, 7-11pm Mon-Thur; noon-midnight Fri, Sat; noon-11pm Sun. **Main course** R$19-$25. **Credit** AmEx, DC, MC, V. **Map** p244 J9 ❸❽ **Health food**
When this restaurant emerged on the scene in 2002, the health-food concept had not yet made headway in Brazil. Seven years and 11 branches later, Wraps has become Paulistanos's favourite snack-bar. The New York loft look reproduced in blacks and reds adds an air of sophistication to the light meals. Fresh salads, tasteful smoothies and the salad granola (invented by chef Carole Crema) quickly gained a loyal following in a city, and indeed a country, that can be a little too dominated by meat and carbs. Here you can have your cake and eat it too: the healthy apple cake with cinnamon ice-cream was recently voted 'best dessert' by local taste arbiter Veja São Paulo.
Other locations throughout the city.

★ Z Deli
Alameda Gabriel Monteiro da Silva 1350, Jardim Paulistano (3064 2058). Bus 107P-10. **Open** noon-6pm Mon-Fri; noon-4.30pm Sat. **Main course** R$39-$49. **Credit** AmEx, DC, MC, V. **Map** p249 G11 ❸❾ **Jewish**

CONSUME

Due Cuochi Cucina. *See p112.*

This run-of-the-mill – albeit charming – deli with few tables and a self-service counter full of delicious salads offers Jewish dining at its best. Gefilte fish can be had here not just on Passover, but all year round. For a taste of eastern-European cuisine, try the *vareniks*, breaded meats and fish. The catch is that as the food tastes better than it looks, you're bound to overeat and spend more time here than you expected. Note that service is slow and the surroundings are not indicative of the prices, so you'll spend more than you expected too, but it's the closest you'll get to Katz's Deli outside of Manhattan.

LIBERDADE

R$ Lamen Aska

Rua Galvão Bueno 466, Liberdade (3277 9682). Metrô Liberdade. **Open** 11am-2pm, 6-10pm Tue-Sun. **Main course** R$12-$13. **No credit cards. Map** p245 O7 **40 Japanese**

The sun has not yet set on one of the few remaining, original Japanese ramen houses in Brazil, but get here quickly before it does. Lamen Aska is no slick Momofuku or Wagamama, but rather a tiny restaurant in the heart of little Japan and an authentically retro place in which to spend your lunchtime. Here you can buy 12 varieties of the ramen dish for around R$12 each and some speciality pork and vegetable gyozas for R$8. It's popular, and there are often queues, but it's worth the wait – if only to be transported to a time at the turn of the century when recent immigrants crowded hundreds of such ramen houses.

PINHEIROS & VILA MADALENA

★ Arturito

Rua Artur de Azevedo 542, Pinheiros (3063 4951/www.arturito.com.br). Metrô Clinicas. **Open** 7pm-midnight Mon-Thur; 7pm-1am Fri, Sat. **Main course** R$36-$66. **Cards** AmEx, DC, MC, V. **Map** p249 F8 **41 International**

Intimate dark wood panelling, austere lighting, and stylish wall-long seating with cushions and throw pillows distinguish this luxurious new addition to the São Paulo scene. It's positively heaving with clientele at the weekend as word has got around about the restaurant and its trendy Argentinian chef and co-proprietor, Paola Carosella. A night time buzz permeates the restaurant, which is on the must-go-to list of every well-to-do Paulistano. Paola's love of fresh ingredients can be felt through the wonderfully varied and ever-changing menu, which includes some uncommon dishes for Brazil, such as leg of lamb, *ceviche* (raw fish marinated in citrus juices) and the Argentine specialty of grilled sweetbread. The menu also features outstanding classics: freshly made pasta, prime beef and pork as well as an extensive wine list. Booking is strongly recommended, especially at the weekend. *Photo p122.*

★ Bistro Robin des Bois

Rua Capote Valente 86, Pinheiros (3063 2795/www.robindesbois.com.br). Metrô Clinicas. **Open** 7pm-midnight Tue, Wed; 7pm-1am Thur; noon-2am Fri, Sat; noon-11pm Sun. **Main course** R$30-$60. **Credit** DC, MC, V. **Map** p249 H8 **42 French**

The food might be fit for a king, but the prices reflect the Robin Hood theme. The candle-lit wooden tables, atmospheric posters, antique-frame mirrors and an intimate outdoor space manage to give just the right Sherwood Forest feel. Try the grilled vegetable salad with goat's cheese as well as the mussels in cream and white wine sauce (perfect as a full meal for two). You're certain to feel like one of the merry men when you're done. For drinks, the Absolut Pepper Bloody Mary delivers a delightful head rush – just don't try shooting your bow and arrow afterwards. Reservations are needed for Friday nights.

★ $ Consulado Mineiro

Praça Benedito Calixto 74, Pinheiros (3064 3882/www.consuladomineiro.com.br). Metrô Clinicas. **Open** noon-midnight Tue-Sun. **Main course** R$19-$64. **Credit** AmEx, DC, MC, V. **Map** p249 G8 **43 Traditional Brazilian**

Step into this creaky yellow house and you may feel like a João Guimaraes Rosa character. (Brazil's most famous modernist novelist was from the state of Minas Gerais.) The homey atmosphere, wooden tables and paintings of the Minas countryside evoke well-preserved colonial towns, like Ouro Preto. As is the custom in Minas, all the plates are intended for two, but really, a third person could easily partake in this hearty, reasonably priced meal. For an appetiser, order the *pão de quiejo*, the cheese bread invented in Minas which rarely tastes as good anywhere else in Brazil. Made from scratch, they should be ordered immediately, as it takes half an hour for the dough and cheese to perfectly meld. For an entrée, try the Tutu Especial or the Tutu á Mineiro, the most famous dishes from this huge central state. The former comes with beans, sausage and eggs, pork cutlets and mandioca (Brazilian yucca) with banana, a *couve* salad (chopped and steamed kale, garlic and butter), and rice. If you're in the mood for home cooking as opposed to a refined meal, this is the place.
Other location Rua Conego Eugenio Leite 504, Pinheiros (3898-3241)

Drake's Bar

Rua Tucambira 163, Pinheiros (3812 4477/ www.drakesbar.com). Bus 177H-10. **Open** noon-2am Tue-Sun. **Main course** R$18-$30. **Credit**: AmEx, DC, MC, V. **Map** p248 D9
㉔ Burgers
Located inside the lush and bright British Council Centre, this restaurant has an inside bar and a gorgeous garden deck area overlooking a small pool surrounded by tropical foliage – a *jardim* created by British garden designer Norinka Ford. The menu offers inventive and delicious burgers as well as some of the finest lagers in town. The British pub inside features live music Thursday to Saturday, with a cover of R$10-R$15.

Filipa

Rua Joaquim Antunes 260, Pinheiros (3083 3868/www.fillipa.com.br). Bus 795P-10, 577P-10, 775P-31. **Open** 11.45am-3.30pm, 7pm-midnight Tue-Thur; 11.45am-3.30pm, 7pm-1am Fri; 11.45-1am Sat, 11.45am-10.30pm Sun. **Main course** R$28-$58. **Credit** AmEx, DC, MC, V. **Map** p249 G10 **㊺ Eclectic**
Following the success of her restaurant, Mestiço, chef Ina de Abreu decided to open Filipa and further expand São Paulo's taste for modern Thai cuisine. Fusing flavors from Thailand, Vietnam, France, Italy and Brazil, the menu features a mix of traditional and creative dishes, from Pad Thai to green curry with filet mignon. If you have an appetite it's worth going all out for a three course meal. Start with the couvert of fig bread and butter and finish with a bang – the coconut sorbet with caramelised ginger and orange really is truly outstanding.

Gardênia Restô

Praça dos Omaguás 110, Pinheiros (3815 9247/ www.gardeniaresto.com.br). Bus 875C-10. **Open** noon-3pm, 7.30pm-midnight Mon-Fri; 1pm-midnight Sat, Sun. **Main course** R$20-$60. **Credit** AmEx, DC, MC, V. **Map** p249 E9 **㊻ International**
The perfect location on Praça dos Omaguás, right by the Fnac bookstore, has kept this romantic restaurant going strong for many years. In 2005, new chef and owner Marina Moraes changed the name, ambience and menu. All that remains from the old Café Gardênia is the ultra-loyal clientele. The primarily middle-aged patrons demand class and the house responds accordingly, with a jazzy feel punctuated by alluring lighting and intimate seating arrangements. The restaurant specialises in lamb, and the regulars' taste for the signature entrée never seems to wane. Don't show up without a reservation: it's an important hobnobbing spot for executives looking to close on important deals.
Other location Gardênia Gabriel, Avenida Gabriel Monteiro da Silva 726, Jardim Europa (3088 3044).

GOA

Rua Cônego Eugênio Leite 1152, Pinheiros (3031 0680/www.gaiavegetariano.com.br). Metrô Clinicas. **Open** noon-4pm Mon-Fri; noon-5pm Sat, Sun. **Main course** R$24-$40. **Credit** AmEx, DC, MC, V. **Map** p249 F8 **㊼ Vegetarian**
GOA chef and owner Augusto Pinto has studied all over the world to become one of the first chefs in São Paulo to use and promote organic materials in cooking. This lovely, warehouse-like restaurant in bohemian Pinheiros is open only for lunch. Try the kibbeh with honey sauce, hummus or couscous. A backyard with a tiny playground is perfectly suited for children and has a number of hammocks that make it a perfect spot for relaxing after dessert.

INSIDE TRACK PIZZERIAS

São Paulo has a very strong Italian community that's been influencing the way the city eats for over 120 years. You'll find the usual deli-style suspects of sundried tomatoes, buffalo mozzarella and rocket, but Brazilian's really push the boat out when it comes to pizza. Look out for chicken with corn and *requeijão* (Brazilian cream cheese) or calabrese sausage with onions. Try both the thin-crust and the thick-crust, and remember that most pizza places in São Paulo are usually only open for dinner.

CONSUME

R$ Integrão

*Rua Joaquim Antunes 377, Pinheiros (3085 3707/
www.integrao.com.br). Bus 715M-10.* **Open** noon-
3pm Mon-Fri. **Main course** R$14-$18. **Credit** DC,
MC, V. **Map** p249 G9 ❹❾ **Vegetarian**
You won't find too much macrobiotic food in São
Paulo, but this simple family restaurant has been
serving fantastic vegetarian and macrobiotic dishes
for over 30 years. Try the delicious Prato Normal,
featuring rice, mandioca balls, a tofu pancake with
carrots, and a light salad of greens on the side. This
is one of the few a la carte vegetarian spots in town,
but while you can find juice and beer on the menu,
due to its macrobiotic adherence, no sodas are sold
here. The food is prepared slowly, transforming the
restaurant into an island of serenity just a few meters
away from the chaos of Avenida Rebouças.

Lola Bistrot

*Rua Purpurina 38, Vila Madalena (3812 3009/
www.lolabistrot.com.br). Metrô Vila Madalena.*
Open noon-3pm, 8pm-midnight Mon-Wed;
noon-3pm, 8pm-1am Thur, Fri; 8pm-1am Sat;
1-5pm Sun. **Main course** R$29-$49. **Credit**
AmEx, DC, MC, V. **Map** p249 E7 ❹❾ **French**
This previously five-table restaurant moved
across the street and now has better decoration
and service, but most importantly, the same great
French food. Chef Daniela França Pinto has a good
hand for meat dishes, especially the poivre steak.
Avoid the pasta if you're hungry, as it can be too
light for a full meal.

Martin Fierro

*Rua Aspicuelta 683, Vila Madalena (3814
6747/www.martinfierro.com.br). Bus 701A-10.*
Open noon-11pm daily. **Main course** R$45-
$65. **Credit** AmEx, DC, MC, V. **Map** p249 E8
❺⓿ **Steakhouse**
If you're a gluttonous, greedy, gormandizing meat
eater, then this Argentinian restaurant is for you.
The eaterie has varied its focus recently and serves
some Brazilian cuts on its menu, but otherwise, you
can pretend you're in Buenos Aires. Some good
choices include the *bife* noix or the *bife de chorizo*
(sirloin). The side salad is a little too simple, but
some empanadas are good options. The restaurant
also makes its own *alfajores* (biscuits with *dulce de
leche*, R$3).

Pasquale

*Rua Amália de Noronha 167, Pinheiros (3081
0333/www.pasqualecantina.com.br). Metrô
Sumaré.* **Open** noon-midnight Mon-Sat. **Main
course** R$23-$40. **Credit** AmEx, DC, MC, V.
Map p249 G7 ❺❶ **Italian**
It's not *Don Pasquale*, Donizetti's most famous
opera, that this restaurant is named after but the
proprietor who was born in the Pugliese region of
Italy. If it's Italy that you're missing, this cosy
restaurant offering the right combination of

antipasti, pasta and wines, should hit the spot. For
antipasti, try the tender marinated eggplant, the
rich and tiny *boursin* cheese balls, and some generous hunks of salami (cured on the premises); it
all might just lead you to attempt a top-of your-
lungs Pavarotti number.

Santa Gula

*Rua Fidalga 340, Vila Madalena (3812 7815/
www.stagula.com.br) Bus 701A-10.* **Open** 8pm-
2am Mon; noon-4pm, 8pm-2am Tue-Sat; noon-
4pm Sun. **Main course** R$40-$60. **Credit**
AmEx, DC, MC, V. **Map** p249 E8 ❺❷ **Eclectic**
Santa Gula is best experienced at night, when the
circa 200 candles are glowing and the multi-level
environment gains a charming and bucolic air.
Walk down the candle-lit alleyway that leads from
the road to the main house, and you'll enter a
dream space. At night, it's ideal for intimate gatherings and popular with families on weekends. The
menu varies from traditional French- and Italian-
inspired dishes to Asian and Brazilian fusion.
Everything you see is for sale here – if you like one
of the rustic sculptures, check the price tag.

Schnapshaus

*Rua Diogo Moreira 119, Pinheiros (3031
9886/www.schnapshaus.com.br). Bus 6262-10
bus.* **Open** noon-3pm, 6-11pm Mon-Thur; 11am-
12.30am Fri, Sat; 11am-5.30pm Sun. **Main
course** R$25-$50. **Credit** AmEx, DC, MC, V.
Map p249 E10 ❺❸ **German**
Fantasizing about homey fare from the Faterland?
Willkommen to the Schnapshaus. In the spirit of
São Paulo's limited German dining options (odd
given the Brazil's sizeable German immigrant history), this is a family-style tavern rather than a cutting-edge eaterie. The well-preserved wooden walls
are still standing, the tablecloths are checkered and
Deutschland posters transport you to a Europe of
schnitzel and beer. The paprika schnitzel is by far
the best dish in the house. The tender pork in moist
paprika sauce with a huge portion of mashed potatoes and the inseparable rice (which gives the meal
a Brazilian touch) make this a memorable stand-in
for grandma's cooking. The entrées, that cost R$45-
R$50, can easily feed two people.

INSIDE TRACK
BEST AÇAI BARS

Açaí (*see p115*) bars are a dime a
dozen in Brazilian cities but here are a
few of our favourites: **Açaí B&B** (Avenida
Doutor Arnaldo 1179, Sumaré, 3062
6850, closed Sun); **Açaí Bar** (Rua Chilon
141, Itaim Bibi, 3045 0505); **Açaí Beach
Bar** (Rua Augusta 1902, loja 3, Jardins,
3159 3240, www.açaibeachbar.com.br).

CONSUME

Profile Mercado Municipal (Mercadão)

The Municipal Market is a foodies' dream.

The **Mercadão** (*see p156*) is a laboratory of the edible, spanning all of the city's most important ethnic cuisines and displaying an incredibly colourful array of fruits and vegetables. It opened on 25 January 1933, and was located alongside the Tamanduateí and Anhangabaú rivers, which in pre-automobile days were the farm-to-market highways. The areas around the market have long since gone to seed, but the market itself recovered from its nadir in the 1970s and was completely restored in 2004.

If you're the kind of traveller with a knack for safely packing

glass jars in your suitcase, you may find some unique treasures. The upper level of the market also has several sit-down joints for lunch with a view of the action. There are 23 restaurants and snack bars here as well as innumerable stores.

There's an abundancy of native fruits, as well as exotic offerings from Asia, and it's possible to get slices of cold pineapple and more uncommon fruit salads for a few *reais*, or taste a piece *pitaya*, *mamey* or *mangostim* as you pass by a shop.

The famous *bacalhau* (Portuguese-style salt-cod), with an aroma of olive oil and a melt- in-your-mouth quality, is a Mercadão favorite. It can be experienced in the form of a pastry at **Hocca Bar**, as well as at other shops further into the labyrinthine market, where the cod is often cheaper. You can also take a piece of salted codfish home from one of the fish shops or emporiums.

The Italian mortadela sandwich is the signature item at the **Bar do Mané**, one of the oldest shops in the market. The generous sandwich is nearly piled as high as the snaking queue that forms for it on weekends. The bar serves up between 800 and 900 *mortadela* orders each day, but it's just one of countless stalls in the market where your jaw may be knocked out of alignment attempting to open wide enough to handle the standard height of the sandwich.

A trip to the market is often combined with cheap shopping on Rua 25 de Março. Arrive at Metrô São Bento around 11am, take a walk around the chaotic street bazaar of Rua 25 de Março, and then it's just a short jaunt over to the Mercadão for lunch – a typical Paulistano Saturday.

CONSUME

Spadaccino

*Rua Mourato Coelho 1267, Vila Madalena
(3032 8605/www.spadaccino.com.br).
Bus 701A-10.* **Open** 7pm-midnight Mon; noon-
midnight Tue-Thur; noon-1am Fri, Sat; noon-
5pm Sun. **Main course** R$26-$44. **Credit** MC,
V. **Map** p249 E8  **Italian**

Chefs Roberto and Paula Lazzarini, brother
and sister, were part of the Brazilian fencing
team for many national and international
championships, including, for Roberto, the
Olympics. Their restaurant is dedicated to the sport
(witness the pictures and fencing paraphernalia on
the walls) as well as to Bolognese cuisine. The soft
gnocchi pasta made of potatoes, beets or manioc,
with a light, well-made tomato sauce or white sauce
is recommended.

Tanger

*Rua Fradique Coutinho 1664, Vila Madalena
(3037 7223/www.restaurantetanger.com.br).
Metrô Vila Madalena.* **Open** noon-3pm, 7pm-
midnight Mon-Thur; noon-3pm, 7pm-1am Fri;
1-4.30pm, 7pm-1am Sat; 1-4.30pm Sun. **Main
course** R$19-$41. **Credit** AmEx, DC, MC, V.
Map p249 E7 **North African**

With leafy walls reminiscent of a desert oasis
and harlequin lamps lighting the image of a Middle
Eastern bazaar, Tanger is a fantasy straight out of
the tales of Scheherazade. This upscale Moroccan
restaurant serves an assortment of mezzes, tagines
and couscous dishes (the lamb in particular is
great). The busiest nights are at the weekend, when
the crowds show up to watch the lively belly dancer
performances.

★ Vinheria Percussi

*Rua Cônego Eugênio Leite 523, Pinheiros
(3088 4920, www.vinheriapercussi.com.br).
Bus 647T-10, 7651-10.* **Open** noon-3pm,
7.30-11.30pm Tue-Thur; noon-3pm, 7pm-1am
Fri; noon-4.30pm, 7.30pm-1am Sat; noon-4.30pm
Sun. **Main course** R$45- $97. **Credit** AmEx,
DC, MC, V. **Map** p249 G9 **Italian**

Family-owned Vinheria Percussi's is known as one
of the best Italian restaurants in São Paulo. It was
Founded in 1985 by Luciano Percussi, an Italian
from Ligúria, it has achieved high consistency and
alluring presentation with the active participation
of Percussi's children. Luciano's daughter, chef
Silvia Percussi, runs the kitchen, while her brother
Lamberto acts as the restaurateur overseeing the
salon and the excellent wine cellar. The delicious
*scaloppine di pollo al limone con gnocchi di ricotta
com spinaci* (a filet of chicken breast in lime sauce
and ricotta gnocchi with spinach) and the marvellous *filetto ao gorgonzola* (filet mignon covered in
gorgonzola sauce and accompanied by delicate
fried potato balls) are standout dishes. To finish,
try the wonderful classic tiramisu made with mas-
carpone and coffee.

Capim Santo. *See p120.*

Yakissoba da Vila

*Rua Fradique Coutinho 695, Pinheiros (3032
2785). Bus 117Y-10.* **Open** noon-10pm Mon-
Thur; noon-11pm Fri, Sat; noon-6pm Sun. **Main
course** R$7-$19. **No credit cards.** **Map** p249
E9 **Japanese**

This hole in the wall is nothing more than a kitchen
area with a table for six, yet it's ideal for picking up
a stir fry or ordering a delivery. It's popular for its
tasty food, reasonable prices and great Japanese
melon ice-lollies. If you're staying in the Pinheiros
or Vila Madalena long enough, you'll probably taste
more than one of the options on the menu.

VILA MARIANA

Sushi Yassu

*Rua Manoel da Nóbrega 199/209, Paraiso (3288
2966/ www.sushiyassu.com.br). Bus 175P-10,
715F-10, 874T-10.* **Open** 11.30am-3pm, 6-11pm
Tue-Fri; noon-3.30pm, 6pm-11.30pm Sat; noon-
10pm Sun. **Main course** R$20-R$90. **Buffet**
R$54. **Credit** AmEx, DC, MC, V. **Map** p244 L9
Japanese

São Paulo is home to the world's largest Japanese
population outside of Japan, and not surprisingly,
it's a sushi lover's paradise. Sushi Yassu offers a
long and varied menu of sushi, sashimi and hot
dishes. On one side of the restaurant is an all-you-
can-eat buffet, but depending on your hunger level
(or how long it seems the fish has been out of the
water), you may want to opt for a combo platter off
the menu instead. The ambience here is nothing
special, but the food is authentic and delicious.
Other Location Rua Tomas Gonzaga 98,
Liberdade (3209-6622).

► *For the best Japanese food in the city, and
consequently the most expensive, head to Jun
Sakamoto (Rua Lisboa 55, Pinheiros, 3088 6019).*

Bars, Cafés & Botequins

Cerveja, Cachaça and coffee.

São Paulo might have a Catholic name, but it sure ain't no saint when it comes to drinking. The city's streets are crowded with bars and *lanchonetes* serving midday snacks as well as beer and cachaças, and more style-conscious bars are popping up all over town, offering beautiful surroundings to match the quality libations. **Augusta** and **Consolação** are especially well known for their trendy drinking establishments, while **Pinheiros** and **Vila Madalena** abound in great traditional *botequins* (Rio-style bars from the early 20th century, with uniformed servers and marble floors). And the café scene in the city is also on the up and up: many travellers who are disappointed that they can't find good coffee in Rio will be pleasantly surprised by the variety of coffee centres in São Paulo.

THE DRINKING SCENE

Brazilians may seem like a rowdy bunch, but most are not hard drinkers, with *cerveja* being the preferred beverage, caipirinhas a distant second and straight cachaça only for the hardiest patrons. Many cooler bars offer a stunning variety of drinks and cocktails, but you should indulge in some of the best caipirinha creations in the world. If you're watching your diet, ask for a caipirinha *sem açucar* (without sugar); it will be strong, but you'll feel better the next morning.

AUGUSTA, CONSOLAÇAO & HIGIENÓPOLIS

Astronete

Rua Matias Aires 183 B, Consolação (3151 4568/www.astronete.com.br). Bus 177H-10, 877T-10, 719R-10. **Open** from 8pm Tue-Sat. **Credit** AmEx, MC, V. **Map** p244 K7 ➊

> ➊ Green numbers given in this chapter correspond to the location of each venue on the street maps. *See pp242-249.*

There's a young, fun, hipster vibe at this dive filled with tattooed patrons. The DJ starts spinning at one or two in the morning, while several club nights offer live music performances. Jack Daniels seems to be the drink of choice with the stylish crowd that isn't quite too-cool-for-school. In fact, some of them might still be doing homework. Admission is R$10 and up.

Bar Leblon

Rua Bela Cintra 483, Consolação (3237 0151/www.barleblon.com.br). Bus 177H-10, 719P-10, 917H-41. **Open** 6pm-3am Mon-Sat. **Credit** DC, MC, V. **Map** p242 K6 ➋

Saudades for the marvellous city? A slice of Rio away from Rio, this pleasant space displays the black-and-white-mosaic tiles of its namesake neighbourhood and offers the balmy music (Marisa Monte and Tim Maia) to comfort a heartsick Carioca. Excellent cocktails include a variety of caipirinha specialities (try the red berry). Look out for occasional live music events.

Bela Tropa
Rua Fernando de Albuquerque 144, Consolação (3120 4952). Metrô Consolação. **Open** 7pm-late Fri, Sat. **No credit cards. Map** p244 K7 ❸
Sick of gringos? Welcome to a locals-only favourite: this delightfully friendly, slightly run-down place hosts great samba and *pagode* parties. The beer-swilling crowd defies the gentrification of this area and subsequently lacks the slick attitude of the patrons at the neighbouring bars. The vibe is open; but those who are glaringly foreign-looking should expect curious stares.

Drosophyla
Rua Pedro Taques 80, Consolação (3120 5535/ www.drosophyla.com.br). Bus 178L-10, 669A-10, 701A-10. **Open** 7pm-1am Mon-Wed; 8pm-2am Thur-Sat. **Credit** DC, V. **Map** p242 K6 ❹
This unmarked house, located in a small passage across from the Cemitério de Consolação, is a bizarre place. The decor is a mix of styles from Asia to Eastern Europe – the result a wonderful mishmash,

which adds another dimension to the great selection of specialist drinks and the outdoor space. The caipirinhas are famous – try the mango with red peppercorns for a fiery take on a national favourite. The owner's cats have made the back of the bar their own: stay up front if you're allergic.

★ Exquisito!
Rua Bela Cintra 532, Consolação (3151 4530/ www.exquisito.com.br). Metrô Consolação. **Open** 6pm-2am Tue-Thur; 6pm-4am Fri, Sat; 6pm-1am Sun. **Credit** AmEx, M, V. **Map** p242 K6 ❺
Journalists and writers converge on this bar like bees on a honey pot. The walls are outfitted with retro posters, while the atmosphere is loud, lively and local. The caipirinhas are sometimes decorated with peppers, and the food hails from all over Latin America, featuring wide-ranging appetisers, from Dominican fare to guacamole and quesadillas.

Salommão Bar
Avenida Angélica 2435, Higienopolis (3257 0390/www.salommao.com.br). Metrô Consolação. **Open** noon-midnight Mon-Wed; noon-3am Thur-Sat. **Credit** AmEx, MC, V. **Map** p244 J7 ❻
Rustic, romantic and royal, this bar, re-fashioned from a 19th-century mansion and drenched in flora, is named after King Solomon. A wide range of imported beer and wine is offered. In the evenings, a guitarist plays bossa nova and MPB (Musica Popular Brasileira) in the garden. Tuesday nights feature stand-up comedy.

★Spot
Alameda Ministro Rocha Azevedo 72, Consolação (3284 6131/www.restaurantespot.com.br). Metrô Consolação. **Open** noon-3pm, 8pm-1am Mon-Fri; noon-5pm, 8pm-1am Sat, Sun. **Credit** AmEx, DC, MC, V. **Map** p244 K7 ❼
A good place to spot and be spotted. Television personalities and movie stars galore appear nightly at this glass palace. It's slightly less fashionable than a decade ago when it opened, but it's still a cosmopolitan meeting place with the best Bloody Marys in town. Suits from the surrounding skyscrapers flock here for lunch. Get here early, or be prepared to wait a good half an hour to be served.

Tapas Club
Rua Augusta 1246, Consolação (2574 1444/ http://tapasclub.com.br). Metrô Consolação. **Open** 8pm-5am Tue-Sat; 6pm-2am Sun. **Credit** MC, V. **Map** p244 K7 ❽
This trippy-looking hotspot reeks of cool, hosting anything from reggae and dub parties to live jazz, short-film screenings and live painting events. The bar offers typical beer and cocktail selections, plus, atypically, a range of Spanish tapas. Admission is often free but can run up to around R$30.

Oscar Café. *See p135.*

Exquisito!

Volt

*Rua Haddock Lobo 40, Consolação (2936 4041/
www.barvolt.com.br). Bus 177H-10, 719P-10,
917H-41.* **Open** 7pm-1.30am Tue-Wed, Sun;
7pm-3.30am Thur-Sat. **Credit** AmEx, DC, MC, V.
Map p244 K7 ⑨

Sunglasses are in order at this fashionable joint,
fit for the American Apparel set. Following the
city's ban on visual pollution, proprietor Facundo
Guerra bought neon lights from the various neighbourhood brothels and placed them in the bar –
hence the name. The variation on the margarita
here is delicious: lemon juice is replaced with a
reduction of ginger and passion fruit juice. The
drinks are priced to kill, but once you taste these
tropical libations, the glasses (and clothes) are
bound to come off. *Photo p133.*

Z Carniceria

*Rua Augusta 934, Augusta (2936 0934/
www.zcarniceria.com.br). Bus 107P-10, 107T-
10, 702N-10.* **Open** 7pm-1.30am Tue-Wed, Sun;
7pm-3.30am Thur-Sat. **Credit** AmEx, DC, MC,
V. **Map** p242 L6 ⑩

Feeling carnivorous? You won't find what you're
looking for in this butcher shop. The newest bar
on the block serves a mostly vegetarian menu in a
restored 1950s slaughterhouse. Fine attention to
historical detail, including *azulejos* (Portuguese
blue tiles) nod to the past. For drinks, try the excellent Bloody Mary, and to experience an authentic
taste of a Brazilian childhood, try the old-
fashioned, cult soft drink Itubaina. The alternative
crowd, excellent decor and less trendy location on
the quieter side of Rua Augusta have already made
it a favourite. *Photo p135.*

BROOKLIN

Buddha Bar

*Vila Daslu, Avenida Chedid Jafet 131 (3044
6181/www.buddhabarbrasil.com.br). Bus 637C-
10, 648P-10, 7710-10.* **Open** 7.30pm-1am Mon-
Thur; 7.30pm-2am Sat, Sun. **Credit** AmEx, DC,
MC, V.

Step inside this enlightened sanctuary and discover
nirvana for the price of a delightful cocktail. Try the
Dark Angel, with cranberries, raspberries, Cointreau
and saké; or the Buddha, one of the many saké and
maracuja drinks on the menu. Located in the exclusive Vila Daslu shopping mall, this branch of the
Buddha Bar chain, which is already a trendsetter in
Paris, New York and Dubai, is filled with the well-
heeled and independent symbols of Paulistano chic.
The huge, golden Buddha dominates everything but
the achingly beautiful clientele.

CENTRO

Amigo Leal

*Rua Amaral Gurgel 165, Centro (3223 6873,
www.amigoleal.com.br). Metrô Republica.*
Open 4pm-1am Mon-Fri; noon-1am Sat; 5pm-
midnight Sun. **Credit** AmEx, DC, MC, V.
Map p243 M5 ⑪

Germans originally popularised beer in Brazil, and
this wood-panelled bar has a credible Rheine River
feel. Its name refers to friendship and loyalty; similarly it has been helping the centre's businessmen
relax after work for more than four decades. The
emphasis here is on quality draught beer, original
pasteis (fried snacks) and a few German dishes, such
as *Eisbein* (pig knees) and *Kassler* (pork chops).

CONSUME

INSIDE TRACK
DRINK AND SNACK

While Brazilian cachaças and caipirinhas are great, one of the best things to try in a traditional Brazilian bar is not the alcohol but the food. Brazilian chefs are at their most creative when they're serving finger foods and fried pastries. Try these places for the best bar food: **Pandoro** for seafood (*see p133*), **Bar Léo** for lunch food (*see p132*) and **Empanadas Bar** for Latin American food (*see p139*).

Bar Léo

Rua Aurora 100, República (3221 0247/ www. barleo.com.br). Bus 701A-10, 9162-10, 1177-51. Metrô Luz. **Open** 11am-8.30pm Mon-Fri; 10.45am-4pm Sat. **Credit** MC, V. **Map** p243 N4 ⑫
Dating back to the 1940s, Bar Léo remains a famous old-time *botequim* with reminders of a time when t-shirts and unaccompanied women were not allowed inside. Its acclaimed reputation rests on serving the creamiest draught beer in town. The accompanying *petiscos* (appetisers) are a must; try the mouthwatering *bolinhos de bacalhau* (fried fish balls) and the canapés. The area directly around Bar Léo is still being revitalised, so it opens and closes very early.

Café Girondino

Rua Boa Vista 365, Republica (3229 4574/ www.cafegirondino.com.br). Metrô São Bento. **Open** 7.30am-11pm Mon-Fri; 8am-6pm Sat, Sun. **Credit** AmEx, DC, MC, V. **Map** p243 O5 ⑬
Named for a famous café in the days when chic hotels were located in the centre and their clients needed an elite spot for a caffeine fix, today's Girondino is more of an island outpost. It's one of the few places in the area where you can go for a coffee on weekends or evenings after hitting an exhibition or a film at the CCBB, or perhaps one of the other cultural institutions nearby. Beer, coffee, tea and a range of cakes and pastries are offered; at midday, there is a full lunch menu, including pasta and meat dishes.

Terraço Itália

42nd floor, Avenida Ipiranga 344, Centro (2189 2929/www.terracoitalia.com.br). Metrô República. **Open** 3pm-12am Mon-Thur; 3pm-1am Fri, Sat; 3pm-11pm Sun. **Credit** AmEx, DC, MC, V. **Map** p243 M5 ⑭
The bar at the top of the landmark Edifício Itália might lack the opulence and glamour of the other penthouse purveyors of liquor, but it makes up for it with an old-school feel, a warm attendance and a 360° expanse of horizon. The furniture is shabby in places, and if you have any inclination towards vertigo steer

well clear, but looking out at the buzzing helicopters and the endless ocean of skyscrapers is enough of a draw for many. The prices are less steep than at comparable establishments, but extended drinking will take its toll on your wallet. Try the caipirinha with saké and basil. The unobstructed view comes at a cost: R$15 will be added to your bill.

LIBERDADE

Choperia Liberdade

Rua da Glória 523, Liberdade (3207 8783). Bus 314J-10, 314V-10, 714C-10. **Open** 7pm-5am Tue-Sun. **Credit** D, MC, V. **Map** p245 O7 ⑮
A gloriously kitsch and decadent atmosphere prevails at this karaoke haven, a bar that's full of hypnotic waterfall holograms. It's popular with the older male locals in the back, who drink litres of saké or whisky until around 5am. Other regulars include surprisingly flawless singers who, with a small range of 1980s hits, continue late into the night. Sushi and skewers of tasty grilled meat are served throughout the never-ending pop concert. Avoid the weekend crowds, and warm up your vocal chords for a weekday visit to ensure your five minutes of fame.

ITAIM BIBI, MOEMA
& VILA OLÍMPIA

★ Bar Ao Vivo

Rua Inhambu 229, Moema (5052 0072/ www.aovivomusic.com.br). Bus 576M-10. **Open** 7pm-2am Mon-Sat. **Credit** DC, MC V. **Map** p246 J14 ⑯
This charming nightspot is a cross between a dark little jazz bar and a jovial pub. It showcases many national musicians – and you can catch anything from a capella singers to instrumental jazz seven days a week. For drinks, try the chef's martini, made with premium vodka, Cointreau and Blue Curaçau, or the Citrontini (citrus vodka), Cointreau and drops of orange and lime juice.

Bar do Arnesto

Rua Ministro Jesuino Cardoso 207, Vila Olímpia (3848 9432/www.bardoarnesto. com.br). Bus 6418. **Open** 5pm-1am Tue-Fri, Sun; 1pm-1am Sat. **Credit** AmEx, MC, V.
You could wear out several livers attempting to taste all the drinks on offer here. Among the options are an outrageous 503 cachaças, a good range of Brazilian and European beers, a respectable South American wine list and a fanciful array of original cocktail suggestions, often very sweet and involving tropical fruits. The kitchen serves up meat dishes and fried snacks. The decor, in its own chic way, tries to recreate a classic 1960s *botequim* – a guise that's easier to fall for when the nightly samba bands circle up to play (around 9.30pm). On saturdays there is a *feijoada* from 1pm to 5.30pm.

Volt. See p131.

Pandoro

Avenida Cidade Jardim 60, Jardim Europa
(3063 1621/www.pandorobar.com.br). Bus 5119.
Open noon-1am daily. **Credit** AmEx, DC, MC, V.
Map p249 F12 ⑰

If you've got a hankering for tuna confit, *chuva de polvos* ('rain of octopuses') or *garoa de lulas* ('a drizzle of squids'), then head to Pandoro. You might then wash away your thirst with a *caju amigo* ('cashew fruit friend'), the establishment's signature drink since its early days. If all that's not enough to make old money feel right at home, there's the 1950s-era decor, mini-botanical garden and aquarium.

JARDINS

Bar Balcão

Rua Dr. Melo Alves 150, Jardim Paulista
(3063 6091). Bus 7245-10, 7545-10, 7598-41.
Metrô Clínicas. **Open** from 6pm Mon-Sun.
Credit AmEx, DC, MC, V. **Map** p244 I7 ⑱

This bar's namesake winding wooden counter replaces tables as a meeting point for patrons, striking a middle ground between the communal and the private. Ranging from umbrella light fixtures to a giant Lichtenstein-style painting that covers an entire wall, the art here only adds to the experimental atmosphere. A favourite of São Paulo's creative set, Balcão is never a big event, but it's always a good night out.

Baretto

Fasano, 88 Rua Vittório Fasano, Jardim Paulista
(3896 4000/www.fasano.com.br). Bus 107P-10,
107T-10, 702N-10. Metrô Consolação
Open 7pm-3am Mon-Fri; 8pm-3am Sat.
Credit AmEx, DC, MC, V. **Map** p244 I8 ⑲

Skye Bar at Hotel Unique may have the city panorama at its feet, but Baretto at Hotel Fasano has arguably the finest live music programming in town. Inaugurated with the launching of Caetano Veloso's 2004 disc, *A Foreign Sound*, Baretto seeks to compete with the likes of New York's Hotel Carlyle in offering a performing platform to world-renowned voices in a classic setting. The dry martini here is magnificent: it's half-served in your glass, while the rest comes in a small bottle with its own tiny ice bucket. Leather and mahogany is the decor of choice, while the architecture reflects the tastes of Isay Weinfeld, São Paulo's newest internationally recognised architect. The covers for musical performances range from R$60 to R$100.

Choperia Opção

Rua Carlos Comenale 97, Bela Vista (3288
7823). Metrô Trianon-MASP. **Open** 4pm-3am
Mon-Thur; 4pm-5.30am Fri, Sat; 4pm-2am Sun.
Credit DC, MC, V. **Map** p244 K8 ⑳

Need a drink after getting acquainted with the beautifully depressing Portinari paintings at the MASP? Make your way to Opção, located directly behind and below the museum; it's known as Avenida Paulista's best happy-hour bar. Featuring a tree-covered patio, a number of large flatscreen TVs and a group of boozers cheering a football game, it's an option that you can't turn down. Lacking originality the shared 600ml bottles of near-freezing beer

CONSUME

Cachaça's Shot at the Top

From moonshine to million-dollar bebida.

Nobel laureate and lush William Faulkner quipped that civilisation began when man happened upon the happy accident of fermentation. By that definition, Brazilian civilisation began with cachaça, the distilled by-product of fermented sugarcane. Its history, while a bit blurry, does date back to the earliest days of Brazil: by some accounts, the *cano* derivative was first produced in the 16th century, in the Captaincy of São Vicente, present day São Paulo state.

Before evolving into the ever-popular caipirinha 400 years later, cachaça was put to many uses: as a medicine; as a means for keeping slaves at arduous labour (the masters claimed it gave them *ânimo*, or drive); as a commodity in African slave trafficking and even as currency within slave communities. During the golden age of navigation, ships travelling the Straits of Magellan route to the Pacific stopped in Rio de Janeiro for repairs and provisions and to keep the crews' *ânimo* up, piled the hold high with the Brazilian 'rum' (though both are made from sugarcane, cachaça is distinctive and tastes more like tequila).

Cachaça even lays claim to British legend: the first boat to transport convicts to Botany Bay, Australia, is believed to have carried cachaça, and the first public drunkenness on the beaches of the land down under was possibly spirited by the high-proof Brazilian fire water. By the 17th century, cachaça's popularity had become so potent that it led the Portuguese crown to attempt production limits, a failed bid to protect commerce in established wine and spirits.

Long considered a poor man's drink, today cachaça is big business. Brazilians raise their glasses with 400 million gallons of cachaça each year, made by more than 30,000 distillers. The export market has surpassed four million gallons annually, and that number is growing, as the hip bars of the world's cosmopolitan capitals discover premium cachaças and endless tropical variations of the once standard lime caipirinha. Steve Luttmann, CEO of New York-based premium cachaça brand Leblon, is even lobbying the US Alcohol and Tobacco Tax and Trade Bureau to make cachaça its own alcohol category.

In São Paulo, you can sample cachaça as a R$20 cocktail in which Amazonian berries bob, or you can keep it *pura*, like the first Australians, and sample a pinga (from the verb *pingar*, which means 'to drip', as the 16th-century sugarcane run-off often did, the first step on its road to becoming a world-renown liquor).

Neighbouring state Minas Gerais is considered top of the shots when it comes to distilling artesanal cachaça: it garnered 11 of the 20 spots when Brazilian *Playboy* compiled its Best Cachaças list. São Paulo is no poor sobriety sister, though, with its *pingas* also at the top of most connoisseur rankings. The state makes the biggest slice of the country's signature spirit: 46 per cent in 2007. The ubiquitous brands, 51 (Brazil's most sold and a São Paulo-based company) and Ypioca, are fine when covered by a mountain of fruit and sugar, but for cachaça sophistication, try a *pinga* of São Paulo state distillations Sapucaia Velha and Mato Dentro, both on *Playboy*'s list.

And remember, cachaça isn't meant to be downed, but savoured sip by sip.

Z Carniceria. *See p131.*

and communal plates of finger food, from bite-sized steaks to classic chips, are the order of the day here.

Cristallo
Rua Oscar Freire 914, Jardim Paulista (3082 1783/www.cristallo.com.br). Metrô Consolação. **Open** 10am-10pm Mon-Sun. **Credit** AmEx, V. **Map** p244 I8 ㉑
Hard to miss on your tour of Oscar Freire, Cristallo's mosaic-like Mona Lisa façade is arguably the most attractive store front on the street. It was the first chocolate/pastry shop opened in 1953 by Italian immigrant Armando Poppa. Since then, Cristallo has been serving the best panettone and panini in town; and don't leave without trying every Brazilian's favourite – *bombas*. Grab a seat outside for an espresso and a spot of people-watching.
Other locations: throughout the city.

O'Malley's
Alameda Itu 1529, Cerqueira César (3086 0780/ www.omalleysbar.net). Bus 177H-10, 719P-10, 719H-41. Metrô Consolação. **Open** noon-5am Mon-Sun. **Credit** AmEx, DC, MC, V. **Map** p244 J7 ㉒
This traditional English pub seems to attract every Englishman living in São Paulo, but it's in fact owned by a delightful Dutchman. The effort the clientele take to out-Cockney each other provides a good English lesson for lone Brazilians wandering in to this expat den. The staff serves beer from countries as diverse as Mexico, the Czech Republic and Belgium, while the patrons drink hard and talk fast.

Oscar Café
Rua Oscar Freire 727A, Jardim Paulista (3063 5209/www.oscarcafe.com.br). Metrô Consolação. **Open** noon-midnight Mon-Fri; 10am-midnight Sat; 10am-10pm Sun. **Credit** AmEx, DC, MC, V. **Map** p244 I8 ㉓
Retro-chic is the word at this Oscar Freire hotspot. The downstairs café offers some of the best espressos in the area. The ambience is accented with framed pictures on the walls, a bookshelf, mirrored tables and, in the back, an area straight from *The Jetsons*: a futuristic TV and lamps create a cosy, relaxed vibe. Upstairs is a bar and restaurant offering a number of set meals (from R$30-R$40 and including a glass of wine) as well as an à la carte menu. *Photo p130.*

Pâtisserie Douce France
Alameda Jaú 554, Cerqueira Cesar (3262 3542/www.patisseriedoucefrance.com.br). Metrô Trianon MASP. **Open** 8am-8pm daily. **Credit** AmEx, DC, MC, V. **Map** p244 K9 ㉔
The owner and pastry chef of this pleasant café in Jardim Paulista Fabrice Le Nud has won numerous awards for his original and mouthwatering creations. A bakery, café and a *sorveteria* (ice-cream parlour) all in one, the glassed-in, European-style veranda and the charming red-velvet parlour inside are perfect settings for a cup of tea or coffee and a sampling of Le Nud's brilliant desserts. Try the Brazilian-themed sorbets, especially the *berimbau*, a mango sorbet in the shape of the stringed instrument that accompanies the martial art of *capoiera*.

CONSUME

Make the most of London life

Suplicy Café.

Other locations: Morumbi Shopping, Area Fashion-Piso Lazer, Morumbi (5189 4584).

Skye

Hotel Unique, Avenida Brigadeiro Luís Antônio 4700, Jardim Paulista (3055 4702/www.skye. com.br). Bus 477A-10, 669A-41, 696P-10. Metrô Brigadeiro. **Open** noon-3pm, 6pm-1am Mon-Thur; 6pm-2am Fri-Sun. *Breakfast* 7-11am daily. **Credit** AmEx, DC, M, V. **Map** p244 I11 ❷
See and be seen at the swankiest spot in town. Hotel Unique's signature poolside bar attracts long-legged models and silver-voiced singers as well as up-and-coming *telenovela* sensations and suits. The glass, glimmer and glow of the setting and city views belie prices that aren't as splendidly high as the bar's elevation. Order a mojito and lounge on one of the outside deck chairs under mood-enhancing lighting. Head there on a weekday if you are in a serenading mood. Skye serves dinner starting at 7pm.

Suplicy Café

Alameda Lorena 1430, Jardim Paulista (3061 0195/www.suplicycafés.com.br). Metrô Consolação, Metrô Trianon-MASP. **Open** 7.30am-midnight Mon-Thur; 8am-1am Fri; 8am-midnight Sat, Sun. **Credit** AmEx, DC, MC, V. **Map** p244 J8 ❷
Suplicy is a small, high-end café chain. The baristas are friendly and the brewers take their coffee seriously; you can watch the beans being roasted in a huge contraption straight out of *Willy Wonka's Chocolate Factory*. Unlike the US café coloniser, Suplicy has not mastered the art of coffee on the go; apparently no-one makes to-go cups in Brazil. Suplicy is a trendier alternative to Starbucks, whose descent on São Paulo can already be seen around Jardim Paulista.
Other locations: throughout the city.

The View

Transamerica International Plaza, Alameda Santos 981, Jardim Paulista (3266 3692/ www.theviewbar.com.br). Bus 669A-10, 669A-41, 714C-10. Metrô Trianon-MASP. **Open** 6pm-2am Mon-Sat. **Credit** AmEx, DC, MC, V. **Map** p244 L9 ❷
As the heavy-handed name suggests, this romantic happy medium between the styles and prices of Fasano and Skye is a penthouse establishment 30 floors up. As a piano bar it attracts both the rendez-vousing barflies and the desperately seeking singles. Better to go with a partner, as seduction is ensured. Only a few wines are below R$100 a bottle. The better bets are the well-made cocktails: the kir royales and margaritas are recommended.

PINHEIROS & VILA MADALENA

Astor

Rua Delfina 163, Vila Madalena (3815 1364/ www.barastor.com.br). Bus 748F-10, 6232-10. **Open** 6pm-2am Mon-Wed; 6pm-3am Thur; noon-4am Fri, Sat; noon-10pm Sun. **Credit** AmEx, DC, M, V. **Map** p249 E7 ❷
Astor recalls the grandeur of the glory days of Americana (the bar was brought over from Philadelphia by boat). An older, more affluent clientele frequents the bar; nevertheless, it maintains an air of jazzy youth. The food is excellent: try a portion of the mouthwatering *feijão* (bean, pork and garlic soup, and a national gastronomic icon). Brazilians have a way with beans in the cauldron that you can't afford to ignore.

Bar Anhanguera

Rua Aspicuelta 595, Vila Madalena (3031 2888/ www.baranhanguera.com.br). Bus 701A. **Open**

CONSUME

The Big Freeze

Beer etiquette in Brazil.

Eccentric billionaires working in tandem with fringe scientists have spent minor fortunes developing cryogenic technology to defeat death. Celebrities too, such as Boston Red Sox slugger Ted Williams, choose high-tech cryogenic freezer over the coffin for when they bite the dust. Yet, despite all the money invested in and and science devoted to the development of cryogenics, the (cheaper) answer is simple: the Brazilian beer refrigerator.

However you decide to down your Brazilian brew, either from the *garrafa* (a big bottle meant for sharing) or *chopp* (a pull of draught, though much smaller than a pint), expect a delightful brain freeze to accompany the flavour. If you arrive at a classic *chopperia* (draught pub), like Posto 6 in Vila Madalena (*see p141*), early enough in the evening, you may even witness the sacred coronation of the tap: a huge block of ice is placed on the head of the *chopp* tank, and so begins a microcosm of Ice Age glacial transfer. After a few hours at the top of the *chopp*, the slow seep of the frigid block transforms the tank's exterior into a glistening wall of ice.

In watering holes where *garrafas* are the rule, the beer-refrigeration technology is no less stupendous and even more high-tech on the surface. The logo of Brahma, Antarctica or Bohemia may adorn the exterior of the appliance, but on any beer refrigerator, there should be a functioning digital display showing second-by-second changes in the interior temperature. If the red numbers on the LCD read-out are in positive territory, or the digital display is blank, you are well advised to leave immediately, as this may not only portend lukewarm beer, but is an affront to proper Brazilian beer etiquette. If the temperature ranges from -1.0 to -3.4, it's safe to order up. (Note: if it dips below -4.0, you may want to wear gloves.)

It's not uncommon to discover a miniature iceberg floating in a *garrafa*. Some consider that intra-drink melting to be the pinnacle and final reminder of just how seriously Brazilians take beer temperature. Ultimately, this sliver of ice could prove vital to much more than just quenching our individual thirst in the tropics. Nations show pride in many accomplishments, from art to athletics to breakthroughs in science. Brazil can point to lofty achievements too – samba, Pelé and Vila-Lobos, to name a few; but it is the Brazilian beer-makers who may be the ones our grandchildren's world places on a pedestal. Cryogenics may be a crackpot's gamble, but with the mass production of enough beer refrigerators, global warming just might become manageable.

6pm-1am Tue-Fri; 3pm-2am Sat; 3pm-midnight Sun. **Credit** DC, MC, V. **Map** p249 F9 ㉙

A beer connoisseur in Brazil might imagine themselves in a land of taste purgatory, given the blandness of major brands and Brazilians' preference for drinking them ultra-cold to mask that fact. Bar Anhanguera will awake you from this nightmare, with a menu devoted exclusively to Brazilian microbrews, all without preservatives. With beers from every part of Brazil, the management claims to have something for every discriminating pub taste.

Bar de Ontem
Rua Cardeal Arcoverde 1761, Vila Madalena (3097 9811/www.bardeontem.com.br). Bus 177Y. MetrôClínicas. **Open** 6pm-late Wed-Sat; 3pm-late Sat; 5pm-late Sun. **Credit** MC, V. **Map** p248 D7 ㉚

While football matches are the norm on many bar screens in Vila Madalena, this defiant joint fill its monitors with concert footage of great MPB performers. The youthful crowd enjoys late-night snacking on the *escondido* (a manioc casserole with cheese and anything from shrimp to chicken). The bartender's favourite poison is a jumbo-sized mix of five hard liquors called the *drink de ontem* ('yesterday's cocktail') that just might be the most deliciously debilitating thing you'll ever taste.

Boteco Santa Laura
Rua Aspicuelta 567, Vila Madalena (3031 1525). Bus 701A. **Open** 7pm-midnight Tue-Wed; from 7pm Thur, Fri; from 6pm Sat; from 2pm Sun. *Concerts* 8pm-12.30am Wed-Sun. **Credit** AmEx, MC, V. **Map** p249 E8 ㉛

The revellers here are every bit as serious about drinking (beer, of course) as in any of the bars along Rua Aspicuelta, but this place also gets people dancing. Fuelling the fun are a mix of DJs and live bands, with samba rock on Wednesdays, *sertaneja* (country music from the interior of Brazil) on Thursdays and samba on weekends. If that's not enough to please everyone, there's a cute mini-electronightclub area in the back room. Cover can range from R$10 to R$15.

★Boteco Seu Zé
Rua Mourato Coelho 1144, Vila Madalena (3034 6382/www.botecoseuze.com.br). Bus 701A. **Open** 6pm-2am Wed-Fri; 1pm-1am Sat, Sun. **Credit** AmEx, DC, MC, V. **Map** p249 E6 ㉜

A traditional Carioca-style samba bar, Boteco Seu Zé gets going quite slowly, with groups of young people sipping ice-cold *chopp* and eating *feijoada*. It livens up as the small band plays louder and faster, and the bow-tied waiters clear out the tables to make room for dancing. The white tiled walls are full of framed caricatures of famous Brazilians named Zé (short for José), and there's a retractable roof to take advantage of sunshine or to avoid rain. Get there early and order a communal *porção de picanha* (top sirloin steak), brought to the table on a sizzling skillet and cooked right before your eyes. Schedule at least three hours for the meal and expect to dance. Artistic covers vary from R$7 to R$10.

Cachaçaria Paulista
Rua Mourato Coelho 593, Vila Madalena (3815 4756/www.cachacariapaulista.com.br). Bus 177Y. **Open** 8pm-5am Fri-Sat. **No credit cards. Map** p249 F9 ㉝

If you can get past the staff's sometimes surly attitude, this is a great place to experience cachaça, as the bar has over 380 varieties from all parts of Brazil on offer. Forget about Manhattans and Cosmopolitans; the next *Sex and the City* movie might feature sweetened cachaças in flavours like kiwi and strawberry that this establishment purveys. For over seven years now, musician Luis Baia has taken the stage here at around midnight to play classic MPB, bossa nova, forró and rock. There's a R$20 cover, R$14 of which includes a drink or two.

Deli Paris
Rua Harmonia 484, Vila Madalena (3816 5911/www.deliparis.com.br). Metrô Vila Madalena. **Open** 7.30am-10.30pm daily. **Credit** V. **Map** p249 E7 ㉞

This Parisian sidewalk café is the perfect place to go for a simple coffee and croissant or a fabulous full-scale Sunday brunch buffet (R$19). Whether you're craving salty or sweet, everything here manages to be superbly delicious. The crepes are to die for and come with a variety of fillings, or try the more veggie-centric offerings such as zucchini quiche or ratatouille.

Empanadas Bar
Rua Wisard 489, Vila Madalena (3032 2116/ www.empanadasbar.com.br). Bus 701A. **Open** 1pm-late daily. **Credit** DC, MC, V. **Map** p249 E8 ㉟

Longing for a quasi-intellectual/leftist hangout or one that once was? Founded in the 1980s by an Argentinian and a Chilean, this joint has the welcome feel of the rest of Latin America – you may even catch several patrons using *portunhol* (a mixture of Portuguese and Spanish). Try the empanadas with *carne seca* (jerky-like beef from the Northeastern part of Brazil).

Filial
Rua Fidalga 254, Vila Madalena (3813 9226/ www.barfilial.com.br). Bus 701A. Metrô Vila Madalena. **Open** 7pm-2.30am Mon-Thur; 7pm-3.30am Fri; noon-3.30am Sat; noon-2am Sun. **Credit** AmEx, DC, MC, V. **Map** p249 E8 ㊱

Somewhat famous, very friendly and a tad bit familial: Filial is owned by the Altman brothers, who opened their first Vila Madalena bar in 1980 and dedicated it to the lovely Brazilian music of *choro*. Since then, the former Clube do Choro has metamorphosed various times and in different locations of this

CONSUME

Posto 6.

neighbourhood; but it is still the after-show bar choice for the *bairros* many musicians. The extensive list of cachaças from Minas Gerais and the caipirinha options are astounding; try the cachaça with *lima da persia* – an odd yet lovely citrus fruit. The best option on a nice night is to sit outside the bar and watch the craziness of Vila Madalena float by. There is a feijoada on Saturday from noon-6pm for R$28.50.

Garagem do Carlão

Rua Lira 129, Vila Madalena (3926 9130). Metrô Vila Madalena. **Open** 6pm-10pm Tue-Fri. Frequently changing hours Sat. **No credit cards**. **Map** p248 D7 ③⑦

The interior design includes a lantern, extension cords, a motorcycle and a few chairs: don't expect to get you car fixed at this tuned-up dive. The authentic garage is one of the warmest establishments to jumpstart an evening with a beer or a caipirinha. It is conveniently located halfway from the *Metrô* station to the neighbourhood's popular music joints on Rua Girasol and Rua Aspicuelta.

Genésio

Rua Fidalga 265 (3812 6252/www.bargenesio. com.br). Bus 701A. **Open** 5pm-4am Mon-Fri; noon-3am Sat, Sun. **Credit** AmEx, DC, MC, V. **Map** p249 E6 ③⑧

From the owners of Filial comes another classic *botequim*, situated just across the street but with an emphasis on fabulous pizzas and pastas. Like its sibling, Genésio is known for its outrageous anthology of cachaças and a similar hipster ambience.

▶ **Other location** Nearby Genial, the third chopperia from the brothers Altman (Rua Girassol 374, 3812 7442) is also a good option for its outdoor seating and tasty meats.

El Guatón

Rua Artur de Azevedo 906, Pinheiros (3085 9466/3807 9647). Bus 795P. **Open** 11am-midnight Mon-Sat; noon-5pm Sun. **Credit** AmEx, DC, MC, V. **Map** p249 G9 ③⑨

This passionately Chilean establishment is your home in Pinheiros for pisco sour, the famous South American cocktail based on the hard liquor distilled from grapes. While most neophytes assume that pisco originated in Peru, it's a point of contention between Peru and Chile, so don't bring it up inside. The friendly staff will also tempt you with empanadas and a variety of fried seafood you won't see much of elsewhere in São Paulo.

El Kabong Grill

Rua Mateus Grou 15, Pinheiros (3064 9354/ www.elkabong.com.br). Bus 715F-10. **Open** 6pm-midnight Mon-Thur; 6pm-1.30am Fri, Sat; 4pm-midnight Sun. **Credit** AmEx, DC, MC, V. **Map** p249 F10 ④⓪

This 1990s rock bar and teen hangout-turned-Tex-Mex restaurant is either your idea of heaven or hell. Modelled on American chains like Applebee's and Outback Steakhouse (surprising hits with the young and the restless), El Kabong brings in the crowds with a brilliant promo scheme. Chic Paulistano thirtysomethings swear by Fridays' classic happy hours and Wednesdays' women-only two-for-one margarita specials. The house offers a double-the-trouble deal Wednesdays, Thursdays and Sundays: order any dish and get the same meal the following Monday and Tuesday, but pay for the service only.

Pé De Manga

Rua Arapiraca 152, Vila Madalena (3032 6068/ www.pedemanga.com.br). Bus 701A. **Open**

6pm-2am Mon-Thur; 6pm-4am Fri; noon-4am Sat; noon-midnight Sun. **Credit** AmEx, DC, MC, V. **Map** p249 E7 ④

Three enormous mango trees give cover to a hoity-toity crowd here. The celebrity-themed sandwiches, the *mini-acarajé* appetiser and various mixed-fruit *caipiroskas* (try the lychee) give this bar a menu outside of the repetitive norm of Brazilian bar food. Well worth an evening with a group of friends.

Pirajá

Av. Brigadeiro Faria Lima 64, Pinheiros (3815 6881/www.piraja.com.br). Bus 477A. **Open** noon-1am Mon-Wed; noon-2am Thur, Fri; noon-2am Sat; noon-7pm Sun. **Credit** AmEx, DC, MC, V. **Map** p248 D7 ④

In imitation of a Carioca *botequim*, Pirajá has classic woodwork and small tables sprinkling out onto the sidewalk. The bar is popular for its beer, a small range of cachaças and some wine. Named after an Amazonian fish and in a nod to Spain, it has a fish-based menu with an emphasis on tapas preparation. If you stretch the imagination a bit, you might smell Rio's salty air or hear children playing on a Mediterranean plaza. Otherwise, prepare to watch through a thicket of foliage as traffic lurches on one of São Paulo's main thoroughfares.

Posto 6

Rua Aspicuelta 644, Vila Madalena (3812 4342/www.posto6.com). Bus 701A. **Open** 5pm-3am Mon-Fri; 2pm-2am Sat, Sun. **Credit** AmEx, DC, V. **Map** p249 E8 ④

Situated on the most popular corner of Vila Madalena, this grand old dame of *chopperias* is a classic old wood-panelled bar. The walls are covered with caricatures of famous personalities, while the vibe harkens back to the good-old 1960s, Rio's golden age. (The name Posto 6 is a reference to the famous lifeguard post, and associated hangout spot, on Ipanema beach.) Whether you're drinking an ice-cold Brahma, or sipping a delicious lime caipirinha, the vibe here is refreshing and the pace is easy. Pair your drinks with the best fried *mandioca* (fried yucca) in town. *Photo p138 and left.*

Salve Jorge

Rua Aspicuelta 544, Vila Madalena (3815 0705). Bus 701A. **Open** 5pm-2am Mon-Fri; noon-2.30am Sat; noon-1am Sun. **Credit** AmEx, DC, MC, V. **Map** p249 E8 ④

The clientele may be ever-so-slightly older, but this bar retains the charm and the noise of a classic Brazilian watering-hole. It may not be the most novel establishment in the *bairro*, but it's a favourite for the let's-get-hammered-in-Vila Madalena set. On weekend nights, you'll need the help of a devoted guardian angel to get a table (don't count on the waiters). But even if your heavenly protector falls sort, you're still in the classic centre of Rua Aspicuelta's bar scene, and many clones are within stumbling distance.

★ São Cristovão

Rua Aspicuelta 533, Vila Madalena (3097 9904). Bus 177Y/778J. **Open** from noon daily. **Credit** AmEx, DC, MC, V. **Map** p249 E8 ④

This wonderful little bar, with a red façade and charming picture-covered walls seems straight out of a Parisian guidebook. Surprisingly, it's Paris by way of Pelé. Devoted to the São Cristovão football team, it sports football photos and memorabilia on positively every square-inch space of wall. From Tuesday to Thursday, root for a Brazilian football team while downing a strong caipirinha. There is a R$12 cover on Mondays (a jazz band plays at 9pm) and a R$8 on Sundays for live samba at 5pm.

Teta

Rua Cardeal Arcoverde 1265, Pinheiros. (3031-1641/www.tetajazzbar.com.br). Bus 117Y-10, 701A-10, 775F-10. **Open** 6pm-5am Mon-Sat. **Credit** AmEx, M, V. **Map** p249 F8 ④

It seems that many of the best spots in São Paulo are next to cemeteries. Teta does not defy this trend, but reflects its rather dark surroundings with a simple yet cosy interior. Specialising in good live music – mostly jazz, bossa nova and *chorinho* (Brazilian music that mostly uses guitars) – it stays open later than most bars in the city, and with neighbours across the street resting for all eternity, there's no chance of rousing them at any hour. The humble decor and a warm bartending team make this a great spot for a night of dedicated melodic pleasure. There is a R$6 happy hour cover for live music, while the primary show covers vary from R$10 to R$15 on weekends.

Vianna Bar

Rua Cristiano Viana 315, Pinheiros (3082 8228). Bus 7245-10, 7545-10, 7598-41. Metrô Clinicas. **Open** 6pm-2am Mon-Fri; noon-2am Sat. **Credit** AmEx, DC, MC, V. **Map** p249 G6 ④

Looking to escape the crowds after an afternoon at the nearby Benedito Calixto Saturday market? Stop by Vianna for food ranging from traditional pastas to Greek *spanakopita* and Lebanese *kafta kebab*, as well as attentive service. The pleasantly smallish patio is a nice place to meet friends for some Brahma in this largely residential area.

THE BEST CACHAÇA

While most places around town serve cachaças, only a small number of spots are known for their variety and flair. Try **Bar do Arnesto** (*see p132*), **Cachaçaria Paulista** (*see p139*) and **Filial** (*see p139*) for a great atmosphere and enough cachaças to satisfy the longing of the most adamant aficionado.

Shops & Services

Shopaholics unite in the tropical land of plenty.

From the chi-chi world of Rua Oscar Freire to the frenzy of indoor and outdoor markets selling knock-off designer wallets and similar cheap goods, and the growing number of good-quality thrift stores sprouting up across the city, São Paulo is a consumer's dream. The only drawback (other than the inflation that affects locals more than it does visitors) is that non-local produced goods – so international brands – can be expensive here thanks to high import tariffs. But Brazil has some good home-produced wares to offer, notably good-quality and affordable leather goods: it's well worth stocking up on bags, belts and boots.

Dedicated shoppers will need to be prepared to travel: the interesting venues are divided between boutiques in the city centre and huge malls futher out.

USEFUL INFORMATION

Weekday hours vary in São Paulo, with some shops closing at 5pm but others open until 7 or 8pm. Some shops shut early on Saturday lunchtime and most are closed all day Sunday. Malls typically stay open until later in the evening (around 10pm), Sundays included.

There are two sale seasons. The first is the post-New Year sale, which starts at the end of January, when the summer season is coming to an end and most people have taken their holidays. The second starts at the end of August. Prices are generally slashed by at least half but, as you'd expect, the range of sizes and colours is limited.

Many of the high-end boutique stores will offer a tax-free refund that you can claim at the airport.

As well as giving a general introduction to shopping in São Paulo, this chapter focusses particularly on Brazilian brands and typically Paulistano shops.

General

DEPARTMENT STORES

At **Lojas Americanas** (www.americanas. com), a wide range of inexpensive goods merits a name referencing the USA. At Lojas, you'll find everything from confectionery to classic Hollywood DVDs, CDs, flip-flops and a range of clothes for men, women and children. Plus you may be glued to the spot for an hour while the whole shop watches the latest Brazilian music video on a big flat screen. Here you can pick up a *sunga* (a pair of Speedos) and other items popular locally.

The clothes chain **C&A** (www.cea.com.br) is very popular in Brazil, selling cheap, wearable and durable garments for all ages. Smaller than the C&A and Lojas Americanas, **Renner** (www.lojasrenner.com.br), has good prices and stocks a decent range of women's clothes, underwear and gym outfits.

MALLS

Cidade Jardim

Avenida Magalhães de Castro 12000, Butantã (3552 1000/www.shoppingcidadejardimjhsf. com.br). Bus 609F-10. **Open** 10am-10pm daily. Hours at stores, bars and restaurants vary. **Credit** varies. **Map** p224 C3.

There are more malls in São Paulo than you could visit in a lifetime, but only one for which Carrie Bradshaw (Sarah Jessica Parker) serves as the public face. The most anticipated opening of 2008, Parque Cidade Jardim is the main facility of a 12-tower complex that's still under construction. Its exclusive mall features Hèrmes, Giorgio Armani, Montblanc and Brazilian designer Carlos Miele. Be sure to check out Chocolat du Jour, the best chocolate store in town.

Where to Shop

São Paulo's best shopping neighbourhoods.

Bom Retiro
The shopping streets in Bom Retiro (3361 9984, www.cdlbomretiro.org), especially along **Rua José Paulino**, **Rua Ribeiro de Lima** and **Rua Aimorès**, are incredibly popular with those looking for bargain-priced clothes. While the majority of the stores are wholesale, some do sell retail. Try to avoid going on Fridays and Saturdays when the pavements are so crowded that frequently you'd be better off walking on top of the cars.

Caninde
Avenida Vaultier in Caninde is the newest centre for off-the-truck goods, including cheap decorations and party knick-knacks.

Centro & around
Rua 25th de Março is lined with stores offering Carnival decorations as well as counterfeit items: think New York's Chinatown. The neighbourhood of **Brás** has the country's and, many claim, South America's largest concentration of shops and wholesalers.

Consolação
The city's best vintage-clothing stores as well as a great number of excellent boutiques can be found here.

Jardim Paulista
National and international designer stores are concentrated in Jardim Paulista, along **Rua Oscar Freire**, **Rua Alameda Lorena** and **Rua Haddock Lobo**.

Liberdade
Pretty much anything can be found for sale on **Rua Galvão Bueno**, located in the Japanese neighbourhood. Small stores can be found on the street and also inside the galleries. Brazilian stones, kitchen utensils, oriental dishes and all kinds of gifts are spread out in hundreds of outlets.

Pinheiros & Vila Madalena
Antiques stores rule around **Rua Cardeal Arcoverde** and **Praça Benedito Calixto** in Pinheiros. **Rua Aspicuelta** and **Rua Harmonia** in Vila Madalena are home to boutiques and used-clothes stores.

★ Daslu
Avenida Chedid Jafet 131, Vila Olímpia (3841 4000/www.daslu.com.br). Bus 6401-10. **Open** 10am-8pm Mon, Wed-Sat; 10am-10pm Tue. Hours at stores, bars and restaurants vary. **Credit** varies.
Movie stars and various gliteratti descend onto the heliport, while the paparazzi (and mortals) arrive in cars at this hybrid boutique-mall of haute couture – no tacky movie theatres or food courts here. Gucci, Pucci and Prada reign, alongside national designers such as Raia de Goeye, Cris Barros and Osklen at the Village on the second floor. Daslu is the meeting point for the crème de la crème of the Paulistano elite – movers and shakers regularly host dinner parties and other events at Terraço Daslu on the top floor.

Eldorado
Avenida Rebouças 3970, Pinheiros (2197 7800/ www.shoppingeldorado.com.br). Bus 577T-10, 702C-10, 715M-10. **Open** 10am-10pm Mon-Sat; 11am-11pm Sun. Hours at stores, bars and restaurants vary. **Credit** varies. **Map** p248 D5.
A fool and his money are easily parted, especially at Eldorado. The building's previous incarnation was as a branch of a 1980s department store, and the shoulder-pad look remains (at least in the design of the interior). Eldorado's two basement levels cater to every need from dog grooming to cellphone repairs. If you need a bit of light relief from conspicuous consumption, the only permanent ice-skating rink in town is located in the second basement (R$25 for 30 minutes).

Praça Benedito Calixto. *See p158.*

CONSUME

Praia de Paulista

No sand and surf on this Paulista turf.

The American Psychiatric Association can debate all it wants about whether shopaholism is an addiction, but in São Paulo, there is no couch or prescription drug that can keep people from the malls. Lacking the signature sand of Brazil's coast, malls are literally referred to as the *praia* (beach) de Paulista (the nickname for state of São Paulo residents), and visiting one is an experience with roots that stretch back to the time of the coffee barons. The triangle formed by Rua Direita, São Bento and 15 de Novembro was concentrated with the most expensive stores, with products that came directly from Europe to the plantation owners' wives and daughters.

The American-style malls (with ruthless linguistic efficiency, simply known as *shoppings*), as well as one of their greatest features – the parking lot – were adopted in Brazil after World War II. **Iguatemi** (*see below*) was the first *shopping* to open its doors far away from the centre, and picky Paulistanos responded with enthusiasm. Iguatemi has the most expensive square-metre rent in all of Latin America today. Malls are to São Paulo what Versailles was to France: all about style and power.

There are more than 50 major *shoppings* in the city. In competition for first place for pilfering Paulistanos' pockets are **Daslu** (*see p143*) and **Cidade Jardim** (*see p142*), which are even more exclusive than Iguatemi due to their lack of public transport and absurd prices for parking – Daslu charges R$30 for the first hour. (Though who knows who'll be hotter

when a super-exclusive JK Iguatemi opens 300 metres away from Daslu at the end of 2009).

Movie theatres have also become a big part of the luxury motif. Dip into the dark at **Bourbon Shopping** (Rua Turiaçú, 2100, 3874 5050, www.bourbonshopping.com.br), which opened its doors in 2008 with an Imax 3D screen, or at Cidade Jardim, which has the most expensive cinema, featuring controllable seats, waiter service and alcoholic drinks. A movie ticket at the latter can cost R$45.

Violence has contributed to the success of malls, as well as to the separation of rich and poor. The *shoppings* are viewed as safe zones: security guards and high walls allow teenagers, mothers with toddlers, and the elderly to recreate a normal city life of shops, restaurants and entertainment.

In the '90s, older shopping galleries helped revive decaying areas. The **Galeria do Rock** (*see p159*) was stuck in an area taken over by the homeless and drug addicts. Music-store owners, attracted to the musical history of the area, started to open their doors and the galeria gained a young clientele. Rua Augusta retains some of the best galleries, like **Ouro Fino** (Rua Augusta 2690), with alternative and designer fashion, and **Le Village** (Rua Augusta 1492).

Paulistano malls employ about 250,000 people, receive an estimated 3,000,000 shoppers per day, and grow ten per cent each year, notwithstanding the current economic crisis.

Ibirapuera

Avenida Ibirapuera 3103, Moema (5095 2300/ www.ibirapuera.com.br). Bus 5318-10, 5318-21, 5342-10, 5369-10. **Open** 10am-10pm Mon-Sat; 11am-10pm Sun. Hours at stores, bars and restaurants vary. **Credit** varies. **Map** p246 I10.
One of the biggest malls in town, Ibirapuera has more than 400 stores and a gourmet area. Charming small stores can be found outside the mall on Ruas Bem-Te-Vi, Gaivota, Pavão and, especially, Normandia.

Iguatemi

Avenida Brigadeiro Luis Antonio 2232, Jardim Paulistano (3816 6116/www.iguatemisaopaulo. com.br). Metrô Brigadeiro. **Open** 10am-11pm Mon-Sat; 11am-10pm Sun. Hours at stores, bars and restaurants vary. **Credit** varies. **Map** p244 L9.

With a chip on its shoulder the size of the Hope Diamond, sophistication and class still rule at the city's oldest shopping centre. Emporio Armani, Louis Vuitton and Ermenegildo Zegna are just some of the designer dreams on display. The jewellery shop Tiffany & Co has a special store on the bottom floor. Check out Brazilian high-fashion shops like Rosa Chá and Maria Bonita, or for slightly more affordable international style, head to Zara and Diesel.

Morumbi Shopping & Market Place

Avenida Roque Petroni Jr 1089, Brooklin (4003 4132/www.morumbishopping.com.br). Bus 7245-10. **Open** 10am-10pm Mon-Sat; 2pm-8pm Sun. Hours at stores, bars and restaurants vary. **Credit** varies.

CONSUME

Morumbi is a favourite with young executives in the area for its first-floor gym (Companhia Athletica) as well as for a branch of the Fnac bookstore that hosts music shows, art events and book releases. The food court has gourmet restaurants including Ganesh (Indian food) and Barbacoa (meat). Brazilian brands Animale, Carlos Miele, Gloria Coelho and Mara Mac are featured.

Pátio Higienópolis
Avenida Higienópolis 618, Higienópolis (3823 2300/www.patiohigienopolis.com.br). Metrô Marechal Deodoro. **Open** 10am-11pm Mon-Sat; 11am-10pm Sun. Hours at stores, bars and restaurants vary. **Credit** varies. **Map** p242 K11.
Located on a pleasantly leafy boulevard in the city's most charming neighbourhood, this mall is at first hard to distinguish from the mansions and 1950s residential buildings around it. The mall is a gathering spot because of its location as well as the new branch of high-end pizza joint Bar des Arts and brands like Calvin Klein underwear and L'Occitane.

Pátio Paulista
Rua Treze de Maio 1947, Paraíso (3191 1100/ www.shoppingpaulista.com.br). Metrô Paraíso. **Open** 10am-11pm daily. Hours at stores, bars and restaurants vary. **Credit** varies. **Map** p245 M9.
Say goodbye to the '90s! The largest mall on Avenida Paulista has just gone through a complete renovation. It's home to big chains like Zara, Luigi Bertolli and Hering. The Pátio's sleek interior appeals to Avenida Paulista businessmen, primarily for midday trips to the food court, while middle-class kids flock to the small three-screen movie theatre.

Villa-Lobos
Avenida Das Nações Unidas 4777, Alto de Pinheiros (3024 4200/www.shoppingvillalobos. com.br). Bus 6262-10. **Open** 10am-11pm Mon-Sat; 11am-10pm Sun. Hours at stores, bars and restaurants vary. **Credit** varies.
Close to Parque Villa-Lobos, this mall has a good selection of quality shops and restaurants. Check out Arezzo, arguably Brazil's best chain store for gorgeous leather bags and shoes (prices rarely dip below R$100 for shoes and R$250 for bags); and Folic, another Brazilian chain with beautifully designed clothing and great bags. The Livraria Cultura on the top floor has a small auditorium.

MARKETS

Brás
Largo da Concórdia, Brás (2694 0823/ www.alobras.com.br). Metrô Brás. **Open** 8am-5pm Mon-Fri; 8am-2pm Sat. **Credit** varies.
Ruas Oriente, Maria Marcolina and Silva Teles, are at the centre of the country's biggest clothing market. The R$7 billion market and its 55 streets have

Feira da Liberdade.

outfitted what used to be an industrial area as a wholesale district. Retail sales occur mostly on Saturdays, on Rua Oriente in particular. For a real South American experience, come by on a Tuesday and meet the *sacoleiros* (bag people) who come from all over the country to sell their wares, or check out Latin America's biggest wholesale mall, Mega Polo Moda (Rua Barão de Ladário 566/670, 3311 2800, www.megapolomoda.com.br). It has a hotel for those who come from outside the state – VIP customers stay for free like casino high rollers.

★ Feira da República
Praça da República, República. Metrô República. **Open** 8am-5pm Sun. **Map** p243 M11.
Running continuously since 1956, the open-air centre has 600 stands and a wide selection of food, including Japanese *yakissoba*, the omnipresent hot dog, and *acarajé*, the deep-fried Bahian shrimp treat. There is also a large open-air gallery where local artists sell paintings – some of them are quite good.

★ Feira de Arte, Artesanato e Cultura da Liberdade (Feira da Liberdade)
Praça da Liberdade, Liberdade (3208 5090). Metrô Liberdade. **Open** 10am-7pm Sun. **Map** p245 O8.
The weekly fair has been ongoing since 1975 and remains one of São Paulo's best-loved. Its 240 stalls mostly compete for your stomach, and just about any Japanese or Chinese fast-food treat can be found at a reasonable price. Jewellery, bonsai trees, aquarium fish and bamboo kitchen utensils are secondary. *Melona* 'creamsickles' – a curious and delicious

Bonpoint

CH
CAROLINA HERRERA

Just like your closet, with your favorite brands.

FURLA

GANT

HERMÈS

LA PERLA

LOUIS VUITTON

MONT
BLANC

Salvatore Ferragamo

TIFFANY & CO.

Livraria da Vila.

South-Korean ice-cream phenomenon – has also become synonymous with Liberdade and is available in most grocery stores and some restaurants.

Rua 25 de Março
Rua 25 de Março, Centro (3227 1473/www. vitrine25demarco.com.br). Metrô São Bento. **Open** 8am-6pm Mon-Fri; 8am-2pm Sat. **Credit** varies. **Map** p243 O10.
The Brazilian government issued a remarkable statement in 2008: around 90% of the designer goods available on the street were counterfeit. Roughly 3,000 shops fill this outdoor market, concentrated in only eight city blocks – where everything from computer games to underwear and watches can be found. More than 400,000 people work and shop here every day. Around Christmas, the number grows to one million shoppers. Don't forget to check inside malls like Mundo Oriental (Rua Barão de Duprat 323, 3229 8089, www.mundooriental.com.br) and Galeria Pagé (Rua Barão de Duprat 315, 3227 3582,www.galeriapage.com.br).

Specialist
BOOKS & MAGAZINES

There are hundreds of bookstores in São Paulo and the most well recognised are French chain **FNAC** (www.fnac.com.br), and the best Brazilian chains **Saraiva** (www.saraiva.com.br) and **Sicilliano** (www.sicilliano.com.br). Some of the newest bookstores, and the ones most interesting from a design perspective, can be found along Avenida Paulista and in the Jardim Paulista district. Unfortunately, books in Brazil still cost a fortune, a sore point for Brazilian intellectuals who are constantly bemoaning the state of their print industry: it doesn't print enough copies of books to bring the prices down. The Centro has a concentration of 40 *sebos* (used book stores), mostly on Rua Álvares Machado.

English-language

★ Livraria Cultura
Conjunto Nacional, Avenida Paulista 2073, Cerqueira César (3170 4033/www.livraria cultura.com.br). Metrô Consolação. **Open** 9am-10pm Mon-Sat; noon-8pm Sun. **Credit** AmEx, DC, MC, V. **Map** p244 K7.
The three-story Livraria Cultura should be your first bookstore stop. The Nobel Prize for Literature winner Jorge Saramago wrote in his blog that the bookstore is 'a cathedral of books, modern, effective and beautiful.' Comfortable couches, a kids' area and inviting art make it perfect for browsing and skimming a few pages, or skipping through album tracks.
Other locations throughout the city.

★ Livraria da Vila
Rua Fradique Coutinho 915, Pinheiros (3814 5811/www.livrariadavila.com.br). Metrô Vila Madalena. **Open** 9am-10pm Mon-Fri; 9am-6pm Sat; 11am-6pm Sun. **Credit** AmEx, DC, MC, V. **Map** p249 E8.
Book releases, signings and short pocket shows (half-hour musical programmes) all feature at this beautiful little bookshop, in the middle of the luxury shopping district. It also contains a nice (but often packed) café. The branch at Alameda Lorena is a concrete grey construction by architect Isay Weinfeld. On the inside, the brutalism recedes as books win out.
Other locations Rua Alameda Lorena 1731, Jardins (3062 1063); Rua Dr Mario Ferraz 414, Itaim Bibi (3073 0513); Shopping Cidade Jardim, Av Magalhães de Castro, 12000 (3755 5811).

Comics

Comix
Alameda Jaú 1998, Jardins (3088 9116/ www.comix.com.br). Metrô Consolação. **Open** 11am-8pm Mon-Fri; 10am-6pm Sat. **Credit** AmEx, DC, MC, V. **Map** p244 E7.

The biggest Manga and comic book store in Brazil. Quality independent and national comics such as *Café Espacial, Garagem Hermética* and *Graffiti 76% Quadrinhos* provide good alternatives (and original presents) to the usual Marvel or DC heroes. Rarities include the X-Men Premium collection.

Used & antiquarian

Red Star

Rua José Bonifácio 215, Centro (3107 1012/ www.sebo-redstar.com.br). Metrô Sé. **Open** 9am-8pm Mon-Fri; 9am-6pm Sat. **Credit** V. **Map** p243 N6.

Boasting a collection of 66,000 items, this *sebo* is well known for stocking old CDs, DVDs, comic books and magazines. Books can be found for as low as R$2. **Other location** Rua Nossa Senhora da Lapa 390, Lapa (3641 5963).

Sebo do Messias

Praça João Mendes 166-140, Centro (3105 6931/www.sebodomessias.com.br). Metrô Sé. **Open** 9am-7pm Mon-Fri; 9am-5pm Sat. **Credit** AmEx, DC, MC, V. **Map** p243 O6.

This messiah has been around for 40 years, and is downtown's most traditional used bookstore. Its collection is catalogued online, so you can shop here without leaving the house, but books, DVDs, CDs, comic books and old magazines are available for perusal at this branch.

Other location Rua Quintino Bocaiúva 166, Centro.

★ Sebo 264

Rua Álvares Machado 42, Liberdade (3101 8811/www.sebo264.com.br). Metrô Liberdade. **Open** 9am-6pm Mon-Fri; 8am-5pm Sat. **Credit** MC, V. **Map** p243 O6.

Looking for rare prints of Semana de Arte Moderna posters (*see p34* **Semana 22**), or first editions of Paulo Coelho novels? This *sebo* has a complete and varied collection of 500,000 items, many of them rare or off the market. The art items receive caring treatment, and the store accepts advance orders.

CHILDREN

Rua Melo Alves in Jardim Paulista, near Rua Oscar Freire, is great for mothers eager to combine parenting with shopping – there are about ten high-end kid-themed venues. What's more, some of the best Brazilian designers began offering kids' collections when their customers complained their little darlings also needed *lojas hypes* (shops of the moment).

Fashion

BestBaby

Rua Dr Melo Alves 413, Jardim Paulista (3083 6444/www.bestbaby.com.br). Metrô Consolação. **Open** 9am-7pm Mon-Fri; 9am-5pm Sat. **Credit** AmEx, DC, MC, V. **Map** p244 I8.

Classic simplicity is the mantra of this cradle outfitter, which is a little on the pricy side and purveys a mix of baby clothes, and toys.

Other location Shopping Iguatemi (3813 8449).

Chicletaria

Rua Dr Melo Alves 417, Jardim Paulista (3063 2264/www.chicletaria.com.br). Metrô Consolação. **Open** 9am-8pm Mon-Fri; 10am-6pm Sat. **Credit** AmEx, DC, MC, V. **Map** p244 I8.

Catering to kids from zero to ten, this pioneer was the first store to settle on Rua Melo Alves. It offers traditional children's clothing in cotton fabrics and pleasant designs.

Other locations throughout the city.

Fit Nina

Rua Oscar Freire 682, Jardim Paulista (3088 6548/www.fitweb.com.br). Metrô Consolação. **Open** Mon-Fri 9am-5pm. **Credit** AmEx, DC, MC, V. **Map** p244 I8.

For *meninas* (girls) only. If you've got a slightly precocious fashionista at home, then Fit Nina is for her. This girlie-centric store on Oscar Freire in Jardins (where else?) presents beautiful fabrics that range from jersey to tweed. It has a gorgeous collection of skirts, shirts, tights and dresses for young females.

Other locations throughout the city.

★ Ronaldo Fraga Filhotes

Rua Aspicuelta 259, Vila Madalena (3816 2181/www.ronaldofragafilhotes.com.br). Metrô Vila Madalena. **Open** 10am-7pm Mon-Fri; 10am-6pm Sat. **Credit** DC, MC, V. **Map** p249 F8.

This store provides a great opportunity for you and your child (and your credit card) to browse Ronaldo Fraga's cutting-edge collections for children and the elderly. Fraga was acclaimed as the best designer of São Paulo Fashion Week Winter 2009.

Toys

★ Plastik

Rua Dr Melo Alves 459, Cerqueira César (3081 2056/www.plastiksp.com.br). **Open** 11am-8pm Mon-Fri; 11am-7pm Sat. **Credit** AmEx, DC, MC, V. **Map** p244 I8.

It's all deeply trendy at this grown-up boys' toy shop. Plastik brings the 'toy art' circuit to São Paulo: the coolly decorated shop also serves as a showcase gallery. Since 2006, the store has stocked not only the niche vinyl toys popular in Japan, the US and Europe, but also creations of national artists that utilise wood, resin and other natural materials. Clothes by labels such as Supreme, Alife and Kid Robot are also stocked.

CONSUME

CONSUME

ELECTRONICS & PHOTOGRAPHY

For electronics, Paulistanos prefer Rua Santa Ifigênia and its hundreds of cell phone and appliance stores. The Brazilian chain **Casa & Video** (www.casaevideo.com.br) is a good one-stop shop for any type of electronic equipment. The French giant **FNAC** has also become popular in Brazil (www.fnac.com.br), and the Pinheiros branch with its pleasant café is a nice way to pass a rainy hour or two. However, tariffs on imported electronics are steep, so best to pack your essentials before coming to Brazil. For electronics repairs, check out the service floors of the **Shopping Eldorado** (*see p143*).

Notebook Computer

Avenida Brigadeiro Faria Lima 1811, stall 518, Jardim América (3812 4046/www.notebook-computer.com.br). Bus 802C-10. **Open** 9am-6pm Mon-Fri. **No credit cards. Map** p249 E11.
Focused specifically on computers and notebooks, this store in the building Palacio das Américas usually has a two-day wait for small repairs. It also sells new equipment and has an online store.

FASHION
Designer

★ Alexandre Herchcovitch

Rua Haddock Lobo 1151, Jardins (3063 2888/ www.herchcovitch.com.br). Metrô Consolação. **Open** 10am-7pm Mon-Fri; 10am-6pm Sat. **Credit** AmEx, DC, MC, V. **Map** p244 J8.
Alexandre Herchcovitch is one of the most daring designers working in Brazil today – he brought back the jelly shoe. His is the voice of a very urban São Paulo, for both men and women. Edgy and full of spark, he's the national John Galliano. A trip to this store is a must for anyone who loves contemporary ready-to-wear fashion.
Other locations throughout the city.

★ Cris Barros

Rua Vittório Fasano 85, Jardim Paulista (3082 3621/www.crisbarros.com.br). Metrô Consolação. **Open** 10am-8pm Mon-Fri; 10am-6pm Sat. **Credit** AmEx, DC, MC, V. **Map** p244 J8.
Cris Barros's creations remind young professional women that they're sexy. It's a simple, sleek and very feminine take on skirts, dresses and shoes.
Other location Vila Daslu, Av Chedid Jafet 131, Vila Olimpia (3846 9833).

Clube Chocolate

Rua Oscar Freire 913, Jardins (3084 1500). Metrô Consolação. **Open** 10am-8pm Mon-Fri; 10am-3pm Sat. **Credit** AmEx, DC, MC, V. **Map** p244 I8.

Clube Chocolate.

Palm trees, sand and clothes merge in an urban beach for this concept store inspired by Paris's Colette. Clube Chocolate mixes its own designs with Brazilian brands. Great for picking up unique gifts or fashionable mementos, and for grabbing a coffee after stomping the streets.

D'Arouche

Alameda Franca 1349, Jardim Paulista (3083 0144/www.eaudarouche.com). Metrô Consolação. **Open** noon-8pm Mon, Wed-Sat; 2-8pm Tue. **Credit** AmEx, DC, MC, V. **Map** p244 J8.
Carolina Glidden-Gannon worked for 12 years alongside Patricia Field while the later master-minded the on-screen glamour of *Sex and the City*. Together with lifelong friend and stylist David Pollak, she created this national label, which stocks well-made basics for city girls, including T-shirts, cardigans and blouses. The price tags are out of reach for most local salaries, but this is an example of Brazilian fashion at its best.

Ellus

Rua Oscar Freire 990, Jardins (3061 2900/ www.ellus.com.br). Metrô Consolação. **Open** 10am-8pm Mon-Sat. **Credit** AmEx, DC, MC, V. **Map** p244 I8.

English models are all the rage in Brazil, and in this vein, Agyness Deyn recently became Ellus' public face. The leading label in premium jeans, Ellus can afford to hire the runway's best, and charge an average R$400 for its Deluxe brand denim. **Other locations** throughout the city.

Iodice
Rua Oscar Freire 940, Jardins (3085 9310/ www.iodice.com.br). **Open** 10am-8pm Mon-Sat. **Credit** AmEx, DC, MC, V. **Map** p244 I8.
R Kelly wore an Iodice T-shirt in his 'That's That' video, and this Brazilian brand gained international recognition almost overnight. Iodice's haute-couture line, Valdemar Iodice, caters only to women, using bright colours and clean lines. The separate Iodice label has a thorough men's line – it's a mixture of Lacoste and the Boss Orange label.
Other location Shopping Iguatemi (3813 2622).

Universo Cecilia Echenique
Rua Peixoto Gomide 1756, Cequeira César (3079 8258/www.ceciliaechenique.com.br). Metrô Trianon-MASP. **Open** 10am-7pm Mon-Fri, 10am-6pm Sat. **Credit** AmEx, MC, V. **Map** p244 J9.
Echinique's beautifully crafted creations for women are hip, sassy and fresh. The collection is stored in a space with a garden, where you can try different blends of coffee and nibble on cakes. Talks and events here are linked to Echnique's mission – that fashion is not always superficial.

General

German immigrants introduced more than just beer and blonde hair to Brazil, and **Hering** (www.hering.com.br), one of the oldest Brazilian chains still in existence, dates back to 1880. The seasonal collections might not be catwalk quality, but the basics – polo shirts, T-shirts, vests and shorts – are well made and a good value. Spinach-eating cartoon heroes and stencilled Seine lovers (Popeye and Pepe le Pew, respectively) are reborn as parodies on the hoodies and T-shirts of comfort-clothes chain **Cavalera** (www.cavalera.com.br). **Zoomp** (www.zoomp. com.br) is a great national store for denim jeans and jackets as well as interesting leather bags and shoes. Expect to pay around R$200-R$300 for a good pair of denim jeans.

Alcides e Amigos
Rua Augusta 3633, loja 23, Consolação (3061 2008/www.alcideseamigos.com.br). Metrô Consolação. **Open** noon-8pm Mon-Fri; noon-7pm Sat. **Credit** MC, V. **Map** p244 K7.
Collector's-item sneakers, excellent eyewear, ironic T-shirts and acid-washed jeans are available at this alternative vintage haven (tucked into the same alley as B.luxo). Alcides also redesigns classic

pieces with contemporary touches in their hooded scarves and fitted plaid shirts for women.

AMP
Rua Augusta 2729, Jardins (3062 8347/ www.amulherdopadre.com). Metrô Consolação. **Open** 10am-8pm Mon-Sat. **Credit** AmEx, DC, MC, V. **Map** p244 J8.
This modern Brazilian label prides itself on its daring look for both men and women. National and contemporary T-shirts add wattage to its own cool sneakers and accessories.

Banca de Camisetas
Alameda Franca 1104, Jardins (3081 5210/ www.bancadecamisetas.com.br). Metrô Consolação. **Open** 10am-9pm Mon-Sat. **Credit** AmEx, DC, MC, V. **Map** p244 J8.
The store only stocks T-shirts made by up and coming national designers, with a focus on national themes. If you dream of your own designs turning heads on the street, you can bring them in, and they'll turn them into T-shirt reality.
Other locations throughout the city.

B.luxo
Rua Augusta 2633, loja 16, Jardins (3062 6479). Metrô Consolação. **Open** 11.30am-8pm Mon-Fri; 11am-9pm Sat. **Credit** MC, V. **Map** p244 J8.
Tucked into a charming alley, B.luxo is a small, savvy cross between a vintage store and a fashion label. It stocks Brazilian variations of European trends as well as its own individual signature line.

Boris & Natasha
Galeria Ouro Fino, Rua Augusta 2690, Jardins (3062 4653). Metrô Consolação. **Open** 11am-8pm Mon-Sat. **Credit** AmEx, DC, MC, V. **Map** p244 I8.
Twins Carolina and Isadora Foes Krieger run their own excellent fashion label, Gemeas, and customise vintage pieces of clothing. Their beautiful store is worth a visit if only to window-shop for vintage toys, oddball antiques and other 'curiosities'.

Doc Dog
Alameda Lorena 1998, Jardins (3063 3343/ www.docdog.com.br). Metrô Consolação. **Open** 10.30am-7pm Mon-Fri; 10.30am-6pm Sat. **Credit** AmEx, DC, MC, V. **Map** p244 I8.
This offbeat store sells alternative urban and pseudo-vintage clothes, as well as sneakers. A small section of the Alameda Lorena store showcases a number of retro and designer toys, including plastic Freddy Kruegers.
Other locations throughout the city.

★ Endossa
Rua Augusta 1360, Jardins (3854 9233/ www.endossa.com). Bus 107P-10, 107T-10, 702N-10, Metrô Consolação. **Open** noon-8pm

CONSUME

Tue-Thur; noon-10pm Fri, Sat; 4-10pm Sun.
Credit AmEx, DC, MC, V. **Map** p244 K7.
One of the first collaborative, commercial shops in
the world, Endossa allows independent designers to
rent out sections of the store. As a result, Endossa
is slightly all over the place, but clothes and accessories from young and hip designers make up the
majority of the merchandise.

ERRE
*Rua Barão de Capanema 551, Jardins (3083
2001/www.erre-sp.com.br).* **Open** 11am-8pm
Mon-Fri; 11am-3pm Sat. **Credit** AmEx, MC, V.
Map p244 I9.
To err is human, to forgive divine: which is why
Claudia and Renata De Goeye, inspired by trial and
error, decided to open this store in March 2008.
Dresses, blouses, shorts and trousers are just some
of the vanguard lines. They are well cut, come in
lightweight, soft fabrics, and are likely to become
attire staples for many years to come.

Forum
*Rua Oscar Freire 916, Jardins (3085 6269/
www.forum.com.br).* **Open** 10am-8pm Mon-Sat.
Credit AmEx, DC, MC, V. **Map** p244 I8.
Instead of promoting Topshop in Brazil, Kate Moss
recently became the new face of this label's Winter
'09 campaign, further staking Forum's claim to
being one of the elite brands of Brazil. The clothes
mainly adhere to contemporary styles, with quality
jeans for men as well as women's jackets and boots.
Other locations throughout the city.

Laundry Club
*Galeria Ouro Fino, Rua Augusta 2690, loja 323,
Jardins (3085 0604/www.laundrysp.com.br).*
Metrô Consolação. **Open** 11am-8pm Mon-Sat.
Credit MC, DC, V. **Map** p244 I8.
Get dressed to the nines in pin-up style at this retro
spot for men and women. This unique store also sells
shoes and lingerie in the same sexy style.

Maze
*Rua Augusta 2500 (3060 8617/www.mazeskate
shop.com.br).* **Open** 10am-8pm Mon-Sat. **Credit**
AmEx, DC, MC, V. **Map** p244 J8.
Definitely the best-stocked skate shop in São
Paulo, it gets the latest apparel from Stussy, 4Star,
Alife, Adidas, Supra, Nike and Mystery. However,
expect to pay dearly: T-shirts start from R$90, and
the sneakers (a mind-boggling selection that are
almost all limited editions) from R$350.

Mulher Elastica
*Galeria Ouro Fino, Rua Augusta 2690, Jardins
(3060 8263/www.mulherelastica.com.br).* *Metrô
Consolação.* **Open** 9.30am-8pm Mon-Sat. **Credit**
AmEx, DC, MC, V. **Map** p244 I8.
This American Apparel clone offers basic cotton/
spandex clothing, from well-cut T-shirts to leggings,

dresses and shorts for girls. They also sell accessories like scarves, bags and leg warmers.

★ Pelu
*Alameda Lorena 1257, casa 2, Jardins (3891 1229/
www.pelu.com.br).* *Metrô Brigadeiro.* **Open** 10am-
9pm Mon-Sat. **Credit** AmEx, MC, V. **Map** p244 J9.
This multi-brand in a cute mews in Jardins is successful with young, hip Paulistanos. The clothes,
resident hairdresser and the bar (which is lively at
happy hour with great DJs and cocktails) have customers lining up out the door.

★ Surface to Air
*Alameda Lorena 1989, Jardim Paulista (3063
4206/www.surface2airparis.com).* *Metrô
Consolação.* **Open** 11am-7pm Mon-Sat. **Credit**
AmEx, DC, MC, V. **Map** p244 I8.
This window to Paris imports seasonal collections,
and the garments on offer are seriously cool – though
exclusive prices can be a deterrent. The store also
stocks some of Brazil's most effervescent labels:
Amapô, PIMP, Neon, Juliana Jabour and dThales.
International DJs host free weekend parties here.

Thrift & vintage

★ Antiguidades Minha Avó Tinha
*Rua Dr. Franco da Rocha 74, Perdizes (3865
1759).* *Bus 875A-10, 875M-10.* *Metrô Barra
Funda.* **Open** noon-7.30pm Mon; 10am-7.30pm
Tue-Fri; 10am-5pm Sat. **Credit** MC, V.
Situated in a three-storey 1920s mansion, this
beloved institution specialises in clothing from the
'30s through the '80s. In fact, it began as an antique
shop, but due to the sheer quality and remarkable
prices of labels like Givenchy, YSL and Louis
Vuitton, it made waves among the city's fashion-
lovers. Miu Miu, Chanel and Prada shoes can be
found at astonishingly pocket-friendly prices.

★ Brechó Frou-Frou
*Rua Augusta 725, loja 2, Consolação (9580 4894/
www.froufroubrecho.blogspot.com).* *Bus 107P-10,
107T-10, 702N-10.* **Open** noon-8pm Mon-Fri;
noon-6pm Sat. **No credit cards. Map** p242 L6.
Vintage Pierre Cardin and Lacoste can be found at
this tiny thrift on Augusta. It won't only outfit you
in style for the rest of your trip: the young and
savvy owner is a great source for tips on the
hippest places in town to show off your purchases.

Juisi by Liquor
*Garden Gallery, Alameda Tietê 43, Jardins
(3063 5766/http://juisi.blogspot.com).* *Bus 107P-
10, 107T-10, 702N-10.* **Open** 11am-7pm Mon-
Fri; noon-7pm Sat. **Credit** MC, V. **Map** p244 J8.
General rarities, vintage dresses and sunglasses
are the staples here. The bubbly staff knows its
stuff and will even offer to give you a personal tour
of the whole store if it's not too busy.

Tunel do Tempo
Rua Major Maragliano 387, Vila Mariana
(5082 1566/www.brechotuneldotempo.com.br).
Bus 577T-10, 5106-31. **Open** 10am-7pm Mon-
Fri; 10am-4pm Sat. **Credit** V. **Map** p245 M12.
Obsessive-compulsion has its advantages. Cláudia
Dib has collected over 5,000 articles of clothing and
accessories for her store, and over the years it has
become the be-all and end-all recycled-clothing stop
for the city's stylists, producers and vintage-lovers.

★ Trash Chic
Rua Capitão Prudente 223, Jardim Paulista
(3815 3202/www.trashchic.com.br). Bus 6245-
10. **Open** 10am-6pm Mon-Fri; 10am-5pm Sat.
Credit AmEx, DC, MC, V. **Map** p249 F10.
Everything in this gorgeous thrift store is mounted
so delicately that it appears to the patron less like
a bargain haven than a fashion house in the
making. Indeed, it's only power labels that you'll
find here: Chanel, Prada, Louis Vuitton, Chloe
and more.

Varal do Beco
Rua Cardeal Arco Verde 1771, Pinheiros
(3032 5074/www.brechovaraldobeco.com.br). Bus
177H-10, 177P-10, 701A-10. **Open** 9am-7.30pm
Mon-Sat. **Credit** DC, MC, V. **Map** p249 E9.
Nutrisport, Poolsport, Daruma, Sela and Karibé
are just some of the second-hand, discontinued
Brazilian labels that are brought back to life here.
For international vintage, look no further than
Pierre Cardin, YSL, Armani, Dior, Colcci, Gucci
and Pucci. Enter through the side street between
Mourato Coelho and Fradique Coutinho.

FASHION ACCESSORIES & SERVICES
Hats & tailors

Two tailor stores are enough to call Rua Augusta
the main tailor street outside of Bom Retiro,
which mostly specialises in commercial tailoring.

Alfaiataria Italiana
Rua Augusta 2192, sobreloja, Jardins
(3064 1399/www.alfaiatariaitaliana.com.br).
Metrô Consolação. **Open** 9am-7pm Mon-Fri;
noon-4pm Sat. **No credit cards. Map** p244 J8.
You can stitch as well as shop for hats here: the
owner established an Italian tailor school in the
same location as the store.

Plas
Rua Augusta 724, Jardins (3257 9919/
www.plas.com.br). Metrô Consolação.
Open 10am-8pm Mon-Fri; 10am-5pm Sat.
Credit MC, V. **Map** p242 L6.
Maurice Plas has been fervently making hats,
berets, ties and vests for the past 45 years. His

devoted clientele includes movie stars, company
execs and fashion designers. A must if you're looking to buy an authentic Panama hat or some red
braces while in São Paulo.

Jewellery

H.Stern (Rua Oscar Freire 652, Cerqueira
César, 3068 8082, www.hstern.com.br) blings
out the Hollywood elite with gorgeous inspired
designs, some based on famous art pieces.
The noble gold collection, a mixture of
precious metals that resulted in a colour
variant of yellow and white gold, is a
particularly special creation. Another,
less high-end national jewellery brand
is **Vivara** (www.vivara.com.br).

Vivi Malek
Galeria Ouro Fino, Rua Augusta 2690,
Consolação (5686 6484/www.vivimalek.weebly.
com). Metrô Consolação. **Open** 11am-8pm Mon-
Sat. **Credit** AmEx, DC, MC, V. **Map** p244 I8.
Vivi Malek makes distinctive bracelets, earrings, neck-
laces and belts for men and women. With her eclectic
style, she works magic on a variety of materials:
rare metals, precious stones and even plastic.

Lingerie & underwear

Thais Gusmão
Rua Oscar Freire 216, Jardins (3085 9426/
www.thaisgusmao.com). **Open** 10am-8pm Mon-Sat.
Credit AmEx, DC, MC, V. **Map** p244 J9.
Retro Betty Boop swing-style lingerie is the speciality of this store, but more traditional underwear can
also be found. Prices start at around R$70 for men's
selections, but the women's start at R$130. The qual-
ity garments are sure to, um, please, at least for those
in a '40s mood for love.
Other locations throughout the city.

Luggage

Le Postiche (Rua Haddock Lobo 1307, Jardim
Paulista, 3081 9702, www.lepostiche.com.br) is
a chain store that specialises in luggage and
leather accessories. It can be found all around
town as well as inside malls.

Repairs

Marise Chá
Rua Fernando de Albuquerque 187,
Consolação (3257 5700). Metrô Consolação.
Open 7.30am-6pm Mon-Fri; 8am-2pm Sat.
Credit DC, MC, V. **Map** p244 K7.
For mid-travel fashion emergencies, this is an
excellent and cheap place to get clothes mended.
Fixing a ripped crotch on a pair of jeans costs
around R$7.

CONSUME

Profile São Paulo Fashion Week

Tropical fashion has arrived – and it's no longer exotic.

Although São Paulo's fashionistas don't need a reason to get all dolled up, this valley of the dolls dresses extra fine during South America's largest fashion show, which takes place in January and June. The elevation of Brazilian tropical wear to haute couture began in 1996 when Paulo Borges, an owner of Luminosidade, the company that now produces São Paulo Fashion Week (SPFW), decided that Brazil – and São Paulo in particular – had arrived on the fashion scene. Little did London, Milan, New York or Paris know that Brazil's largest city, and one whose denizens are well-known for wearing only black, was going to carve out its own niche market in the fashion industry, and produce a viable alternative to the fashion shows in the European and US capitals of style. Since then, the SPFW has been produced with Brazilian themes in mind. From Pelé to Carmen Miranda, it leaves no national icon unturned in order to present a spectacle.

Part of the reason for the show's status is the success that Brazilian fashion models are enjoying success overseas. As well as Giselle Bündchen (the world's highest-paid supermodel, according to *Forbes*), several other Brazilian runway starlets are becoming known in international fashion: Carol Trentini, Fernanda Tavares, Isabeli Fontana, Shirley Mallmann and Hollywood actress Alice Braga are just some of the names to feature in the international press. What's more, Brazilian designers too have been making headway overseas. **Alexandre Herchcovitch** (*see p150*) and **Osklen** (at Daslu; *see p143*) are arguably the Brazilian labels best known internationally; close behind them are Isabela Capeto, Carlota Joakina, Triton, Huis Clos, Lino Villaventura, Tufi Duek and the man who made all the waves at the SPFW in winter 2009, **Ronaldo Fraga** (*see p148*), from the state of Minas Gerais.

The **SPFW** takes place every year in January and June inside Oscar Niemeyer's Pavilhão Ciccillo Matarazzo.

Shoes

Brazil has a number of good and expensive
chain shoe stores, including **Arezzo** (www.
arezzo.com.br), **Andarella** (www.andarella.
com.br) and **Via Uno** (www.viauno.com.br).
Great, one-of-a-kind boutique shoe stores are
harder to find. Check out **Cas** (Rua Fidalga
317, Vila Madalena, 3032 8455, www.casmoda.
com.br) for its retro shoes.

Galleria Melissa

*Rua Oscar Freire 827, Jardins (3083 3612/
www.melissa.com.br).* **Open** 10am-7.30pm Mon-
Fri; 10am-5pm Sat. **Credit** AmEx, DC, MC, V.
Map p244 I8.
There's no south-east Asian art at this gallery sometimes fronted by a massive white elephant statue,
just some fancy footwork. It's an impressive temple
to plastic jelly shoes, but not just any jelly shoes:
expect weird and cutting-edge creations by internationally acclaimed designers like the Campana
Brothers, Karim Rashid and Vivienne Westwood.
The atrium walls serve as a changing exhibition
space for murals, placing it on the Oscar Freire map
as a landmark as well as a shop. The psychedelic
organic shoe displays set the futuristic tone.

Visionaire

*Galeria Ouro Fino, Rua Augusta 2690 Consolação
(3083 2466). Metrô Consolação.* **Open** 10am-8pm
Mon-Sat. **Credit** AmEx, DC, MC, V. **Map** p244 I8.
If violence is to break out over vintage trainers, it's
likely to occur at this sport-shoe mecca. The rarest
editions of Nike, Converse and Lacoste in the city are
available here, and the owner boasts limited-edition
SBs, Dunks and Chuck Taylors. The prices for such
elitism are European.

Swimwear

Rosa Chá

*Rua Oscar Freire 977, Jardins (3081 2793/
www.rosacha.com.br).* **Open** 10am-8pm Mon-
Sat; 1-7pm Sun. **Credit** AmEx, DC, MC, V.
Map p244 I8.
Far from the sands of Rio, but still Brazilian beach
fashion at its finest. Rosa Chá has a huge selection
of bikinis, *sungas* (Speedo-style swimming trunks),
and beach accessories, including sandals, towels
and trainers.
Other locations throughout the city.

Espaço Havaianas

*Rua Oscar Freire 1116, Jardins (3079 3415/
www.havaianas.com).* **Open** 10am-8pm Mon-
Sat. **Credit** AmEx, DC, MC, V. **Map** p244 I8.
The 2004 US election might have been lost on account
of 'flip-flopping', but the original Havaianas concept
store, designed by architecture guru Isay Weinfeld
and opened in 2008, just keeps winning votes. Palm

trees, clean lines, air-conditioning and a sunroof give
a pleasantly breezy feel to the store, while the rain-
bow in the back is made of Havaianas from every hue
of the palette. If these 50-odd shades don't catch your
eye, create your own colour. The store also sells accessories such as towels, key rings and vintage models
of the world-famous sandal.
Other locations throughout the city.

FOOD & DRINK

One of Brazil's most popular high-end
supermarkets, **Pão de Açúcar** (www.paode
acucar.com.br) is usually open 24 hours. It is a
great place to find fine ingredients or alcoholic
beverages late at night. Another chain market,
Emporium São Paulo (Avenida Jurema 271,
Moema, 5054 8000, www.emporiumsaopaulo.
com.br), is the number-one place to get fine
ingredients in the neighbourhood. The newest
fine-food chain market, **St Marché** (Rua Carlos
Weber 502, 3643 1000, Lapa, www.marche.
com.br) started with five units in wealthy
neighbourhoods and bought Emporio Santa
Maria as their classy market. Fresh fruit and
salads are a trademark here.

General

Casa Santa Luzia

*Alameda Lorena 1471, Jardim Paulista (3897
5000/www.santaluzia.com.br). Metrô Consolação.*
Open 8am-8.45pm Mon-Sat. **Credit** AmEx, DC,
MC, V. **Map** p244 J8.
It's located in the heart of Jardins and is full of middle-
aged housewives in the afternoon. Besides the great
variety of fine food and wine, it has a section of soy
protein-based products made for vegetarians.

Empório Santa Maria

*Avenida Cidade Jardim 790, Pinheiros (3706
5211/www.emporiosantamaria.com.br). Bus*

INSIDE TRACK
THE DEATH OF HAVAIANAS

While Havaianas might still be the most
popular flip-flops in the world, in Brazil
they're losing their monopoly as popular
footwear. Whereas several years ago a
pair of these sandals went from R$6 and
up, now it's hard to find ones that cost
less than R$15, a hefty price tag for many
Brazilians, who wear them year round. As
a result, many stores are now offering
competing brands: check out the Olindas
or Ipanemas. They might not yet have
Havaianas' trendy caché, but you can only
buy these in Brazil, and they're only R$7.

Galleria Melissa. See p155.

6200-10. **Open** 8am-10pm Mon-Sat; 8am-9pm Sun. **Credit** AmEx, DC, MC, V. **Map** p249 F12. This market has an exclusive store from a great wine importer, Expand, and a small restaurant on the top floor. Fine-food brands and rare foreign foods are sold here.

Markets

Ceagesp
Avenida Dr Gastão Vidigal 1946, Vila Leopoldina (3643 3700/www.ceagesp.gov.br). Bus 477A-10. **Open** 5am-10am Tue; 4pm-10pm Wed; 5am-10am Fri; 7am-noon Sat; 7am-1pm Sun. **No credit cards**.
If you're interested in buying plants, flowers or fruits, try the state market Ceagesp (also known as Ceasa), located in the west of the city, close to Parque Villa-Lobos. The wholesale market feeds the entire city but offers a number of retail sales as well, with prices that take some beating. Tuesdays and Fridays are plant and flower days. Get there early to find good deals and fresh products. For fruit, Wednesdays (at night) and weekends (in the morning) are the peak times. And if all the heathy, fresh produce and natural aromas get a bit much, outside the entrance you'll find a hot dog stand, open 24 hours a day. They are made the Paulistano way, with mashed potatoes, cheddar, corn and French fries. Delicate stomachs might want to err on the side of caution and abstain.

★Mercado Municipal (Mercadão)
Parque Dom Pedro II, Rua da Cantareira 306, Sé (3313 1326/www.mercadomunicipal.com.br). Metrô São Bento. **Open** 6am-6pm Mon-Sat; 6am-4pm Sun. **Credit** varies. **Map** p243 P4. *See p127* **Profile.**

GIFTS & SOUVENIRS

Presentes Mickey (Rua Oscar Freire 931, Cerqueira César, 3088 0577, www.mickey. com.br) is a traditional high-class wedding-gift store that specialises in fine dishes and kitchen utensils, and carries more than 16,000 items. Another wedding chain store is **Camicado** (Shopping Paulista, 3266 4146,

www.camicado.com.br), which is preferred by Brazilians for mid-priced gifts.

Casa de Velas Santa Rita
Praça da Liberdade 248, Liberdade (3208 7022/www.srita.com.br). Bus 314J-10, 314V-10, 407MM-10. **Open** 8am-6.30pm Mon-Fri; 9am-5pm Sat. **Credit** AmEx, DC, MC, V. **Map** p245 O7.
Looking for some voodoo magic or a spiritual uplift via shopping? Visit this house of candles, which specialises in religious articles, images and sculptures of saints, scented candles and soaps, jewellery, and even Candomblé and Umbanda (Afro-Brazilian religions) souvenirs.

Cullinan Pedras Brasileiras
Alameda Ministro Rocha Azevedo 239, Jardins (3289 7599/www.cullinan.com.br). Bus 478P-10, 478P-31, 577T-10. **Open** 9.30am-7pm Mon-Fri; 9.30am-4pm Sat. **Credit** AmEx, DC, MC, V. **Map** p244 K8.
If you're running out of time to visit the colonial gem towns of Minas Gerais where most Brazilian precious stones are mined, stop by this well-known store that sells exclusively Brazilian stones and objects made from them. Beautiful ashtrays made from Sodalita and chess sets made from Serpentinita stones are among the many unique pieces. And the ubiquitous pink and green watermelon tourmaline is one Brazilian stone you won't find anywhere else in the world.

★ Loja do Bispo
Rua Dr Melo Alves 278, Jardins (3064 8673/www.editoradobispo.com.br). Metrô Consolação. **Open** 11am-8pm Mon-Fri; 11am-6pm Sat. **Credit** AmEx, MC, V. **Map** p244 I8.
Time ceases to exist at Loja do Bispo (Bishop's Shop), the fruit of proprietor Pinky Wainer's vision. She hand-picks pieces from around the world and brings them back to her elegantly crammed shop of curios. You'll come across everything from framed photographs by contemporary artists, to Brazilian folkloric memorabilia, books on contemporary art and life (some published by her own Editora do Bispo), furniture, jewellery and quirky objects.

Loja Loja

*Rua Fernando de Albuquerque 255 (3120 5320/
http://lojaloja.blogspot.com). Bus 177H-10, 719P-
10, 719R-10.* **Open** 7.30-11.30pm Mon; 2-11.30pm
Tue-Fri; 2pm-midnight Sat. **Credit** DC, MC, V.
Map p244 K7.
Novelty-size lighters, comedy door mats, chandeliers
made of plastic, and chests of drawers made from
glass and mirrors are just part of the wide array of
wonderfully oddball products to be found at this
curiosity emporium.

Tabacaria Lee

*Pátio Higienópolis, Avenida Higienópolis 618
(3667 1222/www.tabacarialee.com.br). Bus
177H-10, 719P-10, 719R-10.* **Open** 10am-10pm
Mon-Sat; 2-8pm Sun. **Credit** AmEx, DC, MC, V.
Map p242 K5.
Barack Obama may be lifting some US-Cuban
restrictions, but if you want to buy your boss some
Cubans, this excellent tobacconist, specialising in
imported cigars from Cuba and the Dominican
Republic, should meet your needs. The most
famous cigars sold here are the Cohiba, Montecristo
and Romeo et Julieta. Fine national labels include
Dona Flor and Dannemann. You can also find a
selection of designer pens – Cross and Porsche –
as well as Zippo lighters.
Other locations throughout the city.

HEALTH & BEAUTY
Complementary medicine

Kyron

*Shopping Iguatemi, Avenida Brigadeiro Faria
Lima 2232, Pinheiros (3095 3000/www.kyron.
com.br). Bus 775F-10.* **Open** 10am-10pm Mon-
Sat; 2-8pm Sun. **Credit** AmEx, DC, MC, V.
Map p249 E11.
Located inside Shopping Iguatemi, Kyron was one
of the first day spas to open in the city. It is popular
with brides and offers a number of aesthetic proce-
dures as well as a clinic (for plastic surgery treat-
ments) and a nutritional centre.

Opticians

São Paulo may be a rainy place in many a
season, but **Chili Beans** (Rua Augusta 2690,
Jardim Paulista, 3062 3266, www.chillibeans.
com.br), a national chain, has made its name
designing sunglasses in a variety of styles,
from classic aviator to new models made of
unbreakable, scratch-free plastic composites. You
can even blink twice: if you're not happy with
your original choice, exchanges are easy to make.
Another popular chain for glasses is **Fotoptica**
(Rua Augusta 2710, Jardim Paulista, 3088 2499,
www.fotoptica.com.br), which has 38 units in
town and also functions as a photography store.

Pharmacies & beauty stores

One of Brazil's largest pharmacy chains,
Drogão (Praça Panamericana 50, Alto de
Pinheiros, 3023 0694, www.drogao.com.br)
can be found all around town and offers health
and beauty products. The other huge chain,
Drogaria São Paulo (Avenida Paulista 2073,
Cerqueira César, 3251 0206, www.drogaria
saopaulo.com.br), introduced the all-inclusive
drugstore. Most branches are open 24 hours.

Shops

Ikesaki

*Avenida da Liberdade 146, Liberdade (3111 0060/
www.ikesaki.com.br). Metrô Liberdade.* **Open**
8.15am-7pm Mon-Fri; 8.15am-6pm Sat; 11am-5pm
Sun. **Credit** AmEx, DC, MC, V. **Map** p245 M8.
It started as a wholesale cosmetics store for hairdressers before switching gears and becoming the first
cosmetics megastore in São Paulo.
Other location Rua Galvão Bueno 37, Liberdade.

Spas & salons

There are beauty salons on every corner
in São Paulo. If you have a nail emergency,
don't be afraid to try any small salon you see.
Otherwise, getting a wax is a must during your
stay; from back hair to toe hair, Brazilian salons
are famed for the speed and quality of their
depilação (waxing) methods.

C Kamura

*Rua da Consolação 3679, Jardim Paulista
(3061 5500/www.ckamura.com.br). Metrô
Consolação.* **Open** 9am-6pm Mon, Sat;
9am-9pm Tue-Fri. **Credit** AmEx, DC, MC, V.
Map p244 I8.
Celso Kamura keeps his high-fashion salon in
Jardins filled with beautiful faces. He also developed his own make-up and beauty brand, and is
known for working with Brazilian celebrities.

Kabanah

*Avenida Brigadeiro Luís Antônio 4442,
Jardins (3885 8278/www.kabanahspa.com.br).
Bus 669A-10.* **Open** 9am-10pm Mon-Fri;
9am-7pm Sat. **Credit** AmEx, DC, MC, V.
Map p244 L9.
Longing for Búzios, Bali or Hawaii? This spa's individual, cabana-style rooms allow you to imagine
being on beautiful, famous beaches without leaving the city. Close to Parque Ibirapuera, it offers
pilates classes as well.

★ LUXO

*Rua Aspicuelta 193, Vila Madalena (3031 5511).
Metrô Vila Madalena.* **Open** 10am-7pm Tue-Sat.
No credit cards. Map p249 F8.

Shopping in Liberdade.

The two-barber seat, baby blue salon is popular with trend-setting locals. Ciça, the owner and mistress coiffeuse is the rocker heart and soul of the business. Haircuts can be as trendy or simple as you request, but Ciça will be completely honest if she disagrees with you. And you should trust her, this is one lady who knows her stuff.

MG Hair
Rua Estados Unidos 1862, Jardins (3068 9035/www.mghair.com.br). Metrô Consolação. **Open** 1-8pm Mon; 8am-9pm Tue-Sat. **Credit** AmEx, DC, MC, V. **Map** p244 I8.
Marco Antonio de Biaggi is responsible for the hair on most Brazilian women's magazine covers. His clients have included Naomi Campbell, Carolina Herrera and Ivete Sangalo (Brazil's premier female pop singer).

Studio W
Shopping Iguatemi, Avenida Brigadeiro Faria Lima 2232, Pinheiros (3094 2640/ www.studiow.com.br). Bus 775F-10. **Open** 10am-10pm Mon-Sat; 2-8pm Sun. **Credit** AmEx, DC, MC, V. **Map** p249 E11.
The Brazilian socialite's favourite hairstylist, Wanderley Nunes is responsible for the hairdos of many-a *telenovela* star. He's not always around, so if only Wanderley will do for your do, it's best to make an appointment well in advance.
Other locations Shopping Higienópolis (3823 2233); Shopping Anália Franco (2076 4700).

HOUSE & HOME

The area around Praça Benedito Calixto is full of antique furniture and home furnishing stores. For some vintage collectibles, try the pleasant **Maria Jovem** (Rua João Moura 1019, Pinheiros, 3088 1396, www.mariajovem.com.br).

Antiques

★ Feira de Artes, Cultura e Lazer da Praça Benedito Calixto
Praça Benedito Calixto, Pinheiros (www.praca beneditocalixto.com.br). Metrô Clínicas. **Open** 9am-7pm Sat. **Map** p249 G8.
Surrounded by gift and furniture shops, the Saturday market sells bric-à-brac as well as antique furniture (but be attentive to claimed precedence, as many goods are copies), vinyl, clothes and jewellery. It's busy in the afternoons, when live music, *chorinho*, kicks in from 2.30 to 6.30pm. Vendors' stalls are up early and stand well into the afternoon, but try to get there before 4pm.

Feira de Antigüidades da Paulista (MASP)
Avenida Paulista 1578, Jardins (3252 6382). Metrô Trianon-MASP. **Open** 10am-5pm Sun. **Map** p244 K8.
Family silver, grandmother's lace and antique photographs are just a few of the many things to be found at this beautiful market underneath the hulking body of the MASP. Although the prices can be quite hefty, only one-of-a-kind articles are purveyed here.

★ Feira de Antiguidades e Arte do Bixiga
Praça Dom Orione, Bela Vista (3287 2780). Metrô São Joaquim or Trianon-MASP/bus 475M-10, 475R-10, 967A-10. **Open** 10am-6pm Sun. **Map** p245 M8.
This fair's 300 stalls boast everything from antique clocks and furniture, clothes and records to vintage watches, brooches and sunglasses. There are also a number of excellent food stalls, selling a plethora of delicacies, including home-made Italian cuisine.

General

Carlos Motta
*Rua Aspicuelta 121, Vila Madalena (3032
4127/www.carlosmotta.com.br). Metrô Vila
Madalena.* **Open** 10am-6.30pm Mon-Fri; 10am-
2pm Sat. **No credit cards. Map** p249 F8.
A balanced blend of rustic and chic pervades this
store – and Motta's gorgeous furniture. Definitely
on the bulky side if you plan to take things home
in your luggage but worth the shipping if you find
his style suits yours.

Conceito
*Alameda Gabriel Monteiro da Silva 1522, Jardins
(3068-0380/www.conceitofirmacasa.com.br).*
Open 10am-7pm Mon-Fri; 10am-3pm Sat.
No credit cards. Map p249 F11.
Conceito means 'concept' in Portuguese. Here you'll
find an array of what the management deems to be
the latest and coolest in contemporary design from
around the globe – everything from mementoes
and trinkets to furniture.

★ Dpot
*Alameda Gabriel Monteiro da Silva 1250,
Jardim Paulistano (3043 9159/www.dpot.com.br).*
Open 10am-7pm Mon-Fri; 10am-3pm Sat. **Credit**
AmEx, MC, V. **Map** p249 G10.
Specialising in Brazilian design, Dpot holds pieces
by leading figures of art and architecture such as
Claudia Moreira Salles, Campana Brothers, Lina Bo
Bardi, Paulo Mendes da Rocha and Zanine Caldas,
as well as young up-and-coming designers.

Marcenaria Trancoso
*Rua Harmonia 233, Vila Madalena (3816
1298/www.mtrancoso.com). Metrô Vila
Madalena.* **Open** 10am-7pm Mon-Fri;
10am-5pm Sat. **Credit** AmEx, DC, MC, V.
Map p249 F8.
The name of the store refers to Trancoso, a beautiful beach town in the state of Bahia. Marcenaria
Trancoso specialises in furniture and home
goods, and the focus is on eco-friendly products.
Cutlery, vases, tables and chairs, are just some of
the things on offer here and most are made from
beautiful woods.

,OVO
*Rua Gomes de Carvalho 830 (3045 0309/
www.ovo.art.br).* **Open** 10am-7pm Mon-Fri,
11am-5pm Sat. **Credit** AmEx, DC, MC, V.
Luciana Martins and Gerson Oliveira are the minds
behind ,Ovo (egg, but the comma refers to the age-
old puzzle – which came first, the chicken or egg?)
They inhabit a space of art and design, where metal
tubing is cleverly crafted to form an alluring wall
structure with functioning seats; a chair covered in
lycra looks like a contemporary art object; and
snooker balls become coat hangers.

MUSIC & ENTERTAINMENT

CDs & records

Banana Music Store
*Alameda Lorena 1641, Jardim Paulista
(3085 8877/www.bananamusic.com.br). Bus
107P-10, 107T-10, 702N-10.* **Open** 10am-8pm
Mon-Fri; 10am-6pm Sat. **Credit** AmEx, MC, V.
Map p244 I8.
Banana sells contemporary and classical, national
and international CDs and DVDs.
Other location Shopping Iguatemi (3812 9447).

★ Baratos e Afins
*Galeria do Rock, Avenida São João 439,
loja 314, Centro (3223 3629/www.baratosafins.
com.br). Bus 107P-10, 107T-10, 393H-10.*
Open 11am-7pm Mon-Fri; 10am-2pm Sat.
Credit AmEx, DC, MC, V. **Map** p243 N5.
Founded in 1978 by Luis Calanca, the record shop
turned into a record label when Arnaldo Baptista,
ex-vocalist and bassist for Os Mutantes (*see p191*),
sought out Calanca (the owner of this store) to
release his second solo album. The record label continues, and the shop is an unofficial heritage site
for lovers of Brazilian music. The shop features
cheap vinyl and history galore, and the staff are
cool and knowledgeable.

★ Galeria do Rock
*Rua 24 de Maio 62, Centro (3337 6277).
Metrô República.* **Open** 9am-8pm Mon-Fri;
9am-6pm Sat. **Credit** MC, V. **Map** p243 N5.
This hipster haven is affectionately known as
'Emoland' by city satirists. The Gallery of Rock is a
collection of 450 commercial shops, 190 of them dedicated to the various facets of the music scene. CDs,
vinyl, T-shirts, accessories, flags and posters galore
– you name it, it's here and ready to roll. The prices
are much lower than at equivalent speciality shops
in other areas around the city. The bottom floor is
dedicated solely to hip hop and 'black music' (as
Brazilians term it). On Saturdays, a battalion of
teenage rockers invades.

Rhythm Records
*Galeria Ouro Fino, Rua Augusta 2690, Consolação
(3064 9564/www.rhythmrecords.com.br). Bus
107P-10, 107T-10, 702N-10.* **Open** 11am-8pm
Mon-Fri; 11am-6pm Sat. **Credit** AmEx, DC, MC, V.
Map p244 I8.
A dedicated collection of hip hop, electro, drum 'n'
bass, techno and dance can be found at this record
store specialising in vinyl for spinning DJs.

Musical instruments

Rua Teodoro Sampaio in Pinheiros caters to
three different types of goods: cheap, popular
clothes at the outer end closer to Vila Madalena;

Maria Jovem. *See p158.*

furniture in the middle, close to Avenida
Henrique Schaumann; and musical instruments,
from Praça Benedito Calixto to Rua Oscar
Freire. The national chain **PlayTech** (Rua
Teodoro Sampaio 912, Pinheiros, 3088 0006,
www.playtech.com.br), specialises in percussion
and drums but sells all instruments. Rua Santa
Ifigênia and Rua General Osorio in Centro are
also heavy on musical instruments. Check out
Contemporânea (*see p54*) for its great selection
of instruments and Saturday concerts.

Hendrix Music

*Rua Teodoro Sampaio 709, Pinheiros (3086
4033/www.hendrixmusic.com.br). Metrô Clínicas.*
Open 9am-6pm Mon-Fri; 9am-2pm Sat. **Credit**
DC, MC, V. **Map** p249 G8.
Home to guitars, keyboards, microphones, ampli-
fiers and everything else rock 'n' roll kids need to
make a lot of noise. Its sister store is at Rua Teodoro
Sampaio 719.

SPORTS & FITNESS

Founded in 1955, **Bayard** (Shopping Paulista,
Rua Treze de Maio 1947, Bela Vista, 3191 0400,
www.bayardnet.com.br) is great for sneakers
and clothing and has outlets in most major
shopping malls. **Centauro** (Shopping Santa
Cruz, Rua Domingos de Morais 2564, Vila
Mariana, 5549 4857, www.centauro.com.br) is
another chain specialising in soccer shirts and
accessories as well as general sporting goods.

Decathlon

*Rua Duquesa de Goias 381, Morumbi (2167
0800/www.decathlon.com.br). Bus 609F-10.*

Open 9am-10pm Mon-Sat; 10am-10pm Sun.
Credit AmEx, DC, MC, V.
This sport megastore has a huge variety of goods
on display, and offers everything from clothing to
camp tents and ping-pong tables.

TICKETS

Ticketing services in São Paulo such as
Ingresso.com (4003 2330, www.ingresso.
com.br), **Ingresso Rápido** (4003 1212, www.
ingressorapido.com.br) and **Ticketmaster**
(2846 6000/ www.ticketmaster.com.br) offer
mildly functional, hard-to-navigate websites.
These are useless to foreigners anyway, as
without a valid Brazilian CPF (taxpayer
registration number), you are not allowed to
make purchases either by phone or internet.
If you haven't charmed a CPF out of a
Brazilian yet, head for one of the *pontas de
venda* (sales points) for the particular service
(these are listed on their websites). Tickets for
Ticketmaster and Ingresso Rápido events are
available, for instance, at the electronics
superstore **FNAC** (Avenida Paulista 901,
Jardins, 2123 2000, www.fnac.com.br).

TRAVELLERS' NEEDS

Matueté (Rua Tapinás 22, Itaim Bibi,
3071 4515, www.matuete.com) is a boutique
travel company.
    For baggage shipping, **DHL Express**
(Praça da Republica, Republica, 3259 3766,
www.dhl.com.br) has numerous outlets all
over Brazil. For cellular phone repairs, *see
p149*. For luggage stores, *see p153*.

CONSUME

Arts & Entertainment

São Paulo Fashion Week. *See p152.*

Calendar

Eat, drink and dance 'til you drop at one of the city's annual knees-ups.

Rio de Janeiro will always be carnival destination number one for most people, but São Paulo's financial might and metropolitan style give its annual festival offerings international and cosmopolitan flair. The city's year is packed with events that showcase what this colossal metropolis does best: urban diversity and having a damn good time. São Paulo's cultural calendar covers everything from art to music, cinema to food, and, as in the case of the Gay Pride, cultural affirmation – and that's just for starters. For a complete list of public holidays, *see p231*.

JANUARY-MARCH

Campus Party Brasil
Centro de Exposições Imigrantes (3872 1400/ www.campus-party.com.br). Metrô Jabaquara.
Date Late Jan.
Geeks flock to see the gadgets at the annual São Paulo leg of this global technology innovation and electronics entertainment event.

São Paulo City Anniversary
Various venues (www.prefeitura.sp.gov.br).
Date 25 Jan.
The anniversary of the city's founding, on 25 January 1554, is marked by an extensive (and mostly free) lineup of musical genres: samba, rock, hip hop and classical. In 2007, Os Mutantes played their first gig in the city for nearly 30 years.

São Paulo Fashion Week
Date Jan & June. *See p152* **Profile**.

Chinese New Year
Date Jan.
Celebrated on a Saturday and Sunday in Liberdade with parades and folklore dances.

Carnival Parade
Date mid-Feb. *See pp164-166*.

Mercado Mundo Mix
www.mundomixonline.virgula.uol.com.br.
Date Mar.
São Paulo hosted its first edition of this worldwide creative design festival in March 2009. Held at the Memorial America Latina, the theme was Japanese anime.

APRIL-JUNE

Day of the Indian
Date 19 Apr.
A good time to visit the Museu do Indio (*see p214*) is during the week of this holiday.

Tiradentes
Date 21 Apr.
A national holiday for one of the founding fathers of democracy in Brazil, Joaquim José da Silva Xavier, or Tiradentes (the teeth puller), who was executed in 1789 for plotting a revolt against the crown.

National Choro Day
Various venues. **Date** 23 Apr.
Live shows across the city highlight this day of recognition for one of Brazil's traditional jazz forms.

Virada Cultural
Various venues (http://viradacultural.org).
Date May.
Inspired by Paris's Nuit Blanche, this arts and culture 24-hour non-stop marathon (6pm Sat-6pm Sun) has quickly established itself as a major feature on the city's calendar. In 2008, it featured some 800 performances, attracting around 4 million people. There are film, art, folk, theatre, dance and arts activities aplenty, but the main focus is music.

SP Arte-Feira Internacional de Art e de São Paulo
Pavilhão Cicilio Matarazzo, Avenida Pedro Álvares Cabral, Parque Ibirapuera (3094 2820/ www.sp-arte.com). **Date** late May/early June.
The major national and international art market event on the São Paulo cultural calendar; *see p180*.

Semana Dos Museus (Museum Week)
Date latter half of May.
Brazil's federal government and cities have taken to the international museum week concept with gusto. São Paulo is responsible for making Brazil's museum week commemoration, which hit its seventh year in 2009, one of the largest in the world.

Festa Juninha
Date weekends in June.
Ostensibly a religious holiday honouring three saints, this is a major take-to-the-streets party in most regions of Brazil, and there are fair-like activities, often with a country flair in costume and music, in many São Paulo neighbourhoods.

Gay Pride Parade
Date on a Sunday in late May or early June.
See p187 **Profile**.

Festa Literaria International de Parati
Various venues in Parati. **Date** early June.
This is the major book-market event of the Brazilian year, hosted in a colonial beach town between São Paulo and Rio. It attracts famed international authors: in 2008, Tom Stoppard showed up.

Dia Dos Namorados
Date 12 June.
The Brazilian equivalent of St Valentine's Day. A good way for female tourists to take advantage of their Paulistano-for-a-day right to a second expensive Valentine's Day meal and present.

JULY-SEPTEMBER

Anima Mundi
Various venues (www.animamundi.com.br).
Date July.
International animated film festival that has been colouring Rio and São Paulo for the past 17 years.

Festival of Winter in Campos Do Jordão
www.festivalcamposdojordao.org.br.
Date 4-26 July.
Classical music festival showcasing São Paulo's symphony orchestra that is held in the winter resort town Campos do Jordão (a 2hr-drive from the city).

Nossa Senhora Achiropita
Ruas 13 de Maio, São Vicente & Luiz Barreto, Bela Vista (3105 2789/www.achiropita.org.br). Metrô Brigadeiro. **Date** weekends in Aug.
Sister festival to San Gennaro for São Paulo's Italian community, named after a Catholic figure of note. Tons of Italian food and wine to be sampled.

São Paulo Restaurant Week
Various venues (www.restaurantweek.com.br).
Date late Aug-mid Sept; also held in Mar.
Based on the New York event of the same name, this was originally designed to fill tables during slow periods, but now São Paulo's best chefs and restaurants, along wth armies of foodies, have taken to the concept, which also serves as charity fundraiser.

Independence Day
Date 7 Sept.
Anniversary of the declaration of independence from Portugal, signed by Dom Pedro in 1822.

San Gennaro
Rua San Genarro 160, Mooca (3209 0089/ www.sangennaro.com.br). Metrô Bresser-Móoca.
Date weekends in Sept & Oct.
Taking place on Saturday and Sunday evenings (6pm-midnight), this is the best festival to witness the Italian stamp on the city, in a historic immigrant neighbourhood.

OCTOBER-DECEMBER

Republic Day
Date 15 Nov.
A national holiday that commemorates the date of abdication by the last emperor of Brazil, which was also the first step in the founding of the republic of democratic Brazil.

Black Consciousness Day
Date 20 Nov.
A holiday marking the birth of Zumbi, the leader of a safe haven for escaped slaves, with free concerts and events.

Bienal de São Paulo Art Show
Date scheduled for 2010. *See p181* **Profile**.

Mostra Internacional de Cinema de SP (São Paulo International Film Festival)
Various cinemas, most of them in the Avenida Paulista area (3141 0413/www.mostra.org).
Date late Oct-early Nov.
In a city full of movie enthusiasts, the Mostra has a solid two-week schedule that includes unreleased features, arthouse flicks, career retrospectives and loads of rare reels. The 2008 edition had over 450 films from 75 countries spread over 1,200 showings. Tickets for screenings sell out fast. A good idea is to buy packages of 20 or 40 tickets. Serious buffs should consider the 'permanent' ticket, a one-for-all that allows access to every movie.

Reveillon
Date 31 Dec.
New Year's Eve is a big deal in Brazil, and in São Paulo it is celebrated by revellers on Avenida Paulista. Everyone wears white and parties until the sun comes up. Some Brazilians believe the colour of undergarment worn on New Year's Eve will be the arbiter of one's annual fate, so makes sure you choose carefully.

Carnival

Brazil's business capital proves it can cut loose.

Every year, Paulistanos are faced with a decision about what to do for Carnival. If they can manage it, their first choice is often to flee the city. Rio, Olinda and Salvador are the top destinations for this uniquely Brazilian extreme of pre-Lent bacchanalia, but many locals also escape to beach bashes in places such as Natal and Florianópolis.

They're all fine options, but São Paulo does know how to throw a bit of a party. The city government and business sponsors pour more than $R20 million into the *folia* each year, aiming to build a local scene of note. Besides organising the main spectacle in the Sambódromo, many Paulistanos are involved in samba school rehearsals (*ensaios*), street parades (*blocos*), the January selection ceremony for the carnival's king and queen (Rei Momo and Rainha), and smaller neighbourhood celebrations.

SCHEDULES & INFORMATION

In theory, all of the Carnival madness was originally meant to 'use up' all the carne (meat) before good Catholics started Lent (40 days of fasting and prayer that mirror the period that Catholics believe Jesus spent fasting in a desert). In Brazil currently, however, Lent is at best an afterthought to the phenomenal party that is *Carnaval*.

In São Paulo, the main celebrations begin on the Friday before Ash Wednesday and continue through to Tuesday night. São Paulo can't quite claim the non-stop party of its gaudy little-sister Rio – which tends to get, along with Salvador, most of the overseas visitors – but every day brings events that go on late into the night. These events can range from free to outrageously expensive, from the family-friendly to the toxically debauched. On Ash Wednesday, samba schools gather at their rehearsal sites to watch the *apuração* (reading of judges' scores) and to get drunk one last time to celebrate their win (or to drown their sorrows).

Sources for details of the various events include most newspapers in the week leading up to Carnival, particularly *Folha de São Paulo* on Friday. The official tourism site is www.spturis.com; the city's information site is www.cidade desaopaulo.com; reports on Carnival happenings can be found at http://carnaval.uol.com.br; and the website for serious Sampa Carnival fans is www.spcarnaval.com.br.

SAMBODROMO

São Paulo's carnival schools' parades are worth a visit as they're likely to be the most frivolously lavish live spectacle you've ever seen (unless you've already done Rio's even more extreme version). You have to be a real samba devotee, though, to enjoy the *samba-enredo*, the new samba song belted out, over and over, for the entire hour it takes a samba school to traipse past judges and spectators. To a certain degree, the whole affair is like sports; people root for their favorite samba school and each 'team' is given a score by the judges in a number of categories, including song, costumes and organisation.

The events take place each year in Oscar Niemeyer's **Grande Otelo Gymnasium Complex**, aka the **Sambódromo**, inaugurated in 1991 and expanded over the years to its current capacity of 30,000. This count includes, of course, only those watching the show; 2,000 to 5,000 more parade through the arena each hour. To accommodate them there is a 23,000 square metre staging area at one end of the stadium and, at the other, a 7,000 square metre lot for everyone to disperse after their samba-strut.

TICKETS

Prices for the main parade of samba schools on Friday and Saturday range from R$40 (for

Carnival.

unassigned bleacher seats) up to R$38,400 for the rental of a box seating 25. In theory, tickets are available by phone or internet (4003 2245, www.ingressofacil.com.br) but this will only work if you both speak Portuguese and have a Brazilian taxpayer ID number (CPF). Otherwise, tickets can be purchased in person at ten stadiums around the city. The easiest to reach is Palestra Italia, at Rua Turiassú 1840 in Pompéia; take any Lapa-bound bus from Metrô Marechal Deodoro. For other sales points, see www.ingressofacil.com. br/sif/faq.html or the carnival information section of www.cidadedesaopaulo.com.

BLOCOS

Bloco (street parade) schedules vary every year; check the newspapers and websites for listings. Try to seek out events taking place in **Bixiga** (*see pp59-60*), as this bairro is home to the truly samba-obsessed and it has one of the best schools of the city, Vai-Vai (*see p166*).

Banda do Trem Elétrico
Rua Augusta 1500, Consolação.
Metrô Consolação. **Map** 244 K7.
Metrô workers have run this *bloco* since 1981. They gather at Rua Augusta and Rua Luis Coelho and head to the Teatro Municipal. There, they have buses waiting to take the *foliões* (revellers) to Tatuapé, on the east side of town, where the party continues through the night.

Bantantã
Avenida Waldemar Ferreira 231,
Butantã. Bus 7598. **Map** p248 C10.

INSIDE TRACK
SAMPA SAMBODROMO STATS

45 million R$ generated by tourism.
30,000 Tourists drawn to the city.
5 per cent Percentage of tourists who are foreigners.
4,500 Litres of paint used each year in the Sambódromo.
108 Sound systems blaring.
650 Military police on hand to maintain order.

A big drum band has been playing samba on the west side in Butantã for over 15 years.

Bloco dos Esfarrapados
Rua Conselheiro Carrão 500, Bela Vista.
Metrô Brigadeiro. **Map** p245 M7.
Since 1930, this former section of the Vai-Vai samba school has been keeping samba alive in Bixiga. It's smaller and more relaxed than a Vai-Vai rehearsal, as there's no competition in the works.

Bloco Umes Caras Pintadas
Rua Rui Barbosa 323, Bela Vista.
Metrô Trianon-MASP. **Map** p245 M7.
Kids from 15 to 25 years old form the majority of this *bloco*, organised by UMES (the high school student union).

Butantã
Avenida Escola Politécnica 2200,
Rio Pequeno. Bus 748R.
This parade brought together 16 *blocos* and small samba schools for a crowd of about 20,000 people in 2009 as part of a new initiative to bring together *blocos* that are usually spread around the city.

SMALL TOWN CARNIVALS

More-traditional street carnivals can be found in small towns – some within just an hour of São Paulo. Book ahead for a tiny *pousada* and you can enjoy village calm in the morning, and wild bands parading the streets in the afternoons and evenings. São Luís do Paraitinga has long been a classic Paulista getaway and carries on the tradition of *blocos* with *marchinhas* (marching bands). Itu has a nice street carnival, with music and revelry in the town square. Other nearby cities worth checking out are Salto, Boituva and Sorocaba. Coastal cities' carnivals (particularly Santos) have more going on, with balls, small samba schools and *blocos* on the beach. More random street parades take place in São Vicente, Itanhaém, São Sebastião and Caraguatatuba.

ENSAIOS

Samba rehearsals, or *ensaios,* are not so much drudgery and meticulous choreography as one hell of an excuse to party. It's not surprising, then, that each *escola* (literally, 'school' – but it's more of a bairro samba team) starts preparing for Carnival as soon as they've shucked off last year's costumes.

The several-month lead-up to Carnival is a great time to visit a samba school *ensaio*. You'll get to experience hundreds of neighbourhood fans shouting and shaking to that school's samba song for that year – over and over, for hours and hours. It's a chance for the 250 or so percussionists that form the heart of the school to tighten their act, and for you to learn the lyrics to the song. Cold beer and caipirinhas are usually on sale to soothe your vocal cords, and some schools pass out lyrics sheets (what with the hundreds of drums, distorted amplification and general yelling, this is the only way to make out what's actually being sung). Each school rehearses at least once a week. For schedules and a list of other schools, check listings in *Folha de São Paulo* newspaper on Fridays or visit www.ligasp.com.br.

Carnival.

Mocidade Alegre

Avenida Casa Verde 3498, Limão (3857 7525/www.mocidadealegre.com.br). Bus 9789. **Admission** R$15. **No credit cards.**
This school won the carnival competition in both 2007 and 2009, making the entire northern area of the city proud. Neighbouring schools also worth checking out include Morro da Casa Verde, Acadêmicos do Tucuruvi and X-9 Paulistana.

Rosas de Ouro

Rua Coronel Euclides Machado 1066, Limão (3931 4555/www.sociedaderosasdeouro.com.br). Bus 978A. **Admission** R$20. **No credit cards.**
The school's rehearsal space, in pink and blue with touches of gold, is one of the best in town. Like other schools, there's loud music, drums, cheap beer and crowds; but unlike the others, even when it's full it doesn't feel quite so claustrophobic.

Tom Maior

Rua José Gomes Falcão 215, Barra Funda (3494 9040/www.grestommaior.com.br). Bus 8500. **Admission** R$10-$20. **No credit cards. Map** p242 J1.
This school started out in Pinheiros, but found its neighbours there not so keen on its rehearsals and the attendant noise and craziness. It is now located in the more samba-friendly Barra Funda.

Vai-Vai

Rua São Vicente 276, Bela Vista (3105 8725/ www.vaivai.com.br). Metrô Trianon-MASP. **Admission** R$10. **No credit cards. Map** p245 M7.
This is one of the most traditional schools, located in working-class Bixiga. Since Vai-Vai doesn't have its own rehearsal venue, it simply closes down a few streets in front of its office. Over 3,000 people jam in and, leading up to Carnival, it's quite a party.

Dance Balls

Masquerades, marchinhas and merriment are the Sambódromo alternatives.

While many music halls and nightclubs close over Carnival, as the only Paulistanos left in the city head to free *blocos* in the streets, over the past decade some of the major hotels and clubs have been opening up for their own celebrations. If you're not keen on following a clumsily organised ensemble of musicians through streets packed with drunk revellers, the (relatively) more urbane *bailes* may be for you. Ball attendees are encouraged to dress for the affair and a few balls even require masks. The most traditional are focused on *marchinhas* – the jaunty, lively melodies imported from Portugal and used in the first Brazilian Carnivals. For these

nostalgia-fests, try **Avenida Club** (Avenida Pedroso de Moraes 1036, Pinheiros, www.avenidaclub.com.br), **Hotel Renaissance** (*see p101*) or **Bar Brahma** (*see p192*). Trash 80s puts on a great, polysexual party that can get a little crazy at **Club Caravaggio** (Rua Álvaro de Carvalho 40, Centro, www.trash80s.com.br). **Clube Atlético Juventus** (Rua Juventus 690, Mooca, www.juventus.com.br) holds the classic sort of school-esque ball with kids in their 20s, kissing, drinking and possibly punching each other all in the spirit of Carnival. A more reserved fête is held at **Clube Paulistano** (Rua Honduras 1400, Jardim América, www.paulistano.org.br).

ARTS & ENTERTAINMENT

Children

Theme parks, tropical plants and exotic animals galore.

The metropolises of Brazil aren't usually regarded as ideal destinations for those with kids in tow. However, don't be deterred: São Paulo actually has plenty of activities for children. The traffic and fast-paced frenzy that characterises the city might overwhelm your kids at first, but the laid-back attitude and vibrant energy that are prevalent here combine to make parts of the São Paulo very family-friendly.

To escape the madness, you can't really go far wrong with São Paulo's natural and man-made parks. They're mellow, for one thing, a welcome respite from the crowds. And for another, they're home to a wide variety of animals and plants, many of which are more exotic than those that your kids might be used to seeing at your local park or zoo.

OUTDOOR ACTIVITIES

To start, the **Parque da Água Branca** (Avenida Francisco Matarazzo 455, Água Branca, 3865 4130, www.parqueaguabranca.sp.gov.br), is a pristine space filled with relaxing and eye-pleasing flora and fauna. However, the **Fundação Parque Zoológico de São Paulo** (*see p86*) makes for a wilder ride – it has over 3,000 species of animals and features the Zoo Safari, an actual safari into the natural habitats of park-dwelling wildlife. For a more unusual animal-related outing, consider **Cidade das Abelhas** (City of Bees; *see p168*). You may not be able to touch the fuzzy insects, but you'll learn tons about these misunderstood creatures and leave with a stockpile of delicious honey.

If you and your kids are feeling adventurous, try biking your way around São Paulo's parks. **Parque Anhanguera** (Avenida Fortuna Tadiello Natucci 1000, Perus, 3917 2406) offers a wide range of scenery to take in while cycling, including waterways and swamps that are home to a number of amphibians and reptiles. Birds and mammals can be seen scampering around the grounds as well. The **Parque das Bicicletas** (*see p80*), on the other hand, has a more athletic feel. It comprises 20,000 square metres (215,300 square feet) of areas for biking,

walking and skateboarding. Perhaps even more athletic in atmosphere is **Parque Villa Lobos** (*see p77*). The manicured grounds of this park attract around 20,000 people each weekend to its running and biking tracks, soccer fields, ball courts, gymnastic equipment and amphitheatre.

For some aquatic fun, head to **Parque Guarapiranga** (Estrada Guarapiranga 575, Parque Alves de Lima, 5514 6332, closed Mon), which offers a rather pretty (albeit artificial) lake for swimming, as well as a playground and a number of quality restaurants. **The Horto Florestal** and neighbouring **Cantareira State Park** (*see p58*) are much like the state parks of the United States: lush, natural and full of wild species such as native monkeys. In contrast, the **Parque do Ibirapuera** (*see pp73-75*) is considerably more manicured.

If your kids are in the mood for some serious play, and if you're in the mood for a bit of pandemonium, check out **Parque da Mônica** (*see p169*), an amusement park inspired by a popular and very cute Brazilian cartoon character. **Playcenter** (*see p169*) is another amusement park famous not only in São Paulo but throughout Brazil – it's home to the country's biggest rollercoaster. Yet another option is **Hopi Hari** (*see p169*), which makes a great theme park day trip. Travel to the park is made easier by shuttle buses that leave from selected São Paulo metrô stations.

To rid yourself of a post-amusement park headache, visit **Jardim Botânico** (*see p86*).

About the author
Meieli Sawyer Detoni is a freelance writer based in São Paulo.

Parque do Ibirapuera. *See pp73-75.*

A relaxing wander through the orchid farm, herb garden and the numerous flora-lined paths will definitely put your mind to rest. **Jardim dos Cegos** (located at Parque do Ibirapuera) is another botanical garden, but one with an interesting twist – it's the Garden for the Blind. Nearly all of its plants are highly aromatic and are introduced via labels in Braille. **Parque Previdência** (Rua Pedro Peccinini 88, Jardim Ademar, 3721 8951) has several nature trails and over 50 recorded species of birds, as well as a playground.

INDOOR ACTIVITIES

When you need to take the kids inside to escape the rain or the heat, you're spoilt for choice. Try the **Aquário de São Paulo** (*see p169*), which boasts the title of the largest oceanarium in South America and contains over a million litres of fish-filled seawater.

For an active day trip out of the sun, consider **O Mundo da Xuxa** (*see p169*), which is located in the Shopping SP Market. The World of Xuxa is an indoor amusement park themed after Xuxa Meneghel, the blonde-haired, blue-eyed Latin American kids' idol, and is packed with fun for children up to age 14. **Neo Geo World** (*see p169*) is also good for kids for its Neo Geo Boliche, or 'galactic bowling'. Speaking of galactic, the **Planetário Aristóteles Orsini** (*see p75*), in Parque do Ibirapuera, has an exterior that's as equally space-age as its interior and includes over 40 projectors creating a view of any point in the solar system.

If you're in the mood for some theatrics, pay a visit to the **Unidades do SESC** for multicultural programmes for both children and adults. Lastly, for something that's both indoor and educational, visit the **Instituto Butantan** (*see p83* **The Serpent's Den**). If your kids love snakes, they'll love this

research centre that produces nearly all of the vaccines used in Brazil. It also has one of the largest snake collections in the world.

Aquário de São Paulo
Rua Huet Bacelar 407, Ipiranga (2273 5500/ www.aquariodesaopaulo.com.br). Bus 5108-10. **Open** 9am-6pm Mon-Sun. **Admission** R$10-$20; free under-3s. **Credit** MC, V.
Rare and exotic animals abound at the aquarium but if you're feeling really daring book a *Visita Noturna*. These torchlight night walks are aimed at those interested in the nocturnal habits of fish, sharks and even bats. Tours start at 8pm and cost R$60. Hang on to that flashlight.

Catavento Cultural e Educacional
Parque Dom Pedro II (www.cataventocultural. org.br). **Open** 9am-5pm Tue-Sun, holidays. **Admission** R$6; R$3 reductions; free under-3s. **No credit cards. Map** p243 O5.
Located in the beautiful Palácio das Industrias, Catavento is a participative cultural and educational museum. It is well-laid out and provides children (and adults) with fun and interactive ways to learn, and covers topics including space, the human body, Brazilian geography and wildlife, and physics. No tickets are sold after 4pm.

Cidade das Abelhas
Estrada da Ressaca Km7, Embu das Artes (4703 6460/www.cidadedasabelhas.com.br). **Open** 8.30am-5pm Tue-Sun. **Admission** R$15. **Credit** MC, V.
Did you know that bees are considered the most useful species of insect? You're going to learn that and more when you visit the Cidade das Abelhas, nestled in a spot of the Mata Atlântica (remnant of Atlantic forest) right in Embu. Take a special tour that highlights the life of bees, and then set the kids free on an adventure course of slides and tubes. For bus information, *see p215*.

Hopi Hari

*Rodovia dos Bandeirantes Km 72, Vinhedo
(0800 940 4674/www.hopihari.com.br). Exclusive
'Play Bus' lines from bairro Guarulhos and
Shopping Guarulhos/Metrô Itaquera or Tatuapé or
Tietê or Vergueiro.* **Open** 10am-8pm Sat, Sun.
Admission R$55. **Credit** MC, V.

Certainly no city jaunt, Hopi Hari makes your day
trip worthwhile. Built in 1999 and located 72km (44
miles) outside of São Paulo, the theme park offers
slightly scaled-down thrill rides appropriate for the
younger set; the wooden rollercoaster Montezum is
perfect for adults. Most notable is the park's use of
its own language 'Hopês', which is translated into
Portuguese around the park, and is lots of fun for
locals. For the rest of us there's a Hopês-Portuguese
dictionary sold on site, but good luck translating for
your curious little ones.

Neo Geo World

*Rodovia Presidente Dutra Km 225, Internacional
Shopping Guarulhos, Guarulhos (2086 9999/
www.neogeoworld.com.br). Bus M Brás or Jardim
São Paulo (97).* **Open** 11am-1.30am Mon; 11am-
11pm Tue-Thur; 11am-4am Fri, Sat; 11am-11pm
Sun. **Admission** R$20-$50. **Credit** MC, V.

Bowling has never seemed so fun – or so cool. A DJ
spins for Neo Geo nights, and your teen-approved
trip comes complete with black lights and an over-
sized disco ball hanging above the alleys.
Particularly convenient if you're staying near
Guarulhos International Airport, Neo Geo Boliche
will make you look at bowling in a whole new way.

O Mundo da Xuxa

*Shopping SP Market, Avenida das Nações
Unidas 22 540, Interlagos (5541 2530/
www.omundo daxuxa.com.br). Metrô Praça
da Árvore then to bus Jardim Herplin 695H.*
Open 10am-5pm Tue-Fri; 11am-7pm Sat, Sun.
Admission R$35-$45. **Credit** AmEx, DC, MC, V.

When the weather gets bad, head to the covered O
Mundo da Xuxa – a kiddie homage to one of Brazil's
most bizarrely beloved celebs. The amusement park,
which happens to be located in the Shopping SP
Market, has 19 highly whimsical attractions. Take
a seat on a giant coloured block to watch your tots
frolic in the ball pool or gawp at fantasy displays.

Parque da Mônica

*Shopping Eldorado, Avenida Rebouças 3970,
Pinheiros (3093 7766/www.parquemonica.com.br).
Bus 577T.* **Open** 10am-5pm Wed-Fri; 10am-7pm
Sat, Sun. **Admission** R$29-$42. **Credit** MC, V.
Map p248 D11.

Kids aged 2 to 10 will adore this amusement park,
located in the Shopping Eldorado, which holds over
50 different attractions in a multi-level setup. Enjoy
standard amusement park snacks as your kids discover Mônica's House (a scavenger hunt-type attraction), play with theme park characters, and sit in on

Parque Buenos Aires. *See p64.*

exciting live programmes. Check your email at the
internet café if you need a break from all the bustle.

Playcenter

*Rua José Gomes Falcão 20, Barra
Funda (3350 0199/www.playcenter.com.br).
Metrô Barra Funda/free shuttle to park 9am-2pm
(arrivals) and 4.30pm-close (departures).* **Open**
11am-7pm Fri-Sun. **Admission** R$20-$35.
Credit DC, MC, V.

Wild rides of an adrenaline-pumping nature coexist
with quieter fantasy attractions like the carousel and
mini-train at Playcenter. Many a dedicated
Playcenter employee will tell you that this park has
become a staple for Paulistanos with children, and
they're probably right: the park has been operating
for three decades and counting.

Horto Florestal. *See p58.*

Film

From Cinema Novo to Cannes darling, São Paulo takes its star turn.

The overplayed and reductive cinema cliché, that the world's great cities are their own subject on film, has not always been kind to São Paulo. From Ridley Scott and his *Blade Runner* design team looking to 1980s São Paulo as one of the models for their imagined, frightening, sci-fi Los Angeles, to contemporary Brazilian-directed films like *Blindness*, São Paulo appears as a monstrous urban backdrop, a backdrop as villain or a backdrop as bleak future. But this image of the city is not all its cinema history. Where cliché ends, a long roll of film begins, projecting a more varied history of São Paulo and its star turn in the Brazilian 20th century. From its immigrant roots, artistic avant garde and political upheavals, to the contemporary city, luxury den and den of social inequity, a lot more has been captured by the São Paulo lens than the cliché of the city as urban demon.

CELLULOID SAMPA

As São Paulo was becoming a cosmopolitan capital in the 1920s, film was being used to show an idealised image of the 'country of the future'. Not just by the government, but by the industrial bourgeoisie challenging the old oligarchy. Organised labour and artistic movements like modernism all looked to the camera as a means of communication, with newsreel the most common genre. It was better business for national film companies, however, to distribute foreign films than to pay for expensive camera equipment to produce domestic features. And while the introduction of sound in the 1920s spurred hopes that São Paulo film companies would be able to attract the masses to feature-length movies in their own language, own-grown feature-length films waiting to be made in the city even in the mid 1930s.

But once Getúlio Vargas solidified his power in the 1930s, the national government extended monetary support to the fledgling film industry. Commercial and political propaganda kept the industry alive in São Paulo and Rio de Janeiro through the Vargas era. Ademar Gonzaga's Cinedia Studios worked with the infamous Departamento de Imprensa e Propoganda (Department of Press and Propaganda) to get inspectors to administer public screenings. (In 1940, Cinedia showed more newsreels in São Paulo than the government.)

In 1949, the first attempt to replicate the Hollywood studio system was initiated in São Paulo, with the establishment of Vera Cruz Studios. Vera Cruz tried to bring the techniques of international cinema to Brazilian film, but the production costs far outweighed the potential of the local market, and the studio went bust in 1954.

The explosion of Brazilian artistic cinema came in the late 1950s and early 1960s, after the end of the Vargas-led government, when the push to create a truly independent Brazilian cinema began. It was known as Cinema Novo, and one of its five main directors, Nelson Perreira dos Santos, articulated the movement's ideas in São Paulo film congresses in 1952 and 1953. Like the Brazilian modernism of the 1920s, Cinema Novo would sweep music, theatre, literature and film into one transformational current. The key players initially produced small scale works, however, remembering the failure of Vera Cruz and the success of Italian neo-realist cinema.

The first phase of Cinema Novo (1960-64) mainly tackled national as opposed to local questions; dos Santos made *Vidas Secas* (Dry Lives), based on the famous Brazilian novel about lives of rural poverty. The second phase (1964-68) coincided with the military dictatorship's first years, with filmmakers like dos Santos focusing on the failures of the left in films like dos Santos's *Fome de Amor* (Hunger of Love). As social and cultural repression deepened between 1968 and 1972, the movement turned to more allegorical work linked to the burgeoning Tropicalismo arts scene, such as dos Santos's *Como Era Gostoso o Meu Frances* (How Tasty was My Little Frenchman).

Cinema Novo has been the definitive term for Brazilian cinema ever since dos Santos's early efforts, and São Paulo has provided some of the most important creative spirits and film settings ever since 'the pope', as he's known, set his cameras rolling. The genre has stayed true to its pioneering spirit while evolving along with global cinema trends. The Italian neo-realist influence would carry through to directors like Hector Babenco and his 1981 film *Pixote*, about the brutal life of Paulistano youths in juvenile detention (one of the film's stars would later be shot dead by police in São Paulo). Two decades later Babenco made *Carandiru*, the true story of the massacre of prisoners in São Paulo's largest prison. With a style that married multiple narratives and slick editing flourishes, Babenco's early neo-realist lens had been transformed into an international, Cannes-nominated sensation.

Another famous São Paulo son, Walter Salles, whose father founded one of the largest banks in Brazil, Unibanco, began filming *Central Station* on a small budget, and after two 1999 Oscar nominations, has gone on to produce major Hollywood films like *The Motorcycle Diaries*.

The creative heart of urban film is often identified with large immigrant groups. No one can reference New York City movies without the brutal lens of Italo-American Martin Scorsese, for instance. In São Paulo, the Japanese community has been a major force in film ever since the second generation Nikkei made the move from the rural coffee plantations to the urban *bairro* of Liberdade. Non-Nikkei

filmmakers also became transfixed by movies coming to the city from Japan, including samurai masterpieces, art house films and even soft-core porn, known as *pinku eiga*. Japanese production houses put São Paulo on their distribution map after World War II, and films like Kurosawa's *Rashomon* (1950) played to broad Paulistano audiences. However, in some respects, such films ended up bolstering Brazilian stereotypes of the Japanese community. The 'butterfly syndrome', in which Nikkei actresses were often the sexual focus of São Paulo love stories, either as the demure geisha doll or dragon lady, contrasted with limited roles for male Nikkei actors as samurai sword bearers. However, Nikkei actors also featured widely in Brazilian films, from box-office comedies to Nikkei-specific narratives, as well as in international cinema festival sensations and erotic film escapades. Famed Japanese models made the move to Brazilian cinema in the 1960s and 1970s, including Célia Watanabe, who had a role in *Noite Vazia* (Empty Night), a 1964 Cannes entry directed by major Brazilian auteur Walter Hugo Khouri. By the 1970s, Liberdade had five Japanese-language movie houses, a major step up from the Japanese projector-on-wheels that made the rounds of the plantations in the 1920s and 1930s. Paulistano film buffs would sit in the movie houses not understanding a word, but taking detailed notes on the camera wizardry of the Japanese filmmakers.

The early 1990s was a dark time for Brazilian film, not in terms of quality, but in terms of the financial health of the industry. The withdrawal of governmental support – critical to the industry's survival – under the presidency of Fernando Collor de Mello in 1990, left cinemas

ARTS & ENTERTAINMENT

Pelé, Sly Stalone and Michael Caine team up for *Victory* (1981).

The Silver Screen's Golden Age

The age of grand movie palaces is long-gone – but is a new era beckoning?

Ask elderly Paulistanos about their memories of trips to the flicks, and they are likely to reminisce, misty-eyed, about the grand salons that existed in downtown São Paulo decades ago. They will talk of the Olido, which had its own orchestra. They will remember the vast Cine Ipiranga, with several thousand seats and the majestic debuts of films such as *Ben-Hur*, *Cleopatra* or the latest Marilyn Monroe hit. They will tell you about the chic Arabic decor of the Marrocos and the vast screen of the Comodoro, especially made for higher-resolution 70mm films.

One of the saddest by-products of São Paulo city centre's degradation was the successive tumbling of all of its grandiose movie houses. But São Paulo was not alone in this cultural massacre; it's a process that took place throughout Brazil from the 1980s onwards.

The home video boom, rising violence and the economic decline of inner cities, killed street cinemas up and down the country. The boom in shopping malls fitted with spanking new multiplexes was the final straw. A vast number of cinemas ended up being converted into temples of evangelical

cults, which have been growing in popularity in Brazil since the 1980s. Such was the fate, for example, of the Metro, on once glamorous Avenida São João. Other movie theatres became porn cinemas, parking lots, discount stores or just empty, run-down properties. According to the Ministry of Culture, Brazil had 3,500 cinemas in the 1950s. At the end of the 1990s, that number had dropped to 1,300.

There have been glimmers of hope in the city though, in the wake of strong movements, such as Viva Centro, aimed at revitalising downtown areas. A few years ago, Cine Olido was converted by the city council into a cultural centre, with a gallery, theatre and cute screening room, with wooden chairs and projections of DVDs (tickets cost R$1). Cine Marabá has also recently reopened, completely redesigned by Ruy Ohtake. Rumours suggest that Cine Marrocos will be turned into a new enterprise (possibly a cinema) in the not-too-distant future. Meanwhile, São Paulo's annual film festival, Mostra de Cinema (www.mostra.org), makes an effort to include downtown cinemas in its programme.

in the dark for much of the decade. The resurgence of the film industry at the end of the 1990s (known as the *retomada* (retaking) and the city's fully-fledged re-emergence as a screen starlet a few years earlier, was led by films like *Central Station* (1998) and *Me, You, Them* (2000; Andrucha Waddington), and well as *City of God* (2002) and *Carandiru* (2003). Two new, huge and non-governmental backers of Brazilian film rose in prominence during this period: major Hollywood film distributors and the powerful Brazilian media empire Globo, which extended its reach beyond television and created its own production company, responsible for bringing *City of God* and *Carandiru* to cinema screens.

Cinema Novo continues to be the master reel when referencing Brazilian movies today. Its favourite locations and settings, the favelas and the *sertão*, continue to be mined by filmmakers striving to express the Brazilian experience: the massive cities, the myriad mazes of poverty in the urban *morros* (hills) and the rural backwaters where electricity can still seem a marvel. Many critics today, though, find the best work of Brazilian filmmakers to be less overtly political,

and more a merger of politics with the personal. Instead of lashing out at the higher classes for neglecting social ills, a previous common thread of Cinema Novo, the focus of much current Brazilian celluloid is the web of corruption that underscores much of Brazilian society today.

CINEMAS

Bristol
Avenida Paulista 2064, Cerqueira César (3289 0509/www.playarte.com.br/Cinema). Metrô Consolação. **Open** 1pm-midnight daily. **Tickets** R$14-$25. **Credit** MC, V. **Map** p244 K7. *See p174* **Kinoplex Itaim**.

★ Centro Cultural São Paulo
Rua Vergueiro 1000, Paraíso (3397 4002/ www.centrocultural.sp.gov.br). Metrô Vergueiro. **Open** 4-11pm Tue-Sun. **Tickets** free. **No credit cards. Map** p245 N10.
São Paulo's aerodynamic-looking Cultural Centre, perched atop a steep hill beside the Avenida 23 de Maio thoroughfare, is quite an impressive and clever architectural feat. From vintage Hollywood flicks to

current Brazilian production, programming is diverse. This cinema is the budget-lovers favourite, with free entry; just pick up your ticket one hour before the film starts.

Cidade Jardim Cinemark

Avenida Magalhães de Castro 12000, Cidade Jardim (3758 1670/www.shoppingcidade jardimjhsf.com.br). Bus 5118, 5119, 6200. **Open** 11.25am-midnight daily. **Tickets** R$16-$21. *Luxury screening rooms R$35-$46.* **Credit** AmEx, DC, MC, V. **Map** p248 C9.

Ever wanted to see a movie you love on a real golden screen? Does a cinema with leather seats, popcorn made with olive oil, a bar and waiter service (even during screening), and champagne and wine on the menu, sound good enough? Shopping Cidade Jardim, the city's flashiest mall brings you the ultimate cinema experience; for over-the-top (and pricey) movie viewing, this is the place to go. The mall is an elitist fortress, and the real film buff is bound to revel in the perfect sound and image, and first-class seating arrangements (there's plenty of room between your seat and the other rows).

★ Cine Bombril

Avenida Paulista 2073, Conjunto Nacional (3285 3696). Metrô Consolação. **Open** 1.30pm-midnight daily. **Tickets** R$5.50-$8.50. **Credit** MC. **Map** p244 K7.

Lavishly refurbished a few years back, this old cinema house is also a marquee screening place during the annual São Paulo International Film Festival, and often features the best in Brazilian documentary filmmaking and non-commercial features.

Cinesesc

Rua Augusta 2075, Jardins (3087 0500/ www.sescsp.org.br). Metrô Consolação. **Open** 2pm-midnight daily. **Tickets** R$8-$12; reductions R$4-$6. **Credit** AmEx, MC, V. **Map** p244 J7.

If you fancy sipping a caipirinha while watching a Pasolini film on the big screen in the company of arty types, then this place is for you. The bar inside the movie room of the Cinesesc is isolated by walls and a large glass panel, and sells drinks throughout the screenings. This traditional address is for those who avoid mainstream blockbusters like the plague, with the programme unsurprisingly featuring a lot of arthouse, European and Asian cinema, as well as documentaries. Many festivals and exhibitions take place here.

Espaço Unibanco Augusta

Rua Augusta 1470 e 1475, Consolação (3288 6780/www.unibancocinemas.com.br). Metrô Consolação. **Open** 1.30pm-midnight daily. **Tickets** R$12-$16. **Credit** DC, MC, V. **Map** p244 K7.

With five cinemas and a consistently good selection of movies ranging from mainstream to arthouse, this is the kind of place where you can drop by without planning what to see – there's always a good chance that there'll be something interesting being screened. It has two bookshops, good snacks on offer, beer and a large foyer that is regularly used for premières and parties. Just off Avenida Paulista, the cinema is also convenient for a pre-drinking/clubbing session, as several good bars and clubs are just down the road on Rua Augusta.

Nelson Perreira dos Santos. *See p170.*

ARTS & ENTERTAINMENT

On the set of *Blindness*.

Espaço Unibanco Bourbon Pompéia

3rd floor, Shopping Bourbon, Rua Turiassu 2100, Pompéia (3673 3949/www.unibanco cinemas.com.br/index.asp). Metrô Barra Funda. **Open** 1pm-midnight daily. **Tickets** R$10-$18. *IMAX* R$20-$30. **Credit** AmEx, MC, V.

Start your day with a spending spree and finish it watching a 3-D film with the kids. One of the newest shopping malls in town, the Bourbon is home to Brazil's first and only IMAX theatre. There are 11 screens and the programming is reasonably diverse, although the focus tends to be on the latest Hollywood features.

Frei Caneca Unibanco Arteplex

3rd floor, Shopping Frei Caneca, Rua Frei Caneca 569, Consolação (3472 2365/www. unibancocinemas.com.br/index. asp). Metrô Consolação. **Open** 1pm-midnight daily. **Tickets** R$13-$22. **Credit** AmEx, MC, V. **Map** p242 L6.

Frei Caneca shopping mall is a favourite spot for gay Paulistanos. Its cinema complex has eight different sized screens, where films ranging from arty to box-office smashes are featured. The complex also has a pretty good café and bar.

Gemini

Avenida Paulista 807, Jardins (3289 3566). Metrô Brigadeiro or Trianon-Masp. **Open** 2pm-midnight daily. **Tickets** R$10-$16. **No credit cards.** **Map** p244 L9.

The decor seems to have stayed untouched since the 1970s, but don't let the worn-out carpets and tacky panels on the walls deter you. This place is worth checking out because it always features good flicks, often European, that left the regular circuit a while ago. If you missed the latest Woody Allen or Fernando Meirelles there is a good chance that it will still be showing at the Gemini.

HSBC Belas Artes

Rua da Consolação 2423, Consolação (3258 4092/ www2.hsbc.com.br). Metrô Consolação. **Open** 2pm-midnight daily. **Tickets** R$8-$16; reductions R$4-$8. **Credit** DC, MC, V. **Map** p244 J7.

Originally opened in 1967, this street complex quickly established itself as a mecca for arty and alternative flicks. After closing for a while, it underwent a complete refurbishment a few years ago. It has six pretty comfortable screens that offer mostly new European and American releases, without ever resorting to mainstream shopping-mall fodder.

Kinoplex Itaim

Rua Joaquim Floriano 466, Itaim Bibi (3131 2004/www.kinoplex.com.br). Bus 106A, 477A. **Open** 2pm-midnight daily. **Tickets** R$16-$22. **Credit** MC. **Map** p244 I12.

This and the Bristol (*see p172*) are devoted to the more commercial end of film production. But if you want to catch up on the latest Hollywood blockbusters, you'll find comfortable seating and quality screens. Kinoplex is a good alternative if you are in the Itaim Bibi-Vila Olimpia-Jardim Paulistano area.

Reserva Cultural

Avenida Paulista 900, Jardins (3287 3529/ www.reservacultural.com.br). Metrô Brigadeiro or Trianon-Masp. **Open** 1pm-midnight daily. **Tickets** R$13-$19. **Credit** V. **Map** p244 L8.

Reserva Cultural is a great central option for quality films, from mainstream to odd-ball. There are four good screens of different sizes plus a restaurant, bar, bakery and a specialist bookstore. Fridays and Saturdays feature midnight screenings.

★ Sala Cinemateca

Largo Sen. Raul Cardoso 207, Vila Mariana (3512 6111/www.cinemateca.gov.br). Metrô Vila Mariana. **Open** 3-10pm daily. **Tickets** R$8; reductions R$4. **No credit cards.** **Map** 247 M13.

In the 1940s, a group of students and film-lovers founded what was to become the main archive of Brazilian cinema, Cinemateca Brasileira. Today, it holds more than 200,000 film reels plus thousands of memorabilia items such as posters, books, magazines, original screenplays and photos. The Cinemateca has two movie halls that make the most of its film library: mini-festivals, classics, rare films old and new, foreign and Brazilian make up the eclectic schedule.

Galleries

Sample folk, indigenous and naïf art in Sampa.

Two major movements dominated Brazilian art during the 20th century, Brazilian Modernism and Tropicalismo, and these created an exceptional reputation for the scene here. The wealth and creativity of São Paulo's residents have enabled an enormous and thriving art market, the largest in South America. The city offers the fruit of its labour in a large array of swish venues that deal in everything from cutting-edge contemporary work to early Brazilian modernist pieces, as well as street and Japanese-Brazilian art. Over the last ten years the scene has burgeoned and today São Paulo has its own art fair, SP-Arte, which premiered in 2005.

COMMERCIAL GALLERIES

Barra Funda

★ Galeria de Babel
Rua Dr Sérgio Meira 230/61 Torre 1, Barra Funda (3825 0507/www.galeriadebabel.com.br). Metrô Barra Funda. **Open** 10am-5pm Mon-Sat. **No credit cards. Map** p242 K2.
A one-of-a-kind gallery in São Paulo, Galeria de Babel is a haven for lovers of photography. The names in its collection include established fashion photographers like Otto Stupakoff and Bob Wolfenson, along with the likes of Gui Mohallem, Joel Meyerowitz, Marcelo Brodsky, Martin Parr and Zak Powers.

Bela Vista

Galeria Deco
Rua dos Franceses 153, Bela Vista (3289 7067/ www.galeriadeco.com.br). Bus 475M-10. **Open** 9am-6pm daily. **No credit cards. Map** p245 M8.
Galeria Deco has been promoting art by Japanese and Nikkei (Japanese-descended) artists since 1981. Here, you can find excellent works by names such as Yayoi Kusama, Futoshi Yoshizawa, Kimi Nii, Nobuo Mitsunashi, Yashusi Suzuki and Yutaka Toyota.

Galeria Polinésia
Rua Pedro Taques 110, Bela Vista (3129 4401/ www.galeriapolinesia.com). Bus 719P-10.

About the author
Camila Belchior *is a São Paulo art critic who has worked on the Brazil: Body and Soul exhibition at the Guggenheim in New York.*

Open 2-8pm Wed-Sat. **No credit cards. Map** p242 K6.
This trendy gallery is installed in a whitewashed house and is visited frequently by young folk in fashion circles. You'll come across all sorts of work by artists from Brazil and around the world. Nathan Gray's works on paper, all the way from Australia, are a delight.

Butantã

Galeria Leme
Rua Agostinho Cantu 88, Butantã (3814 8184/www.galerialeme.com). Bus 177P-10. **Open** 10am-7pm Mon-Fri; 10am-5pm Sat. **No credit cards. Map** p248 C10.
This is a unique space, showcasing thought-provoking and eye-catching work in different media from Brazilian and international artists. The gallery space, designed in bare concrete by architect Paulo Mendes da Rocha, is striking. There's an annex across the street that serves as an artists' studio. *Photo p180.*

Centro

SOSO Arte Contemporânea Africana
2nd floor, Avenida São João 313, Centro (3222 3973/www.soso-artecontemporaneaafricana.com). Metrô São Bento/bus 4112-10. **Open** 11am-7pm Mon-Fri; 11am-4.30pm Sat. **No credit cards. Map** p243 N5.
SOSO's mission is to bridge the distance between Brazilian and African cultures by promoting contemporary African production. It invites artists to Brazil and offers them residency programmes in

Luciana Brito.

partnership with Fundação Sindika Dokolo, and highlights their shows at the gallery. Installed on the 2nd floor of a Niemeyer building in the heart of São Paulo's historic city centre, SOSO boasts a 200sq-m exhibition space. There is also an archive of contemporary African art.

Higienópolis

Galeria Pontes
Rua Minas Gerais 80, Higienópolis (3129 4218/ www.galeriapontes.com.br). Metrô Consolação/ bus 719P-10. **Open** 10am-7pm Mon-Fri; 10am-5pm Sat. **Credit** AmEx, MC, V. **Map** p242 J6.
If folk art is what you are looking for, Galeria Pontes is the ideal stop. Installed in a heritage house in Higienópolis, the gallery offers sculptures and paintings by artists from around the country. Edna Matosinho de Pontes, the owner, is a collector herself and a wonderful source from which to learn the symbolism and origins of the pieces she has for sale.

★ Galeria Vermelho
Rua Minas Gerais 350, Higienópolis (3138 1520/ www.galeriavermelho.com.br). Metrô Consolação/ bus 719P-10. **Open** 10am-7pm Mon-Fri; 11am-5pm Sat. **Credit** AmEx, MC, V. **Map** p244 J7.
A leading art space in town, Galeria Vermelho is devoted to contemporary art. The gallery was designed by Paulo Mendes da Rocha. It makes the most of a mews area that includes a large outdoor patio where its very own restaurant, Sal Gastronomia (*see p109*), is a perfect way to end a morning. The façade of the gallery is often used by exhibiting artists in group or solo shows. The shows emphasise the creative process (there's plenty of conceptual art) and all media. Look for works by Chelpa Ferro, installations by Chiara Banfi, photos of indigenous tribes by Claudia Andujar, as well as works by Dias & Riedweg, Héctor Zamora, Marilá Dardot, Rosângela Rennó and Nicolás Robbio.

Itaim Bibi & Vila Olímpia

Casa Triângulo
Rua País de Araújo 77, Itaim Bibi (3167 5621/ www.casatriangulo.com.br). Bus 5119-21. **Open** 11am-7pm Tue-Sat. **No credit cards.** **Map** p249 G12.
One of the main galleries in town dealing in contemporary art, Casa Triângulo is a platform for both Brazilian stars and international names. Casa Triângulo's team includes established artists such as Sandra Cinto, Marcia Xavier, Lucia Koch, Nazareth Pacheco and the internationally acclaimed collaborative team of *assume vivid astro focus* (avaf). There are also interesting works by Pier Stockholm, Valdirlei Dias Nunes, Rogério Degaki and Adriana Gallinari.

Galeria Baró Cruz
Rua Clodomiro Amazonas 526, Itaim Bibi (3167 0830/www.barocruz.com). Bus 6401-10. **Open** 11am-7pm Tue-Fri; 11am-5pm Sat. **No credit cards.**
Since 2004, Galeria Baró Cruz has been promoting and dealing in contemporary art from Brazil and around the globe. It has a stable of established names as well as up-and-coming bets. If you are in the neighbourhood, pop in and check out the fabulously imaginative installations by Henrique Oliveira, photos by Claudia Jaguaribe and Michael Wesely, paintings by Fabiano Gonper and works by Pablo Siquier and Pablo Vargas Lugo.

★ Luciana Brito
Rua Gomes de Carvalho 842, Vila Olímpia (3842 0634/www.lucianabritogaleria.com.br). Bus 6401-10. **Open** 10am-7pm Mon-Fri; 11am-5pm Sat. **No credit cards.**
This gallery specialising in contemporary art is well worth the trek to Vila Olímpia. Luciana Brito represents artists from Brazil and abroad, including iconic names in the international art milieu, like Marina Abramovic. Works are high calibre and new exhibitions tend to cause a stir in São Paulo. Large-scale photographs by Brazilian Caio Reisewitz and famous Bahian photographer Mario Cravo Neto, installations by Argentine Leandro Erlich, and works by Allan McCollum and Liliana Porter are unmissable.

Jardins

AC Galeria de Arte
*Rua José Maria Lisboa 1008, Jardim Paulista
(3063 3707/www.acgaleria.com). Metrô
Trianon-MASP.* **Open** 10am-7pm Mon-Fri.
No credit cards. Map p244 K8.
The gallery focuses on works from the 1960s and
1970s by Brazilian artists. Ivald Granato, José
Roberto Aguilar, Claudio Tozzi and Gregório Gruber
are just a few of the artists represented here.

Bolsa de Arte – Galeria Bergamin
*Rua Rio Preto 63, Jardim Paulista (3062 2333/
www.galeriabergamin.com.br). Bus 702P-42.*
Open 11am-7pm Mon-Fri. **No credit cards.
Map** p244 J9.
This modernist-looking space functions both as an
auction house and gallery. It auctions Brazilian classics and Brazilian modernists, but has recently
branched out into contemporary art and design as
well. Exhibitions vary in nature, so you may come
across a very contemporary show or one that
specialises in modernist paintings. This diversity
makes it an interesting stop on the Rua Oscar Freire
tour, and should be followed by a coffee at the Santo
Grão café just around the corner (Rua Oscar Freire
413, 3082 9969, www.santograo.com.br).

Collectors Arte Século XX
*Rua Dr Melo Alves 369, Jardim Paulista
(3062 4805). Metrô Consolação/bus 7545-10.*
Open 10am-7pm Mon-Fri; 10am-2pm Sat.
No credit cards. Map p244 I8.
If you adore Art Deco, this lovely gallery is for you.
The household specialities are deco furniture,
bronzes and glasswork. The space also holds works
by modernist painters and Brazilian designers such
as Joaquim Tenreiro, Sérgio Rodrigues and José
Zanine Caldas.

★ Dan Galeria
*Rua Estados Unidos 1638, Jardim Paulista
(3083 4600/www.dangaleria.com.br). Metrô
Consolação.* **Open** 10am-7pm Mon-Fri; 10am-
1pm Sat. **Credit** AmEx. **Map** p244 I9.
A well-established gallery in the milieu, Dan Galeria
regularly organises retrospective shows of Brazilian
modernists and exhibitions of established contemporary artists in the gallery's collection. From time
to time there are also shows of works by international artists from the '20s. You'll certainly come
across A-list artists here: Anita Malfatti, Guignard,
Alfredo Volpi, Antonio Bandeira, Bruno Giorgi,
Cícero Dias, Emiliano Di Cavalcanti, Lasar Segall,
León Ferrari, Lygia Clark, Lygia Pape and Tomie
Ohtake, to name just a few.

Emma Thomas
*Rua Augusta 2052, cj 03, Jardim Paulista
(8219 6452/www.emmathomas.com.br).
Metrô Consolação/bus 702P-10.* **Open**
4-8pm Wed-Sat. **No credit cards.
Map** p244 J8.
Since 2006, the Emma Thomas gallery has promoted
artists at the start of their careers and helped structure the work of young curators. It represents a constant flow of new talent, which is wonderful for
adventurous and risk-taking collectors, as well as
collectors in the making, since prices are more accessible than at comparable galleries.

Galeria Berenice Arvani
*Rua Oscar Freire 540, Jardim Paulista
(3088 2843/www.galeriaberenicearvani.com).
Metrô Consolação/bus 702P-42.* **Open** 10am-
7.30pm Mon-Fri. **No credit cards. Map** p244 I8.
Since 2001, Galeria Berenice Arvani has been
dealing in contemporary art from Brazil and abroad.
Ask to see works by Hélio Nomura, Hércules
Barsotti, Mira Schendel and Rubem Valentim.

ARTS & ENTERTAINMENT

Nara Roesler. *See p178.*

Choque Cultural. *See p179.*

Galeria Luisa Strina

Rua Oscar Freire 502, Jardins (3088 2471/
www.galerialuisastrina.com.br). Bus 702P-42.
Open 10am-7pm Mon-Fri; 10am-5pm Sat.
No credit cards. Map p244 J8.
Galeria Luisa Strina is one of the cornerstones of
the contemporary circuit. It is a good option for the
cognoscentie, and for the curious who have a good
eye and don't mind the sometimes frosty reception
– it's part of the show. Luisa Strina is one of the
most iconic art dealers in town. Her space on the
corner of Oscar Freire has a wonderful rooftop
deck, which, during openings or installations of
exhibits, offers visitors a hangout in the heart of
the Jardins. Strina represents artists from all
around the globe. Her premise is solid, thought-
provoking contemporary art in all media. There are
well-established emblematic artists such as Marepe
and Cildo Meireles, who is currently Brazil's fore-
most conceptual artist and is known in the main
art hubs throughout the world. Young mid-career
artists such as Alexandre da Cunha, Edgard de
Souza, Jarbas Lopes and Renata Lucas are also
shown here.

Monica Filgueiras

Rua Bela Cintra 1533, Jardim Paulista
(3081 9492). Metrô Consolação. **Open**
10.30am-7.30pm Mon-Fri; 10.30am-2.30pm
Sat. **No credit cards. Map** p244 J7.
Monica Filgueiras is a delight to talk to and has been
dealing contemporary art in São Paulo for decades.
She represents a varying array of artists whose works
range from multimedia to sculptures. She has pieces
by classic modernists such as Victor Brecheret, as
well as by videomakers, photographers and graffiti
artists: Ozi, Bugre and Gejo to name a few.

Nara Roesler

Avenida Europa 655, Jardim Europa
(3063 2344/www.nararoesler.com.br).
Bus 702N-10. **Open** 10am-7pm Mon-Fri; 11am-
3pm Sat. **No credit cards. Map** p249 G11.
An avid player in the market, Galeria Nara Roesler
represents contemporary artists working in different
media. The array of artists varies in style from the 'old
school contemporary', as in the work of Tomie Ohtake,
and the geometric and kinetic creations by Julio Le
Parc, to the more cutting-edge experimentations of
Hélio Oiticica. There are also fashionable young talents led by the painter Rodolpho Parigi, Cao
Guimaraes and Alberto Baraya. The gallery sits next
door to Thomas Cohn on Rua Colômbia, amid
luxury car dealerships and design stores. *Photos*
p175 & p177.

Passado Composto

Rua da Consolação 3198, Jardim Paulista
(3064 0805/www.passadocomposto.com.br).
Metrô Consolação. **Open** 10am-7pm Mon-Fri;
10am-3pm Sat. **Credit** AmEx. **Map** p244 I8.
At two different addresses, Passado Composto deals
in 18th- to 20th-century glasswork (on Rua
Consolação) as well as furniture by major-league
Brazilian designers from the 20th century, such as
Joaquim Tenreiro and Sérgio Rodrigues (at the
Alameda Lorena location).
Other location Alameda Lorena 1996, Jardim
Paulista (3088 9128).

Paulo Kuczynski Escritório de Arte

Alameda Lorena 1661, Jardim Paulista
(3064 5355). Metrô Consolação.
Open 9.30am-6.30pm Mon-Fri.
No credit cards. Map p244 I8.

A specialist on Alfredo Volpi, super-dealer Paulo Kuczynski showcases Brazilian modernists. Find exemplary works here by Brazilian masters Portinari and Di Cavalcanti, iconic scenes by Guignard, seascapes by Pancetti and the striking work of Franz Krajcberg.

Thomas Cohn
Avenida Europa 641, Jardim Europa (3083 3355/www.thomascohn.com.br). Bus 702N-10. **Open** 11am-7pm Tue-Fri; 11am-6pm Sat. **No credit cards**. **Map** p249 G11.
Thomas Cohn is the local dealer for British sculptor Tony Cragg, but also has a very good eye for painting. He represents the household names Oscar Oiwa and Leonilson, plus two recent additions: the emerging Brazilian Ana Elisa Egreja and Russian Julia Kazakova, both young and up-and-coming talents.

Perdizes

Gravura Brasileira
Rua Dr Franco da Rocha 61, Perdizes (3624 0301/www.gravurabrasileira.com). Metrô Barra Funda/bus 875A-10. **Open** 10am-6pm Mon-Fri; 11am-1pm Sat. **No credit cards**. **Map** p242 I3.
The only gallery in town dedicated entirely to dealing in prints (*gravuras*) by new stars and high-calibre established artists from around the country. A hub for anyone interested in the medium, it is a drawing force in the milieu. With dozens of artists in the collection, you'll have plenty to paw through.

Pinheiros & Vila Madalena

Amoa Konoya Arte Indígena
Rua João Moura 1002, Pinheiros (3061 0639/www.amoakonoya.com.br). Bus 701A-10. **Open** 9am-6pm Mon-Sat. **Credit** AmEx, DC, MC, V. **Map** p249 G8.
Amoa Konoya means 'tortoise' in indigenous dialects. Indigenous crafts of all shapes, sizes and functions have travelled across the country from 60 settlements throughout Brazil. This is without a doubt the best place for these unique artefacts. Informative videos and books are available on site for those keen to learn more about Brazil's first residents.

★ Casa da Xiclet Galeria
Rua Fradique Coutinho 1855, Vila Madalena (2579 9007/www.casadaxiclet.multiply.com). Bus 748N-10. **Open** 2-6pm Mon, Wed-Sun. **No credit cards**. **Map** p249 G8.
Casa da Xiclet is at the heart of art criticism in Brazil. This unique space, run by Xiclet, doubles as her house and a gallery for contemporary art. Her shows are organised around themes that either engage the art scene in a dialogue, critique the art scene or present polemic subjects for further discussion. If you're at Fortes Vilaça Gallery (*see below*), you ought to pop in here too.

★ Choque Cultural
Rua João Moura 997, Pinheiros (3061 4051/ www.choquecultural.com.br). Bus 701A-10. **Open** noon-7pm Tue-Sat. **Credit** V. **Map** p249 G8.
Prepare to be shocked and enlightened at one of the highlights of the Brazilian art front. Situated in a small townhouse, Baixo Ribeiro's gallery is wholly dedicated to promoting Brazilian urban art, from graffiti artists to skateboard designers and fashion creatives. If you catch Baixo in the house, you'll most definitely come out of the visit a whole lot wiser on the subject. You can pick up prints at very reasonable prices, as well as sculptures, paintings and drawings. Check out works by Speto, Titi Freak, Pjota, Zezão, Silvana Mello and Daniel Lannes.

★ Fortes Vilaça
Rua Fradique Coutinho 1500, Vila Madalena (3032 7066/www.fortesvilaca.com.br). Bus 748N-10. **Open** 10am-7pm Tues-Fri; 10am-5pm Sat. **No credit cards**. **Map** p249 E8.
Arguably one of the most well-established Brazilian contemporary art galleries on the international circuit, Galeria Fortes Vilaça represents up-and-coming and established artists from the world over. Some of the star holdings include the chocolate, dust, diamond or litter 'drawings' of classic art or historical works, photographed by Vik Muniz. There are also striking tile works and paintings by Adriana Varejão; the clinical perfectionism of Iran do Espírito Santo; and the oneiric graffiti-inspired paintings of Os Gêmeos. Foreign

ARTS & ENTERTAINMENT

artists include Gerben Mulder, Cerith Wyn Evans, Franz Ackerman, Hiroshi Sugito, Nobuyoshi Araki and Los Carpinteros among many others. The annex warehouse is slightly out of the way, but is well worth a visit, which should be booked in advance. A must for those into contemporary art. **Other location** Warehouse, Rua James Holland 71, Bom Retiro (3392 3942, closed Sat & Sun).

Gabinete de Arte Raquel Arnaud
Rua Artur de Azevedo 401, Pinheiros (3083 6322/www.raquelarnaud.com). Bus 177Y-10. **Open** 10am-7pm Mon-Fri; noon-4pm Sat. **No credit cards. Map** p249 G8.
A trailblazer in contemporary art, Raquel Arnaud has been working since 1973 and focuses on constructivist and kinetic art as well as installations, sculpture and painting. Look out for Carmela Gross, Carlos Zilio, Cruz-Diez, Frida Baranek, Georgia Kyriakakis, Iole de Freitas, Silvia Mecozzi, Waltércio Caldas and Sergio Camargo.

Galeria Virgilio
Rua Virgilio de Carvalho Pinto 426, Pinheiros (3062 9446/www.galeriavirgilio.com.br). Bus 177Y-10. **Open** 10am-7pm Mon-Fri; 10am-5pm Sat. **No credit cards. Map** p249 F9.
Galeria Virgillio's location is an asset: the large space in a mews makes for a pleasant visit, detached from the monotony of Pinheiros. The exhibition space is dedicated to contemporary art. However, the gallery doesn't just deal in art; the annex offers courses and lectures. The focus is on home-grown artists like Wagner Morales, Daniel Murgel, Diego Belda, Edith Derdyk, José Rufino and Marcelo Solá, among several others.

Millan
Rua Fradique Coutinho 1360, Vila Madalena (3031 6007/www.galeriamillan.com.br). Bus 748N-10. **Open** 10am-7pm Mon-Fri; 11am-5pm Sat. **No credit cards. Map** p249 E8.
Dealing in contemporary art, André Millan is a mainstay of the Brazilian art market, representing artists such as Amilcar de Castro, Artur Barrio, Mira Schendel and Tunga. The stable of artists also includes Paulo Climachauska, a local artist who makes figurative paintings where the lines are formed by arithmetical equations (mainly adding and subtracting). Another high-calibre addition is Miguel Rio Branco, arguably one of the most impressive photographers currently working. The gallery also offers courses and gatherings in the annex under the name of b_arco.

Vila Mariana

Galeria Jacques Ardies
Rua Morgado de Mateus 579, Vila Mariana (5539 7500/www.ardies.com). Bus 675N-10. **Open** 10am-6.30pm Mon-Fri; 10am-4pm Sat. **No credit cards. Map** p245 M12.
Naïf art is sometimes not fully appreciated or valued, but Jacques Ardies has been dealing in Brazilian naïf art since the early '80s. He has been pivotal in promoting the work in the country and abroad, with shows in galleries all over the country as well as in New York, Paris and Tel Aviv, to name but a few. A vast array of paintings, sculpture and prints are available in this restored old house in Vila Mariana. Even though it may feel a little out of the way, if this is the art of your choice, make a point of stopping.

David Bachelor's *Backlights* at Galleria Leme. *See p175.*

Bienal and SP-Arte

The art fairs that amuse, inform and spark controversy.

The first **Bienal de São Paulo** took place in 1951 as a result of the efforts of its patron, Francisco Matarazzo Sobrinho – known as Ciccillo Matarazzo (*see p40* **The Count of São Paulo**). The creation of this gateway to foreign art came around at the same time as several other major art-world initiatives, including the birth of the major cultural institutions such as MASP and the MAM.

The first Bienal brought Pablo Picasso's *Guernica* to São Paulo, along with works by Giacometti and Magritte. Over the years, it has given the Brazilian audience access to Jackson Pollock, Constantin Brancusi and Kurt Schwitters, to name a few. However, the format of the Bienal has changed over the years; insurance for art of this calibre became prohibitively expensive, and slowly the Bienal lost its prestigious historic component. Today, it is the main international exhibition of contemporary art in Brazil, and it is in the good company of the Venice Biennale and Documenta in Kassel in terms of prestige.

Back in 1983, the first sight to greet visitors was a big American car wrapped in bread rolls. It was an instant hit and established a tradition for the provocative. The 2008 edition of the Bienal was especially controversial. An entire floor

floor of the building was left empty: you guessed it, like a blank canvas. But when a well-known group of tag kids descended to spray signatures and protest phrases on its white walls, security was called and two of the gang were arrested.

This led to a huge public debate, with one of the issues being whether or not the Bienal placed itself above street demonstrations. It also seemed that the cognoscenti might have missed a trick when it came to street art, given that São Paulo has become one of the world capitals of graffiti and several galleries of urban art have flourished in the city over the last few years as a new generation of Paulistanos take an interest in new forms.

The striking Bienal building designed by Oscar Niemeyer is also home to **SP-Arte**, Brazil's only art fair. It hasn't stolen the Bienal's limelight yet, but it certainly has injected the circuit and market with a whole new dynamic. Perhaps comparable in South America only to ArteBA in Buenos Aires, SP-Arte gains influence and attendance every year.

The Bienal de São Paulo (http://bienalsaopaulo.globo.com) runs in even-numbered years and the SP-Arte (www.sp-arte.com) is held over a long weekend every year in April or May.

Gay & Lesbian

Stepping out, Sampa style.

Gay São Paulo may not have the cachet of New York or London as being one of the world's signature scenes – or even the sexy, over-confident swagger of Rio de Janeiro or Buenos Aires – but make no mistake, Sampa deserves diva status. If the ten per cent rule applies (and the Parada do Orgulho GLBT – the world's largest gay pride event – suggests that's a conservative estimate), São Paulo's gay and lesbian population is in the range of two million. The precise number of the GLBT population is less important, though, than the fact that gay and lesbian Paulistanos are standing up and being

counted. From Barbies (Brazilian muscle Marys), go-go boys, *bolachas* (girls) and the over-50s, all the way to the sex workers and escorts mining the club crowd, the city has a style all of its own when it comes to gay love and life.

GETTING OUT & ABOUT

In South America, the cosmopolitan gay scenes often reflect the images of their parent cities. Rio is still the pretty one, sunning itself and basking in its own beauty, while Buenos Aires seduces as a value-for-money location, with its combination of cheap and chic thrills.

Compared to Sampa's year-round gay and lesbian nightlife, though, scenes in other South American hot spots can seem a little quaint. São Paulo's gay scene mirrors the makeup of its parent megalopolis, spread out across the diverse neighbourhoods on a gargantuan, sprawling city map. And in a typically Brazilian manner, social class and income seem to divide citizens more than sexual orientation. While GLBT is the official acronym for the gay scene and is common in the city (especially on gay pride parade day), Brazilians, Paulistanos included, also use the phrase GLS – meaning gays, lesbians and sympathisers – which encompasses not only Paulistano homosexuals but their mates in the straight world. This acronym hints at the social fabric of the city, where the mingling of gays and straights is common across the swankiest restaurants, bar and clubs.

About the author
Ricardo Bairos *is a Brazilian journalist who currently resides in New York City.*

As such, strictly queer places are becoming less prevalent. This means there are fewer gay ghettos, but there are still areas where gay and lesbian establishments are more concentrated. Most of the neighbourhoods on the São Paulo social map offer options for a tailored clientele as well as for a mixed straight-gay crowd, from the glitziest places to dive bars and hardcore hangouts. In Pinheiros and Vila Madalena, where the watering hole per capita ratio is hard to beat, there are venues that cater to the girls specifically, such as **Bar da Fran** (*see p186*), mega-clubs, and some of the sexier behind-closed-door spots, like **Termas Fragata** (*see p186*).

Upscale Jardins is as fashionable with the GLS crowd as it is with everyone else, and a tell-tale sign of this social integration is the gay stamp on the Jardins location of café chain **Fran's** (*see p183*). Nearby Bela Vista is fast becoming the most popular district, with some of the best underground and over-the-top clubs, including **Glória** (*see p199*), where famed Brazilian designer Alexandre Herchcovitch regularly hosts weekend bashes. Lower Augusta, too, is on the rise among party-bound Paulistanos.

The former warehouse district of Barra Funda is São Paulo's club central now, with multi-dance floor GLBT landmarks close by. Gay temple **The Week** (*see p185*), in Lapa, Barra Funda's neighbour, is one of the most popular clubs, gay or otherwise, in the city right now, with thousands of devotees coming here to worship until the wee hours.

Glória *See p199.*

CAFES AND RESTAURANTS

In keeping with the general going-out vibe, where straight and gay mix from dinner to late-night, there are lots of gay-friendly restaurants in São Paulo. **Mestiço** (*see p109*), one of the best dining options, is popular with gay people. The fusion dishes here mix Asian with a whole range of cuisines, and its location near the blossoming nightlife scene in lower Augusta and Consolação makes it perfect for a pre-party meal.

Fran's Café

Rua Haddock Lobo 586, Jardins (3083 1019/ www.franscafe.com.br). Metrô Consolação. **Open** 24hrs daily. **Main courses** R$13-$20. **Credit** AmEx, DC, MC, V. **Map** p244 J7.

Starbucks may have lured most of the easy-to-please world into licking whipped cream from its coffee creations, but São Paulo's home-grown café scene has put pressure on the US bean empire. Fran's presents a great alternative to the US chain, and its Jardins location has the added benefit of being the gayest of its many city branches. Being open 24/7 might have something to do with it: it's a popular hang-out for the boys' post-club hopping (this being Sampa, that's generally around breakfast time). **Other locations** throughout the city.

L'Open

Alameda Itu 1466, Jardins (3060 9013/www.lopen. com.br). Metrô Consolação. **Open** 7pm-1.30am Tue-Thur, Sun; 7pm-2.30am Fri, Sat. **Main courses** R$20-$43. **Credit** AmEx, V. **Map** p244 J7.

Open your heart to this traditional Italian spot with a non-traditional Italian food-loving clientele. Founded in 2003, L'Open is São Paulo's only out-of-the-closet gay restaurant. It offers a full Italian menu of meats, pastas and salads, as well as a pizza bar with straight-from-the-oven classics heaped high with fresh mozzarella and more exotic variations. While the interior design, with a sleek bar and interior palms rising from the floor, doesn't evoke your typical Italian joint, the food is great in the classic Italian-cuisine way. L'Open also hosts art shows.

CLUB NIGHTS AND VENUES

Club culture is alive and well in São Paulo, and the gay community is a big reason for its strong pulse. There are at least a few options for parties and clubs almost every night of the week. On weekends, the scene approaches overload proportions. This isn't just a boys' club either. Lesbian visitors will be surprised by the number of bars and parties designed specifically for the girls. So find a scene, and *se joga* (literally, 'throw yourself in').

ABC Bailão

Rua Marquês de Itu 182, Vila Buarque (3361 7964/www.abcbailao.com.br). Metrô Santa Cecília. **Open** 9pm-late Wed, Thur, Sun; 11pm-late Fri, Sat. **Admission** R$15-$20. **Credit** MC, V. **Map** p243 M5.

A favourite with the over-50 crowd and their admirers. The music ranges from vintage pop to sertanejo (Brazilian country) and from axé (Bahian music) to slow songs for romantic fools. The ABC stands for Amigos Bailam Comigo (friends dance with me). Over-50s get an admission discount most nights, and girls often pay a premium entrance price.

Blue Space

Rua Brigadeiro Galvão 723, Barra Funda (3666 1616/www.bluespace.com.br). Metrô Marechal Deodoro. **Open** 11pm-6am Wed, Fri, Sat; 7am-1am Sun. **Admission** R$17. **Credit** AmEx, DC, MC, V. **Map** p242 K2.

This strictly gay mega-club with a capacity of 1,500 has some of the funniest drag shows and hottest go-go boys. Most of the stage productions have inspired a cult following on YouTube, are so elaborate they could teach Cher a thing or two about

Parada Orgulho LGBT. *See p187.*

costume changes. On the main dancefloor, the music is usually an uninspired *bate-estaca* (jackhammer), but on the smaller floor the beats are more interesting. The crowd is mixed: post-adolescents share space with Barbies (muscle Marys). There's also a darkroom. Sunday tea dances are popular.

Bubu Lounge & Disco
Rua dos Pinheiros 791, Pinheiros (3081 9659/www.bubulounge.com). Bus 107P-10. **Open** midnight-late Wed, Fri, Sat; 7pm-late Sun. **Admission** R$15-$60. **Credit** AmEx, DC, MC, V. **Map** p249 F10.
A straight-friendly gay mega-club with three main spaces spanning across more than 1,000sqm. A lounge area has live music, usually samba or other classic Brazilian beats. House and techno reign on the main dancefloor, while both old and contemporary pop tunes are floated on the upper floor. Saturday night's Top! party is popular with straight couples. For a date with a diva, it's worth checking out the matinée party Top of the Sundays, presented by drag queen Léia Bastos. For lesbians, there's the popular monthly party Bubu Só Para Elas (Bubu Only for the Girls).

Cantho
Largo do Arouche 32, Centro (3723 6624/www.cantho.com.br). Metrô República. **Open** 11pm-late Wed-Sun. **Admission** R$20-$30. **Credit** AmEx, DC, MC, V. **Map** p243 M4.
'Old' is a word that comes up in reference to this club: it's the main nightspot in the older and grungier downtown gay-friendly area of Largo do Arouche; it's a popular destination for the older gay crowd; and the dominant musical style is vintage pop, with hits from the '70s, '80s and '90s on the

playlist. But old doesn't mean dead: you won't see this place slowing down until the sun rises. With three bars, a mezzanine and, most importantly, a giant disco ball that illuminates the 800 people that the club can accommodate, it's a pop heaven that keeps even the most mature guys young at heart.

Farol Madalena
Rua Jericó 179, Vila Madalena (3032 6470/www.farolmadalena.com.br). Metrô Vila Madalena. **Open** 7pm-1am Wed, Thur; 7pm-2am Fri, Sat; 5pm-midnight Sun. **Admission** R$5-$7. **Credit** DC, MC, V. **Map** p249 E7.
This venue is a three-headed GLS social monster, with a bar, restaurant and concert hall. While it serves a full menu of traditional Brazilian *petiscos* (appetizers) and entrées named after Brazilian beaches, what sets the Farol apart is its standing as a music hall. Offering a change of musical pace from the typical club thumping tunes and '70s disco, Farol Madalena features contemporary Brazilian music *ao vivo* (live), including MPB, pop and samba rock. It's been open since 1997 and has become a particularly popular destination for the ladies.

Flex
Avenida Marquês de São Vincente 1767, Barra Funda (3611 3368/www.flexclub.com.br). Metrô Barra Funda. **Open** midnight-7am Wed-Sat. **Admission** R$30-$50. **Credit** MC, V.
One of the Week's (*see p185*) main competitors for Saturday night parties with its Top Notch fest, Flex has a similar vibe – tribal-house music and a crowd of flexing *descamisados* (shirtless boys). Its owned by the same club promoters who produce the E-Joy (www.ejoy.com.br) series of famed circuit parties that occur frequently in São Paulo, Rio de Janeiro and Florianópolis and always feature a major international DJ lineup.

Freedom
Largo do Arouche 6, Centro (3362 9207/www.freedomclub.com.br). Metrô República. **Open** 11pm-late Fri, Sat; 3pm-10pm Sun. **Admission** R$5-$20. **Credit** AmEx, DC, MC, V. **Map** p243 M4.
Strippers, go-go boys and drag queens – oh my! Add the laser light show, and what more does one need to trip the club light fantastic? A younger crowd liberates itself most nights at Freedom, often under the tutelage of a generous helping of drag queens. Weekend nights highlight lady strippers, but there are go-go boy shows too. A variety of DJs play, but

a favorite musical style is *bate-cabelo* (literally, hair-shaking). The Sunday matinées, from 3pm to 10pm, sometimes attract a big crowd.

Nostro Mondo

Rua da Consolação 2554, Jardins (3661 6813/ www.nostromondo.com.br). Metrô Consolação. **Open** 11.30pm-5am Fri; 11pm-5.30am Sat; 6pm-midnight Sun. **Admission** R$7-$12. **Credit** DC, MC, V. **Map** p244 J7.

São Paulo's pioneering gay club opened in 1971. Nearly four decades later, it is still going strong, with go-go boys who wow the crowds with risqué performances. If you happen to be in the city on 1 January, you can hit the new year running – Nostro Mondo features a bevy of drag queens performing the gay version of the Corrida de São Silvestre (the oldest and most famous long-distance running event in Brazil) right outside its doors. *'Olha a polícia!'* (Look, the police!) is the starting cry, harking back to the early '70s when police brutality against the marginalised scene was common.

Tunnel

Rua dos Ingleses 355, Bela Vista (3285 0246/ www.tunnel.com.br). Metrô Brigadeiro. **Open** 11pm-late Fri, Sat; 7pm-late Sun. **Admission** R$12-$15. **Credit** DC, MC, V. **Map** p245 M8.

One of São Paulo's oldest gay clubs, with 16 years of tunneling under its belt, this spot is known for its camp drag shows and competitions. A roster of house DJs commands the turntables, and weekend

---

INSIDE TRACK
GAY GOOGLE

Like the rest of the world, gay São Paulo has gone online. The best guide you'll find to work out what's going on right now comes in the form of two scene-specific websites. The first, **Mix Brasil** (www.mixbrasil.com.br), is Brazil's ultimate gay website. Founded by André Fischer (publisher of the gay magazine *Junior)*, the Roteirão section has listings of events in São Paulo. Fischer also organises a very popular gay and lesbian film festival, which had its 17th anniversary in 2009. Next to type into your browser should be **Guia Gay Brasil** (www.guiagaybrasil.com.br), which has tons of nightlife and entertainment listings. It's in Portuguese, but an English version is in the works. Two important Brazilian lesbian networking sites are **Leskut** (www.leskut.com.br), an offshoot of **orkut.com.br**, which is the Facebook of Brazil, and **Parada Lésbica** (www.paradalesbica.com.br), which promotes various nightlife events in the city.

---

shows are highlighted by the fabulous Nany People, one of Brazil's most famous drag queens, who has been featured in film and on radio, and has even taken her turn at performing Brecht. The space has been renovated over the years, with many touches, including mosaic walls and floors in the manic mode of Gaudi, harking back to years gone by.

Ultradiesel

Rua Marquês de Itu 284, Centro (3338 2493/ www.ultradiesel.com.br). Metrô República. **Open** midnight-late Wed-Sun. **Admission** R$20-$25. **Credit** MC, V. **Map** p243 M5.

This huge downtown club has room for 1,300, and every person in the sea of people risks being made deaf and blind by the high-tech assault of lights and sounds. With a 50,000-watt sound system, wall images intended to intensify the hallucinogenic stylings of the resident and international DJs (often from the USA, Israel and Germany), and 360-degree 3D technology, Ultradiesel is the all-night club as big-budget Hollywood popcorn movie. Saturdays are often known as Super Dyke, followed by a popular after-hours party on Sunday mornings.

Week

Rua Guaicurus 324, Lapa (3868 9944/ www.theweek.com.br). CPTM Lapa. **Open** midnight-late Sat. **Admission** R$35-$65. **Credit** AmEx, DC, MC, V.

The Week is what every other club (gay or straight) is trying to copy. Think Ibiza in the heart of São Paulo's concrete behemoth. It's the city's main gay club and a gay brand all over Brazil, with summer-season clones in Rio de Janeiro and Florianópolis, and an average of 2,000 muscle boys, straight couples, celebrities and hipsters crowding its two huge dancefloors and outdoor space (including a swimming pool) every Saturday. The Week may soon go international, too, with its circuit parties already having popped up in Barcelona. Saturday night is the signature Babylon party, but look out for weekday special events and the ocasional daytime pool lounging.

PUBS AND BARS

Many of São Paulo's best bars are favoured gay hangouts and clustered around Jardins, including **Volt** (*see p131*), **Ritz** (*see p122*) and **Spot** (*see p130*).

Bar da Dida

Rua Dr Melo Alves 98, Jardins (3088 7177). Metrô Consolação. **Open** 6pm-1am Tue-Sun. **No credit cards. Map** p244 I7.

The *boteco* is the quintessential Brazilian bar experience, and in less clichéd terms, the country's version of the hole-in-the-wall drinking establishment. The crowd in this humble place spills over onto the pavement and the parking lot of a building

ARTS & ENTERTAINMENT

next door. It started out as a lesbian hang-out but has become a relaxed attraction for an eclectic crowd, favoured by artsy types and professionals fleeing the more generic happy-hour doldrums. A cold beer is the most common request, but a starfruit and basil caipirinha offers a more memorable contrast to Dida's simple surroundings.

Bar da Fran
Rua dos Pinheiros 735, Pinheiros (3081 1643/ www.bardafran.com.br). Bus 107P-10. **Open** 9pm-5am Fri, Sat. **Credit** AmEx, MC, V. **Map** p249 F10.
This new *bolacha* (Paulistano slang for lesbian) hang-out in Pinheiros has a casual and cosy bar with pool tables and occasional art shows. It's close to Bubu Lounge & Disco, so it's a great place to prime the party pump before hitting the dancefloor.

Flyer
Rua Peixoto Gomide 67, Consolação (3129 8985). Metrô Consolação. **Open** 6pm-2am Tue-Sun. **Credit** MC, V. **Map** p244 K7.
Flyer has an inviting atmosphere for the start of any evening, with thousands of party invites covering the walls of this crazily busy bar. The buzz doesn't undercut its charm, and it's located in the vicinity of Rua Frei Caneca, so a stroll of the Caneca gay scene, including Shopping Frei Caneca, can start here.

Gourmet
Alameda Franca 1552, Jardins (3064 7958). Metrô Consolação. **Open** 10pm-3am Tue-Sat; 9pm-3am Sun. **No credit cards. Map** p244 I7.
One of São Paulo's most beloved gay drinking spots, Gourmet (aka Director's Gourmet) is a small stage star that premiered in 1990. Its modest interior is decorated with movie posters, and it's a great pre-club spot for a quiet *esquenta* (pre-party drink).

SEX CLUBS, SAUNAS & GYMS

269
Rua Bela Cintra 269, Consolação (3120 4509/ www.sauna269.com.br). Metrô Consolação. **Open** 24hrs daily. **Admission** R$29. **Credit** AmEx, MC, V. **Map** p242 K6.
A relatively new sex complex (it opened in 2007), 269 is home to the biggest sauna in the country, which has a capacity for an astounding 400 patrons, so you can't fail to bag yourself *um gatinho* (a hottie). Its 24/7 schedule includes rooms for the night. There is no shortage of ways to fill a full day inside here. The ground floor has a bar, computers, jacuzzi, sauna and steam room, while the top floor has the common 'inter-active' area. 269 is also big on special events, like toy parties (bring your own or buy something in the sex shop) and naked nights, when the dress code doesn't even allow towels. Rooms start at R$38 for a single and R$56 for a double, for 12 hours. Prices go up slightly between Friday and Sunday.

Bio Ritmo – Paulista
Avenida Paulista 2073, Jardins (3365 0800/ www.bioritmo.com.br). Metrô Consolação. **Open** 6am-11pm Mon-Fri; 10am-6pm Sat; 10am-4pm Sun. **Admission** R$80. **Credit** AmEx, MC, V. **Map** p244 K7.
This fancy gym in the heart of Avenida Paulista has tons of classes, a moneyed crowd (businessmen from the area) and a pleasant staff.
Other locations throughout the city.

Fórmula Academia (Cerqueira César)
Rua da Consolação 2970, Jardins (3062 0193/www.formulaacademia.com.br). Metrô Consolação. **Open** 24hrs daily. **Admission** R$299 monthly. **Credit** MC, V. **Map** p244 I7.
The first 24-hour gym in São Paulo serves as a pre-party for muscle guys to buff up before heading over to the Week, or any other late-night spot. If you don't fancy pumping some iron, there's also a steam room.
Other locations throughout the city.

Station
Rua dos Pinheiros 352, Pinheiros (3898 1293/ www.stationvideobar.com.br). **Open** 9pm-3am Mon-Thur, Sun; 10pm-5am Fri, Sat. **Admission** R$13-$15. **No credit cards. Map** p249 G9.
Brazil's pioneer cruising/sex bar, Station takes after similar places in Europe. It's busiest between 11pm and 1am.

Termas Fragata
Rua Francisco Leitão 71, Pinheiros (3085 7061/ www.termasfragata.com.br). **Open** 2pm-midnight daily. **Admission** R$30. **Credit** AmEx, DC, MC, V. **Map** p249 G9.
One of São Paulo's most traditional saunas, with a very casual atmosphere. Escorts work the crowd.

Profile Parada Orgulho LGBT (Pride Parade)

Over three million people are out and about at Sampa's coming-out party.

Rio might get the kudos for Carnival but come to São Paulo in June and you'll find one serious party at the world's largest Gay Pride parade. The first **Parada de Orgulho GLBT de São Paulo** was organized in 1997 and brought together 2,000 people on Avenida Paulista. Cut to 2008 and there were 3.4 million people dancing behind *trios elétricos* (floats) for 3.5 kilometres for seven hours.

Like Carnival in others cities, the parade attracts more and more tourists to São Paulo (about 300,000 in 2008) and as such it's become one of the most important holidays in a city mainly used to business tourists. Foreign gays are starting to flock to the event and its several circuit parties, just like they do for New Year's and Carnival in Rio de Janeiro.

The difference is that São Paulo's gay pride is entirely participatory. It has more to do with the Love Parade, in Berlin, say, than with the Gay Pride in New York. People dance along

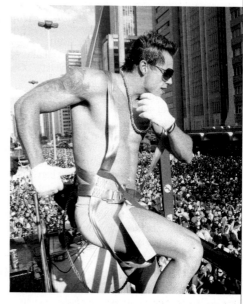

Avenida Paulista and Rua da Consolação, all the way to Praça Roosevelt.

There are other official events during the weekend, like the Feira Cultural LGBT, a four-day arts fair at Vale do Anhangabaú, with concerts and plays. The day before the parade is mainly known for the Caminhada Lésbica e Bissexual (a lesbian mini-parade) as well as the Gay Day, at amusement park Playcenter.

As well as all the locals, out-of-towners, Brazilians and foreigners partying in the streets to international DJs, the Parada also has a political message behind all the fun and games. The theme for 2009 was 'No Homophobia, More Citizenship, Equal Rights'. Sadly, as if to counteract this message, a homemade bomb went off during 2009's Parada, injuring 21 people.

For listing see p163.

ARTS & ENTERTAINMENT

Music

From samba kings to trippy mutants, Sampa's song is ever-changing

São Paulo has served as a muse for many generations of Brazilian musicians – in a culture that loves to mix pleasure and pain, the city provides a bounty of both. And since the best musicians from Brazil all head for this sober business centre at some point (following the money, if nothing else), this wonderful, challenging city has long been on a collision course with the Brazilian lyrical imagination. Even musicians who aren't devoted enough to write an ode to the city seem to end up living or at least playing here, and it's not unusual to find world-class artists doing weekly gigs at places like **Bar Brahma** or **Studio SP**. And in addition to the bands from all over Brazil who come to town to make it big, Sampa soil has also proven fertile for home-grown city talent. For audiences, this means it's impossible to understate the variety and quality of live music on offer.

INFORMATION

Sources for concert listings include the excellent *Guia de Folha*, included in the newspaper *Folha de São Paulo* on Fridays; the magazine *Veja*, released every Saturday (or with hard-to-navigate listings at http://vejasao paulo.abril. com.br); and a roundup of samba and *choro* concerts on www.samba-choro.com.br/casas/sp.

Many larger venues offer substantial discounts if you call ahead or send an email to get your name placed on their list (check venues' websites for details). The cover for men in some establishments can be up to double that for women. Many upper- and middle-class Paulistanos will only go to venues that charge a cover for 'security' reasons (they'll even admit that it is to avoid the sort of people who can't afford to pay an entrance) – but all free and cheap venues listed here are perfectly safe.

The absolute best way to catch top-quality artists in all genres, from Brazilian superstars to total unknowns, is at the various **SESC** installations around town (*see p205*). The Centro Cultural Vergueiro brings in some great, cheap shows (*see p69*). Many large venues give student discounts.

Tickets for stadium and large-scale auditorium concerts in São Paulo can generally be purchased through one of three major ticketing services (*see p160*).

FORRÓ

Forró is an emotional experience – though it's pretty hard to say which way your emotions should fall. *Forró* lyrics read like a series of catastrophic, near-suicidal, heart-rending complaints ('why, oh why, doesn't she love me?'), but the melodies are happy, goofy party music (ignoring the actual ancestry, think polka hopped up on samba), and the dancing style (couples fused together, from cheek to thigh) makes it impossible to ignore any potential chemistry with your partner.

Forró can refer to almost any traditional music from the northeast of Brazil, but in São Paulo the emphasis is on *arrasta-pé* ('foot-dragging' – the ultra-fast traditional style) and *xote* (more influenced by pop music). The traditional and most frequently used *forró* arrangement is a trio comprised of accordion, large bass drum and triangle, along with vocals.

Forró music sounds a bit like polka, while the dance steps remind many foreigners of salsa. *Forró* is on a two-count whereas salsa is on four, and though some of the twists and turns from salsa resemble *forró universitario* (the non-traditional style danced outside of the northeast), *forró* dancers often forgo these fancy manipulations and just take small steps, their bodies glued together. This makes the basics far easier to learn than salsa – an hour-long class at the beginning of the night is enough to get most people moving on the beat.

In addition to these listings, Açaí Praia has forró on Saturday afternoons (*see p190*).

Buena Vista Club

Rua Atílio Innocenti 780, Vila Olímpia (3045 5245/www.buenavistaclub.com.br). Bus 6418. **Open** 8pm-late Mon, Tue, Thu-Sun. **Cover** $R10-$25. **Credit** AmEx, MC, V.

This is a congenial spot for serious dancers. Mondays are for *forró*, and other days of the week each have their own theme: salsa and merengue, *pagode*, zouk and Latin pop, with both live shows and DJs. Late in the night, expect a dizzying mix of all of the above. Some evenings begin with fast-paced classes, moving from the most basic steps to semi-advanced moves within the hour.

★ Canto da Ema

Avenida Brig. Faria Lima 364, Pinheiros (3813 4708/www.cantodaema.com.br). Bus 177Y. **Open** 10.30pm-5am Wed-Sat; 7pm-5am Sun. *Classes* 8.30pm Thur-Sat; 5.30pm Sun. **Cover** R$7-$23. **No credit cards. Map** p248 D10.

This is a classic and a popular home to some of the best *forró* musicians around. All classes and ages press onto a dance floor drenched in sweat and pheromones.

Remelexo

Rua Ferreira de Araújo 1076, Pinheiros (3034 0212/www.remelexobrasil.com.br). Bus 477A.

Open 11pm-5am Fri, Sat; 8pm-2.30am Sun. *Classes* 7.45-9.30pm Fri, Sat; 4.45-6.30pm Sun. **Cover** R$8-$20. **No credit cards. Map** 248 D10.

Thanks to the team of very passionate dance instructors who divide the class into groups from absolute beginners to advanced, this is the best spot for a pop-in *forró* class in São Paulo, whether honing your moves or just grasping the basic steps. Later the place packs in the young and enthusiastic, and the trios taking to the stage astound on both ends of the expertise spectrum.

HIP HOP & RIO FUNK

Brazilian hip hop often resembles its North American counterpart, although many artists, like Curumin or Chico Science & Nação Zumbi have found ways to make it distinctly and wonderfully Brazilian. Meanwhile, the word 'funk', to Brazilian listeners, has nothing to do with how James Brown gets down, but rather it's a school of hip hop with ultra-fast, heavy beats and wildly sexual lyrics that came out of Rio under the influence of Miami bass.

It's a generally rough going for hip-hop fans to consistently find quality live shows in São Paulo, where the genre is looked down on. Some nightclubs that otherwise specialise in dub or electronic music have hip-hop nights, often with live acts. Some to check out include **Clash Club** (*see p202*) on Tuesdays, **Dj Club Bar** on Thursdays (Alameda Franca 241, Jardins, www.djclubbar.com.br), **Jive Club**

ARTS & ENTERTAINMENT

Bar do Cidão. *See p193.*

Elza Soares at **Bar Brahma**.
See p192.

(Alameda Barros 376, Higienópolis, www. jiveclub.com.br) on Wednesdays, **Mood Club** (Rua Teodoro Sampaio 1109, Vila Madalena, www.moodclub.com.br) on Fridays and Saturdays, and **Vegas** (*see p199*) on Tuesdays. Another recommended option is the **Casa do Hip Hop de Diadema** (Rua 24 de Maio 38, Jardim Canhema, Diadema, 4075 3792), a non-profit community centre dedicated to black music and culture with an information centre, workshops and some Saturday afternoon performances.

JAZZ & BOSSA NOVA

Bossa nova started in the late 1950s in Rio as 'music for playing in the living room' and quickly became a worldwide craze. It's been *desafinando* ('singing off-key' – the early, misguided criticism of bossa singers) ever since.

Bar B
Rua General Jardim 43, Centro (3129 9155/ http://barbsp.com.br). Metrô República.
Open 5.30pm-late Tue-Sun. **Cover** R$5-$7.
Credit MC, V. **Map** 243 M5.
The decor and the clientele scream hippy chic; this is one of the establishments on the front end of revitalising São Paulo's centre. The emphasis is on 'contemplative jazz', but you could also show up to find far-fetched electro-punk and any number of other fascinating experiments in progress.

★ Bourbon Street Music Club
Rua dos Chanés 127, Indianópolis (5095 6100/ www.bourbonstreet.com.br). Bus 5362. **Open** 9pm-late Tue-Sun. *Shows* 11pm Tue-Thur; midnight Fri, Sat; 11pm Sun. **Cover** R$25-$45 **Credit** AmEx, DC, MC, V.
Upper-class Paulistanos come to this sanitised version of New Orleans trying not to look tired after a long day at the office. Jazz, blues and pop music are on offer, with some huge Brazilian names in the line up.

Sindikat Jazz
Rua Moacir Piza 64, Jardins (3086 3037/ www.syndikat.com.br). Metrô Consolação.
Open 9pm-late Tue-Sat. *Shows* 10.30pm. **Cover** R$8-$12. **Credit** AmEx, DC, MC, V. **Map** 244 J7.
This laid-back bar offers top-quality performances in its non-smoking basement and a friendly upstairs area for performers and the audience to mingle between sets. The crowd is composed of serious jazz heads, many of whom bring their instruments and find a moment to join in.

ROCK

Countless young Paulistanos think samba is silly, *forró* is so yesterday, *música sertaneja* (Brazilian country) is for ignorant hicks and *pagode* (a samba heavy on percussion) is the least classy of any of these. (As sad as this outlook is, they do have a point about the schmaltzy excesses of some mega-hits in the home-grown Brazilian genres.) But those who dismiss samba in favour of rock aren't necessarily throwing out their heritage – Brazil's rock acts have adopted the genre with significant creative success. The largest Sampa venues host Brazilian and international stars, while smaller rock joints usually deliver excellent cover bands playing the hits in Portuguese and English. There is also a smaller but vibrant scene for new indie bands as well.

Açaí Praia
Horácio Láfer 285, Itaim Bibi (3078 8725/ www.acaipraia.com.br). Bus 967A. **Open** 5pm-late Mon-Fri; 2pm-late Sat; 4pm-late Sun. **Cover** R$8-$15. **Credit** AmEx, DC, MC, V.
A younger crowd, particularly hailing from the northeast, is drawn here for the beach theme and live surf, pop rock and reggae music. A dedicated and very friendly *forró* crowd gathers on Saturday afternoons and stays late into the night. The entrance is on Avenida Brigadeiro Faria Lima.

Lucena Bar
Avenida Ermano Marchetti 1058, Lapa (3617 4172/3617 4174/www.lucenabar.com.br). Bus 847. **Open** 7pm-late Wed-Sat. **Cover** free-R$22. **Credit** AmEx, MC, V.

Teenage Mutants

Os Mutantes, Sampa's gift to psychedelic rock.

In the late 1960s, a small gang of Brazilian musicians took bossa nova, Bahian song, and international rock on a trip called *Tropicália*. Despite some wild experimentation, the Bahians leading the charge, Caetano Veloso and Gilberto Gil, remained sonically rooted to their home state. But São Paulo's main contribution to the scene, the teen trio **Os Mutantes**, dived unreservedly into the international late-'60s psychedelic-pop soundscape – not surprising, considering they came from a city whose gaze always wanders abroad.

Rita Lee, the band's vocalist, once told the New York Times that unlike other schoolgirls, 'I didn't want to marry a Beatle. I wanted to be a Beatle.' In 1968, Lee, along with her boyfriend, Arnaldo Baptista, and his brother, Sérgio Dias Baptista, formed a band and style whose debt to the Beatles is unmistakable. So much so that Veloso complained he and Gil would play Os Mutantes for their Londoner friends only to have it misconstrued as a 'Beatles rip-off'.

But Os Mutantes were creating something beyond anything that the Beatles or anyone else did at the time. They careened from straight pop to interesting if barely listenable noise to gorgeous screwball circus melodies, intentionally straying from comprehensibility in order to remain subversive while under the watch of the dictatorship's censors. And even when nothing they sang made sense, it still sounded steadfastly ironic (even their cover of Jorge Ben Jor's heartfelt serenade 'Minha Menina' sounds a bit sarcastic).

The band broke up in 1973, after a too-short run and numerous member changes. A supposed key cause of the break was a fraternal dispute over whether Fendor guitars were better than Gibsons, but there were other things to contend with both then and post-Mutantes: love spats, psychotic episodes and an attempted suicide. It seems Os Mutantes were ahead of their time in now de rigueur intra-band melodrama. Lee went on to superstardom in her solo career, but the band was pretty much forgotten (and outside of Brazil, never widely known) until David Byrne released a best-of compilation on his Luaka Bop record label in 1999. The short run of Tropicália is now credited with giving birth to the subsequent MPB (Popular Brazilian Music) movement, and a wide range of artists, such as Marisa Monte, Beck and Kurt Cobain, have paid homage to São Paulo's trippy mutants. With all this cachet both inside and outside of Brazil, the brothers finally reunited for a tour in 2006 (with the unwilling Lee replaced by Zélia Duncan).

At the time of writing, no further Os Mutantes tours have been announced, but the band's story remains a strong argument for tuning into São Paulo's still-eclectic, internationally aware music scene. Who knows which kook rockers now gracing Paulistano stages have landed there a few decades ahead of their time?

This bar hosts *música sertaneja* groups on Wednesdays and MPB and pop rock other nights, with late-night electronic DJs. The two dance floors fill up with pretty youngsters and enough artificial fog to complicate their ogling fests.

★ Piu Piu

Rua 13 de Maio 134, Bixiga (3258 8066/ www.cafepiupiu.com.br). Bus 475M.
Open 9.30pm-late Thur-Sat; 8.30pm-late Sun. **Cover** R$10-$15. **No credit cards.** **Map** 245 M7.

This beautiful and relaxed café-bar is a Sampa institution and puts quality music first. There's a three-sided stage around which tables are packed, and beyond that, people standing and dancing. The place is known mainly for pop-rock covers but also has nights for MPB, *choro*, tango, blues and more.

Tonton

Alameda dos Pamaris 55, Moema (3804 0856/ 3804 0857/www.tonton.com.br). Bus 5126.
Open 7pm-late Tue-Sun. **Cover** R$8-$20. **Credit** V.

At this friendly, wood-panelled venue, patrons mix easily at long tables and listen to a decent line-up of groups playing both original music and covers of rock hits in English and Portuguese.

MPB & SAMBA ROCK

MPB stands for *música popular brasileira* (Brazilian popular music), a genre that arrived on the coat-tails of bossa nova and updated that swinging lilt with other Brazilian influences and international pop rock to create a 'national' style in the mid-1960s. The *trópicalistas* like

Os Mutantes (*see above*) were a subset of the genre, and other key artists have been as well, including Elis Regina, Novos Baianos, Marisa Monte, Gilberto Gil, Caetano Veloso and Chico Buarque. Its concurrent sister movement, samba rock, is a combination of samba, soul and American funk put forth by artists like Jorge Ben Jor and Tim Maia. MPB is thriving and evolving today but also often serves as more of an umbrella term for all Brazilian popular genres.

★ Bar Brahma

Avenida São João 677, República (3333 3030/ www.barbrahmasp.com). Metrô República. **Open** 11am-late daily. *Shows* 10.30pm weekdays; 2pm & 9pm Sat; 1.30pm Sun. **Cover** R$7-$55. **Credit** AmEx, MC, V. **Map** 243 N5.

Another Sampa institution, this bar overlooks the intersection Caetano Veloso popularised in his song 'Sampa' (*see p46*). The neighbourhood went to seed, but the reopening of Bar Brahma in the late '90s partially revived its popularity and fame. The drinking holes Caetano frequented on this corner have changed hands over time and gone a bit more upscale, but Bar Brahma's resident star line-up of samba, MPB, *choro*, jazz and pop groups is sure to get your ticker bopping too. It's a bit touristy – Paulistanos automatically bring any out-of-town guests here – but still a must-see for a reason. There is a main room and several smaller performance areas (all of them intimate) offering a grand total of around 140 performances per month. The cover charge varies greatly depending on the room you choose.

Citibank Hall

Avenida Jamaris 213, Moema (2846 6232/ www.citibankhall.com.br). Bus 5154. **Tickets** (through Ticketmaster only; *see p160*) R$60-$300. **Map** 246 J15.

This beautiful 3,000-capacity concert hall has hosted the voices of Brazilian legends like Roberto Carlos, Tom Jobim and Chico Buarque, as well as international icons on the Brazilian legs of their tours.

★ Grazie a Dio

Rua Girassol 67, Vila Madalena (3031 6568/ www.grazieadio.com.br). Bus 714C. **Open** 8pm-late Tue-Sun. *Shows* 10pm Tue, Wed; 11pm Thur-Sun. **Cover** R$10-$25. **Credit** AmEx, DC, MC, V. **Map** 248 F8.

This is a relatively small space for such a scorching weekly line-up of resident samba rockers. The joy of these five-to-ten-piece groups is so evident that you get the feeling they're playing as much for themselves as for the undulating public just inches from the stage.

Studio SP

Rua Augusta 591, Consolação (3129 7040/ www.studiosp.org). Metrô Consolação.

Open 9-11pm Tue-Sat. **Cover** free-R$35. **Credit** DC, MC, V. **Map** 242 L6.

In its few short years of existence, this space has become famous for attracting innovators from across Brazil's pop-music spectrum, whether it's MPB, hip hop, rock or electronic. There's a line-up of resident Paulistano acts as well as guest appearances by big Brazilian and international names. The walls are decorated by street artists and VJs.

MÚSICA SERTANEJA

Like its sister, American country music, Brazil's *música sertaneja* (music from the backlands) has evolved from traditional rural folk genres into a sort of saccharine processed pop with a cowboy hat. *Música sertaneja* has its roots in *música caipira*, plaintive singing over a ten-string guitar. The much slicker version now popular in Brazil's interior borrows from rock, Mexican mariachi and American country. While not nearly as appreciated in big city São Paulo, *música sertaneja* has a few night-time outposts, where famous *sertaneja* acts (typically fraternal duos) play for crowds pounding their boots in pairs and, yes, in lines. It's enough to make you forget urban Sampa's aloofness and for a moment believe you're lost in the Brazilian *sertão* (hinterland) – or, for that matter, Kansas.

Of course, the best way to hear top *sertaneja* acts is by going to a rodeo; these take place in towns around São Paulo from March to September. For schedules, go to www.marcoscowboy.com.br (also a source for *sertaneja* dance classes) or www.brasil western.com.br.

The following listing is Sampa's queen of *sertaneja*, but also worth checking out are **Lucena Bar** on Wednesdays (*see p190*) and **Rancho do Serjão** (Avenida Pedroso de Morais 1008, Vila Madalena, www. ranchodoserjao.com.br).

Villa Country

Avenida Francisco Matarazzo 774, Barra Funda (3868 5858/www.villacountry.com.br). Metrô Barra Funda. **Open** *Restaurant* from 8pm daily. *Bars & dancefloors* 11pm-late daily. *Concerts* from midnight daily. **Cover** R$20-$35. **Credit** DC, MC, V. **Map** 242 I2.

The Disneyland of *sertaneja* nightclubs, this sprawling, faux-rustic saloon features a restaurant, clothing shop, photo studio, candy store, bars, dancefloors, stages and, oh yes, some great musicians. Thanks to its scale, a number of bands currently perform here, and in a single night you can traverse the full range of down-home Brazilian and American country styles. Friday nights are recommended for the sheer volume of entertainment and the gorgeous crowds using cowboy gear as a fashion statement.

SAMBA, CHORO & PAGODE

Paulistano samba, as a distinctive musical genre in lyrics and sound, was created in the music of a handful of musicians from the city, who went on to become just as famous as their Carioca counterparts. At the helm are Adoniran Barbosa (*see p197* **The Troubadour of Bixiga**), Paulo Vanzolini, Eduardo Gudin, and Demônios da Garoa. If you want to pay your respects to Adoniran Barbosa and see the town that he immortalised in his most famous song 'O Trem das Onze' ('The 11 O´clock Train'), visit the **Museu do Jaçanã** (Rua São Luiz Gonzaga 156, Jaçanã, 2241 4286 , http://museudojacana.blogspot.com, closed Mon). Choro can be heard all around town but most often at street markets at **Feira do Bixiga** (*see p158*) and at **Praça Benedito Calixto** (*see p158*) on Sundays, and at **Contemporânea** (*see p54*) on Saturdays.

Banda Gloria @ Aldeia Turiassú

Rua Turiassú 928, Perdizes (8515 1112/ http://bandagloria.com.br). Bus 874T. **Open** 11pm-late Fri. **Cover** R$25-$35. **Credit** MC, V. Normally reserved for private events, this gorgeous, laid-back dance hall opens to the public biweekly to host one of the sharpest samba ensembles in São Paulo. For more than a decade, Banda Gloria has been reviving and re-engergising classic samba, but the owners are not afraid to throw some MPB, '50s rock and swing into the mix. The crowd is a healthy mix of devoted *gafieira* dancers (ballroom samba) and those who can't even tap their beer cups on the beat.

Bar do Alemão

Avenida Antartica 554, Agua Branca (3879 0070). Bus 117Y-10. **Open** 10am-2am Mon, Tue; 10am-4am Wed-Sat; 6pm-2am Sun. *Shows* 10pm daily. **Cover** R$7-$10. **Credit** DC, MC, V. Although this old samba and *choro* hangout is not conveniently located, it is one of the few places where live music can be heard every single night. The two-level bar is straight out of an Alpine village, but the walls are incongruously covered with photos of famous sambistas. The cover might be the cheapest in town, and every table gets a free basket of popcorn once the music starts. Monday is *choro* (a Yamaha, flute and *pandeiro*–tambourine), Tuesday is *seresta* (romantic music accompanied by acoustic guitars), Wednesday is jazz, Thursday is samba, Friday to Sunday is *choro*. The music starts at 10pm, but get to the bar by 9.30pm at the latest to secure a table – even on a Monday, the bar fills up fast.

★ Bar do Cidão

Rua Deputado Lacerdo Franco 293, Pinheiros (3813 3111/www.bardacidao.com.br). Bus 117Y-10. **Open** 7pm-late daily. **Cover** R$7.50. **Credit** V. **Map** 249 E9. This São Paulo institution is to Paulistanos what Bip-Bip is to Cariocas; in other words, a local joint for everyone of every age, but mostly for regulars, who crowd the tables to listen to the numerous bands that play here every night of the week. Cidão, the owner, has had a hundred different professions, from cabbie to truck driver and beyond, like his Carioca counterpart, Alfredo. He finally bought this tiny little spot, where he mans the bar and listens to the music with his wife and young son. A

Bar Saravah. *See p194.*

ARTS & ENTERTAINMENT

favourite of famous international personalities like Hanna Schygulla, who frequents Cidão's every time she's in São Paulo – well, she's only been there twice, but Cidão always mentions that famous *moça* (girl) who really likes the bar.

Bar Mangueira
Rua Claudio Soares 124, Pinheiros (3034 1085/ barmaguierasp.com.br). Bus 177P-10. **Open** 9.30-4am Thur, Fri; 1.30-10.30pm Sat; 5-10.30pm Sun. **Cover** R$10-$20. **Credit** MC, V. **Map** 249 E10.

If you aren't able to travel to Rio, go to Bar Mangueira. An outpost of Rio's most famous samba school (founded by the great sambista Cartola) – and subsequently, Brazil's as well – this packed dance hall is located on the Largo da Batata. The crowd is decidedly Paulistano, with few, if any, tourists. This music joint is famous for the huge *pagode*, samba and samba-rock bands that play until the wee hours of the morning for dedicated samba fans who come to drink Brahma, dance and celebrate birthdays. Call for free classes given before the bands begin to play.

★ Bar Saravah
Rua João Moura 796, Pinheiros (3081 6010). Metrô Sumare. **Open** 4pm-3am Fri, Sat; 5pm-1am Sun. **Shows** 5pm, 9.30pm Fri, Sat; 5pm Sun. **Cover** R$5-R$10. **Credit** MC, V. **Map** 249 G8.

This hopping spot, with its bright colours and walls decorated with old music scores and beautiful frames, entertains some of the best samba bands in town. A projection screen hangs in an alcove, although almost everyone ignores it as they are too

busy *fofocando* (gossiping). It's filled with hipsters, Pinheiros regulars and trust-fund kids dancing samba on Fridays, Saturdays and Sundays. The owner, Sara Tomazelli, speaks fluent English and is always around the bar to hang out with regulars or the occasional tourist. Beer goes for R$4, while the caipirinhas come in many delicious fruit flavours – besides lime, try strawberry or kiwi. Next door is the Tomazelli family's vintage home-decoration store, Maria Jovem (*see p158*).

Calo na Mão
Escola Estadual Professor Antonio Alves Cruz, Rua Alves Guimarães 1511, Pinheiros (8298 1209/www.calonamao.com.br). Metrô Sumaré. **Open** 2-5pm Sat. **Cover** free. **Map** 249 F7.

This bloco promotes the Pernambucan music of *maracatu*, a mix between African, Amerindian and European sounds. Their rehearsals are open to the public every Saturday.

★ Ó do Borogodó
Rua Horácio Lane 21, Pinheiros (3814 4087). Bus 117Y-10. **Open** 9pm-3am Mon-Fri; 1pm-3am Sat; 7pm-midnight Sun. **Cover** R$15 Mon-Fri; R$20 Sat, Sun. **Credit** MC, V. **Map** 249 G8.

This is hands-down the best samba venue in town if you want to dance, drink and sing along to incredible new and old sambas. At the weekend, the crowd pours outside the doors, and there's never a place to sit. It's mellower during the week, when the clientele is older and more genteel. The large warehouse space hosts top-notch samba bands most nights, with the musicians playing guitars and *cavaquinhos*. As good as anything in Rio's Lapa.

Pau Brasil Bar.

Bar Manguiera.

★ Pau Brasil Bar
Rua Inácio Pereira da Rocha 54, Vila Madalena (3816 1494). Metrô Vila Madalena/bus 117Y-10. **Open** 10pm-late Wed-Sun. **Cover** R$7-$10. **No credit cards**. **Map** p249 F8.

This little hole in the wall harks back to the authentic joints of the Cidade Maravilhosa. It's pretty hard to find, as there is no sign and the door typically looks closed, but once you've located it, you won't want to leave. The Pau Brasil (the Brazilian tree that the country was originally named for, and its first export) is an exceptionally good samba spot, with a *roda de samba* (samba circle) on most nights, a cute little bar filled with cachaças and beers, which has a loyal following. Once the joint gets full, there's no room to breathe, but everyone's crowded round the *roda*.

Salve Simpatia
Rua Mourato Coelho 1329, Vila Madalena (3814 0501). Metrô Vila Madalena. **Open** 9pm-4am Fri, Sat. *Shows* 11pm. **Cover** R$15-$20. **Credit** AmEx, DC, MC, V. **Map** 249 E8.

The music here is top notch, with great samba and *pagode* bands playing several times a week. The atmosphere, on the other hand, smacks of a meat market, with partially dressed couples crowding around the band stands. The service is quite unremarkable, and at times downright unpleasant, but if you're strictly after excellent music, then this is truly one of the best samba spots in the city.

Tocador de Bolacha
Rua Patizal 72, Vila Madalena (3815 7639/ www.tocadordebolacha.com.br). Metrô Vila Madalena. **Open** 7pm-2am Tue-Sat. *Shows* 9pm Wed, Thur; 10pm Fri, Sat. **Cover** R$12. **Credit** V. **Map** 249 E8.

Many of Sampa's live-music spots fit into one of three categories: classic samba clubs, dive bars or Vila Madalena traditional *botequims* that feature live samba to fuel the drinking of *chopp*. Tocador fits none of these descriptions. Tucked into a side street in the nightlife capital of Vila Madalena, it appears more like a small country villa or Spanish-style cottage in the Hollywood hills, with old LPs decorating the walls. There's plenty of outdoor space, if you're lucky enough to get good weather; both the patio off the main room and the side deck spanning the length of the bar make the environs feels like a backyard party. Tocador has a fine touch with caipirinhas, and talented musical acts play anything from straight jazz to a mix of all the classic Brazilian genres.

Villaggio Café
Rua Teodoro Sampaio 1229, Pinheiros (3571 3730/www.villaggio.com.br). Metrô Clínicas. **Open** 6pm-late Mon-Sun. *Shows* 9pm daily. **Cover** varies. **Credit** DC, MC, V. **Map** p249 G8.

This café/bar in Pinheiros has music every night of the week, and its pleasant chill-out atmosphere is perfect for those looking to relax, listen to some quiet music and sip a few drinks. There is a stage, and on Monday nights the bar is home to a bevy of singer-songwriters. On other nights there is samba and *choro*. It's also worth checking out the samba schools' rehearsals (*see pp164-166*).

Bar do Alemão. See p193.

FESTIVALS

'Annual' electronic and pop-music festivals come and go, according to mysterious whims – even organisers aren't sure whether a successful event will be repeated the following year. But a few to look out for are the **Helvetia Music Festival** around October (www.hmf.art.br), **Skol Sensation** in April (www.skolsensation.com.br), and **Skol Beats** in September or October (www.skolbeats.com.br), and the **Häagen Dazs Mix Music** in November (www. haagendazs.com.br). The **Festival Nacional da Canção** (National Song Festival) takes place in September in five cities in the south and southeast of Minas Gerais, about 300 kilometres from São Paulo, and has become one of the premier showcases for new Brazilian talent (www.festival dacancao.com.br).

One mega-event you can definitely count on is São Paulo's birthday festivities every 25 January, when the city sponsors free outdoor concerts by superstar artists, who in past years have included Jorge Ben Jor, Daniela Mercury and Beth Carvalho; *see p162*.

During the May **Virada Cultural** (*see p162*), launched in 2005, the city hosts concerts, street art, a circus, performance art and theatre events for an entire 24 hours straight.

Check newspapers for special concerts and events at music venues and plazas around the city during the **Festa Junina** (Saint John's Day) on 24 June. The emphasis is on food and traditions from the northeast, so this is a great time to go *forró* dancing.

October's **TIM Festival** is the largest music festival in Latin America, occuring simultaneously in Rio de Janeiro, São Paulo and Vitória. Recent line-ups for the Brazilian corporate rock fest have run the musical gamut from Bjork to Kayne West, Cat Power and Sonny Rollins.

INSIDE TRACK
WRITE YOUR OWN SAMBA

A samba routine may not be your route to the centre stage of *Britain's Got Talent* or *American Idol*, but even a gringo lacking any semblance of skill with Portuguese syllabics can begin his or her career as a musical poet – or at least sing along in a São Paulo bar – without major embarrassment. The most important words for any samba are *saudade* – the untranslatable word for longing; *alegria* – pure happiness; *tristeza* – plain and simple sadness; *maravilhoso/a* – marvelous; and *no morro/morro* – literally, 'on the hill', or hill, the most common term for a Brazilian favela.

You can sing any combination of these words in any order and approximate a samba. It's that simple (sort of). Though, of course, the best sambas and samba lyricists are among the best songwriters in the world. But it's a beginning, at least, and like a course of medicine, all you need to do for samba health is to repeat the lyrical doses, as necessary.

The Troubadour of Bixiga

The sambista who put São Paulo on the samba map.

São Paulo isn't famous for its samba scene. In fact, many have derided its musical heritage, with Vinicius de Moraes, the leading bossa nova lyricist, once dismissing it as 'the grave of samba'. But as Vinicius himself well knew, that's far from the case. Vinicius wrote one of his most famous songs, 'Bom Dia Tristeza' (Good Morning Sadness) in 1957 with **Adoniran Barbosa**, the father of Paulistana samba.

Adoniran, the man who revolutionised Brazilian samba, was easily recognised for most of his life by his hat, bow-tie and grainy voice. Born into a large Italian family in 1910, João Rubinato, as he was then called, dropped out of school at the age of nine to help out his family. He began working with his father on the railway in Jundai, São Paulo. From then on, he held a number of different posts, from waiter to painter, even selling socks at one point.

During the long walks that would take him to his jobs, Adoniran began to sing and compose sambas. These were not the sambas of Rio's favelas; yes, they were about the poor, but the location and regional make up was different. Adoniran eulogised the industrial city, a behemoth of immigrants, and introduced lyrics about Sampa's working class and the poor – prostitutes, day labourers and chauffeurs.

Adoniran came to become a key player in the cultural scene of the neighbourhood of Bixiga (now officially part of Bela Vista), which maintains a strong samba tradition to this day. His gravelly voice was initially a hindrance to a fully fledged singing career, but eventually his emphasised heavy Italian accent became part of his act.

In 1933, he began singing on Rádio Cruzeiro do Sul and eventually went on to record records and become a host on Rádio Record. There he created a number of immigrant personalities that stereotyped and caricatured both immigrant groups and city dwellers. During the hugely popular comedic programme, he made fun of Italians, the French, the English, Afro-Brazilians and Jews – no group escaped his parody. It was the language and accents of these radio characters that gave birth to Adoniran's innovations in samba lyrics and music. The linguistic tendencies of his on-air personalities took over his songs, leading to more wrath from the samba purists in Rio, who railed at the corruption of the Portuguese language that was coming from São Paulo.

When Adoniran met the samba group Demônios da Garoa (still Sampa's most famous samba band, who continue to perform to this day), his music gained its best interpreters. Adoniran had an amazing number of hits, with most of his songs being recorded by famous musical stars, including Beth Carvalho, João Bosco and Rita Lee. To this day, Adoniran's sambas are the most popular songs in the city's samba clubs – at least a third of the playlist will have sprung from the mind of this talented man. Despite his fame and acclaim, he died in relative poverty in 1982.

ARTS & ENTERTAINMENT

Nightlife

How Brazil's powerhouse gets its kicks.

São Paulo's nightlife easily competes with that of New York or London: new places open frequently, and intense competition means that owners constantly strive to outdo each other on design and atmosphere. It's a fast-moving scene, with the attendant irritation that underground clubs can find themselves flavour of the month almost overnight – and so proceed to hike up their prices. Trends develop so quickly that you might enjoy a decent amount of elbow room at the bar of a new club one week but go back the next only to find it packed to capacity. But that's all part of the experience. There are enough great venues in São Paulo for there always to be somewhere good to move on to, regardless of what might be in vogue.

THE CLUB SCENE

The best way to keep up to date with the ever-changing roster of what's in and what's fun is to befriend a savvy Paulistano, or to pick up the newspaper *Folha De São Paulo* on a Thursday, as it contains the Guia Da Folha – the city's weekly entertainment guide. It'll give you the lowdown on more mainstream music and arts scenes as well as tipping you off to decent DJs and new underground hotspots.

A range of high-profile venues including the local outpost of Ibiza's **Pacha** (*see p202*) and **D-Edge** (*see p201*), cater to the affluent set, while the more underground places, such as **Bar Secreto** (*see p201*) and the Party Intima evenings at **Audio Delicatessen** (*see p201*), are good for those not so into the super club vibe.

Unfortunately the Metrô system closes shortly after midnight, so you'll need to take the bus or a taxi home. The bus network is extensive and runs all night; with forward planning even the most obscure locations should be reachable. See p225 for more on night buses. Taxis offer a more secure way of getting around, but the city is huge and, as many a Paulistano will complain, taxi drivers often have no problem taking the scenic route, even with locals in the back. For

About the authors

Camilo Rocha *has worked as a journalist and DJ in São Paulo for over two decades. For writer* **Karim Alexander Khan**, *see p63.*

all purposes, it is best to call ahead for a radio taxi, or to get a cab at one of the *pontos de taxi*, which can be found throughout the city. For recommended taxi companies, see p225.

CENTRO

★ Love Story

Rua Araújo 232, República (3231 3101/ www.danceterialovestory.net). Metrô República/bus 178L-10, 669A-10, 702C-10. **Open** midnight-late Wed-Sat. **Cover** R$25-$50. **Credit** MC, V. **Map** p243 M5.

There are several reasons why Love Story is one of the most famous nightclubs in São Paulo: Mike Tyson once partied and got arrested here, and when rocker Nick Cave lived in São Paulo, he was a frequent visitor. It only gets started after 2.30am, when everyone finishes work and needs to let off steam. The club exudes raunch and trashiness and wild times are to be had inside. People dance on tables and flirt hard on the dancefloor. At once inclusive and exclusive, Love Story calls itself the 'House of all Houses' and expects you to party until you drop to techno and house with all manner of nightlife creatures.

CONSOLACAO

Funhouse

Rua Bela Cintra 567 (3259 3793/www.funhouse. com.br). Bus 177H-10, 719P-10, 719R-10. **Open** midnight-late Wed-Sat. **Cover** R$10-$15. **Credit** MC, V. **Map** p242 K6.

Vegas.

ARTS & ENTERTAINMENT

This great little two-floor club mainly attracts a fashionable alternative crowd with rock and bassline-heavy electronic music. Some excellent national DJs such as Bo$$inDrama have made appearances and live bands (mainly of the post-rock/grunge variety) also play on the tiny dancefloor. There is a jukebox on the second floor that offers classic punk, rock and some Britpop.

Lôca

Rua Frei Caneca 916 (3159 8889/www.aloca. com.br). Metrô Consolação/bus 107P, 478P, 669A. **Open** noon-6am Tue-Thur; noon-10am Fri, Sat; 7pm-6am Sun. **Cover** R$15-$25. **Credit** DC, MC, V. **Map** p244 K7.

Twelve years on and still going strong, A Lôca has become an underground institution. Very underground. Transvestites dance next to fashionistas, and technoheads hit on party girlies. There are nights dedicated to techno, house, classics and pop. It's dirty, sleazy and a bit of a shot in the dark: some nights can be really special; others can be a druggy freakshow. This is only for the more adventurous.

★ Vegas

Rua Augusta 765 (3231 3705/www.vegasclub. com.br). Bus 107P-10, 107T-10, 702P-41. **Open** 5am-5am Tue-Thur; 11pm-7am Fri; 11pm-11am Sat. **Cover** R$15-$25. **Credit** V. **Map** p243 L6.

One of São Paulo's foremost clubs attracts DJs from all over the world: Fischerspooner and Surgeon have performed here, and quality national talent

plays out every week. The local rockabilly/swing band that provides the soundtrack on some weeknights is also lots of fun. A cool young crowd steams up the two downstairs floors to dance and techno. Saturdays get a dose of rock via DJing sisters the Meninas do Rock. The crowd is GLS (gay-mixed).

BELA VISTA

★ Drops

Rua dos Ingleses 182 (2503 4486/www.dropsbar. com.br). Buses 175P, 477A, 477U. **Open** 8pm-1am Wed, Thur; 8pm-2am Fri, Sat. **Cover** R$10-$15. **Credit** DC. **Map** p245 M8.

This trendy bar is set up in a gorgeous mansion from the 1930s. The musical menu is eclectic and can go from rock to Latin to jazz to lounge, depending on the night. This is more of a place to sway to the music than to go mad on the dancefloor (in fact, there isn't one). There's a good food and drink selection.

★ Gloria

Rua 13 de Maio 830 (3287 3700/www. clubegloria.com.br). Bus 475M-10, 967A-10. **Open** midnight-late Thur-Sat. **Cover** R$15-$50. **Credit** DC, MC, V. **Map** p245 M8.

A former church, Gloria attracts the fashionistas of São Paulo thanks to its opulent decor, with beds, mirrors and champagne bars. Expect a GLS (gay-mixed) crowd, especially one Friday every month for its now-famous (and packed) Vai! nights, when changing dress codes such as 'demonic' or

São Paulo DJs Go Global

From Sampa to superstardom.

Brazilian composer Tom Jobim once famously said that the best route for a musician in his home country was to the airport. Although one of Brazil's most celebrated musicians, he felt that national talent earned greater recognition and paychecks abroad.

Many São Paulo DJs would agree with that, as they are always heading overseas. Brazil's most vibrant and interesting nightlife city has been a hotbed for spinning and knob-twisting artists for the last ten years. Names such as Renato Cohen, Wrecked Machines, Murphy, Click Box, Pet Duo, Drumagick and Wehbba, all born and bred in São Paulo, are now touring the world's dancefloors.

As you read this, Paulistano Gum Boratto is probably performing at some major festival in the northern hemisphere: Coachella, Sónar, DEMF… you name it. He's come far in a few years: 'My debut abroad was at the Nitsa club, in Barcelona. I was pretty nervous but I was surrounded by friends, guys like Michael Mayer, DJ Koze and Matias Aguayo. It was a great night, everyone got into it.' This was the beginning of a prodigious international career. Boratto's two albums, *Chromophobia* and *Take My Breath Away*, earned widespread acclaim, and he's remixed tracks for

Pet Shop Boys and Goldfrapp.

Before Boratto, the most famous São Paulo DJ worldwide was Marky (*pictured*). Raised in the drab eastern São Paulo suburb of Cangaíba, Marky and fellow drum 'n' bass DJ Patife, tired of being neglected in their home town, made a legendary trip to London in 1998 in an attempt to promote their work.

Marky went on to become a staple of the UK scene. He has since had a record in the British top 20 and has often been hailed as best drum 'n' bass DJ.

Patife hasn't reached such stellar heights, but nonetheless, he has played countless international gigs, including festivals like Barcelona's Sónar. He said about his first gigs, 'At home, you know what you have to play. But the first times you play abroad, you don't really know what to do. It was pretty nerve-wracking.'

Coming from the hip hop side of things (although nowadays he's much more diverse) is Zegon, also known in town as Ze Gonzales. Zegon splits his time between São Paulo and LA. There he met US contemporary Squeak E Clean, with whom he formed NASA (North America South America, geddit?). In 2009, they released their debut album, *The Spirit of Apollo*, packed with famous collaborators such as George Clinton, David Byrne, Tom Waits and Kanye West.

'futuristic' ensure outrageous outfits. The music at Vai! plays second fiddle, and you can expect lashings of Britney Spears and other bubble-gum (but bass-heavy) pop. For fans of music rather than glamour, Thursday nights cater to hip hop lovers, and Saturdays are electronica and rock.

Milo Garage

Rua Minas Gerais 203A (3129 8027/www.milo garage.com). Bus 177H-10, 719P-10, 917H-41. **Open** 10.30pm-late Wed, Fri, Sat. **Cover** R$10-$15. **Credit** V. **Map** p244 J7.

Milo used to be a record store until people started hanging out there more than they should have. It's a small, sweaty venue that opens out into a small conservatory between two skyscrapers, giving an amazing view for when you want to escape the dancefloor furnace for a bit. Wednesdays are lo-fi and alternative rock spun by the maestro Milo himself, Fridays play hip hop, soul and dub (with DJ Kbça, who also appears at Pacha), and on Saturdays it's indie rock, electro and '80s gems.

★ Sonique

Rua Bela Cintra 461 (2628 8707/www.sonique bar.com.br). Metrô Consolação/bus 107P, 669A, 805L, 875A. **Open** 6pm-2am Tue, Wed; 6pm-3am Thur-Sat. **Cover** free. **Credit** MC, V. **Map** p242 K6.

One of a kind, this ultra-stylish new bar has a dancefloor that proposes to be a 'warm-up' for other clubs and parties. A notice board that looks like an airport flight panel announces what's happening around town. A van and taxi service can be arranged from here to other venues. The idea is to close earlyish, but often the goings on get good enough to make revellers stick around all night long. Note: the no cover policy is offset by a R$40 minimum food and drink charge.

PINHEIROS & VILA MADALENA

Audio Delicatessen

Rua Mourato Coelho 651 (3097 0880/www.audio delicatessen.com.br). Bus 177H-10, 177Y-10, 771P-10. **Open** 11pm-late Fri-Sat. **Cover** R$15-$30. **Credit** AmEx, DC, MC, V. **Map** p249 E9.

The surrounding area of Vila Madalena is renowned for its conservative, almost preppy atmosphere, which is why the ambience at Audio Delicatessen comes as such a breath of fresh air. The two-storey disco has a more chilled-out area downstairs, while the clubbing really gets going on the first floor. From Thursday to Saturday, the programme mainly revolves around rock and electro. An especially good night here is Party Intima, one Friday per month.

★ Bar Secreto

Rua Alvaro Anes 97 (www.sitedobar.com). Bus 875C-10, 7013-10, 7043-10. **Open** 10pm-late Tue-Fri. **Cover** free. **Credit** MC, V. **Map** p249 E9.

Bar Secreto has no telephone number, no cover fee, and yet it has been the site of both Madonna and Justice after-parties. It also plays host to a plethora of well-known DJs (think Soulwax and Mehdi) in its small enclosure. The free entry is offset by relatively hefty drinks prices (R$25 for a vodka and orange juice). However, you won't be able to see your favourite DJs so up close and personal anywhere else in the city.

BARRA FUNDA

★ Berlin

Rua Cônego Vicente Miguel Marino 85 (3392 4594/www.clubeberlin.com.br). Bus 148P-10, 148P-31, 177C-10. **Open** 10pm-late Tue-Sun. **Cover** R$12-$15. **Credit** DC, MC, V. **Map** p242 L2.

A retro-decorated club that has an exceptional Tuesday night live jazz showcase. It attracts younger, more danceable acts that sometimes border on swing. Thursdays are alternative, and Fridays a mishmash of disco, rock and garage. It also functions as an analogue recording studio.

CB

Rua Brigadeiro Galvão 871 (3666 8971/www.cb bar.com.br). Bus 407M-10, 719R-10. **Open** 10pm-5am Tue-Sat. **Cover** R$10-$20. **Credit** DC, MC, V. **Map** p242 K2.

A legitimate rock 'n' roll diner-turned-club. It's dark, but very well decorated in neon and red vinyl, topped off by the working Wurlitzer jukebox in the corner. The bands it attracts vary from rockabilly to dirty blues to straight rock but are always of a good quality – notables include the Forgotten Boys and As Cobras Malditas.

Clash

Rua Barra Funda 969 (3661 1500/ www.clashclub.com.br). Metrô Barra Funda or Marechal Deodoro/bus 175P, 177C, 177P. **Open** 11pm-late Tue; midnight-late Thur-Sat. **Cover** R$20-$60. **Credit** MC, V. **Map** p242 K2.

This is São Paulo's main techno temple. The best Brazilian DJs, plus regular guests from abroad, keep the large room going until the wee hours. The crowd is quite young, quite ravey and very up for it. It's not all techno, though: on Tuesdays it hosts Chocolate, one of the best hip-hop nights in town.

D-Edge

Alameda Olga 170 (3667 8334/ www.d-edge.com.br). Bus 177C-10, 177C-22, 177C-23. **Open** midnight-late Mon-Sat. **Cover** R$15-$25. **Credit** AmEx, DC, MC, V. **Map** p242 J2.

There's no doubt that this is one of the most visually impressive clubs in São Paulo. The wall on one side of the place acts like a huge equaliser, pulsing in time to the music – mainly of the electro, rock

ARTS & ENTERTAINMENT

Sonique. *See p201.*

and techno varieties. Superlative DJs like Richie Hawtin, Tiga and Ricardo Villalobos spin when in town, bolstering the already impressive nights put on by local producers, such as CREW (Tuesdays), which gets a team of nine DJs sharing the stage.

Neu

Rua Dona Germaine Burchard 423 (listaneu @gmail.com). Bus 877T-10, 938C-10, 978J-10. **Open** 11p-late Wed-Sat. **Cover** R$10-$15. **No credit cards. Map** p242 I2.
Neu is a minimal space, without any kind of decoration whatsoever in what is essentially a no-frills, 1940s-style house with a terrace. What it does have is an excellent music policy, bringing in smaller international acts and national gems that made its former nights at Milo Garage (*see p207*), so great.

Pacha

Rua Mergenthaler 829, Vila Leopoldina (2189 3700/www.pachasp.com.br). Bus 178T-10, 802C-10, 278A-10. **Open** 10pm-8am Fri, Sat. **Admission** R$60-$120. **Credit** MC, V.
If you don't like superclubs, don't bother. São Paulo's branch of Spain's stalwart is glamourous, sexy and fiendishly expensive – if you want to party VIP, it'll cost you R$2,000. Yes, that is three zeros. The club has space for 8,000 clubbers, and is majestic, from the inner, domed main arena, to the glorious open-air dancefloor outside. Regularly attracting some of the world's most famous DJs (from hip hop to house to techno) and, with them, some of the world's most attractive crowds, it's a must if you're in town to party with the city's well-heeled and pour champagne on the dancefloor.

Performing Arts

All the world's a stage, especially in São Paulo.

Brazilian theatre and dance have been well-respected on the international stage for decades, being renowned for both creativity and, especially impressive for a developing country, high-quality performances. **Thiago Soares**, the principal ballet dancer at the Royal Ballet Company, represents Brazil overseas as one of the most brilliant dancers of the 21st century. The **Theatre of the Oppressed**, formed by Augusto Boal, has inspired hundreds of similar movements in different countries. Meanwhile, the **Orquestra Sinfônica do Estado de São Paulo**, has been lauded by *Gramophone* magazine as one of the three most promising emergent orchestras in the world.

CLASSICAL MUSIC

São Paulo's classical music scene benefits from the constant updating of its European-style theatres, and from being home to one of the best symphony orchestras in Latin America. The Paulistano love for music also permits even the city's most snobbish venues to play host to some of the country's best popular musicians: you can now take in both a symphony or a samba from the same velvet-lined box that once seated a royal, with important music and performing arts venues including **Auditório Ibirapuera** (*see p74*), **Caixa Cultural** (*see p52*), **CCBB** (*see p52*), **Citibank Hall** (*see p192*), **HSBC Brasil** (*see p173*) and **Via Funchal** (*see p80*).

★ Sala São Paulo

Praça Julio Prestes 16, Luz (3367 9500/ www.salasaopaulo.art.br). Metrô Luz. **Box office** 10am-6pm Mon-Fri or before concert; 10am-4.30pm Sat on performance days; 2hrs before concert Sun. **Tickets** R$20-$110. **Credit** AmEx, DC, MC, V. **Map** p243 N3.
One of the most modern concert halls in Latin America, Sala São Paulo is also an impressive work of architectural rebirth, constructed in a 1938 train station that was originally patterned on the style of Louis XVI. The station's redesign as a cultural centre and concert hall was carried out with meticulous

attention to the acoustic needs of its resident, the Orquestra Sinfônica do Estado de São Paulo (OSESP). After a series of spats and scandals in the classical music world, in 2009, John Neschling, the director of the orchestra since 1997, was replaced by the Frenchman Yan Pascal Tortelier.

★ Teatro Municipal

Praça Ramos de Azevedo s/n, Centro (3397 0300/www.teatromunicipal.sp.gov.br). Metrô Anhangabaú. **Box office** 10am-7pm Mon-Fri; 10am-5pm Sat, Sun. **Tickets** R$10-$80; reductions R$5-$4. **Credit** AmEx, DC, MC, V. **Map** p243 N5.
This European-style classical theatre, designed by Ramos de Azevedo, opened to the public in 1911 at the height of the city's coffee wealth. It has hosted the likes of Maria Callas, Enrico Caruso, Arturo Toscanini, Ana Pavlova, Isadora Duncan, Rudolph Nureyev, Margot Fonteyn, Mikhail Baryshnikov, Duke Ellington and Ella Fitzgerald. In more recent years, Yoko Ono and Bobby McFerrin, as well as the most important Brazilian musicians, have played for the city. *Photo p205.*

About the author

Mose Hayward *is the author of* Explosexuawesome Career Guide *and over 30 episodes of* Leonart *for Televisión Española.*

Theatro São Pedro

Rua Barra Funda 171, Barra Funda (3667 0499/
www.theatrosaopedro.or.br). Metrô Marechal
Deodoro. **Open** 4pm-performance time.
Tickets vary. **Credit** V. **Map** p242 L3.
São Paulo's second oldest theatre was inaugurated in 1917, becoming the cultural centre of Barra Funda and the surrounding districts. The beautiful neoclassical building first served as a theatre for plays, then as a cinema, and it's currently a venue for classical music. The theatre underwent a huge refurbishment in the 1990s, reopening in 1998 with modernised lighting and improved acoustics. Concerts are often free.

Subversive Stages

Playwrights and theatres that helped to define the city as a theatrical powerhouse.

Theatre has been used as a tool of resistance and subversiveness by writers, from Molière to Brecht, the world over, and Brazilian playwrights are no exception.

In 1948, Italian industrialist Franco Zampari created the **Teatro Brasileiro de Comédia** (TBC). The theatre was the first of three major Paulistano companies to have a major influence on the Brazilian theatre scene, but it closed in 1958; as its ideology moved ever leftward, the middle-class bourgeoisie and the government that had supported the theatre found less and less incentive to pay to see performances in which they were, more often than not, the laughing stock.

In the 1960s, **Teatro Oficina** was one of the greatest avant-garde theatres in the western hemisphere. It produced plays by Oswald de Andrade like *O Rei da Vela*, and revolutionised others that were part of the European canon, such as Molière's *Dom Juan*, which was performed by the theatre in 1971 as a rock opera.

The socially aware **Teatro de Arena** was founded in 1956 by **Augusto Boal** and Gianfrancesco Guarnieri. As well as the Brecht plays, it produced the groundbreaking musical works *Arena Conta Zumbi* (1965) and *Arena Conta Tiradentes* (1967). Both of these plays focused on the retelling of important historical stories from the country's past, involving topics such as slavery and the first attempted revolution against the Portuguese led by Tiradentes (the young dentist and revolutionary who was executed for plotting against the Portuguese crown).

Later, Boal took up the theme of the favela. One of the pivotal plays for the Teatro de Arena was Guarnieri's *Eles Nao Usam Black Tie* (*They Don't Wear Black Tie*), which depicted life in a favela. It focused on the generational struggles of a father, who is attuned to the needs of his community, and his son who wants to reject his shanty town background.

By the 1960s, the Teatro de Arena was no longer interested in mainstream productions, and a bored Boal revolutionised the city's theatre scene by presenting the Corniga system, in which he sought to break with theatrical norms. In his format, characters were played by several different actors during the course of a play, and multiple narrators would tell the same story. In 1971, Boal wrote *Arena Conta Bolívar*, which was prohibited by the dictatorship from being staged. Boal was subsequently imprisoned and exiled, and the theatre was forced to close in 1972.

When Boal returned from exile in Europe in 1983, he resumed work in the theatre, and in 1986 founded the **Centro de Teatro do Oprimido** (Centre of the Theatre of the Oppressed, www.theatreoftheoppressed.org). The centre developed a methodology for revolutionising the art form by introducing theatre to poor communities and making it more accessible to everyone, but especially the impoverished. Boal died in May 2009.

São Paulo playwright **Plinio Marcos** shares top billing with Augusto Boal in the city's provocative theatre history. His first seminal work was *Barrela* (*Gang Bang*). Marcos's brutal play was influenced by an article he had read about a young man who, after a drunken bar fight, was thrown into a cell with criminals who proceeded to beat and rape him. The victim subsequently turned to a life of violence and sought revenge on the police responsible for his loss of innocence. This play got the controversial ball rolling for Marcos's work and was banned in Brazil for more than 20 years. During the dictatorship, Marcos was arrested numerous times and had more plays banned than any other Brazilian writer – a notable artistic achievement. He believed in theatre for the masses, and took his plays to many favelas. He also often acted as a clown, a method which he used as a way to interact with people in the poor communities where he worked.

ARTS & ENTERTAINMENT

Teatro Municipal. *See p203.*

DANCE

São Paulo's preeminent dancers can usually be seen at the SESCs (*see below*) and **Centro Cultural São Paulo** (*see p68*),but various smaller venues, generally offering both classes and performance spaces, are also worth noting. The most active include **Galeria Olido** (*see p46*), **Lugar** (Rua Augusta 325, Consolação, 3237 3224, www.ciacorpos nomades.art.br) and **Sala Crisantempo** (Rua Fidalga 521, Vila Madalena, 3819 2287, www.sala crisantempo. com.br).

Some of the more innovative dancers and companies to watch out for are **Companhia Nova Dança 4**, **Companhia Nova Dança 8**, **Diogo Granato**, **Key Zetta e Companhia**, **Jorge Garcia** and **Zé Maria**.

NOVO CIRCO

Small Brazilian companies of circus artists have taken up the New Circus movement with gusto. In the early 1990s the Brazilian press didn't know what to make of modern dance that made use of acrobatics or theatre borrowing on clown techniques, but now the companies practising these arts form a small but important part of the performance landscape, mainly appearing at SESCs. Interesting groups to watch out for are **Circo Mínimo** (www.circominimo.com.br), **Circo Zanni** (www.circozanni.com), **Grupo Acrobático Fratelli** (www.acrobaticofratelli. com.br), **Nau de Ícaros** (www.naudeicaros.com. br) and **Namakaca** (www.namakaca.com.br).

Academia Brasileira de Circo

Avenida Regente Feijó 1560, Jardim Anália Franco (2076 0087/2076 0001/www.academia decirco.com.br). Bus 3139. **Box office** 9am-6pm Mon-Fri; 2-9pm Sat, Sun. **Tickets** R$10-$25. **No credit cards**. **Map** 243 O1.
Founded in 2004, this troupe's show is focused on traditional circus entertainment like juggling, magic, balancing feats, contortionism and trapeze. Advance tickets also available from www.ingresso.com.

SESC

The impact on the performance scene of the non-profit SESC centres scattered throughout Brazil is simply enormous. Even in São Paulo, where there is such a large number and variety of shows on offer, the SESCs remain the best providers of quality and value for money when it comes to theatre, dance and music shows.

Created in 1946 as a way for Brazilian commerce to assure the social well-being of the general workforce, **SESC** (Serviço Social do Comércio – the commercial sector's social services) has become a giant, well-funded non-profit institution in Brazil, thanks to laws stipulating contributions by all commercial enterprises. Its aim is to promote culture, health and education to the Brazilian public and it has centres in every Brazilian city of a decent size.

In São Paulo itself there are 16 SESC venues, which function as major athletic, performance and exhibition centres. World-class music, dance, theatre and circus are on offer and ticket prices are always reasonable (around $R5-$25) and often even free. Performance spaces range from traditional proscenium stages to black-box experimental labs, to live music beer halls (the Choperia do SESC). For information on programming at all of São Paulo's SESCs, visit www.sescsp.org.br. Tickets for events must be purchased in person at any SESC installation around the city (not necessarily the one holding the event) during the building's general hours. All SESCs accept credit cards.

The most important SESC buildings for performances are **SESC Consolação** (Rua Dr Vila Nova 245, 3234 3000); **SESC Paulista** (Avenida Paulista 119, 3179 3700, closed Mon); **SESC Pinheiros** (Rua Paes Leme 195, 3095 9400, closed Mon); and **SESC Vila Mariana** (Rua Pelotas 141, 5080 3000, closed Mon). **SESC Pompeia** (Rua Clelia 93, Pompeia, 3871 7700, closed Mon) is famous as a place to catch shows by some of Brazil's top contemporary music performers, like the divas Mart'nalia and

Teatro Alfa.

Fernanda Takai. The complex is an architectural landmark designed by architect Lina Bo Bardi (who was responsible for the MASP).

THEATRE

That there's something unique and wonderful about Brazilian theatre was not lost on Paulistano playwright Oswald de Andrade (1890-1954). His *movimento antropofágico* (anthropophagy – or ritualistic cannibalism – movement) sought to digest external influences and make them wholly Brazilian, rather than simply using them to imitate Europe. Taking de Andrade's call as their rallying cry, Paulistano playwrights and directors have produced a theatre culture that is unlike any other.

Espaço Parlapatões

Praça Roosevelt 158, Centro (3258 4449/ www.parlapartoes.com.br). Metrô Anhangabaú. **Box office** 4-10pm Tue-Sun. **Tickets** $R10-$30. **Credit** AmEx, DC, MC, V. **Map** p243 M6.
The acting troupe that calls this theatre home started out in 1991 with street theatre performances. Eventually the group's skits and circus stunts morphed into plays. Since then, the group has continued to produce theatre with circus influences and an emphasis on audience involvement, whether for a mega-production in a space like the sambódromo or for a couple of performers with a low-key setup in its own, more intimate space.

SESI

Avenida Paulista 1313 (3146 7000/www.sesisp. org.br). Metrô Trianon-Masp. **Box office** noon-8pm Tue-Sun. **Tickets** free-R$10. **Credit** AmEx, DC, MC, V. **Map** p244 L8.
SESI is to the industrial sector what SESC is to commerce; mandatory contributions from Brazilian industry get funnelled into this independent nonprofit institution to promote the social welfare of the masses. The SESI building on Avenida Paulista hosts first-rate theatre, dance, cinema and music, including some free productions. Call ahead to find out the right time to queue up for a ticket.

Teatro Alfa

Rua Bento Branco de Andrade Filho 722, Santo Amaro (5693 4000/0300 789 3377/ www.teatroalfa.com.br). Bus 6039. **Box office** 11am-7pm daily. **Tickets** R$60-$130. **Credit** AmEx, DC, MC, V.
Brazil does Broadway. Just over a decade old, this large performance space hosts big-budget dance, opera, orchestra, pop music, theatre and, in particular, international musicals. Tickets can be purchased by phone or from the box office without a Brazilian CPF.

Teatro Oficina Uzyna Uzona

Rua Jaceguai 520, Bela Vista (3104 0678/www. teatroficina.com.br/uzyna_uzona). Metrô Liberdade. **Box office** 1hr before performances. **Tickets** R$5-$100. **No credit cards. Map** p245 N7.
For more than 50 years this São Paulo institution has been challenging the city both politically and artistically. During the dictatorship era the theatre attempted to find workaround, metaphorical ways to resist power through its plays, though it still ended up being censored. It continues to be run by one of its original founders, José Celso Martinez Corrêa, and now receives state funding as well as recognition for its historical role.

Teatro Sérgio Cardoso

Rua Rui Barbosa 153, Bela Vista (3288 0136/ www.teatrosergiocardoso.org.br). Bus 5106. **Box office** 3-7pm Wed-Sun. **Tickets** free-$20. **Credit** V. **Map** p245 M7.
Named after a legendary Brazilian actor, this theatre has a main stage for large-scale national and international dance, theatre and classical music performances as well as a smaller space, the Sala Paschoal Carlos Magno, for experimental productions.

Teatro da Vertigem

Rua 13 de Maio 240, Bela Vista (3255 2713/ www.teatrodavertigem.com.br). Bus 967A. **Box office** 1hr before performances. **Tickets** free-R$20. **No credit cards. Map** p245 M7.
Formed in 1991, Teatro da Vertigem is an experimental artists' collective. The group is as comfortable putting on work in the metrô or on the banks of the Rio Pinheiros as in a theatre space. The collective relentlessly digs into its own psyche and experience for material and creates its performance pieces in a democratic fashion.

TICKETS

For details of where to buy tickets, *see p160*.

ARTS & ENTERTAINMENT

Sports & Fitness

São Paulo kicks off its plans for the 2014 World Cup.

The chance to banana kick Brazil back into global glory on home turf is still five years' away (the country is hosting the FIFA World Cup in 2014 for the first time since 1950, when the national squad suffered a shocking loss to Uruguay), but there is plenty of sporting action throughout the year in São Paulo. A trip to watch a match of the 'beautiful game' is a requisite of any trip (with the city's stadiums due to be renovated for 2014), but visitors will also find a host of opportunities for exercising outdoors, from hiking to cycling to skating. And in a country where body sculpting is a national obsession, the plethora of gyms and fitness classes should come as no surprise.

MAJOR STADIUMS

Though many of the Brazilian cities hosting World Cup games will need to build new stadiums, in São Paulo and Rio renovation of existing arenas is more likely. São Paulo's Estádio do Morumbi is likely to be the host stadium for the opening game in 2014, and will be upgraded in time for the event. (Games held in Rio's Estádio do Maracanã, meanwhile – the stadium in which Brazil lost to Uruguay in the final of the 1950 World Cup – will be watched with a poetic zeal.)

Estádio do Morumbi

*Praça Roberto Gomes Pedrosa 1 (3749 8000).
Bus 765A-10.* **Open** 9am-6pm Mon-Sat;
10am-4pm Sun. **Tickets** R$30-$120.
No credit cards.
Morumbi is home to São Paulo Football Club (SPFC), and also hosts the state championship games, known as *clássicos*. The stadium's official name is Estádio Cicero Pompeu de Toledo, and it is the largest in the city with a capacity of 80,000. It was designed by the famed modernist architect João Batista Vilanova Artigas, with the inaugural match taking place in 1960. The lower tiers offer cheaper tickets and general seating, which means you will be standing shoulder-to-shoulder among the faithful, but with a limited view of the field. The middle tier has the most expensive tickets, and provides a numbered seat or access to private boxes, as well as the best views. The expansive open-air *arquibancada* (stadium seats) up top may lack the civility of the middle tier, but wins hands down for having the best, and most interactive, atmosphere.

Estádio do Pacaembu

*Praça Charles Miller s/n, Pacaembu (3664 4650).
Bus 408A-10.* **Open** 11am-5pm daily. **Tickets**
R$30-$120. **Map** p242 J5.
The official name of this ground is Estádio Municipal Paulo Machado de Carvalho, and it is the home turf for football club Corinthians. It is much smaller than Morumbi, with a capacity for 40,000 fans. The stadium is mainly open-air, the majority of the tickets sold are for general seating. In the event of rain a stretch of numbered (*numerada*) seats running down one side of the field is the only section of the stadium that is partially covered. The stadium plaza also serves as home to the city's Museu do Futebol (*see p65*). The museum's most valued artefact is the shirt that was worn by Pelé during the 1970 World Cup Final in Mexico. *Photo p208*.

SPECTATOR SPORTS
Football

O jogo bonito (the beautiful game) may be a clichéd Brazilian tourist experience, but it should still be on every visitor's to-do list. While matches can be intense, a little common sense should prevent visitors from encountering any problems. The best approach is to go casually dressed (T-shirt, shorts and tennis shoes), and it's a good idea to make sure you are not wearing the colours of the opposing team. Also make sure you have bought a seat in the right section, since being the lone home green in a sea of white enemies at a game is definitely not the way to make friends during a heated game.

Estádio do Pacaembu. See p207.

Like football matches elsewhere in South America, this is the sports version of a mosh-pit, so be prepared to dance and sing from your seat, as well as possibly be called on to help wave a parachute-sized flag or dodge falling fireworks.

Tickets are affordably priced for general seating, making the need to buy from touts outside the box offices unnecessary at most matches. Numbered seats are more expensive, and all prices rise during championships. Be prepared to pay in cash at stadium box offices. Some box-office windows only sell tickets to 'membership holders' who pay annual dues; but if you are lucky and know a word or two of Portuguese, it is not difficult to find a member who will present their membership card to buy you a ticket.

Corinthians (white and black shirt) has one of the largest fan bases in São Paulo, and is known as the 'working class' team of the outer-borough neighbourhoods. After relegation to the B league only a few years ago, there is excitement among fans again with the return of Ronaldo to the club. **São Paulo** (white shirt with red and black) is supported by the jet-set Brazilian playboys, and has recently had a number of successes in the Brazilian championships, as well as in the Latin American Champions League, Libertadores. **Palmeiras** (green shirt), one of the most-followed teams in the country, is the club of choice in the centrally located neighbourhoods of São Paulo, where there is a large population of Brazilians with Italian heritage. **Santos** (black and white striped shirt or white) is a club from a coastal city located one hour from the capital of São Paulo, but is considered the city's unofficial fifth team, and is more popular than the beleaguered **Portuguesa** (red and green shirt). Santos is where Pelé got his start, the Bethlehem of Brazilian *futebol*.

Parque Antárctica
Rua Turiassa 1840, Água Branca (3874 6500). **Open** 10am-5pm Wed, Sun. **Tickets** R$30-$120. **Map** p242 I3.
After the major venues Pacaembu and Morumbi, this is one of the city's most accessible stadiums. Its official name is Palestra Itália and it serves as

home to Palmeiras. The stadium has a limited capacity of 32,000 fans. The box office opens 72 hours before a game.

Vila Belmiro
Avenida Princesa Isabel 77, Santos (13 3257 4000). **Open** 10am-6pm Fri; 9am-6pm Sat, Sun. **Tickets** R$20-$60.
Officially called Estádio Urbano Caldeira, this stadium is the home ground of the port city of Santos (one hour outside of São Paulo). It is perhaps the most popular Brazilian stadium for families, and its design brings the spectator closer to the field than in the other city stadia; expect an intimate, club-like atmosphere in a ground that only holds 20,000.

Formula 1 Racing

Brazilians are as crazy about their racing car drivers as they are about their football stars, especially when it comes to racing legend Ayron Senna (*see p211* **King of the Road**). The **Autódromo de Interlagos** (Avenida Sen. Teotônio Vilela 261, 5041 3233, www.gpbrasil. com.br), so-named because it is located in between two enormous reservoirs and reminded early admirers of Interlochen in Switzerland, is the home of the Formula 1 Grande Premio do Brasil. Interlagos has been the signature race circuit in Brazil since the early part of the 20th century, except for the years 1980-89, when the municipal government refused to invest in renovations and Rio de Janeiro stole the Grande Premio race from São Paulo. Interlagos was the site where British hotshot Lewis Hamilton claimed the annual Formula 1 championship on 2 November 2008, even though Brazilian driver Felipe Massa finished in first place.

Horse-racing

Long after the *bandeirantes* had galloped across the interior of Brazil, São Paulo's horse-racing history began with the founding of the original jockey club in 1875. It was an important socialite stomping ground for the early Paulistano elite, but it wasn't until 1941 that the current site of the *hipódromo* in Cidade Jardim was built, replacing a race ground in Moóca. Today the

Jockey Club de São Paulo.

Jockey Club hosts major races throughout the calendar year. You can watch the horses in full stride, and lose money without speaking a word of Portuguese. *Boa sorte* (good luck).

Jockey Club de São Paulo
Avenida Lineu de Paula Machado 1263, Cidade Jardim (2161 8300/www.jockeysp.com.br). CPTM Hebraica-Rebouças. **Open** 6.30-11.30pm Mon; 2pm-8pm Sat, Sun. **Admission** free. **Map** p248 D12.

Running

Paulistanos typically move around the city at a quick pace, and the city's **Corrida Internacional de São Silvestre** (www. saosilvestre.com.br) has been channelling that mass energy into a 15-kilometre (ten mile) race for 85 years. Brazilian journalist Casper Libero found time in between fighting against Getulio Vargas, being exiled and becoming a pioneer in communications to promote some of the most famous sports events in São Paulo, including this one. The race, held on 31 December, is now a major event. It was a strictly Paulistano race for its first 16 years, but the São Paulo supremacy was broken in 1941 with the victory of a runner from neighbouring Minas Gerais. By 1947, the event had become international. The results of the 2008 run looked much like the results of any major global race. At 15 kilometres, it doesn't compare to the torture of a marathon, but the race is famed for its course, which places runners under the duress of São Paulo's concrete ups and downs.

PARTICIPATION SPORTS

Personal fitness regimens are easy to satisfy in São Paulo, with exercise opportunites ranging from park hikes to cycling. Skate enthusiasts can take advantage of all that concrete.

Cycling

If you have your bike and helmet with you, one of the most interesting rides you can do is with the **Night Bikers**, a group of friends that meets every Tuesday night for some joyrides. The meeting point is always on the same street (Rua Pacheco de Miranda, Moema, ww.nightbikers. com*)* and always at the same time of 8.45pm, but the routes vary from week to week. Several city parks also have dedicated trails for cyclists, including **Parque Villa-Lobos** (*see p77*), where bikes are available to rent at the entrance, and **Parque das Bicicletas** (*see p80*), which is a small park exclusively for bikers with a 3,000-metre (9,850-feet) long track, close to massive **Parque Ibirapuera** (*see pp73-75*). **Parque do Carmo** (Avenida Afonso de Sampaio e Souza 951, Itaquera, 6748 0010*)*, a former farm and one of the biggest parks in town, has a cycle track that is best for mountain bikes and on which you can really get away from it all.

Dance studios

Casa de Artes OperÁria
Rua Sacramento Blake 88, Mooca (2618 5540/ www.operaria.com.br). Metrô Bresser-Mooca. **Open** 9am-11pm Mon-Sat. **No credit cards**. This facility conjures up the sweat and aspirations of the movie *Fame*; it's a small New York City-like dance and musical theatre school with regular tap, jazz and ballet classes.

Wolf Maya
3rd floor, Shopping Frei Caneca, Rua Frei Caneca 569, Cerqueira César (3472 2444/ www.escoladeatoreswolfmaya.com.br). Metrô Consolação. **Open** 1-11.30pm Mon-Sat. **Credit** MC, V. **Map** p242 L6.
This dancing (and acting) school was created by TV and musical theatre director Wolf Maya. Some of the faces currently to be seen on Brazilian TV have studied here. Fernanda Chamma, a big name in Brazilian musical choreography, is in charge of the studio.

Football

Rolley Ball
Rua Galeno Castro 479, Jurubatuba (5523 6598/ www.rolleyball.com.br). **Open** 9am-11pm Mon-Sat. Football as a kick-about game and social event is very popular in São Paulo. Football training is given to children starting at 7 years-old.

Grand Marquise in
Parque Ibirapuera. See p209.

Golf

Though São Paulo is no keen golfer's dream destination, **FPG Golfcenter** will at least allow you to keep your swing from getting too rusty. It is one of the few golf courses in the city and charges from R$30 to R$60 per person. The driving range costs R$15 for 60 balls.

FPG Golfcenter
Rua Dep. João Bravo Caldeira 273 (5587 5844/ www.fpggolfcenter.com.br). **Open** 4-10pm Mon; 7am-10pm Tue-Fri; 7am-8pm Sat, Sun. **Credit** AmEx, D, MC, V. **Map** p246 A18.

Gyms

São Paulo has plenty of high-quality gyms with advanced equipment. But if you'd rather not spend the money, head to **Praça Esther Mesquito** (*see p64*) in Higienópolis; the tiny square has exercise machines that are free to all.

Bioritmo
Conjunto Nacional, Avenida Paulista 2073, Cerqueira César (3365 0800/www.bioritmo. com.br). **Metrô Consolação.** **Open** 6am-11pm Mon-Fri; 10am-6pm Sat; 10am-4pm Sun. **Credit** MC, V. **Map** p244 K7.
This is a typical Paulistano gym: full of beautiful people and popular with the gay scene. Good equipment and fitness classes make it one of the best in town.
Other locations: throughout the city.

Cia Athletica
Morumbi Shopping, Avenida Roque Petroni Júnior 1089, Brooklin (5506 3000/www. ciaathletica.com.br). **Open** 5am-midnight Mon-Fri; 8am-5pm Sat, Sun. **Map** p250 C18.
Located inside a mall, this is a three-floor sport complex with swimming pools and advanced workout equipment. It has a special Pilates studio.
Other locations: throughout the city.

Competition
Rua Cincinato Braga 520, Bela Vista (3171 2777/ www.competition.com.br). Metrô

INSIDE TRACK
PRISON BREAK

One of the most infamous prison massacres occurred at São Paulo's Carandiru lockup in 1992, forcing it to be shut down by the government. Now, the land has been reborn as **Parque da Juventude** (Avenida Zaki Narchi 1309, Carandiru, 2251 2706). Ten courts, including two tennis courts, were built in the huge complex that used to be the prison. Skaters, cyclists and rollerbladders are welcome. Green areas are used for jogging and walking, and you don't even have to head back to a cell after the recreation period ends.

King of the Road

In Brazil, Ayrton Senna has permanent pole position.

Football is generally considered the be-all and end-all of sporting passion in Brazil, but it will never lap Formula 1 racing. *Milhões* of *corações* still get revved up over the career of racing legend **Ayrton Senna**, who died 15 years ago, on 1 May 1994, when his car veered off the Imola track during the San Marino Gran Prix, hitting the concrete wall at the Tamburello corner to the horror of millions watching on television.

Senna won three world championships and 41 grand prix races, took 65 pole positions and made 162 grand prix starts in his ten year career; a track success that earned him a firm spot in the Formula 1 Hall of Fame.

Love for Senna goes well beyond the numbers, though. It was his intense approach to success, and the velocity at which he lived his life both on and off the track that to this day make him a hugely popular figure both in the world of racing in general and in his native land.

Senna's intensity often led to controversy. His talent was so great that anything less than victory was intolerable to him. He waged an infamous battle with rival and teammate Alain Prost that ultimately led Senna to take out Prost's car during the first turn of a 1990 title-winning race (he was also exacting revenge for a similar move Prost had made the year before in winning the title).

It was, however, in his relationship with himself that Senna's intensity reached its most extreme. He related that during the 1988 Monaco Grand Prix qualifying event, he could not keep himself from going faster and faster even though he had the pole position, and his pushing against the limits of consciousness frightened him into pulling off the track. 'Every time I push, I find something more, again and again,' Senna said.

Senna's ability to manoeuvre around tight corners extended beyond the world of Formula 1; he had an acute understanding of the double-edged sword that defines many elements of Brazilian society. Born into a wealthy São Paulo family, shortly before his death Senna began talking to his relatives about the idea of creating an organisation for underprivileged Brazilians. The **Instituto Ayrton Senna** (http://senna.globo.com), run by his sister Viviane, was established a few months after his death, and 100 per cent of royalties from *Senninha* – Senna's comic book and cartoon character – and from licencing of his image, go to the Institute's mission. Since 1994 Instituto Ayrton Senna has provided help to more than 11 million Brazilian children, educated more than 500,000 teachers and donated more than R$203 million to social programmes in 26 Brazilian states. In 2009, the Institute is supporting 2,188,921 children in 1127 Brazilian cities.

Senna was fond of responding to critics and controversy by saying, 'I am Senna', but his mercurial nature was ultimately less a hindrance than a help in creating a legacy of worldwide respect. Even after their heated feud, Alain Prost helped carry the coffin at Senna's state funeral. Current British champion Lewis Hamilton idolised Senna, shed tears the day of his death, and now wears a crash helmet painted in Senna's signature yellow.

Visitor to São Paulo travel down the road now named after Senna, heading from Guarulhos airport to the city centre. Fans can also pay their respects at the Cemiterio do Morumbi, not far from the city's famous Interlagos track, where today's Formula 1 stars like Hamilton, and Brazilians Rubens Barrichello and Felipe Massa, battle for the pole and podium.

There is a modest bronze plaque marking Senna's grave: 'Ayrton Senna da Silva 21.3.1960 – 1.5.94. *Nada pode me separar do amor de Deus.*' (Nothing can separate me from the love of God).

Or from the love of his fellow *Brasileiros*.

Praça Esther Mesquito. *See p210.*

Brigadeiro. **Open** 6am-11pm Mon-Fri; 10am-4pm Sat, Sun. **Credit** MC, V. **Map** p245 M9.
A comprehensive sports club located at the heart of Avenida Paulista, this gym also has a Pilates studio and yoga classes.
Other locations throughout the city.

Horse-riding

If you're looking to saddle up while in the city, then head to **Parque da Água Branca**, which has a horse-riding school, as well as a small zoo.

Parque da Água Branca
Avenida Francisco Matarazzo 455, Água Branca (3673 0978). Metrô Barra Funda. **Open** 6am-6pm Mon-Sun. **Map** p242 I2.

Pilates

Galeria Pilates
Rua Natingui 1536, Pinheiros (3476 0279/ www.galeriapilates.com.br). **Open** 8am-9pm Mon-Fri. **Credit** MC, V. **Map** p248 D7.

Pilates Studio
Avenida Cidade Jardim 411, Itaim Bibi (3078 1381/www.pilates.com.br). **Open** 7am-9pm Mon-Fri; 8am-12pm Sat. **Credit** MC, V. **Map** p249 F12.

Sky-diving

The Brazilian sky-diving capital is just an hour's drive from São Paulo. The city of Boituva has what is considered to be the perfect 'drop zone' for the sport, and was host for the World Skydiving Championships in 2004. You won't find a better place to skydive in South America, and maybe even the world. For your winged chariot and a shove out the open aeroplane door, try **Páraquedismo Boituva** (15 3263 1645/ www.boituvaparaquedismo.com.br).

Yoga

There are as many places to strengthen and stretch those muscles in São Paulo as there are yoga positions. The following also offer alternative therapies.

Espaço Girassol
Rua Girassol 602, Vila Madalena (2925 9000/ www.espacogirassol.com). Metrô Vila Madalena. **Open** 10am-9pm Mon-Fri; 9.30am-5pm Sat. **Credit** MC, V. **Map** p249 E7.

Prema Yoga
Rua Maria Figueiredo 189, Cerqueira César (3283 0884/www.premayoga.com.br). Metrô Brigadeiro. **Open** 7am-10pm Mon-Fri. **Credit** MC, V. **Map** p245 M9.

INSIDE TRACK
URBAN TREKKING

The city's parks are a great place for an afternoon stretch of the legs, yet some offer more than simply a walk around a man-made lake with a stop to feed the ducks. **Parque da Cantareira** (*see p58*) has a nine-kilometre trail around the biggest urban forest in the country. It takes a whole day to complete and you can hike it on your own, but if you want to take a guide then contact **Ecoturismo Brasil** (3903 0277, www.ecoturismobrasil.com.br).

Opened in 1939, **Parque da Aclimação** (Rua Muniz de Souza 1119, 5573 4180) has a huge lake and a pleasant tree-lined track around the water. It's a great walk even on busy weekends, when live music often accompanies your steps. It's open 5am to 8pm daily.

Escapes & Excursions

Embu das Artes. *See pp214-215.*

Escapes

It's all fun and games on São Paulo's beaches.

São Paulo may not be associated with days spent on the beach or wandering down cobblestoned remnants from the colonial era, but it's closer than the traveller might think to sun, sand and signs of times gone by, all providing quick relief from an overwhelming city. Within an hour's ride is a 16th-century town that conjures up the atmosphere of the earliest landowners and pioneering Jesuits. Within a few hours are gorgeous tropical getaways with ample opportunities for outdoor pursuits: from trekking in the rainforest above the ocean and showering in waterfalls to surfing, or just lazing on the beach with a caipirinha. São Paulo can be too much sometimes, so do as Paulistanos do, and sneak off to one of a number of hideaways within easy reach of the city.

EMBU DAS ARTES

São Paulo is an overnight bus trip away from some of Brazil's colonial gem cities, but if 12 to 16 hours in a semi-reclining double-decker seat watching bad Hollywood DVDs with the jokes cracked in dubbed Portuguese is not your idea of a holiday, then consider Embu das Artes, less than one hour from the city. While not a colonial masterpiece like Ouro Preto, Embu offers a quick country escape that can be condensed into half a Sunday. Well-to-do Paulistanos make the journey with regularity to reset the urban stress meter. Set in verdant rainforest hills, even the ride here will display more green than a full week in São Paulo. If your Brazilian itinerary includes the famous colonial cities, Embu das Artes may not live up to expectations; but otherwise, it could be your best chance to experience a little pre-20th century Brazil – something you won't find much evidence of in São Paulo.

This *aldeia* (village) dates back to the 1550s, and its original name, M'Boy, signified 'great snake' in the Tupi-Guarani language of the native Indians. In 1624, the land was donated to the Jesuits so that they could found a church; they later established a convent which is now the **Museu de Arte Sacra**.

The Feira de Arte e Artesanato (9am-6pm) takes over the streets of the *centro historico* and the main plaza, the Largo 21 de Abril, most days, though weekends are definitely the best time to go, as it's a much larger affair on Saturdays and Sundays. Crafts from jewellery to porcelain to musical instruments, and a wide range of decorative arts on display that make excellent gifts. It began in 1969, and now, in addition to stalls, there are many artists' studios and shops set in historic buildings that offer crafts, artisanal cachaças and sweet liqueurs in a large range of flavours.

INSIDE TRACK
EMBU'S ANGEL OF DEATH

One name linked with Embu is that of **Josef Mengele**. Dr Mengele, notorious for carrying genetic experiments using twins at Auschwitz during World War II, fled to South America in 1949, dying in an Embu swimming accident in 1979. He was buried there under his assumed name of Wolfgang Gerhard, but the body was later exhumed and was proved to be his.

Rumours have been rife that the high rate of twins born in the southern Brazilian town of Candido Godoi (one in every five pregnancies, against an average of one in every 80) is somehow connected with Mengele's visits there in the 1960s. However, geneticists insist that genetic isolation and inbreeding are more plausible explanations.

The **Museu de Arte Sacra dos Jesuitas** (Largo dos Jesuitas 67, 4704 2654, closed Mon), is a Jesuit complex that dates back to the 17th century. The **Centro Cultural Embu das Artes** (Largo 21 de Abril 29, 4781 4462) has three exhibition rooms and is located on the main plaza. The **Museu do Indio** (Rua da Matriz 54, 4704 3278, closed Mon) is a little beyond the main square, on the side opposite to the Centro Cultural.

Where to eat & drink

Embu's historic centre has no shortage of restaurants and bars. **Emporio São Pedro** (Viela das Lavadeiras 28 and 75, 4781 2797) is on a tiny side street off Rua Siqueira Campos. A colonial edifice with a pretty garden, it now serves as an emporium of antiques as well as as a restaurant. The place has a high-end menu with dishes from R$34 to R$58, or a complete tasting menu for $R110. It's open Wednesday to Sunday from 10am to 6pm.

If you're more in the mood for the pub experience and a simpler, albeit eclectic, menu, **O Garimpo** (Rua da Matriz 136, 4704 6344, www.ogarimpo.com, R$20-$48) offers something of a Hard-Rock-Café-meets-House-of-Blues vibe. Its **Bar Graf Zeppelin** pours a selection of imported German and Brazilian premium draughts. It's open from 11.30am to 10pm daily, with evening music – anything from Pink Floyd and Bee Gees cover bands to Dixieland jazz – and lunchtime shows (1-4.30pm) on weekends.

Getting there

Embu is less than an hour from the city. The best route is highway BR 116, which can be accessed from Marginal Pinheiros, Rodovia Raposo Tavares or Avenida Francisco Morato. On BR116, you can take Km 279 or Km 282 to Embu. Buses run from the city's Tietê bus station (Rodoviaria do Tietê), which is linked to Tietê metrô stop. The buses, marked 'Embu/Engenho Velho', leave from Avenida Cruzeira do Sul, which is below the main ramp that connects the metrô stop to the interior of the bus terminal. There are one or two services an hour. You can also catch a bus from the neighbourhood of Pinheiros, at the Largo da Batata, run by the Soamin bus company and with the route also marked 'Embu Engenho'.

Tourist information

Centro de Atendimento ao Turista
Largo de Abril 21 s/n, (4704 6565). **Open** 9am-5.30pm Mon-Fri; 9am-6pm Sat, Sun. A map of the town and its sites of interest, which will take all of three minutes to master, is available.

GUARUJA

Just 86 kilometres from São Paulo is the attractive resort town of Guaruja. Previously known as the island of Santo Amaro, it was used as a hiding place for contraband slaves until the mid 19th century. In 1892, it was turned into a bathing room for well-to-do Paulistanos, but the construction of a motorway linking the island with the mainland created an unfettered explosion in tourism, buildings and new settlers in the 1970s and '80s. This put a huge strain on the town's infrastructure and created favelas on the outskirts.

The town stretches along Pitangueiras beach, where its development began; behind it are lots of shops, hotels, restaurants and private accommodation. This huge stretch of beach becomes Enseada beach, the largest one in Guaruja, full of hotels and apartments and the main area for going out at night. Bars and restaurants take over the beachfront as well as the beach itself. The beach ends at the promontory of Sorocotuba Hill where the land curves inward again. Visitors with a car can drive near to the beautiful little beach appropriately called Eden. You must park your car and follow a trail down through the forest, but the waters are crystalline, and it's worth it simply to escape the crowds. After that come the attractive Pernambuco and Perequê beaches, well known for their restaurants serving fantastically fresh fish and seafood.

Guaruja boasts the largest aquarium in Latin America – **Acqua Mundo** (Avenida Miguel Stefano 2001, Praia da Enseada, 13 3398 3000, www.acquamundo.com.br, closed Mon) – with over 30 tanks and 700 different species of fish and aquatic animals, such as sharks, penguins and seahorses. Admission ranges from R$12 to R$20, or R$52 for a family of four. Watersports such as surfing, windsurfing and jet-skiing are very popular here. Check out www.ondas.com.br for further information.

Where to stay

There is plenty of accommodation in Guaruja catering to all budgets, from hotels to apartments for rent; there's even a campsite.

For a luxurious stay, check into the five-star **Hotel Sofitel Jequitimar** (Avenida Marjory da Silva Prado 1100, Praia de Pernambuco, 13 2104 2000, www.accorhotels.com, doubles R$735-R$1000). For a mid-range option, try the **Delphin Hotel** (Avenida Miguel Estefano 1295, Praia da Enseada, 13 3797 6000, www.delphinhotel.com.br, doubles R$220-$360) or **Ferraretto Guarujá Hotel** (Rua Mário Ribeiro 564,

Centro, 13 3023 6600, www.ferraretto hotel.com.br, doubles R$140-$160). For a cheap and cheerful *pousada*, try **Pousada Solar da Ilha** (Rua José da Silva Figueiredo 144, Praia da Enseada, 13 3351 8664, www.solarda ilha.com.br, doubles R$110-$150), and for camping, head to **Pousada e Camping** (Avenida Santa Maria 900, Praia Enseada, 13 3355 3977, www.guia guaruja.com.br/pousadaecamping).

Where to eat & drink

On the roads behind *praias* (beaches) Pitangueiras and Enseada are plenty of bars and restaurants to suit all tastes and pockets. A good place at which to watch the world go by and eat table snacks or a pizza *rodizio* (all you can eat) is **Boteco Avelino's** (Avenida Leomil 772, Pitangueiras, 13 3355 6798). For those hankering after Asian food, there's a Thai place on the beachfront, **Thai Restaurant** (Avenida Miguel Stefano 1001, Enseada, 13 3389 4000).

For clubs during high season, try the 3,000-capacity **Sirena de Guaruja** (Avenida Miguel Stéfano 1001, Enseada, 13 3885 5511). Or dance to traditional *axé* and reggae at **Perequê Praia Show** (Rodoviaria Guarujá-Bertioga in Perequê, 13 3353 5353), or at Phoenix (Avenida Miguel Stefano 1087, Enseada, 13 3355 4192), a 2,000-square-metre club with three rooms and five bars.

Tourist information

Get clued in about Guaruja at Avenida Marechal Deodoro da Fonseca 723 in Pitangueiras (13 3344 4600, www.visit eguaruja. com). It's open from 9am-5pm daily.

Getting there

By car from São Paulo, get on to the motorway Anchieta-Imigrantes, and after the mountain descent, exit on Rodovia Piacagueira-Guaruja.

If travelling by bus, take a direct service from Jabaquara Bus Station (*see p224*), or from the Tietê Bus Station to Santos, from where you can take the ferry across.

ILHABELA

Safe, clean and gorgeous, Ilhabela is a favourite island hideaway for Paulistanos.

For a long time, people struggled to find a moniker suitable to this delightful morsel of nature. And we're not speaking metaphorically. Ilhabela means 'beautiful island', but the name was only settled on in 1944. Before that, it spent six years as Formosa (gorgeous), and before that, for more than a century, it was known as Villa Bella da Princeza (the princess's beautiful town). When Amerigo Vespucci came through back in 1502, he called it the Island of Saint Sebastian (for the Catholic saint day on which he 'discovered' it), and the archipelago's main island is still officially Ilha de São Sebastião (though everyone calls it Ilhabela). Stepping back even further, the place's original residents, the Tupinamba people, called their home Ciribai, or 'tranquil place'.

Words such as 'tranquillity', 'beauty' and 'serenity' often spring to mind on trips to the island; suffice to say, the place is rather pretty but very popular as a result. Currently, Ilhabela hosts some 20,000 year-round residents, but upwards of 100,000 tourists pass through during the summer months. Its key attractions – the beaches – are some of the safest and the cleanest along the coast of either Rio or São Paulo states,

and the 346-kilometre **Parque Estadual de Ilhabela** (Ilhabela State Park), still covers 83 per cent of the island, thanks to laws limiting further development. Wildlife enthusiasts come here to spot otters, monkeys, lizards, wild cats and the island's 800 species of birds, while divers head to Ilhabela for the marine life and the array of undersea shipwrecks. Also on offer are watersports, jungle hikes, 400 waterfalls, boat and jeep excursions and, of course, simply lying back on beaches.

During the peak summer months and on Brazilian holidays, the island's strips of sand can be packed, but go any other time of year, and you'll have all the space you could want, even on the most popular beaches.

Tourist information

Upon arrival you will pass the **Tourist Information Office**, just past the ferry terminal (Avenida Princesa Isabel 3249, 12 3895 1041, www.visitilhabela.com.br, closed Tue). It's worth stopping in at to pick up a map and has a well-stocked array of flyers for restaurants, pousadas and tour agencies. The office's website also offers some good information and a hotel reservation service that allows you to check which hotels are available for the dates you wish to travel – useful in the busy summer months.

The best online English source for information about the island's wildlife, greenery, political past, pirate shenanigans and ways to give back to its environment is the somewhat outdated www.ilhabela.org, an NGO dedicated to protecting the island's natural heritage. Another good source for a wide range of practical tourist information is www.ilhabela.com.br.

Where to stay

Lodging options on Ilhabela are never great value compared to elsewhere in the state, and from mid December to the end of February and for the month of July, prices are much higher, going absolutely crazy around the new year and Carnival. During high season, minimum stays of up to five days are expected. Also, quoted prices generally do not include the ten per cent service tax tacked on to the final bill.

For luxury, head to the **Hotel Itapemar**, with spectacular suites overlooking the coast (Avenida Pedro Paula de Moraes 341, 12 3896-1329, www.itapemar.com.br, double rooms R$260-$550). Ornate nautical decor can be found at the **Pousada do Capitão** (Avenida Almirante Tamandare 272, 12 3896 2253, www.pousadado capitao.com.br, doubles R$193-$233). A relaxing, decent-value option immersed in plant life is the **Pousada Tamara** (Rua Jacob Eduardo Toedli 163, 12 3896 2543 or 3896 2630, www.pousada-tamara.com.br, doubles R$99-$129). The cheapest option is, of course, to camp; a great spot in front of a beach (Praia Grande) with its own waterfall can be found at **Camping Canto Grande** (Avenida Riachuelo 5638, 12 3894 1506/1713, www.cantogrande.com.br, R$25 per person, $R5 per vehicle).

Where to eat & drink

For excellent and reasonably priced seafood on the beach with jovial service, it's hard to beat **Pescador Bar** on Praia das Cabras (Avenida Brasil 1701, 12 3894 1576, burgers from R$6, fish courses R$18-R$34). For a more upscale lounge atmosphere overlooking the water, head to **Kyox** (Avenida Princesa Isabel 245, 12 3896 1645, www.captains.com.br, burgers from R$9, Italian and Japanese main courses R$28-R$47). Making its mainly Paulistano clientele feel right at home, Ilhabela has a lot of Japanese dining options; a good one is **Tori** (Avenida Pedro Paula de Moraes 1030, 12 3896 1521, mains R$30-$38).

For laid-back electronica in an attractive space with a young and touristy beach vibe, head to **Creoula** (Avenida Força Expedicionária Brasileira 31, 12 3896 3403, www.creoula.com.br), which is free every day except Saturday (R$25).

Scuba diving

A combination of unusual conditions has provided Ilhabela with Brazil's largest undersea ship junkyard, which brings in curious divers from all over the world. Among the reasons for all the nautical carnage are the high levels of magnetite around Ilhabela, which has confused sailors' compasses for centuries. Strong winds to the south of the island and sharp submarine rock outcroppings are additional factors.

There's also a great variety of marine life thanks, in part, to fishing restrictions, and those diving near Búzios Island may even spot dolphins or whales. Finally, and most intriguingly, there's Ilhabela's history as an early pirate hideout (it was apparently an ideal place to lie in wait and ambush passing ships), ensuring tales of hidden sunken treasures.

Tours and daily courses are provided by **Narwhal** (Avenida Princesa Isabel 170, 12 3896 3807, narwhal.com.br), which also runs a pousada catering to divers' needs. It has many offices in São Paulo to help you organise your trip beforehand.

INSIDE TRACK
BORRACHUDOS

The downside to Ilhabela's clean water are the *borrachudos* (sometimes known as black flies in English). These teensy-weensy vampirish horrors are particularly attracted to unpolluted waterways. *Borrachudos* fly low to the ground and make much less noise and cause less tactile sensation than mosquitoes as they suck your blood, leaving large itchy welts. The best prevention is to cover exposed skin and pick up an insect repellent cream (*creme repelente*) at a pharmacy before your trip.

Beaches

Among the beaches easily accessible by road (whether by car, bike or public bus), the best are generally those on the southwestern side of the island. The **Praia da Feiticeira** is clean and gorgeous; the **Praia do Curral** is similarly wonderful, and offers kayak rentals, boating excursions, free public bathrooms and a shower, plus there's a stand serving quite possibly the island's best *pasteis* (fried snacks – try the shrimp). The **Praia Pedras Miúdas**, as the name suggests (if you speak Portuguese), has pebbles as you step further out, but its shallow areas and calm waters make it very popular for those with young children.

Those who want to suffer a bit to earn their beach paradise can hike or bike to the **Praia do Jabaquara** in the north or take a boat or an

Embu das Artes. *See p214.*

overland 4x4 to the **Castelhanos**, a heavenly two-kilometre expanse where white sand meets big waves. Several agencies organise these day-long excursions, including **Maremar Turismo** (Avenida São João 574, 12 3896 1418/2443, www.maremar.tur.br).

Getting there

The only bus company with service from São Paulo to São Sebastião (dropping you right next to the ferry to Ilhabela) is **Litorânea** (11 3775 3861, www.litoranea.com.br), with eight departures daily from the Tietê Terminal. The trip takes three and an half hours in good traffic conditions, and a one-way ticket costs R$41.

The ferry between São Sebastião and Ilhabela runs 24 hours and leaves every 20 minutes or so. Pedestrians and cyclists cross for free. A round trip for a car on weekdays is R$12; on weekends, it's R$17. Travellers in cars may want to jump the queues (particularly on summer weekend rush times) by making a reservation at 3358 2743 or 3358 3088, though they'll pay more than five times the normal fee for the privilege.

PARANAPIACABA

Paranapiacaba was built by the British in the late 19th century as a control centre for the São Paulo Railway as well as to house its workers, allowing people and goods to be transported to and from São Paulo and the port of Santos. Considered an engineering miracle due to the steep escarpment of the Serra do Mar to the coast, the railway to Santos is no longer in operation. But it's a fascinating historical town to visit, and the original workers cottages, the locomotive sheds and the funicular cable station are very well preserved.

Take a trip on the **Maria-Fumaça steam train** (R$5), an enjoyable 20-minute ride through the foothills of the Serra do Mar, and visit the **Funicular Museum**, full of old British railway paraphernalia. Wander around **Castelinho** (R$2), the well-preserved Victorian-style house of the chief British engineer. Now home to the **Centro Preservação da Historia de Paranapiacaba**, it displays old maps and photographs of the railway's early years, and offers lovely views from its hill-top position.

The town has its own mini Big Ben, and, although shrouded in fog on many afternoons, on clear days the views are stunning; in fact, in Tupi-Guarani, the name means 'from where you can see the sea'. Many visitors come here to hike in the **Parque Estadual da Serra do Mar** (*see right*) a beautifully preserved Mata Atlântica noted for its orchids and bromeliads, as well as a variety of birds and

attractive waterfalls. Hikes must be done with a guide; remember to bring food, drink and sturdy footwear, and be aware that the weather here is changeable. There are many companies offering walking tours and adventure sports in the town, and several pousadas for those interested in staying longer. Call **Paranapiacaba Tourist Information Centre** on 11 4439 0237 (English is spoken).

Getting there

By train Take the CPTM Train Line 10 at Luz Station to Rio Grande Da Serra (R$2,55/1hr).
By bus Take the AOL 424 to Paranapiacaba (R$2,50/20minutes).

UBATUBA

Only five per cent of Brazil's original Atlantic Forest has been preserved in the 500-plus years since the Portuguese arrival, but going to **Vale do Paraíba**, an untouched forest, is a revelation to those who travel down Tamoios road. The mountains announce the wild beauty of this place, but it is not until you reach the Rio-Santos road that you realise how magnificent it is to be so close to nature. Ubatuba is not just a city on the beach. It is one of the best natural areas in Brazil. About 80 per cent of its original rainforest is preserved. It is so impressive that the government turned the wild area into the **State Park of Serra do Mar**.

The blue sea is cut by a 90-kilometre coast with lots of small bays, sometimes so small that the beach is deserted. There are over 70 different beaches in the area, and they are mostly easy to access by car from the Rio-Santos road, though some of them are not easy to find. The northern side of the city has more wild beaches, with lots of vegetation, but the tourism services are a let-down. *Pousadas* here allow their customers to taste a bit of the natural style of living.

Paranapiacaba. *See p219.*

The southern side is focused on big resorts and high-class housing.

But the city is not just about nature. The name Ubatuba means 'lots of boats' in Tupi-guarani, the language of Tupinambás, the Indian tribe that lived in the region in the 16th century. They fought for their land against the Portuguese until a peace agreement was reached in 1563. By 1637, Ubatuba was considered a village and began to base its economy on sugarcane, making sugar and cachaça for the region of Minas Gerais. What once was a hard-to-bypass path through Vale do Paraíba is now the Oswald Cruz road that connects Ubatuba to Taubaté. But that road wasn't there until 1932. Before that, the city endured difficult times trying to get its economy organised and did not meet with much success. The centre was almost abandoned, and the city lost most of its historical architecture. The region had always been very isolated, and that's the reason why 80 per cent of its natural forest is untouced. It was not until 1972 that Ubatuba started to see real progress, starting to reach its potential as a tourist haven with the construction of the Rio-Santos road.

Things have changed a lot since then. Ubatuba's centre has been revitalised, and it now sports a fantastic dining area, with many restaurants serving local cuisine based on seafood. São Sebastião, Ilhabela, Bertioga, Caraguatatuba and Ubatuba have all become top places for Reveillon (New Year's Eve), summer vacation and long weekends. Ubatuba was especially fortunate; by being the last city on the state coast, it didn't succumb to the ugly, development fate of many other major tourist destinations. There was development but at a slow pace, having an overall smaller effect on

nature than it did in cities like Bertioga and Caraguatatuba. Additionally, Ubatuba is adjacent to Parati on the Rio de Janeiro border, which is great for tourists who want to spend a day in the sedate colonial village of Parati and come back to the cozy pousadas of Ubatuba.

How to get there

By car Take Rodovia Ayrton Senna/Carvalho Pinto until São José dos Campos (70 minutes); Rodovia dos Tamoios to Caraguatatuba (50 minutes), or go through Rodovia Rio-Santos, going north to Ubatuba (40 minutes). Alternatively, you can take Rodovia Ayrton Senna/Carvalho Pinto or Via Dutra until Taubaté (1hr 50 minutes) or Rodovia Oswaldo Cruz to Ubatuba (1hr). The latter road gets steep towards the end, so double check your brakes before you go.

By bus From Tietê Terminal (Metrô Portuguesa-Tietê), go to Litorânea. The company has daily buses to Ubatuba for R$56. Don't forget: the phone code for Ubatuba is 12.

Sightseeing

Aquário de Ubatuba

Rua Guarani 859, Itaguá (3832 1382/ www.aquariodeubatuba.com.br). **Open** 10am-8pm Mon, Tue, Thu, Sun; 10am-10pm Fri-Sat. **Admission** R$14; R$7-R$13 reductions; free under-5s.
A private facility created by oceanographers who work in the region, this complex has one of the biggest salt-water tanks in the country, with 80,000

litres of water. Here it's possible to find lots of local and foreign species, like seahorses, morays, sharks, batfishes, groupers and globefishes. There's a room where people can touch invertebrates like sea cucumber or starfishes. An area for Magellan penguins opened in 2009.

Ilha Anchieta

The biggest island in town has its own private park. Boats from Saco da Ribeira take tourists to see three of the island beaches: Engenho, Palmas and Presidio. A prison projected by Ramos de Azevedo was active until 1955, and it's still possible to visit the cells and headquarters.

Parque Estadual da Serra do Mar

Núcleo Picinguaba, BR 101 km 08. **Open** 9am-5pm Mon-Sun. **Admission** free.
The biggest state park in São Paulo, with over 300,000 hectares, has its most famous sight, the Núcleo Picinguaba, in Ubatuba. Declared a park in 1977, this area remains almost intact and some of the old farm lots have already returned to their wild form. In the park, professionals from many fields work in botanical and cultural preservation. There are five beaches within the park area (Brava da Almada, da Fazenda, Picinguaba, Brava de Camburi and Camburi), and they are the final five before arriving in Parati. Two fishing villages are situated here. Some sights within the forest, like Sertão de Picinguaba, can be explored with a local guide. This area has a number of trails with different levels of difficulty. Jatobá, the nearest, starts at Casa da Farinha, a sugar and alcohol factory made in the 19th century, retrofitted by the State Park authorities and now used as a manioc meal factory. The Jatobá trail takes off to Poço da Rasa, and is a three-hour walk. If you're really prepared, you can try getting to Morro do Corisco. It's a nine-hour, one-way trip that ends in Serra da Bocaina, in Parati. You can check into one of the hotels or *pousadas* on the Picinguaba or Almada beaches.

Projeto TAMAR

Rua Antonio Atanázio 273, Itaguá (3832 6202/www.tamar.org.br). **Open** 10am-6pm Mon, Tue, Thu, Sun; 10am-8pm Fri, Sat; closed on Wed. **Admission** R$6; free over-65s and children under 1.2m. **Credit** MC.
This sanctuary was created in 1980 to protect ocean turtles and their environs. TAMAR keeps its urban base in Ubatuba (they have more than 20 along the coast), and it's one of the important research centres.

Ruínas da Lagoinha – Praia da Lagoinha

BR 101, km 72 to Caraguatatuba
Going north on Rio-Santos, close to km 72, you will find a small road that goes 500 metres inside the forest. There, the thick walls of an old aqueduct are one of the few historical sights in Ubatuba. The

aqueduct was built at the beginning of the 19th century and was part of a sugar and cachaça factory. The aqueduct harks back to an old rich Ubatuba, when the city had an active port and was an important part of the state's revenue. The surrounding trails lead to a waterfall nearby.

Hotels

Casa do Sol e da Lua (Rua do Refúgio do Corsário 580, BR 101 to Parati, Km 67.5, Praia da Fortaleza, 3848 9412, www.acasadosole dalua. com.br, doubles R$160-R$280) is a pousada right on Fortaleza beach, on the south side of the peninsula, so guests are ten steps away from the sea. Fortaleza is well located and accessible by a 7-kilometre road out of praia Dura. The beach has a trail that leads to Cedro and Bonete, two of the best beaches in Ubatuba. Having only seven rooms, the owners pamper guests with surprise drinks and snacks. There's a DVD room and a library.

Casa Milá (BR 101 km 13 to Parati, Praia da Almada, 3832 9021, www.casamila.com.br, doubles R$190) is about 150 metres above sea level. The downside of it is that you are only one kilometre away from Almada, the thin white-sand beach on the north side of town. The upside: the view from this height is simply breathtaking. The owners are architects and are always making improvements to the house. As it's almost on the border with Rio de Janeiro state, a one-day trip to Parati is a must.

The wild waves, the quiet river on the side and the mangrove that is a part of the hotel grounds make **Itamambuca Eco Resort** (BR 101 to Parati, KM 36, Itamambuca, 3834 3000, www.itamambuca. com.br, doubles R$418-R$538) special. Exotic birds, lizards and even blue crabs can be found. It was built on the site of a campsite that's still in use. Campers can use the pool and restaurants from the resort.

A small resort on an easily accessible beach, **Pousada Maranduba** (Avenida Marginal 899, Praia de Maranduba, 3849 8378, www.pousada maranduba.com.br, doubles R$300-R$ 400), on the south side, is a good option for more urban tourists. The Rio-Santos road offers full access to the beach, which means it has infrastructure and can get very crowded on summer weekends. The rooms hold up to four people, making them ideal for families. Rates include dinner.

The charming all-inclusive **Pousada Picinguaba** hotel (Rua G 130, BR 101 km 7 to Parati, Vila Picinguaba, 3836 9105, www.picinguaba.com, R$250-R$300) is located on Praia de Picinguaba, an untouched fishing village. There are no signs on the grounds, as Emmanuel Rengade, the French owner, demands a private environment for his guests. There's also a house 20 minutes from the hotel that offers even more privacy. Rates include a fantastic breakfast and dinner based on *caiçara* food (mostly fish with bananas). TV, internet and air-conditioning are not available, as this is a place to forget you ever had a more frantic life, but you can watch movies in the home-cinema room.

Restaurants

Peixe com Banana (Rua Guarani 255, Praia do Cruzeiro, 3832 1712, mains R$100 for two, with drink and service) takes its name (fish with bananas) from the dish of the house. Green bananas are cooked in an iron pan – which makes them look blue – then mixed with fish and Brazilian spices. Located on Cruzeiro beach downtown, this is a good option for dinner.
Solar das Águas Cantantes (Estrada do Saco da Ribeira s/n, Praia do Lázaro, 3842 0178, www.solardasaguascantantes.com.br, closed Tue mains R$100 meal for two, with drink and service) has a family vibe which has made it one of the most popular places here for over 25 years. Located inside a hotel on Lazaro beach on the south side, it serves seafood and great moquecas (fish or shrimp stew).

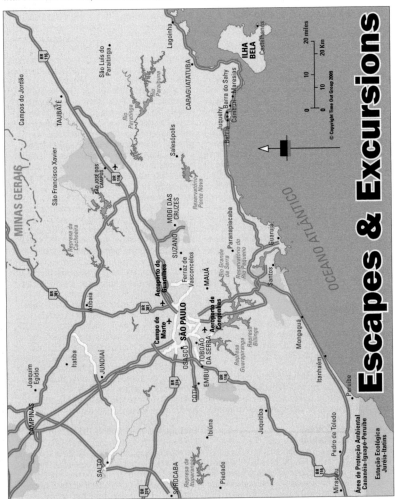

Escapes & Excursions

Directory

Getting Around

ARRIVING & LEAVING

By air

Guarulhos International Airport (GRU; 6445 2945, www.infraero.gov.br), also known as Cumbica, is São Paulo's major international airport. GRU is located 40 kilometres (25 miles) from the city centre and is served by major domestic and international airlines. Guaracoop (6445 7070, www.radiotaxiazulebranco.com.br) runs a taxi service from outside the arrival area. Rates are fixed and range from R$75 to R$100 depending on the neighbourhood you are going to. For R$30 there is also an airport shuttle bus (3775 3861, www.airportbusservice.com.br) that stops in São Paulo's central neighbourhoods, at major hotels, and at the Tietê bus terminal (*metrô* access). The most budget-friendly (and time-consuming) option is to take a local bus (Bus 25; R$2.30).

São Paulo's other major airport, **Congonhas** (CGH; 5090 9000), serves domestic flights and is just eight kilometres (five miles) from the city centre. Your transportation options from CGH are the same as above: taxi (R$30-$40), shuttle bus (R$30), or public transport (875A, 875M; R$2.30). Deciding which to take will depend on your budget, destination and the amount of baggage you are carrying.

Ninety-nine kilometres (62 miles) outside São Paulo, near Campinas, is **Viracopos-Campinas** airport (3725 5000). Its code is VCP or CPQ. The airport is mostly used for cargo transport, but a new airline, Azul (3003 2985, http://viajemais.voeazul.com.br), has started running passenger flights from here to many Brazilian cities.

The website www.toandfrom theairport.com provides detailed information about getting to and from the airports. The general code for the airports serving São Paulo is SAO.

Major airlines

Aerolineas Argentinas *0800 707 3313/www.aerolineas.com.* **Air Canada** *3254 6600/ www.aircanada.ca.*

Air France *0800 888 9955/ www.airfrance.com.* **American Airlines** *4502 4000/ www.aa.com.* **British Airways** *4004 4440/ www.britishairways.com.* **COPA** *0800 771 2672/ www.copaair.com.* **Gol** *0800 280 0465/ www.voegol.com.* **Iberia** *3218 7130/www.iberia.com* **TAM** *0800 570 5700/ www.tam.com.* **United Airlines** *1800 538 2929/ www.united.com.*

By bus

There are three main bus terminals in São Paulo, all connected by *metrô*. The largest bus station is **Rodoviária do Tietê** (Avenida Cruzeiro do Sul 1800, 3235 0322), which serves international destinations and most destinations to the north. This is the station you are most likely to visit if you take any long-distance buses in Brazil. Some buses going to southern and south-western destinations leave from **Rodoviária da Barra Funda** (Rua Maria de Andrade 664, 3392 2110), as well as from **Rodoviária de Jabaquara** (Rua dos Jequitibás, 5012 2256). Buses leaving from the latter also serve coastal cities like Santos and Guarujá.

Unfortunately, there is no centrally organised website listing times and routes of domestic and international buses. SOCIOCAM (www.sociocam.com.br), however, allows users to search which companies serve which destinations; and many private bus companies operate their own websites. These sites can be useful for collecting information; but without a CPF (Brazilian social security number) you will probably be unable to make a purchase online. Instead, tickets can be bought at the ticket window in the bus station. Tickets do sell out, especially in the summer (Dec-Feb) and during holidays, so it is a good idea to purchase in advance.

Some of the main bus operating companies include: **Expresso Brasileiro** (6221 0155, www. expressobrasileiro.com); **Gontijo** (2109 1333, www.gontijo.com.br); **Rápido Federal** (2142 7100,

www.rapidofederal.com.br) and **Cometa** (4004 9600, www.viacometa.com.br).

By rail

Brazil does not have a national rail network so, unlike in Europe, train travel is not an option for most destinations. São Paulo does have a commuter train network (CPTM). For more information, *see right.*

PUBLIC TRANSPORT

São Paulo's public transport system is extensive. The *metrô* is clean, safe and relatively straightforward. However, many trips will require at least one transfer, and some neighbourhoods aren't served at all. Luckily, where the *metrô* doesn't go, a bus usually does. Tourists will find the bus system rather confusing at first but it is a decent way to get around if you are up for the challenge.

Fares & tickets

If you are going to be in the city for a while and will be using public transport, it is worth getting a **Bilhete Único**. This electronic card allows for discounts and free transfers between buses, the *metrô*, and CPTM. For R$3.75 you can take one *metrô*/CPTM ride and up to three bus rides during a period of two hours. The Bilhete Único can be obtained at most *metrô* stations. In essence the card is free, but it must be charged with a minimum of R$20 to start.

Metrô

São Paulo's underground system is called the *metrô* (3291 7800, www.metro.sp.gov.br). There are four *metrô* lines with a fifth under construction. Each line is identified by a colour and a number and there are maps conveniently located in all *metrô* stations (*see p256*). A ride to any destination costs R$2.55, and tickets can be bought at the booth labelled *bilheteria*. Transfers are often necessary, but it is free to switch lines and trains run frequently. With some exceptions, the *metrô* operates from 4.30am to midnight.

City buses

São Paulo is served by a large network of buses regulated by **SPTrans** (0800 771 0118, www.sptrans.com.br). A 24-hour hotline, 156, provides information on buses around the city. Bus schedules and routes are published on the SPTrans website, which also has a route-mapping service. Google maps (http://maps.google. com) also allows you to map your route by inputing your start and end point, and also provides public transport directions for *metrô*, CPTM and buses. The front and side of each bus is labelled with street names indicating the bus's route; but if you don't know which bus to take your best bet is to ask other waiting passengers or the bus driver. Once on the bus you will have to pay R$2.30 to the *cobrador* (bus conductor) and pass through the turnstile. If you are not sure where to get off, ask the *cobrador* for help.

CPTM

The Companhia Paulista de Trens Metropolitanos (0800 055 0121, www.cptm.sp.gov.br) is essentially an extension of the *metrô* which serves farther-flung suburban destinations as well as parts of the city that the *metrô* does not reach. The tickets cost R$2.55, and transfers between the *metrô* and CPTM are allowed.

Helicopters

São Paulo state has one of the largest helicopter fleets in the world, with around 500 choppers (approximately half the number registered in all of Brazil), 300 of which serve São Paulo city alone.

Helimarte *2221 3200/ www.helimarte.com.br*
Master *2221 5498/ www.masterhelicopteros.com.br*
LCR *2221 2177/www.lcr.com.br*

TAXIS

São Paulo taxis are white with a green sign on the roof. The safest way to take a cab is to call a radio taxi or find one at a *ponto de taxi* (these are easy to find and are located throughout the city). *Taxis comum* (common taxis that are owner driven) can also be hailed on the street, though this is somewhat less secure. Taxis use electronic meters, and fares start

at R$4.55. Each additional kilometre costs R$1.80, and the charge for sitting in traffic is R$0.40/min. After 8pm and on weekends, the price will be 25 per cent higher. Most rides will cost between R$20 and R$50.

Coopertaxi *6941 2555.*
Delta Rádio Táxi *5572 6611.*
Ligue-Taxi *3866 3030.*

DRIVING

Car hire

Driving in São Paulo is not for the faint of heart – drivers are aggressive, and cars weave through the sprawling megalopolis with little semblance of order. Traffic and parking can be a nightmare, especially during peak hours. Though cars are a part of daily life for many Paulistanos, driving is not a necessity during a visit to São Paulo (and pedestrians will thank you for not contributing to the city's high levels of pollution).

However, rental firms will happily hand you a set of keys as long as you have a driving licence and a credit card. The minimum age required to rent a car is usually 25, though some companies will rent to 21-year-olds. Rental companies can be found in the airport and in the city centre.

Avis *3256 0411/www.avis.com.*
Budget *5093 6622/ www.budget.com.*
Hertz *3258 9384/www.hertz.com*
Thrifty *7818 8484/ www.thrifty.com.*
W Rent a Car *3089 4720/ www.wrentacar.com.br.*

Fuel stations

Ethanol is just as common in Brazil as traditional fuels, so make sure you know which fuel your hired car runs on.

Parking

During business hours, there is a per hour parking fee of R$2 on streets in commercial areas downtown, so be aware of signs and road markings. Booklets of tickets (*Cartão Zona Azul*) can be purchased at newsstands (ten tickets cost R$20). For each hour a car is parked a ticket must be filled out and placed visibly in the window. After business hours, many streets have self-employed guards who 'watch' your car for

you while it is parked. You don't have much choice in the matter, so to prevent your vehicle from being damaged it is best to pay these 'freelancers' R$2 for the service. Many restaurants and bars also offer a valet service for a small fee.

Rotating transit policy

From 7am to 10am and from 5pm to 8pm, there is a rotating transit policy in the expanded city centre, which is based on licence plate number and day of the week. On Mondays, licence plate numbers ending in one or two cannot circulate; on Tuesdays, numbers ending in three or four are prohibited; on Wednesdays, five or six; on Thursdays, seven or eight; and on Fridays nine or zero.

Night driving

Due to the risk of carjacking, it is legal (and recommended) to simply slow down, rather than stop, at a red light at nighttime when the roads are clear of traffic.

CYCLING

There are very few *ciclovias* (cycle paths) in São Paulo but Parque Ibirapuera and Cidade Universitária are good places to find some. Cycling is safer and more pleasant at the weekends when there is less car traffic. On weekends and holidays, bicycles are allowed on the metrô; and a new bike-share programme has even been instituted in which some metrô stations rent bicycles free of charge. For more on cycling, *see p209.*

WALKING

Though São Paulo is a car-oriented city, it is possible to explore many areas on foot. Walking can be a great way to slow down and see the sights. The best neighbourhoods for wandering around on foot are the historical Centro (it is less safe at night), Vila Madalena and Jardins. Rua Oscar Freire is a pedestrian-friendly street with many designer stores and great people watching opportunities. Parque Ibirapuera is also a nice place to stroll as it has many trails. Neighbourhoods like Jardim Paulista, Higienópolis, Consolação and Bela Vista are quite hilly. When crossing streets watch out for speeding traffic as cars rarely slow down for pedestrians.

DIRECTORY

Resources A-Z

DIRECTORY

ADDRESSES

In Brazilian addresses, the street name (often followed by a comma) precedes the street number. The room, suite or apartment number usually appears after the street address, followed on the next line by postal code, city name and a two-letter state abbreviation. The abbreviation for São Paulo state is SP.

AGE RESTRICTIONS

In Brazil the legal age to drink, drive, smoke and have sex is 18.

ATTITUDE & ETIQUETTE

Meeting & greeting

Brazilians tend to be very warm, so it is not difficult to meet locals and make friends. Cheek kisses are customary in Brazil as a form of meeting, greeting and saying goodbye. The number of kisses depends on the region – in São Paulo one kiss is standard. Women will kiss women and men will kiss women, but two men will usually just shake hands. When unsure just follow the lead of others.

Punctuality

Brazilians are not known for their timeliness. It is acceptable, and often expected, to arrive late to social functions, so do not be surprised if you are kept waiting. Do, however, aim for punctuality in business situations; but be aware that due to traffic and other transportation delays, arriving 15 to 20 minutes late is generally excusable.

Dress

In many situations Brazil is more casual than the US and Europe when it comes to dress (due in part to the hot climate). São Paulo, however, is the financial capital of Latin America and is therefore more conservative than cities like Rio when it comes to clothing. In a business context it is always important to look neat and clean, and to present oneself well.

BUSINESS

Networking is very important in Brazil as many business transactions come about through word-of-mouth contacts. Many professionals will have studied English, but it never hurts to be prepared with a few Portuguese phrases (*see p232* **Language & Vocabulary**).

Conventions & conferences

Each year São Paulo hosts three-quarters of the business trade shows that take place in Brazil. Many hotels host conferences and conventions; listed below are a few other expo centres:
Centro de Convenções Rebouças *3898 7850/ www.convencoesreboucas.com.br.*
Frei Caneca Convention Center *3472 2000.*
World Trade Center *3043 7117 /www.worldtradecentersp.com.br.*

Couriers & shippers

Bike Courier *5549 6422.*
DHL *3062 2152/www.dhl.com.*
FedEx *5641 7788/ www.fedex.com.*

Office services

Cophel Comércio e Fotocópia Copiadora Ltda *Rua Teodoro Sampaio 2534, Pinheiros (3819 0086).* Bus 6250-10, 702U-21. Open 8am-6pm Mon-Fri. **No credit cards. Map** p249 E9.
EDITEMA Translation Company *Rua André Ampère 153, sala 115 (5105 3170/www.editema.com.br).* Bus 5121-10, 607G-10. Open 8am-5pm Mon-Fri. **No credit cards**.

Useful organisations

BM&F Bovespa (São Paulo Stock Exchange) *Rua 15 de Novembro 276, Centro (3272 7373). Metrô São Bento.* Open 10am-5pm Mon-Sat. **Map** p243 O5.
British Chamber of Commerce & Industry in Brazil *Rua Ferreira de Araújo 741, 1st floor, Pinheiros (3819 0265).* Bus 117Y-10, 5100-10. Open 8.30am-5.30pm Mon-Fri. **Map** p248 D9.

CONSUMER

In 1990, a consumer-rights law took effect in Brazil to protect the public from false advertising and defective products. For more information contact:
Fundação de Proteção e Defesa do Consumidor (PROCON São Paulo) *Rua Barra Funda 930, 4th floor (3826 1457/www.procon. sp.gov.br).*

CUSTOMS

Visitors may enter Brazil with up to US$500 of foreign-bought

goods. In addition to this they may purchase up to two litres of spirits and goods from the duty-free shop, up to a maximum of US$500. Travellers may return to the UK with one litre of spirits and one carton of cigarettes or 50 cigars. Those returning to the US may take one litre of spirits and up to US$800 worth of goods.

DISABLED

São Paulo is unfortunately not the most accommodating city for visitors with disabilities. Higher-end restaurants and hotels are more likely than other places to cater to individual needs. Public transport is difficult to access. There is no central government agency providing information for the disabled. Private tour agency **Go in São Paulo** (3289 3814, www.goinsaopaulo.com.br) provides touristic services and assistance for the handicapped, while non-profit agency **Centro de Vida Independente** (www.cvi.org.br) also provides assistance and information for the disabled.

DRUGS

In 2006 the minimum prison term for traffickers was increased but the penalties for possession were reduced. Drug possession is still a serious crime, though those caught will not necessarily be sent to prison. However, it is not a good idea to entangle yourself with the Brazilian legal system and the sometimes-corrupt police force. It is best to stay away from all forms of drugs and to be especially careful in clubs, on buses, and on highways where you may run into police checkpoints. Possession of coca leaves is illegal, so be sure not to bring any into the country if arriving from Andean regions.

ELECTRICITY

Use caution when plugging in electronic devices because voltage varies across Brazil. São Paulo is usually 110V, but you will also find 220V. Most sockets accept the flat two-pronged pins found in the US and Canada, and the rounded two-pronged pins found in most of Europe. A world adaptor might not be necessary in São Paulo but could come in handy, especially for travel to other regions of the country.

EMBASSIES & CONSULATES

Australia Consulate *9th floor, Santos 700, Cerqueira Cesar (2112 6200/3171 2851/ www.cdasp.org.br).*
Canada Consulate *16th floor, Avenida Nações Unidas 12901, Brooklin (5509 4321/www. canadainternational.gc.ca/ brazil-bresil).*
Ireland Consulate *Alameda Joaquim Eugenio de Lima 447 (3147 7788/hcisp@yahoo.com).*
New Zealand Consulate *15th floor, Alameda Campinas 579, Cerqueira Cesar (3148 0616).*
UK Consulate *Rua Ferreira Araújo 741, 2nd floor, Pinheiros (3094 2700/ www.ukinbrazil.fco.gov.uk).*
US Consulate *Rua Henri Dunant 500, Chácara Santo Antonio (5186 7000/ http://brasilia.usembassy.gov).*

EMERGENCIES

For hospitals, *see right*; for helplines, *see p228*; for the police, *see p229*. Other 24-hour emergency numbers in Brazil are as follows:

Ambulance *192.*
Civil Defense *199.*
Civil Police *197.*
Federal Police *194.*
Fire *193.*
Military Police *190.*
Transit emergency *194.*

GAY & LESBIAN

Associação da Parada do Orgulho GLBT de São Paulo *Praça da República 386, sala 22, Centro (3362 8266/ www.paradasp.org.br).*
Defensoria Homossexual *Avenida Doutor Altino Arantes 83, Vila Clementino (aiessp@hotmail.com).*
Grupo Pela Vidda *Rua General Jardim 566, Vila Buarque (3259 2149/www.aids.org.br or www.pelavidda.org.br).* Non-governmental organisation for people with AIDS/HIV.

The Gay and lesbian tourism association **Associação Brasileira de Turismo para Gays (ABRAT)** (www.abratgls.com.br) provides information and assistance for the GLBT community. Information in English can be accessed through its website.

HEALTH

In the event of unforeseen illness and emergencies, visitors to Brazil can receive treatment in public hospitals. However, these hospitals are often busy and are not required to treat existing conditions or assist patients once their health has become stable. Travellers are strongly advised to take out health insurance beforehand.

Vaccinations are not required for entry into Brazil except for travellers arriving from yellow-fever infected areas in the Americas and Africa. For visitors remaining in São Paulo, no vaccinations are necessary, though those travelling on to remote areas in Mato Grosso and the Amazon regions will need a yellow-fever vaccine and anti-malaria medication. The vaccination takes two weeks to take effect, so plan accordingly.

It is safe to drink tap water in São Paulo, though many locals avoid doing so, drinking filtered water instead.

Disque Saude *Rua Doutor Eneas de Carvalho Aguiar 188, Cerqueira César (150/ www.saude.sp.gov.br).*

Accident & emergency

Albert Einstein Hospital *Avenida Albert Einstein 627, Morumbi, (3747 1233/ www.einstein.br). Bus 756A-10, 5119-10.*
Benificência Portugesa *Maestro Cardim Street 769, Bela Vista (3505 1000/www.beneficencia. org.br). Metrô Vergueiro.* **Map** p245 M9.
Hospital das Clinicas *Avenida Dr. Enéas de Carvalho Aguiar 255, Cerqueira César (3088 5829/ www.hcnet.usp.br). Metrô Consolação.* **Map** p244 I7.
Hospital Samaritano *Rua Conselheiro Brotero 1486, Higienópolis (3821 5300/ www.samaritano.org.br). Metrô Marechal Deordoro.* **Map** p242 J4.
Hospital São Paulo *Rua Napoleão de Barros, Vila Clementino (5576 4522/ www.unifesp.br). Bus 577T-10.* **Map** p247 M14.
São Luiz *Rua Dr. Alceu de Campos Rodrigues 95, Itaim Bibi (3848 8726/www.saoluiz.com.br). Bus 477P-10.*
Sírio Libanês *Rua Dona Adma Jafet 91, Bela Vista (3155 0900/*

www.hospitalsiriolibanes.org.br).
Metrô Consolação or Trianon-MASP. **Map** p244 K8.

Contraception & abortion

Abortion is illegal in Brazil
except in cases that put the
woman's life at risk, or when
pregnancy is the result of rape.
Contraceptives can be bought
at pharmacies or obtained for
free from the Prefeitura de Saude
(Rua General Jardim 36,
Vila Buarque, 3397 2000,
www.prefeitura.sp.gov.br).

Dentists

Centro Odontológico *Avenida
Angélica 1007 (3822 1008/
www.cohigienopolis.com.br.
Bus 874T-10.*
**Instituto Bibancos de
Odontologia** *Maurício Francisco
Klabin 401, Vila Mariana
(5579 5453/5573 2208/
www.bibancos.com.br).
Metrô Chácara Klabin.*
**Odontomax - Pronto Socorro
Dentário** *Avenida Dom Pedro I
697, Ipiranga (2273 7959/2274
6668). Bus 174M-10.*

Hospitals

See p227 **Accident
& emergency**.

Opticians

See p157.

Pharmacies

Branches of Drogão, as well
as other pharmacy chains (*see
p157*), can be found throughout
the city.

STDs, HIV & AIDS

The government runs various
programmes related to AIDS
and HIV treatment. For more
information, contact the
Prefeitura de Saude (*see p227*
Contraception & abortion).
For counselling and information,
see below **Helplines**.

HELPLINES

All numbers are open 24hrs unless
otherwise stated.

Alcoholics Anonymous
3315 9333.
English speakers available
upon request.

Child Abuse *3104 4850.*
Open 9am-5.30pm Mon-Fri.
HIV/AIDS *0800 16 25 50.*
Open 8am-6pm Mon-Fri.
Narcotics Anonymous
9990 5535.

ID

Everyone in Brazil must carry
identification. For security
reasons, it is best not to carry
an original passport around,
but foreign visitors can get a
copy of their passport certified
by a notary. A student ID is
also very handy in São Paulo
as it frequently allows for
discounted prices.

INSURANCE

Visitors are strongly advised
to take out travel and medical
insurance before travelling. For
more information, *see p227*
Health.

INTERNET

For internet access, visit a
cyber café or LAN House.
These can be found in most
neighbourhoods. Many hotels
have at least a cable connection
to hook a laptop up to the internet.
Some hotels, restaurants and
bars also offer Wi-Fi (free or
prepay), but bear in mind that
Wi-Fi is harder to find in Brazil
than in the US and UK.
Centro Cultural *See p69.*
Free Wi-Fi hotspot.
Galeria Olido Cibernarium
*Avenida São João 473, Galeria
Olido (3223 3694/www.projeto
fabrica.com.br). Metrô São Bento
or República.* **Open** 9am-8pm
Mon-Sat; 2-8pm Sun. **Map**
p243 N5.
Part of a non-profit, international
programme designed to combat
digital exclusion, internet use
is free as long as you show
identification.
Suplicy Café *see p137.*
Branches throughout the city
offer free Wi-Fi.
Starbucks *www.starbucks.com.br.*
Many branches offer free wireless
access with activation of a
Starbucks gift card.
For a list of website providing
further information, *see p233.*

LANGUAGE

Most middle- and upper-class
citizens have studied some
English. However, do not expect

your average cab driver or sales
clerk to be fluent in any language
other than Portuguese. You will
have the most luck finding English
speakers in places that receive
many tourists, such as hotels
and high-end restaurants. A
phrasebook is always nice to have,
especially when going out to eat
(many places will not provide an
English menu). For further
reference, *see pp232-233.*

LEFT LUGGAGE

There is a left luggage service
in the arrivals area of Guarulhos
airport. Prices range from R$6
to R$32, depending on baggage
size. Congonhas airport has self-
service lockers (R$7/24 hrs)
between the arrivals and
departures area and an office for
larger items. Luggage lockers
are also available in the bus
stations (R$7/24 hrs). In Tietê
they can be found in the
downstairs level near the
taxi stand. Look for the sign
marked 'guarda volumes'.

LEGAL HELP

English speaking lawyers in
São Paulo include **Suchodolski
Advogados Associados** (24th
Floor, Rua Augusta 1819, 3372
1300, www.suchodolski.com.br)
and **Ary Oswaldo Mattos
Filho** (Alameda Joaquim Eugênio
de Lima 447, 3147 7600, www.
mattosfilho.com.br). For further
assistance, *see p227* **Embassies
& consulates**.

LIBRARIES

Biblioteca Mário de Andrade
see p53.
Centro Cultural São Paulo
see p69.

LOST PROPERTY

If you leave something in a taxi
or on public transport contact the
relevant company directly, and
hope for the best. For lost credit
cards, *see p229.*

MEDIA

Magazines

Caras
Portuguese for 'faces' (think
People magazine), this weekly
celebrity gossip magazine will
keep you up-to-date on the
lives of Brazil's rich and famous.

Época
A popular news magazine published by the media conglomerate Rede Globo.

Veja
The *Newsweek* of Brazil, this weekly news magazine covers current events, politics, health, technology and entertainment.

Newspapers

Folha de São Paulo
This paper is well respected and well read throughout the country, boasting the largest circulation in all of Brazil.

O Estado de São Paulo
A daily newspaper nicknamed Estadão (Big State), this is the second most popular paper after Folha.

Radio

Alpha FM 101.7 FM
Specialises in tunes from the 1970s and '80s.

Eldorado FM 92.9 FM
Eldorado plays a contemporary mix including jazz, blues, MPB (Música Popular Brasileira) and Bossa Nova.

Kiss FM 102.1 FM
São Paulo's station for classic rock and rockabilly.

Transamérica 100.1 FM
This pop station plays the latest hits and is popular among the younger crowd.

Television

Globo
Headquartered in Rio but reaching viewers across the Americas, this is Brazil's most popular television network.

Rede Record
Brazil's oldest network and the second most popular channel.

Sistema Brasileiro de Televisão (SBT)
This channel airs a number of imported shows and is especially popular among kids and pre-teens.

MONEY

The Brazilian currency is the *real* (plural, *reais*). One hundred *centavos* equals one *real*. It is always advisable to carry a supply of coins and small-denomination notes because it can be difficult to break larger bills when paying on buses or purchasing from street vendors. Bank notes come in denominations of 100 (light blue), 50 (brown), 20 (yellow), ten (red or

blue/orange polymer), five (purple), two (dark blue) and one (green). Coins come in denominations of one real and 50, 25, ten and five centavos. There are two versions of each coin in varying colors of silver, gold and copper, but the value is easy to identify by simply looking at the number on the coin.

Most shops and restaurants accept major credit cards such as Visa (V), MasterCard (MC), and American Express (AmEx). Diners Club (DC) is also usually accepted. Some places only accept cash. It's a good idea to notify your bank and credit card companies before travelling abroad to prevent an account freeze.

Banks & ATMs

It is easy to find banks and ATMs throughout the city – it is not so easy to find ones that will accept foreign ATM cards. The key is to be persistent and to try different ATM machines until you find one that works. Travellers tend to have the most success with CitiBank, HSBC and Banco do Brasil. Look for ATM machines with a Visa or Cirrus logo.

Bureaux de change & travellers' cheques

Travellers' cheques are less common than they used to be. The best places to change them are in bureaux de change (*casas de cambio*), generally in the main branch of the major banks. Take your passport for ID purposes.

Lost & stolen cards

American Express
800 268 9824.

Diners Club
4001 4444/0800 784480.

Mastercard
1 636 722 7111.

Visa
1 636 722 7111.

Tax

There is no standard sales tax in Brazil.

NATURAL HAZARDS

Flooding can happen from time to time during the rainy season. Protect yourself from mosquitoes by using repellent and by wearing trousers and long-sleeved tops. Though malaria is not present in São Paulo, there have been cases of dengue fever.

OPENING HOURS

Public transport systems operate normally during holidays. For more information, *see p224* **Public transport**.

Banks 10am-4pm Mon-Fri.
Bars varies. Some bars open at noon and stay open through the night; others open late and are booming until the early morning. It is best to check with individual bars to verify opening and closing times.
Businesses 9am-6pm Mon-Fri.
Post offices 9am-5pm or 6pm Mon-Fri, with some larger branches opening Saturday mornings.
Shops varies, but generally 9am-6pm Mon-Fri and 9am-1pm Sat. Shopping centres usually stay open until 10pm. Many shops close on Sundays, but some pharmacies and large stores remain open.

POLICE

DEATUR (Headquarters of the Specialised Tourist Police)
Avenida São Luiz 91, Centro (*3214 0209/3120 3984*).
Police Station at Congonhas Airport *Avenida Washington Luis, Moema* (*5090 9032/ 5090 9043/5090 9041*).
Police Station at Cumbica/Guarulhos International Airport *Rua Dr João Jamil Zarif, Guarulhos* (*6445 3064/6445 2686*).
Port & Airport Police Division *5th Floor, Rua São Bento 380, Centro* (*3107 5642/3107 8332*). Special services for tourists.

POSTAL SERVICES

Post offices are called **Correios** (look for a yellow sign with blue text). Ordinarily, international mail under 20 grams costs about R$1.50-$2, depending on the destination. Bear in mind that service can be slow. International mail can be received through the *posta restante* system. Watch out, though, as packages shipped to Brazil from abroad are sometimes slapped with heavy import taxes upon pick-up.
Correio Central *Rua Líbero Badaró 595* (*3242 6084/ www.correios.com.br*).

RELIGION

Brazil is a culturally diverse country with many religions.

WEATHER REPORT

MONTH	AVERAGE HIGH	AVERAGE LOW
January	27°C (81°F)	18°C (64°F)
February	28°C (82°F)	18°C (64°F)
March	27°C (81°F)	18°C (64°F)
April	25°C (77°F)	16°C (61°F)
May	23°C (73°F)	13°C (55°F)
June	22°C (72°F)	12°C (54°F)
July	22°C (72°F)	12°C (54°F)
August	23°C (73°F)	13°C (55°F)
September	24°C (75°F)	14°C (57°F)
October	24°C (75°F)	15°C (59°F)
November	26°C (79°F)	16°C (61°F)
December	26°C (79°F)	17°C (63°F)

The primary religion is Catholicism but a number of other religions are practised as well, including various other forms of Christianity, Judaism, Islam, African-influenced Candomblé and Umbanda.

Listed here are a few of São Paulo's many places of worship.

Busshinji Temple For listing, see p62.
Brazil Mosque *Avenida do Estado 5382, Cambuci (3208 3726/www.arresala.org.br).* Bus 571T-10, 3391-10, 3391-51.
First Baptist Church in São Paulo *Praça Princesa Isabel 233, Campos Elíseos (3331 7393/ www.pib.org.br).* Bus 2001-10, 119C-10. **Map** p243 M3.
God is Love Pentecostal Church *Avenida do Estado 4568, Glicério (3347 4700/www.ipda .com.br).* Bus 309N-10, 309T-42.
Israeli Congregation of São Paulo *Rua Antonio Carlos 653, Cerqueira César (2808 6299/ www.cip.org.br).* Bus 805L-10, 177H-10. **Map** p244 K7.
Methodist Church - Brazil National Headquarters *Avenida Piassanguaba 3031, Planalto Paulista (2813 8600/ www.metodista.org.br).* Metrô São Judas.
Mormons of the Latter-Day Saints in São Paulo *Avenida Prof. Francisco Morato 2390, Caxingui (3723 7607/ www.mormon.org.br).* Bus 627R-10, 775P-10.
Orthodox Cathedral For listing, see p67.
São Paulo Association of the Seventh-Day Adventist Church *Rua Gabrielle D'annunzio 246, Brooklin (3545 0900/ www.paulistana.org.br).* Bus 476A-10, 775M-10.
Sé Cathedral For listing, see p49.
Spirit Federation of the State of São Paulo, *Rua Maria Paula 140, Bela Vista (3115 5544 /www.feesp.com.br).* Bus 393C-10, 408A-10. **Map** p243 N6.
Sukyo Mahikari *Rua Paracatú 1004, Saúde (5594 5936/ www.sukyomahikari.org).* Metrô Saúde. **Map** 247 O18.
Superior Organisation of Umbanda of the State of São Paulo *Rua Mendes Junior 41, Brás (2694 3294/ www.souesp.com.br).* Bus 271F-10, 311C-10.
World Messianic Church in Brazil *Rua Sena Madureira 1008, Vila Mariana (5087 2000/ www.messianica.com.br).* Bus 475R-10, 5106-10. **Map** p247 M13.

SAFETY & SECURITY

Just like in any large metropolis, crime is a serious issue in São Paulo. Taking certain precautions will reduce your risk of becoming a victim of theft. Be careful with personal belongings at all times, especially at night and in the city centre. Be particularly cautious if carrying a laptop. Avoid sitting near a window if using your laptop in a café, as you will be an easy target to spot and more susceptible to theft. Do not wear flashy clothing or expensive jewellery, and be discreet when taking photos or talking on a cell phone.

Most places in São Paulo are safe to walk in during the day but at night it is best to avoid dark streets where there are few people. High-risk areas for crime and pickpocketing include eastern São Paulo and Praça da Sé, as well as São Paulo's 'red light district' which covers Rua Augusta north of Avenida Paulista and the Estaçao de Luz metro area. Be especially wary of young men on motorcycles, as armed theft by these means has become more common. If you are approached by a mugger, do not resist – many thieves carry weapons and are not afraid to use them.

If you are renting a car, be aware that car-jacking is common in São Paulo. As a result, drivers tend to ignore traffic lights and stop signs, particularly at night. Proceed cautiously when approaching an intersection, paying close attention to both oncoming traffic and pedestrians; and make sure car doors are locked at all times.

SMOKING

Smoking in São Paulo is banned in enclosed spaces such as shopping malls, buses and hospitals. Most restaurants have a section for *fumantes* (smokers) and *não-fumantes* (non-smokers). Smoking is permitted in *baladas* (bars and clubs).

STUDY

São Paulo is home to Brazil's largest and most respected university, **Universidade de São Paulo** (Avenida Prof. Almeida Prado 1280, Butantã, 3091 4600, www.usp.br).. São Paulo's other main universities include **Pontifícia Universidade Católica de São Paulo** (Rua Monte Alegre 984, Perdizes, 3670 8000, www.pucsp.br), which was founded in 1946 it was an important institution in the resistance against the dictatorship. The **Fundação Getúlio Vargas** (Avenida 9 de Julho 2029, Bela Vista, 3281 7777, www.fgv.br) is another important learning and cultural institution. Students with a valid ID can get significant discounts on shows and other events. For this reason, an International Student Identity Card (ISIC) (www.isiccard.com) is a worthwhile investment.

Language classes

Many language schools offer courses to foreigners interested in studying Portuguese. Courses may last from a week to up to many months. It is possible to study with a private tutor or take a class with other students. Language institutes include **Alumni** (Rua Pe João Manoel 319, Jardins, 5644 9700, www.alumni.org.br); **Fast Forward** (Alameda Lorena 684, Casa 4, Jardins, 3051 7112, www.fastforward.com.br); and **Senac São Paulo** (Rua Dr Plinio Barreto 285, 4° andar, Jardins, 2182 6900, www.sp.senac.br). For further language reference, see pp232-233.

DIRECTORY

TELEPHONES

Dialing & codes

Brazil's international country code is 55. All cities have a two-digit city code followed by an eight-digit telephone number. The area code for São Paulo is 11. When making a local call to a São Paulo number from within São Paulo only the eight digit number is necessary. When making a national call in Brazil you must first dial 0, then a telephone provider code (15, 23, or 21 will usually work), followed by the two-digit city code, then the eight-digit number. You also need the telephone provider code when making international calls. In this case it woud be 00 + telecom provider code + country code + area code + number. (Bear in mind that Skype tends to save money and a lot of the headache.)

Other major Brazilian city city codes are as follows: Rio de Janeiro 21, Belo Horizonte 31; Curitiba 41, Porto Alegre 51 and Brasilia 61.

Mobile phones

Mobile phones usually use 900Mhz and 1800Mhz wavelengths (or sometimes the 850Mhz wavelength). Usually European dual band phones will work. If you have a GSM phone from the US it may work, but you will probably need to call your provider and have international restrictions removed. To purchase minutes, prepaid SIM cards can be bought at pharmacies and newsstands. Mobile phone providers include Claro (www.claro.com.br), Tim (www.tim.com.br), Nextel (www.queronextel.com.br) and Vivo (www.vivo.com.br).

Operator services

To make local collect calls without an operator dial 9090 + the number and to make non-local collect calls dial 90 + telecom company number + area/ country code + number.

Public phones

There are public telephone booths on practically every block. In order to use one you must first purchase a *cartão telefónico* (phone card) for R$5 or more, available at shops or newsstands. There are also special phone cards you can buy to make international calls, so be sure to specify to the sales clerk.

TIME

São Paulo, Rio de Janeiro, and Brasilia all share the same time zone: GMT minus three hours. São Paulo's daylight savings occurs during the southern hemisphere's summer. Clocks go forward one hour at the end of November and go back one hour in the end of February.

TIPPING

Restaurants bills generally include a ten per cent service charge for meals, and tips are not expected beyond that. If you were impressed with the service you can certainly give more. Taxi drivers do not expect tips either, but it is customary to let them keep the change. Tips are given for home deliveries, to porters in hotels and to hairdressers.

TOILETS

There's a distinct lack of public toilets in São Paulo. Your best bet is to buy something cheap in order to use the restroom in a petrol station, store or restaurant. Shopping malls and fast food outlets are also good options. Toilet paper is generally not flushed in Brazil (it goes in the wastebasket beside the toilet).

TOURIST INFORMATION

São Paulo's official tourism site is www.cityofsaopaulo.com. There are several tourist information offices including ones in Guarulhos airport (*see p224* **By air**) and Tietê bus station (*see p224* **By bus**). The most central tourist office is downtown on Avenida São João 473.

On Thursdays at 8pm there is a free two-hour walking tour through central areas. It starts at the Municipal Theater. Call 3256 7909 or 3019 8831 for further information.

VISAS & IMMIGRATION

Brazil has a reciprocity policy when it comes to visas. Travellers from the UK, Ireland and New Zealand need only a passport to enter Brazil, valid for at least six months before departure. Visitors from Canada, Australia and the United States must apply for a tourist visa in advance through a Brazilian embassy. Tourists are granted a 90-day stay which may be extended another 90 days in-country through the Policía Federal. Those who disobey these time limits will be fined at the airport.

WEIGHTS & MEASURES

Brazil uses the metric system. Therefore distances are measured in metres, weights are measured in grams, and temperature is measured in degrees Celsius.

WHEN TO GO

Climate

Summertime is from December to March. Warm-weather clothing is suggested for the sun and heat of the urban jungle. Raingear is also useful as afternoon showers are a frequent occurrence in the summer (umbrella sellers sprout up on every corner as soon as the sky turns grey).

In spring and autumn the climate is generally warm and pleasant. The average winter temperature is 16 degrees Celsius (61 degrees Farenheit), with the coldest month being July when it can sometimes get quite chilly. Many buildings in São Paulo do not have heating so sweaters and a light jacket are suggested.

Public holidays

New Year's Day (1 Jan); **Carnival** (Mon and Tue before Ash Wed); **Good Friday** (2 Apr 2010, 22 Apr 2011); **Easter Sunday** (4 Apr 2010, 24 Apr 2011); **Tiradentes Day** (12 Apr); **Labour Day** (1 May); **Corpus Christi** (June, varies); **Independence Day** (7 Sept); **Children's Day** (12 Oct); **All Soul's Day** (2 Nov); **Proclamation of the Republic Day** (15 Nov); **Black Awareness Day** (20 Nov); **Christmas Day** (25 Dec).

WOMEN

There is some machismo culture in Brazil but it is not as strong as in other parts of Central and South America. São Paulo is a modern city and lone women travellers will have no problem fitting in.

WORKING IN SAO PAULO

A work visa is required to be legally employed in Brazil, and any potential employer will have to apply for one through the Ministry of Labour & Employment. There are some hoops one must jump through to invest in or start a business in Brazil. For more information and details it is best to contact your embassy (*see p227*) or seek advice from a law firm (*see p228*).

Language & Vocabulary

Written Portuguese seems reassuringly familiar if you speak Spanish, with many recognisable words. The shock comes when you hear it spoken. The pronunciations given in this section are specifically for Portuguese as spoken in São Paulo. Brazilian accents vary widely but if you can understand Cariocas, you should have no problem with people from other regions.

PRONUNCIATION

Once you know how each letter is pronounced, Portuguese is actually pretty much phonetic. Stress falls on the penultimate syllable in most words, on the last syllable for words ending in consonants (except for **s**, and in most cases **m**). Words with accents have the stress on the syllable with the accent.

Vowels

Many Portuguese vowel sounds are nasal and don't really have equivalents in English. Nasal voewls in written Portuguese are usually seen with a tilda (~) over the **o** or **a**. **ão** is similar to the 'ou' in *lounge* but is much more nasal. **ãe** is like the 'i' in *mine*, again more nasal. **õe** is similar to the 'oin' in *boing*.

Some vowels are also nasalised when they're followed by **m** or **n** at the end of a syllable. An example of this everyone will hear here is in *sim* (yes).

a is close to the English 'a' in *cat*
e is like the English 'ey' in *they*
é or **ê** is like the English 'e' in *bet*
e unstressed at the end of a word is like the English 'ea' in *tea*
i is also pronounced like 'ea' in *tea*
o is usually like the English 'o' i n *local*
ó, **ô** and occasionally **o** is like the 'o' in *hot*
final **o** is like the 'oo' in *foot*
u is also pronounced like the 'oo' in *foot*

Consonants

The letters **b**, **f**, **k**, **p**, **v** and **w** are pronounced as in English. So are **d**, **g** and **t**, except when they're followed by **i** or an unstressed **e**. In these cases they are softened: d becomes

like the 'dg' in *judge*; t becomes like the 'ch' in *cheese* ; g becomes like the 's' in *pleasure*. This sound is also the way to pronounce the Portuguese **j**.
c is hard like the 'c' in *canal*, except when it has a cedilla (ç) or is followed by **e** or **i**, which soften the sound to like the 'c' in *ceiling*.
h is always silent. When **l** follows a vowel it becomes like an English **w**.
lh together make the sound like the 'lli' in *million*.
m and **n** at the end of a word or syllable and immediately following a vowel will nasalise the vowel.
r at the beginning or end of a word, and **rr**, are pronounced like the Scottish 'ch' in *loch*.
s is like the English **s** except when it's between two vowels then it's pronounced like an English **z**. In the middle of a word followed by a consonant it's pronounced either like the **s** in *pleasure* or like the English **sh** depending on the consonant.
x is usually pronounced like the English **sh**, but can sometimes be pronounced like the English **s** or **x**.

BASICS

hello *oi; olá*
goodbye *tchau*
good morning *bom dia*
good afternoon *boa tarde*
good evening/night *boa noite*
yes *sim*
no *não*
maybe *talvez/pode ser*
how are you? *como vai?; tudo bem?*
Please *por favor*
thanks *obrigada* (if you are female); *obrigado* (if you are male)
sorry *desculpa/perdão*
excuse me *com licença*
I don't speak Portuguese *não falo português;*
do you speak English? *Você fala inglês?*
I don't understand *não entendo*
good *bom/boa*; **well** *bem*
bad/badly *mal/ruim*
small *pequeno*; **big** *grande*
a bit *um pouco*; **a lot/very** *muito*
with *com*; **without** *sem*
and *e*; **also** *também*
this *este/esta*; **that** *aquele/aquela*
because *porque*
what? *o quê?*; **who?** *quem?*;
when? *quando?*; **which?** *qual?*;
why? *por quê?*; **how?** *como?*;
where? *onde?*; **where to?** *para onde?*

I am English *sou inglês/inglesa*;
Irish *irlandês/irlandesa*; **American** *dos Estados Unidos*; **Canadian** *canadense*; **Australian** *australiano/a*; **a New Zealander** *neozelandes/neozelandesa*
what time is it? *qué horas são?*
forbidden *proibido*
out of order *não funciona*
bank *banco*; **post office** *correios*

EMERGENCIES

Help! *socorro!*
I'm sick *estou doente*
I need a doctor/hospital *preciso de um médico/um hospital*
there's a fire! *tem um incendio!*

GETTING AROUND

airport *aeroporto*
station *estação*
ticket *passagem*
one-way *ida* **roundtrip** *ida e volta*
bus/coach station *rodoviária*
entrance *entrada*; **exit** *saída*
left *esquerda*; **right** *direita*
straight on *direto/em frente*
street *rua*; **avenue** *avenida*;
motorway *estrada*
map *um mapa*
speed limit *limite de velocidade*
petrol *gasolina*

SHOPPING

how much? *quanto custa?*
expensive *caro*; **cheap** *barato*;
sale *liquidação*
is there.../are there... *tem/têm...*
i would like... *eu gostaria de...*
what size? *qual tamanho?*
can I try it on? *posso experimentar?*

DAYS, MONTHS & SEASONS

morning *manhã*; **afternoon** *tarde*
night *noite*; **tomorrow** *amanhã*;
yesterday *ontem.*
Monday *segunda-feira*; **Tuesday** *terça-feira*; **Wednesday** *quarta-feira*; **Thursday** *quinta-feira*;
Friday *sexta-feira*; **Saturday** *sábado*; **Sunday** *domingo*
January *janeiro*; **February** *fevereiro*; **March** *março*; **April** *abril*; **May** *maio*; **June** *junho*; **July** *julho*; **August** *agosto*; **September** *setembro*; **October** *outubro*; **November** *novembro*; **December** *dezembro*.

Further Reference

BOOKS

Non-fiction

Fernando Cardoso *The Accidental President of Brazil: A memoir* Part autobiography, part history book, this memoir provides a wonderful introduction to the country's recent past and a basis for understanding how Brazil fits into the global community of the 21st century.
Jeffrey Lesser *Discontented Diaspora: Japanese Brazilians and the Meaning of Ethnic Militancy, 1960-1980* A sharp dissection of the Japanese immigrant milieu and identity in São Paulo.
Tracy Peixoto and Leslie Nasr *Living in São Paulo: The L & T Guide* An informative guide for visitors and expatriates relocating to São Paulo.
Tracy Novinger *Communicating with Brazilians: When 'yes' means 'no'* Novinger hits the nail on the head in this book as she discusses cultural differences between Brazilians and North Americans.

Literature

Jorge Amado
Seara Vermelha (Red Harvest)
This novel won the Stalin Prize in the 1951, so swept was the Communist awarding committee by the exploitation of the poor by Brazil´s rich. The novel is about *nordestinos* (north-eastern migrants) who came to São Paulo to escape drought and to seek jobs.
Zelia Gattai Amado
Anarquistas Graças a Deus
The book that made Jorge Amado´s wife famous in her own right, focused on the history of Italian anarchists in early 1920s São Paulo.
Mário de Andrade
Paulicéia Desvairada (Hallucinated City) This book of poems about São Paulo launched Brazilian modernism and predated Caetano Veloso's tribute to Avenida São João by about 40 years.
Carolina Maria de Jesus
Quarto de Despejo (Child of the Dark)
This diary written by a woman who lived in a São Paulo favela in the 1960s is one of the most poignant retellings of slum life.

Patrícia Melo
O Matador: Roman (The Killer: A Psychological Thriller) The story of a killer told by an omniscient narrator.
Patricia Pagu
Parque Industrial: Romance Proletario (Industrial Park: A Proletarian Novel)
Dedicated to the proletariat of the Paulistano neighbourhood Brás, the novel was written by Oswald de Andrade´s first wife and an ardent Communist.
Drauzio Varella
Estação Carandiru
The story of a doctor's interviews with inmates inside the infamous Paulistano penetentiary.

FILM

Blindness *dir. Fernando Mereilles* (2008) Based on José Saramago's novel, the film, shot in a post-apocalyptic looking São Paulo, explores the disintegration of a society when everyone goes blind.
O Bandido da Luz Vermelho *(The Red Light Bandit) Rogério Sganzerla* (1968) The story of a bandit who always used a red flashlight to break into houses at night. A classic of Cinema Marginal, the film has stunning cinematography.
Carandiru *dir. Hector Babenco* (2003) A film based on the true story of the Paulistano police massacre of 111 prisoners. Written by Dr Drauzio Varella who was doing AIDS research at the penitentiary and who became close to the convicts.
Cidade dos Homens *(City of Men) dir. Fernando Meirelles* (2002-2005) This 19 part series offers the best of Brazilian television. Two best friends from a favela in Rio, are seen growing up and dealing with poverty, race and violence on a daily basis. Episode *Hip Sampa Hop* is set in São Paulo
Estômago *(Stomach) dir. Marcos Jorge (2007)* One of the best films to come out of Brazil: Estômago, shot in São Paulo, reuses the favourite obsession of the Modernists – eat or be eaten.
O Grande Momento *(Grand Moment) dir. Roberto Santos* (1958) Italian immigrants on the periphery of São Paulo, and a young couple who don't have the money to pay for their nuptials: it all makes

for a touching story with a happy ending.
A Hora da Estrela *(Hour of the Star) dir. Suzana Amaral* (1985) Based on the troubling novel by the same name written by Clarice Lispector. The story of Macabea, a poor immigrant from the north-east, is set in Rio, the movie was shot in São Paulo.
Noite Vazia *(Eros) dir. Walter Hugo Khouri* (1964) An erotic portrayal of São Paulo at night, married men, prostitutes, and sexy '60s cinematography.
Pixote: A Lei da Mais Fraco *(Pixote: The Law of the Weakest) dir. Hector Babenco* (1981) A sad and violent tale of Paulistano street kids growing up in a youth detention centre.
São Paulo, Sociedade Anônimo *(São Paulo, Anonymous Society) Luis Sérgio Person* (1965) The auto-industry and the city itself serve as great themes for what is arguably the best São Paulo movie.
O Ano em Que Meus Paes Saíram de Ferías *(The Year My Parents Went on Vacation) dir. Cao Hamburger* (2006) A touching story about a young boy who goes to live with his Jewish grandfather in Bom Retiro while his parents are fleeing from the dictatorship.

MUSIC

Adoniran Barbosa *Trem das Onze*
Demônios da Garoa *60 Anos Ao Vivo*
Eduardo Gudin *Um Jeito de Fazer Samba*
Rita Lee *Bossa n' Beatles*
Os Mutantes *Os Mutantes*
Paulo Vanzolini 'Ronda'
Caetano Veloso 'Sampa'
Tom Zé 'São, São Paulo'

ON THE WEB

www.couchsurfing.com
Networking site for travellers.
.http://tltc.la.utexas.edu/brazil pod/tafalado Great resource for Portuguese language learners.
www.samba-choro.com.br
www.fiquemaisumdia.com.br
Tourist guide to São Paulo.
www.totalspguide.com
Like the city's graffitied walls and funky bohemian haunts, this insider web site to São Paulo bursts with colour and hip, urban flavour.

DIRECTORY

Index A-Z

INDEX

INDEX

Advertisers' Index

Please refer to the relevant pages for contact details

Maps

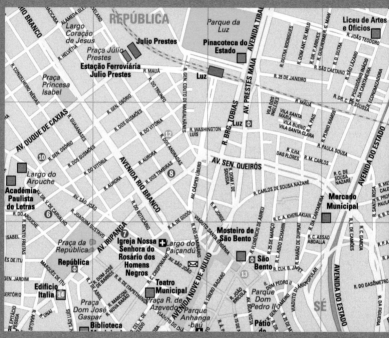

Legend	
Major sight or landmark	▮
Railway Station	▮
Metro Station	⊕
Park	▮
Hospital	✚
Area	JARDIM PAULISTA
Avenue	▯
River	▮
Church	✚
Airport	✈
Highway	▰
Pedestrian road	▯

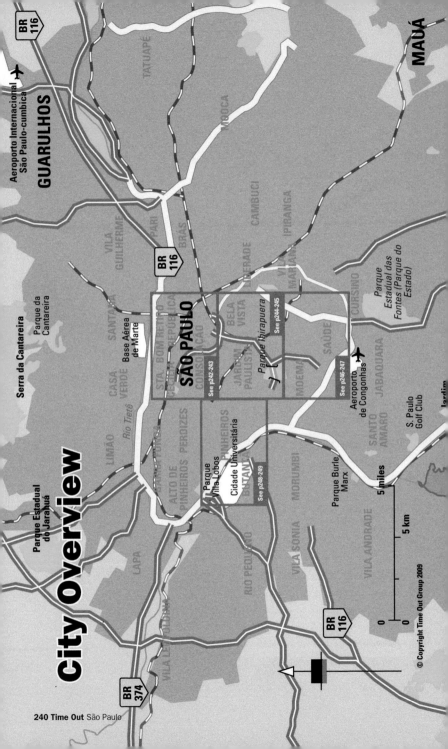

City Overview

© Copyright Time Out Group 2009

São Paulo Metrô

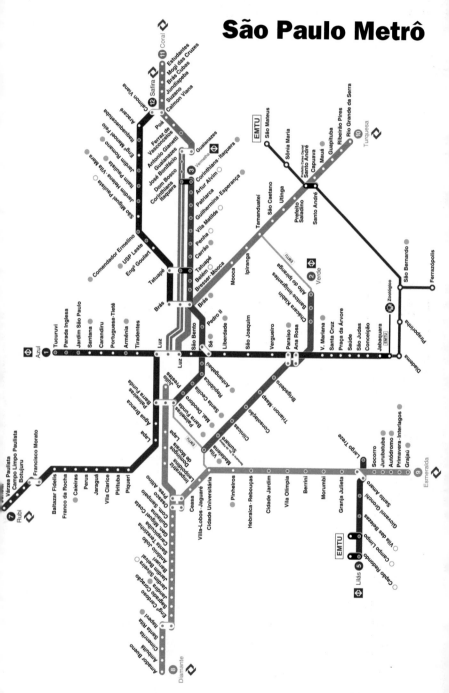

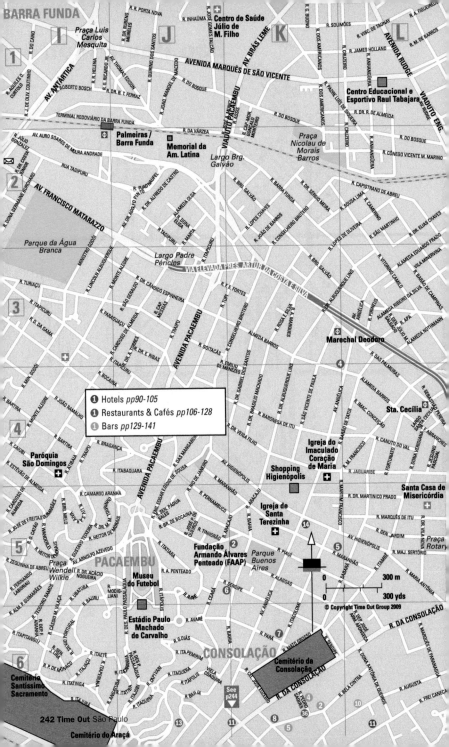

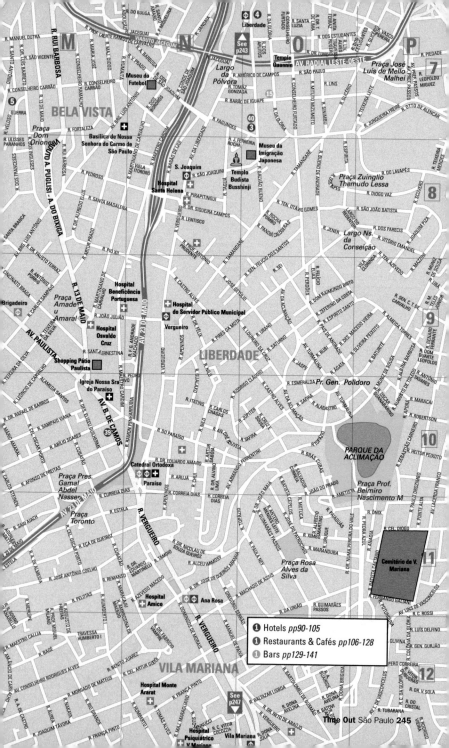

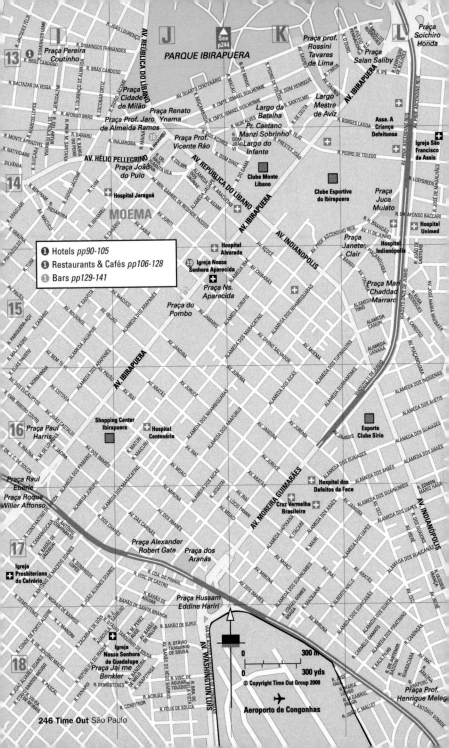

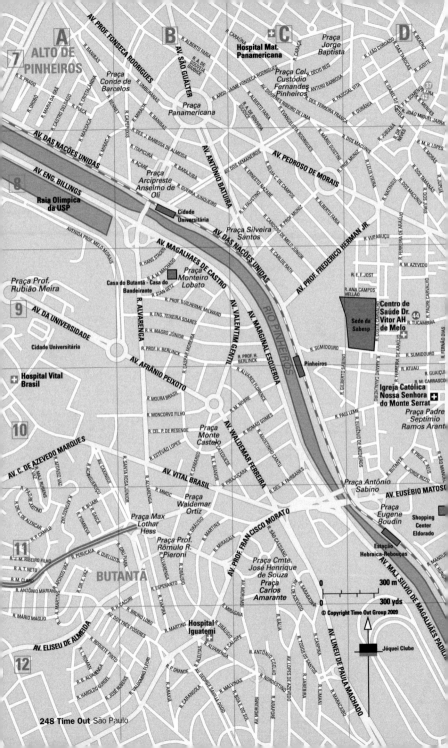

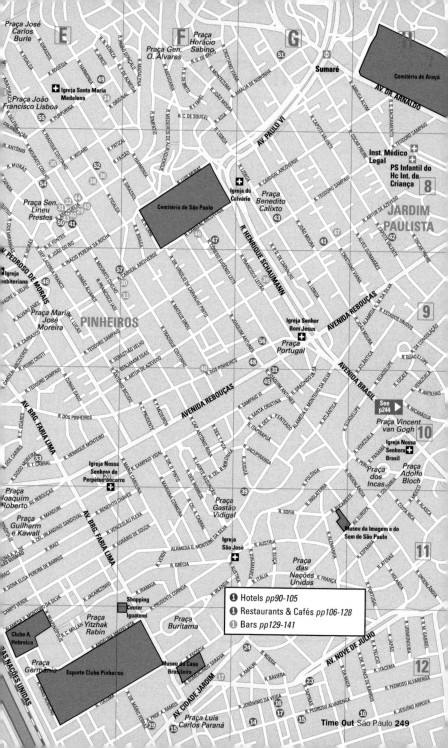

Street Index

STREET INDEX

Street Index

STREET INDEX

Street Index